NEW PRODUCT VENTURE MANAGEMENT

NEW PRODUCT
VENTURE MANAGEMENT

by

DELMAR W. KARGER

Ford Foundation Professor of Management
Rensselaer Polytechnic Institute

and

ROBERT G. MURDICK, PH.D

Professor of Management
College of Business and Public Administration
Florida Atlantic University

GORDON AND BREACH
New York   London   Paris

Copyright © 1972 by
Gordon and Breach, Science Publishers, Inc.
440 Park Avenue South
New York, N.Y. 10016

Editorial office for the United Kingdom
Gordon and Breach, Science Publishers Ltd.
42 William IV Street
London W.C. 2

Editorial office for France
Gordon & Breach
7-9 rue Emile Dubois
Paris 14e

PREFACE

The essence of business is risk. For most firms, this risk appears in the many decisions related to the management of new product ventures. Many great companies have been started on the basis of hunches about a new product idea and many small firms survive for a time on the basis of intuitive new product decisions. In the long run, however, a more systematic and scientific approach to new product venture management (NPVM) is required if a company is to survive the sophisticated competition of today.

Despite the importance of the subject matter of NPVM, most books treat the subject in a recipe fashion. We have tried in this book to emphasize the nature of risk and cost in every new product decision. We have covered the diverse areas which are involved in NPVM to provide modern systematic approaches for the business manager. At the same time, we have supplied adequate conceptual material and references to make this book qualify as a college text in the marketing or planning disciplines. Most of this material has been tested in the new product problems course given at Rensselaer Polytechnic Institute.

Additional validity has been given to specialized topics by two practicing authorities: Dr. Enrico Petri, a highly experienced public accountant and currently Associate Professor of Accounting at the State University of New York (Albany) provided a careful review and many suggestions for Chapter 11. Dr. Richard E. Stanley, a former advertising agency account executive, and currently Associate Professor of Marketing, University of South Carolina, has written Chapter 13 especially for this book. We are extremely grateful for their contributions.

No preface would be complete without acknowledging the encouragement of our wives, Ruth and Emily. Also, the dedicated secretarial, editing, and typing services of those who make the book possible must also be remembered here; we gratefully acknowledge the assistance of Emily Murdick and Ruth Ashley.

D. W. KARGER
R. G. MURDICK

CONTENTS

Preface v

CHAPTER 1
New Products – Opportunities and Risks 1

CHAPTER 2
Product Planning 19

CHAPTER 3
Organizing for Product Planning and Development 47

CHAPTER 4
Technological Innovation 59

CHAPTER 5
Obtaining New Product Ideas 75

CHAPTER 6
Research and Engineering 89

CHAPTER 7
Legal Risks . . . . , . . . 111

CHAPTER 8
The Role of Marketing in the New Product Process 129

CHAPTER 9
Marketing Research for Decision Making 141

CHAPTER 10
Evaluating New-Product Projects 165

CHAPTER 11
How to Cost the New Product 201

CHAPTER 12
How to Price for Life-cycle Profit 227

CHAPTER 13
Promoting the New Product (by Dr Richard E. Stanley)   241

CHAPTER 14
Securing Capital and Going Public   263

Index   277

CHAPTER 1

NEW PRODUCTS – OPPORTUNITIES AND RISKS

As long as we are unable to forecast the future exactly as it will come to pass, there is a risk of misfortune from our actions. It is in the very nature of commerce to accept risk in the hope of gain. In recent years, companies of all sizes have been struggling to cope with the swollen costs and increasing risks of developing and launching new products. The purpose of this book is to provide practical guidance for evaluating and minimizing risk in such new product ventures (1) providing information and procedures for a planned systematic approach to each major new product activity, and (2) discussing the risk aspects of key decisions. *New services for a service organization are synomous with new products, the same considerations apply.*

This book is directed to would-be entrepreneurs. Entrepreneurs will take risks which would make a professional manager break out in a cold sweat. He sees opportunities for big gains long before the market researchers have gathered their data and made their analysis. He is "one-up" on the large corporate teams. Entrepreneurship can, however, be introduced into the large corporations to a far greater extent than it now exists. The corporation may accomplish this by providing the right climate, the money, and adequate freedom to take risks for entrepreneurial people it hires. At the same time, a more systematic and rational approach to new product venture management as covered in this book may save some individual private business entrepreneurs from disaster. Ventures are business enterprises in which there is the opportunity to make high profits in a situation characterized by great uncertainty.

IMPORTANCE OF NEW PRODUCTS

Research has shown that it is commonplace for major companies to have 50 % or more of current sales in products new in the past ten years. About 75 % of the nation's growth in sales volume over the next three-year period can be expected to come from new products.[1] Figures 1a, 1b, and 1c show the contribution of new products to sales for major industry classifications. New products are the basis for survival and growth of a company!

Great companies have been founded on the introduction of a single new product as the history of the Xerox Corporation will attest. Small companies

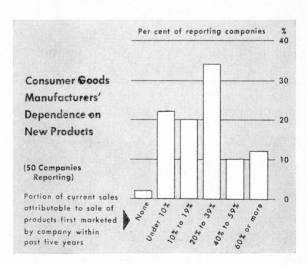

Figure 1-1a Consumer goods manufacturers' dependence on new products
Source: Roger M. Pegram and Earl L. Bailey, "The New-Products Race", *The Marketing Executive Looks Ahead*, 1967, National Industrial Conference Board, p. 39

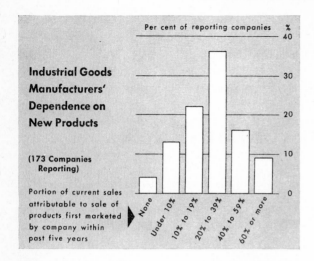

Figure 1-1b Industrial goods manufacturers' dependence on new products
Source: *Ibid.*, p. 39

How much of 1972 sales will be in new products?

INDUSTRY	Percent of 1972 sales	Billions of 1968 dollars
Iron and steel	7	2.88
Nonferrous metals	11	2.34
Electrical machinery	20	11.80
Machinery	21	17.58
Autos, trucks and parts	17	9.93
Aerospace	51	20.59
Other transportation equipment (RR equipment, ships)	10	0.83
Fabricated metals and instruments	20	13.18
Stone, clay and glass	15	2.93
Other durables	21	9.58
TOTAL DURABLES	21	91.64
Chemicals	16	10.04
Paper and pulp	12	3.86
Rubber	8	1.52
Petroleum	6	1.56
Food and beverages	8	9.39
Textiles	18	5.08
Other nondurables	5	3.64
TOTAL NONDURABLES	10	35.09
ALL MANUFACTURING	16	126.73

Figure 1-1c How much of 1972 sales will be in new products?
Source: New York: Economics Research Department, McGraw-Hill Publications Co., by permission

have grown large by the introduction of new products as illustrated by International Business Machines and General Electric. Other companies have stagnated or died because they failed to develop new products to meet new demands and new competition. The moral is that the successful finding, developing, and introducing of new products and services is vital to the success of almost any business—whether a manufacturing, commercial, financial, or service organization. Even non-profit foundations and government agencies are caught up in the problems and opportunities associated with new products.

The opportunities are great. With the temporary monopoly afforded by a new product, profit margins are widened, and capital earned can be "ploughed back" into the business to cause it to grow even faster. New products can cause sales and profits to increase even during recessions and depressions. However, there is another side to the picture. *The risks are great.* Experience indicates that only one in about 60 new product ideas, on the average, is a success. Figure 1-2 shows how ideas are discarded or fail as they move through the new product development process.

It seems rather evident from the above that new products present both an opportunity and a risk—a risk that the ordinary company must take. The problem is to *minimize the risk and maximize the chances for a success.* Another view is that a company should move toward the best, not merely away from the worst; it is a much-to-be-preferred action. This movement is towards risk, not toward safety. Safety is an illusion in business as Lockheed Aircraft Corp. and General Dynamics Corp. discovered when they came to the verge of bankruptcy. The chief executive officer of a company and his board of directors are often called upon to *bet their company* when one or more of the following factors appear:

1. A new opportunity appears which is too good to pass up. This may be a major technical breakthrough or it may be a simple new product, either of which could restructure the industry and realign future competitors.
2. The traditional business of the company is gradually eroding and something must be done to

change the trend, or the company will slowly fail. Major diversification is the only alternate to going out of business.

3. The high rate of earnings yields cash flows which are beyond the reinvestment plans of the basic business. In today's "new business environment" large cash reserves are tempting targets for corporate raiders, hungry stockholders, or the Internal Revenue Service.

Risk—the probability of exposure to loss—is an inseparable companion of opportunity. Business judgments are based upon experience, analysis, and intuition. The risk is not taken until somebody *acts*. The entrepreneur, in many cases, may take the same action as the large corporation but he assumes it *earlier* when the risk is greater.

Expressions of judgment about the future and about the value of alternative ventures have tradi-

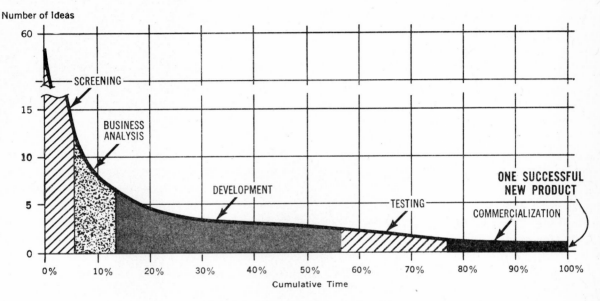

Figure 1-2 Mortality of new product ideas
Source: *Management of New Products*, Booz, Allen & Hamilton, Inc. Management Consultants, 1968

4. A new product is apparently succeeding to some degree, but it will require cash far beyond the existing resources of the company in order to fully exploit the product. New debt or equity capital must be obtained. There is no assurance that success will be achieved; however, not to take advantage of the possibility is to throw away a major opportunity. (The Haloid Corporation which became Xerox Corporation is the classic case).

THE NATURE OF RISK

The opportunities and the profits offered by the introduction of new products represent only one side of the coin. On the other side are risk and loss.

tionally been vague and ill-defined. It is advantageous for the venture manager to attempt to express his beliefs in a way which permits comparisons. This involves careful and precise definition of beliefs and facts coupled with some kind of rating or index scale. For this purpose, it is convenient to use a scale ranging from 0 to 1.00 for which zero represents the very unlikely and 1.00 represents the practically certain event. This degree-of-belief index is also called the subjective probability of an event. While we readily admit that expressing a judgment that a new product's chance of success is 0.85 does not necessarily add to the accuracy of the words "very likely", however, it does have several advantages. It forces the manager or entrepreneur to think a little more carefully about what leads up to his conclusion. It permits combining judgments about many events which make up the future. And finally, it permits comparison of views among people in an organization through use of a common language. For these reasons, we will include some elementary applications of quantitative judgments in venture management throughout this book.

RISK AND NEW PRODUCT VENTURES

As we noted earlier, a business *venture* is directed toward profits with a significant risk attached. If we simply invest a sum of money in AAA rated bonds with the expectation that our capital will eventually be returned and we will receive a stream of dividends, this is not a "venture". The risk is negligible and the return on investment is practically certain and minimal. A business venture is characterized by a wide range of profit (or loss) possibilities and a risk which is significant enough to deter the masses of investors with their aversions to high risk.

The foreboding estimates of the percentage of new products which fail indicate that product innovation is indeed a venture. In 1968, for example, 9450 supermarket lines were introduced, but less than 20% met their sales goals. A single product failure in this field may cost from $75,000 in test marketing stage to $20,000,000 for national introduction.[2]

While such figures may cause panic in the faint-hearted, the true entrepreneur is aware of some more cheerful facts about a new product venture. First, rarely does a good manager *bet his company* on a *single* venture; therefore, complete failure does not usually result in complete disaster. At the same time, the issue is not usually one of facing overwhelming success vs. complete disaster such as betting our fortune on a spin of the roulette wheel. There are various gradations of success and gradations of loss. The skillful entrepreneur seeks to minimize his loss on the downside and maximize his profits on the upside. His ingenuity in finding ways to do this is what sets him apart from the traditional management of most large companies.

Preventive measures are usually better than after-the-failure measures. It is well to plan and manage a venture so that the probability of success increases more rapidly than the cumulative investment in the venture. In Figure 1-3, Curves A and C show the undesirable cases which are so common and Curve B shows a better approach to be sought.

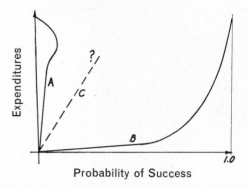

Figure 1-3   Risk and expenditures for new product ventures

Since risk is expressed by action based upon judgment about the future, the objective of the entrepreneur should be to improve his predictions. This is not as difficult as it might first appear. There are many fairly reliable tie-points for him to connect to. Projections of GNP, technological forecasts, industry forecasts, trends in consumer tastes, and government policies are a few. For the local business there are such assists as city planning, demographic trends, and regional economic studies. The main point is that the manager rarely faces a situation in which he is completely uncertain about future events. Some information is available and more is obtainable for him to base some predictions. The skillful entrepreneur will seek *key* information and plan systematically rather than plunge blindly into the future.

To help identify the decision areas relating to ventures of which the entrepreneur must be cognizant so as to move intelligently toward profit and away from hazard, F. H. Krantz developed Figure 1-4. The kinds or varieties of hazards associated with the decision areas identified above are shown in Figure 1-5.

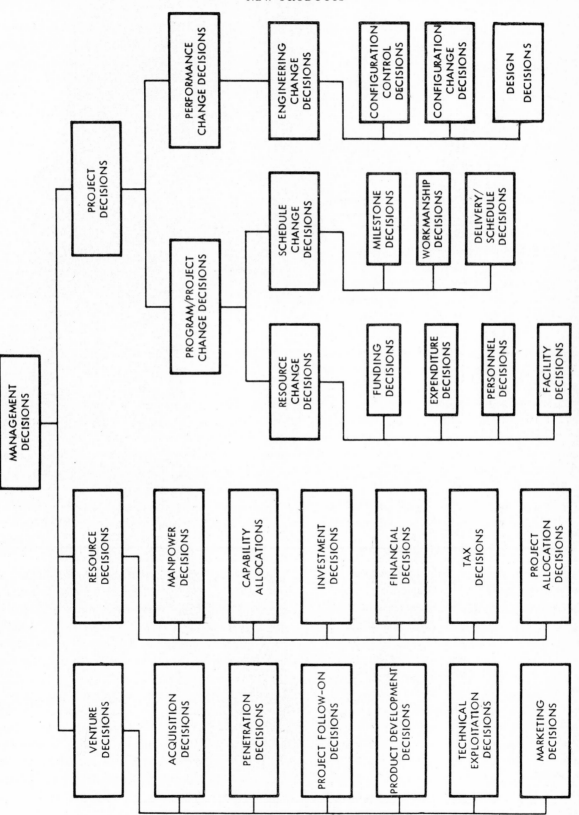

Figure 1-4 Decision areas important to the entrepreneur

Source: F. H. Kranz, "The Hazards of Project Decisions", The Institute of Management Sciences Presentation, North American Rockwell Corp., 1969

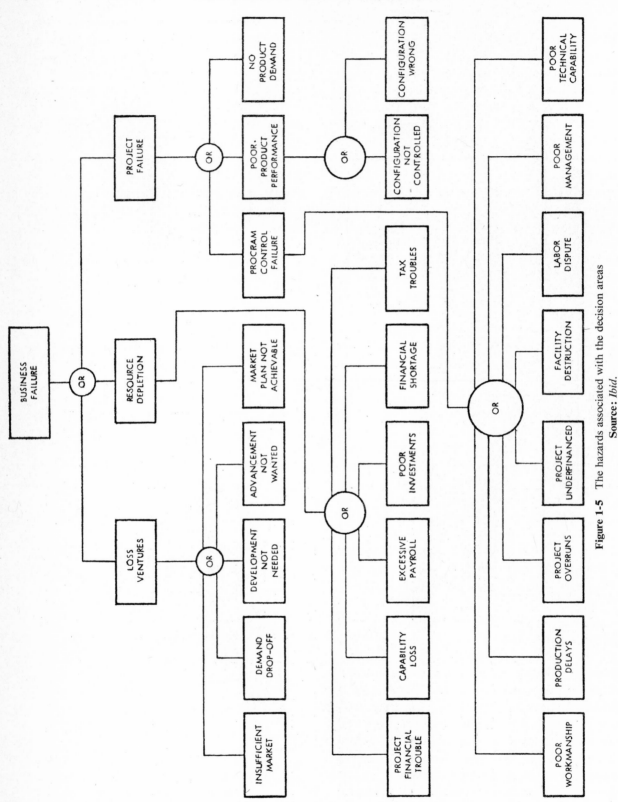

Figure 1-5 The hazards associated with the decision areas

Source: *Ibid.*

RISK AND GROWTH

Most businesses attempt to minimize risk by innovating around the edge of present products. The result is that rapid changes in market needs and revolutionary products produce unpleasant and unprofitable surprises. Instead of designing today yesterday's needs, the venture-oriented firm designs ahead to be ready for tomorrow's needs. He forecasts new needs, seeks to uncover felt but undefined needs, and attempts to capitalize on constantly changing technology and manufacturing methods. Growth is the watchword of the entrepreneurial management. This growth is achieved not only by getting the jump on competition through major innovations, but also by investing in an increasing number of ventures. American business has generally been unwilling to utilize the funds available by increasing its debt/equity ratio. In balancing the risk of illiquidity associated with potential rapid growth against the certainty of slow growth and safety of liquidity, United States firms have opted for the security blanket. As the sophisticated Boston Consulting Group puts it:

American companies rarely have debt levels exceeding 50% of book equity, whereas Japanese companies on average use debt equal to *four times* or more of stated equity. It is not at all surprising that Japanese companies, with *significantly lower profit margins*, grow two or three times faster than their American Competitors; no more surprising is the rapidity of Japanese economic growth relative to that of the United States.[3]

RISK AND TIME

It seems reasonable to assume that there is more risk involved in the expectation of receiving a dollar of revenue ten years from now that of receiving a dollar next year. When a product is assumed to have a long life, therefore, later revenues should be discounted for risk. New products by competitors, changes in consumers' tastes, or specific technological innovations may shorten the anticipated life of a product.

Long-range forecasts of such environmental factors are always less reliable than short-range forecasts.

Since the actual values of a stream of future revenues should be discounted for time, discounting for risk gives a further reduction of the present value of revenues anticipated for a new product. In comparing alternative new product proposals, therefore, products with high initial sales and short lives will be favored over those providing modest revenues over a long period of time. This introduction of risk into evaluation criteria will therefore require a constant search for new products that will likely yield high return on investment.

As we mentioned previously, the *timing* of action is an important aspect of risk and venture gains. Early entry into the market in the case of a successful product has four advantages:

1. It may assure a major share of the market over the life of the product
2. The firm which maintains the major share of the market always leads his competitors in experience with resulting lower costs
3. Resources are converted into revenues earlier in time so that the present value of returns from the project is greater
4. A first-in first-out policy takes advantage of the life-cycle peak of most products so that resources may be continually reinvested in the high-profit phase of product life cycles.

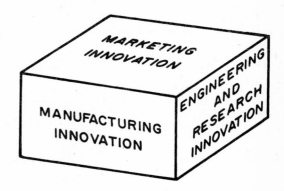

Figure 1-6 The three dimensions of product newness
Source: D.W.Karger and R.G.Murdick, "Product Design, Marketing, and Manufacturing Innovation", Copyright, 1966 by the Regents of the University of California. Reprinted from the *California Management Review*, Vol. **IX**, No. 2, p. 41, by permission of the Regents

INCREASING MARKET NEWNESS			
Expand sales into new classes of customers.	No change in product, but new classes of customers reached. Probably involves finding some new uses for product. Can occur without expansion of sales to old classes of customers; can even occur when sales to old classes of customers are decreasing. Finding new uses for product may involve technical or new product assistance.	No change in product, but new classes of customers reached. Probably involves finding some new uses for product. Can occur without expansion of sales to old classes of customers; can even occur when sales to old classes of customers are decreasing. Finding new uses for product may involve technical or new product assistance.	Expanded sales to new classes of customers will not automatically occur. If such expanded sales occur it will be principally for same reasons and in same manner as those for an unchanged product.
Strengthened market in existing classes of customers.	Remerchandising and/or other sales effort to expand sales. Sell more customers of the same types previously served.	Remerchandising and/or other sales effort to expand sales. Sell more customers of the same types previously served.	Market coverage for present classes of customers likely to increase due to improvements in product characteristics and merchandisability. Since there is an effect on price, however, the general aim is always to reduce cost, increase profit margin, and only increase price when absolutely necessary.
No market change.	No change in product characteristics and no change in market penetration.	No change in product characteristics and no change in market penetration.	Positive market change likely to result; however, some adverse market parameters could hold sales constant, or even let them slip.
	No product change.	Product characteristics remain same but changes in components, formulation, production techniques, etc., made to keep costs in line and quality at same relative level.	Minor design modification. Improvements in product characteristics to yield greater utility to customers and/or increase merchandisability. Example: side-burn trimmer on Sunbeam electric shaver.

INCREASING PRODUCT

Figure 1-7

WHAT CONSTITUTES A NEW PRODUCT

A "new" product is a product which is differentiated from other similar products already on the market, including those of the company introducing it. The problem is to specify the degree of differentiation which makes a product "new". A new product must be sufficiently different from older designs or products or reach new markets such that the physical, functional, or psychological benefits can be dis-criminated by customers after reasonable promotion by the firm. In some cases, a minor revision from a technological viewpoint of an existing product could have a greater market impact than a completely new product. Since there is considerably less risk in introducing a redesigned product than a completely new product, small companies should consider carefully such an alternative. The purpose of new product development is, after all, to maintain the life and profitability of the company. Each company must

In effect, the marketing function is here concerned with what is essentially a new product, complete with all the problems associated with a new product.	Opening of new markets because of introduction of a replacement product does not automatically follow. Unless changes in characteristics and/or resultant price obviously opens new markets, new applications must be actively sought and aggressively exploited when found in order to reach new classes of customers.	Addition of new product lines makes it possible to attract new classes of customers, especially where previously incomplete line made it necessary for certain classes of customers to buy from several manufacturers. New marketing programs involving promotion, channels of distribution, and emphasis required.	Addition of new product lines makes it possible to attract new classes of customers, especially where previously incomplete line made it necessary for certain classes of customers to buy from several manufacturers. New marketing programs involving promotion, channels of distribution, and emphasis required. If company is the first to use the new technology, coordinated marketing program may mean entirely new markets.
With major design modification of a product, is usually a strengthened market, because the sales department has new ideas to promote.	Replacement product usually lends itself to a remerchandising campaign resulting in greater penetration of existing markets.	If new product will be used by existing customers, the hold on them will be strengthened, especially if new product relates in some manner to existing product line.	If new product will be used by existing customers, the hold on them will be strengthened, especially if new product relates in some manner to existing product line. If company is the first to use the new technology, significant market gain may result.
Positive market change likely to result; however, some adverse market parameters could hold sales constant.	Product changes drastic enough to change market penetration. Example (possible little effect on market): synthetic resin instead of shellac in Johnson's Glo-Coat in 1950.	Not applicable.	Not applicable.
Major design modification. Example: IBM Selectric Typewriter.	Replacement of an existing product by new but related technology. Example: replacing tube-type portable radio with transistorized model.	Diversification: addition of a new product line (could be a new company introducing the product) involving existing technology, but new to the company. Examples: Bulova Accutron watches, Tensor lamps, G.E. computers.	Diversification or product line expansion using new technology. Involves development and/or expansion of the new technology.

NEWNESS ————————————➤

Marketing vs product newness

seek a direction which capitalizes upon its talents, whether these are engineering, marketing or manufacturing. Figure 1-6 illustrates the ways in which a firm may progress in its new product development.

In order to illustrate more clearly what we mean by degrees of newness of a product and how a company can have new products without new markets and vice versa, two interfaces of the matrix illustrated in Figure 1-g will be found in Figures 1-7 and 1-8. These figures are titled respectively Marketing versus

Product Newness and Manufacturing versus Product Newness. It is important for the new product venture manager to carefully study these figures so that all of the implications are understood and practical applications may be achieved.

While Figures 1-7 and 1-8 show the range of measurement of innovation in relatively fine steps, we might still wonder how much change produces a truly new product. A few examples which may provide some insight are listed below:

Technical	Technical	Manufacturing	Marketing
Ballpoint pen	Jet aircraft	Industrial diamonds	Drop shipping
Computer (new generations)	Three-way light switch	Timex watches	Discount stores
Laser equipment	Dial telephone	IBM "Selectric" typewriter	Rotating charge accounts
Safety glass	Penicillin	Printed circuits	Games and prizes
Atomic power plant	Touch-tone push button telephone	Integrated circuits	Trading stamps
Television	"Acutron" watch		

INCREASING PROCESS NEWNESS ↑

New - to - the - world manufacturing processes. Examples: "Float" plate glass. High energy metals forming. Use of lasers.	Not applicable.	Not applicable.	Not applicable.
Introduction of a new type of processing. Examples: Replacing electromechanical with electronic switching (assistance from engineering required). New products designed by engineering) to either expand existing line or begin a new line.	Not applicable.	Not applicable.	Not applicable.
Major modification of existing processing methods and/or materials. Example: batch vs. continuous production.	Not normally applicable. No change in basic product or its characteristics but changes in quantity or cost projections may necessitate reprocessing.	Not normally applicable.	Not normally applicable.
Minor modification of existing plant processing (materials and/or methods).	Minor modification in processing often made with consequent minor effect upon cost and/or quality.	No change in basic product characteristics, but minor changes in manufacturing methods to keep costs in line.	Production costs may increase or decrease. Major manufacturing process changes not usually required. Volume may increase and reduce costs.
No processing change.	No change in product or manufacturing.	Not applicable.	Not applicable.
	No change.	Product characteristics remain the same, but changes in components, formulation, production techniques, etc., to keep costs in line and quality at the same relative level.	Minor design modification. Improvements in product characteristics to yield greater utility to customers and/or increase merchandisability. Example: Addition of side-burn trimmer to Sunbeam electric shaver.

INCREASING PRODUCT

Figure 1-8

All of the above represented to the purchaser something completely new. Examination of the technical innovations indicate three methods by which major leaps were made: (1) accidental discovery, (2) invention, and (3) long or intensive laboratory research effort. In the case of computers, many small improvements combined with new arrangements are held up for economic reasons until a really new product—a new generation of computers—can be made available. In contrast, once television appeared on the market, no major new generation of television sets appeared until color TV.

Consider the first crude black and white TV set compared with the color-controlled, instant start, remote controlled set of today. The latter would certainly be classified as a new product if it had been

Not applicable. Could be involved, but not usually.	Could be involved, but not usually.	Could be involved.	Required.
May be required.	May be required.	New-to-the-company processing or major modification is usually required.	Often required, sometimes in combination with above.
Major changes in processing usually involved and often is one of the major reasons for design modification. Cost quality, and/or product characteristics affected.	Major modification (or introduction of new processing) is required.	Major modification (or introduction of new processing) is required.	Major modification (or introduction of new processing) is required.
Major change in process usually involved.	Not applicable.	Not applicable.	Not applicable.
Not applicable.	Not applicable.	Not applicable.	Not applicable.
Major design modification. Example: IBM Selectric Typewriter.	Replacement of existing product by new but related technology. Example: Replacing tube-type portable radio with transistorized model.	Diversification: addition of new product or product line (could be new company introducing product) involving existing technology but new to the company. Examples: Bulova Accutron watches, Tensor lamps, G.E. computers.	Diversification or product line expansion using new technology. Involves development and/or expansion of the new technology. Examples: G.E. nuclear power plants. Douglas's rocket system.

NEWNESS——————————————→

Manufacturing vs product newness

Source: D.W.Karger and R.G.Murdick, "Product Design, Marketing, and Manufacturing Innovation", Copyright, 1966 by the Regents of the University of California. Reprinted from the *California Management Review*, Vol. IX, No. 2, p. 16, 17, by permission the Regents

the immediate successor of the black and white set. This is typical of many products.

It is possible to plot a "progress function" of an index of merit vs. time. A "new" product could be considered to be one for which either the figure of merit jumped the equivalent of 10 years of progress. While these particular numbers are arbitrary, they nevertheless indicate how a really new product could be defined. Similar reasoning could be applied to manufacturing and marketing innovations.

SOME NEW PRODUCT BASICS

We have assumed up until now that the meaning of a "product" was well known. In actuality, we have placed major emphasis on the *physical* product (except for the marketing implications). A product, at least a commercially successful one, is something which satisfies a bundle of needs of the buyer. Functional, psychological, social, and cultural dimen-

sions are associated with each product. Each of these aspects influences the buying decision of the customer. The nature of these dimensions are discussed in more detail in subsequent chapters.

The nature of new product development is also greatly affected by the *type* of purchaser. Therefore, we should consider new products in terms of the three major classes of purchasers:

1. Consumers who use up the product for personal satisfactions
2. Industrial purchasers who use products in the production of products to achieve added value to their products
3. Government, which purchases products to fill political or social needs.

In addition to the purchase decision influences and the market characteristics, products are characterized by four types of time cycles:

1. Long cycles of social or cultural swings. Fashion cycles typify these. Snug fitting suits for men, vests, cuffs, clothes, use of cosmetics and beards.

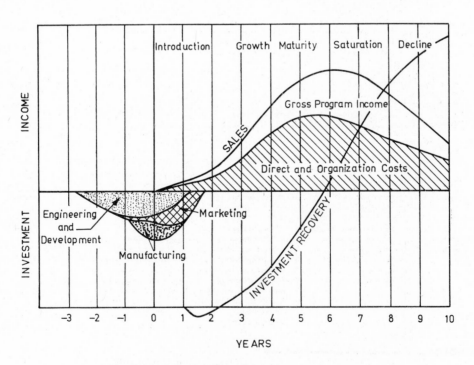

Figure 1-9a   Product life cycle and investment recovery
Source: Harry L. Hansen, *Marketing: Text, Techniques and Cases*, Homewood, Ill.: Richard D. Irwin, Inc., 1969, p. 90

Similarly, for women one can cite such things as lengths of skirts, high waist or low waists, and amount of decolletage.

2. "Life cycles" for products which may be as short as a few days or as long as a decade. The life cycle of a manufacturer's product may be terminated by the economics of a highly competitive market, by technological progress, or by changes in consumers' tastes.

3. Planned obsolescence cycles in which the manufacturer terminates the life of a product by making minor changes in either function or appearance and discontinues production of the superceded product.

4. "Sudden death" cycles in which the government orders the production of a particular product to be ended. Examples, include drugs, foods, and items which are hazardous to the user in other ways such as radiation from TV, fireworks, aircraft with suspected defects.[4]

Most products, and many services, have a life cycle similar to that illustrated in Figures 1-9a and 1-9b. Sales do not bring in revenue until a considerable investment has been made. Usually sales rise

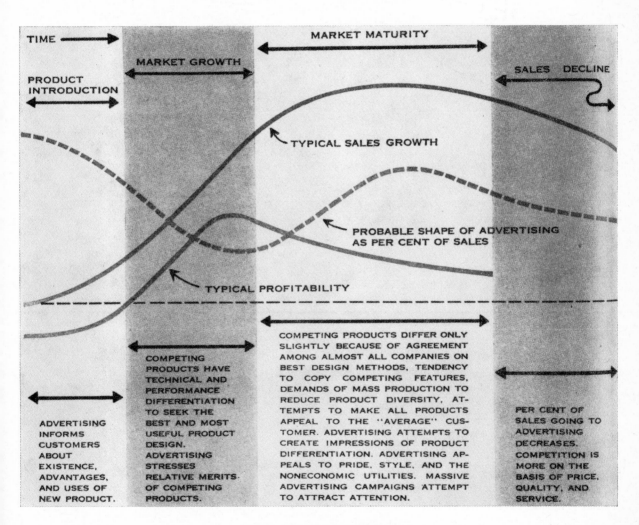

Figure 1-9b   Product life phases
Source: J. W. Forrester, "Advertising: A Problem in Industrial Dynamics", *Harvard Business Review*, March–April, 1959

gradually at first until the product has become known and accepted. There are, of course, meteoric rises such as in the cases of ballpoint pen, Tensor lamp, polio shots and Xerox equipment.

As competitors enter the market, the sales of the product innovator usually continue to increase, but at a slower rate. As the market becomes saturated,

Earlier, the mortality rate of new products as they go through the various stages of development and evaluation was mentioned and described in Figure 1-2. Figure 1-12 shows the typical cumulative expenditures over time as determined by the Management Research Department of Booz, Allen & Hamilton, Inc.

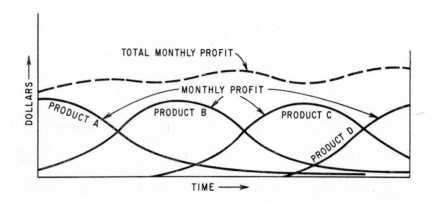

Figure 1-10 How profit contributions from a company's products vary with time
Source: D. W. Karger and R. G. Murdick, *Managing Engineering and Research*, New York: The Industrial Press, 1969

sales begin to drop. With production facilities in full operation, each firm attempts economies, lower prices, and tries to obtain a larger share of a declining market. Profits decline with decreasing volume and decreasing profit margins. At this point, the life cycle of the product is ending and additional innovations are needed.

The determination in advance of the shape and length cycle is important to the entrepreneur who seeks to move to new products as the market saturates. Methods for fitting curves to early data to forecast the shape of life cycles have been developed.

The new product venture manager needs to keep in mind that if products do have a life cycle similar to that shown in Figure 1-9a, that a continuous stream of new products needs to be introduced merely to keep revenues at a reasonable constant level as is illustrated in Figure 1-10.

It is possible to redesign and revise an existing product so as to cause the general configuration of the life cycle to take the form shown in Figure 1-11

It is simple to conclude by viewing Figure 1-2 and Figure 1-12 that it is more profitable to kill off the unsuccessful product early in the development stage. This is why screening and business analysis, about which more will be said later, is so very important.

There is another lesson to be learned from this same Booz, Allen & Hamilton study about where the losses in terms of expense dollars are likely to occur. This information is shown in Figure 1-13.

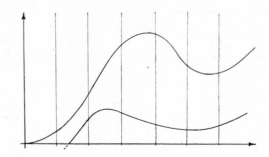

Figure 1-11 Life cycle of a product which is renewed

These facts should not lead us to believe that we cannot succeed in new product ventures. The same management consulting firm studied 54 prominent companies and found that 57 per cent of 366 new products recently marketed were successful; 23 were doubtful; and only 10 per cent were known failures. This is a strong indication that new product risks can be successfully managed.

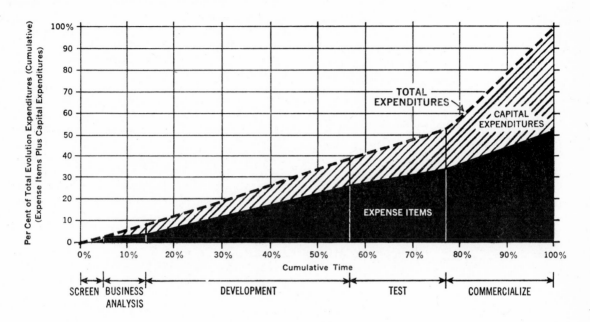

Figure 1-12 Cumulative expenditures and time

Source: *Management of New Products*, Booz, Allen and Hamilton, Inc. Management Consultants, New York, 1968

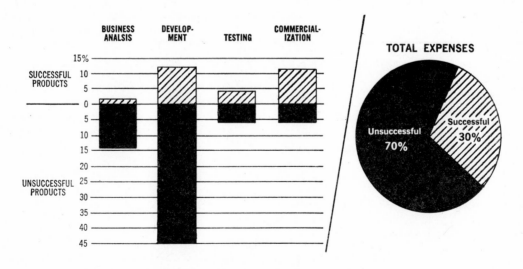

Figure 1-13 Effectiveness of new product expenditures

Source: *Management of New Products*, Booz, Allen and Hamilton, Inc. Management Consultants, New York, 1968

REFERENCES

1. *Management of New Products*, Booz, Allen & Hamilton, Inc., Management Research Consultants, 1968.
2. Theodore L. Angelus, "Why New Products Fail", *Marketing Insights*, May 12, 1969, p. 14.
3. The Boston Consulting Group, Inc., "Risk and Economic Growth", Perspective #57, Boston, 1969.
4. W. E. Cox, Jr., "Product Life Cycles as Marketing Models", *Journal of Business*, October, 1967. See also Brockhoff, K., "A Test for the Product Life Cycle", *Econometrica*, July–Oct., 1967.

BIBLIOGRAPHY

"A Conglomerate Bucks the Trend", *Business Week*, July 11, 1970.

Andersen, Sigurd L., "Venture Analysis a Flexible Planning Tool", *Chemical Engineering*, March, 1961.

"A Rough Sacking for Viyella Chief", *Business Week*, Dec. 20, 1969, p. 23.

"As I See It", *Forbes*, June 1, 1969, pp. 53–57.

Berg, Thomas and Shuckman, Abe, *Product Strategy and Management*, Holt, Rinehart, and Winston, New York, 1963.

"Bet Your Company", The Boston Consulting Group, 1969.

Brockhoff, Klaus, "A Test for the Product Life Cycle", *Econometrica*, July–October, 1967.

Carters, C. F., G. P. Meredith, and G. L. S. Shackle, *Uncertainty and Business Decisions*, Liverpool U. Press, 1962, pp. 43–44.

Cole, Arthur H., *An Approach to the Study of Entrepreneurship: A Tribute to Edwin F. Gray*, Cambridge: Harvard U. Press, 1965.

Collins, Orris S., David G. Moore, and Darab B. Unwalla, *The Enterprising Man*. East Lansing, Michigan, Michigan State U. of Business Studies, 1964.

Cox, W. E. Jr., "Product Life Cycles as Marketing Models", *Journal of Business*, October 1967.

Dean, D. V., *Evaluating, Selecting and Controlling R & D Projects*, American Management Association, Inc., 1968.

"Divestment and Growth Perspectives", The Boston Consulting Group, 1969.

"Du Pont's 'answer machine'", *Business Week*, December 20, 1969.

"Entrepreneurs are Made, Not Born", Forbes, June 1, 1969, pp. 3–57.

Furst, S. and Sherman, M., *The Strategy of Change for Business Success*, Clarkson & Potter, Inc., 1969.

Fusfeld, Alan R., "The Technological Progress Function: A New Technique for Forecasting", working paper #438–70, Sloan School of Management, M.I.T., January, 1970.

"Gallery of Business Wonders", *Fortune*, Jan. 1969, pp. 80–83.

Gee, E. A., Andersen, S. L., and Gee, R. E., "New Venture Planning, A Quantitative Approach to Managing Risks", Development Department E.I. du Pont de Nemours & Company, Willmington, Delaware, June 2, 1965.

Cole, Arthur H., *Business Enterprise in its Social Setting*, Cambridge, Harvard U. Press, 1959.

Gerlach, J. T. and Wainwright, C. A., *Successful Management of New Products*, Hastings House, 1958.

Gough, J. W., *The Rise of the Entrepreneur*, New York, Shocken Books, 1969.

Grossman, Adrian J., "An Approach for Formalizing Entrepreneurial Processes in Business", CIOS, 1963 XIII.

Hanan, Mack, "Corporate Growth Through Venture Management", *Harvard Business Review*, January–February, 1969.

Hilton, P., *Handbook of New Product Development*, Prentice Hall, New Jersey, 1961.

Hilton, P., *New Product Introduction for Small Business Owners*, Small Business Administration, Washington, 1961.

"How the High Fliers Take Off", *Business Week*, Nov. 22, 1969, pp. 112–114.

"Improving on the General", *Forbes*, April 15, 1970, p. 78.

Jackson, Myles, "New Product Development as a Normal Part of General Management Activity", The President's Association, American Management Association, Inc., 1966.

Jackson, Myles, *The President's Involvement in the Development of New Products*, AMA, New York, 1966.

Karger, D. W., *The New Product*, Industrial Press, 1960.

Karger, D. W. and Jack, A. B., *Problems of Small Business in Developing and Exploiting New Products*, Rensselaer Polytechnic Institute, Troy, N.Y., 1963.

Kunstler, Donald, A. "Corporate Venture Groups: Vanguard of Innovation", *Marketing Insights*, December 2, 1968, pp. 14–16.

Levy, Robert, "The Go-Go World of the Risk Manager", *Dun's Review*, November, 1967.

Ludwig, S., "Gambling on Ideas for Fast Growth", *International Management*, Nov. 1968, pp. 26–27.

Marting, E. (ed), *New Products, New Profits and Companies Experience* in New Product Planning, AMA, New York, 1964.

Management of New Products, Booz, Allen and Hamilton, Inc., New York, 1968.

McClelland, David C., *The Archieving Society*, Princeton, N.J., Van Nostrand Co., Inc., 1961.

Merrill, M. A., "A Primer for the Prospective Entrepreneur", *Circuits Manufacturing*, Dec., 1969.

Miller, S. S., *The Management Problems of Diversification*, Wiley, 1963.

"New Ventures Grow Up", *Chemical Week*, Dec. 17, 1969, pp. 47–48.

"Perspectives on Corporate Strategy", The Boston Consulting Group, Boston, Mass., 1968.

Perspectives on Experience, The Boston Consulting Group, 1968.

Petersen, Russell W., "New Venture Management in a Large Company", *Harvard Business Review*, May–June, 1967, pp. 68–76.

"Profiles of Venture Capitalists", *The Institutional Investor*, Jan., 1970, pp. 51–52.

Roberts, E., "What It Takes to be an Entrepreneur ... And to Hang on to One", *Innovation*, New York, N.Y., 1969.

Sayigh, Jusif A., *Entrepreneurs of Lebanon*, Cambridge, Harvard U. Press, 1962.

Schoen, D.R., "Managing Technological Innovation", *Harvard Business Review*, May–June, 1969.

Scrase, R.R., (ed), "New Products: Concepts, Development and Strategy", Sixth Annual New Products Marketing Conference, 1956, University of Michigan, Graduate School of Business Administration, 1967.

Singer: "A New Way to Make Money", *Dun's Review*, Jan., 1970, pp. 22–23.

"Smart Money Draws a Crowd", *Business Week*, Feb. 28, 1970, pp. 92–95.

Steinmetz, Lawrence L., John B. Kline, and Donald P. Stegall, *Managing the Small Business*, Homewood, Illinois, Richard D. Irwin, Inc., 1968.

"They Gamble on New Technology", *Business Week*, Nov. 1, 1969, p. 128.

Tull, Donald, "The Relationship of Actual and Predicted Sales and Profits in New-Product Introductions", *The Journal of Business*, July, 1967.

"U.S. Business Trends", *Time*, May 10, 1963.

"Venture Capitalist With a Solid Intuition", *Business Week*, May 30, 1970, pp. 102–103.

"Venture Management", publication of The Center for Venture Management, Milwaukee, Wisconsin, Fall, 1969.

Wallenstein, G.D., "Concept and Practice of Product Planning", American Management Association, Macmillan, 1968.

"Wall Street: In On the Ground Floor," *Newsweek*, Feb. 10, 1969, p. 70.

Warshaw, M.R. and Murphy, G.P., editors, *New Product Planning for Changing Markets*, Seventh Annual New Products Marketing Conference, 1967, University of Michigan Graduate School of Business Administration, 1968.

"What Makes Entrepreneurs Tick?", *Steel*, Sept. 1, 1969, pp. 29–30.

"What Will He Think of Next?", *Sports Illustrated*, May 4, 1970, pp. 38–42.

"Why They Go By Themselves", *Forbes*, June 1, 1969, pp. 53–57.

CHAPTER 2

PRODUCT PLANNING

A company may be formed by an entrepreneur on the basis of a brilliant idea, an ingenious new product, or a gamble to fill a dormant need with a modified product. Once the company has passed the initial formative stage, the odds in favor of success are greatly increased by formalized short and long-range planning. Why? The business of management is the management of change.

The fact that leading large corporations have generally established a position of Director or Vice President of Corporate Planning indicates the importance of formal planning. As early as 1966 more and more companies were formalizing their long-term planning, and this was especially noticeable for the *Fortune* 500 list.

The principal link between the customers and the firm are the products of the firm. Therefore, the central focus of planning must be on products. Products represent the bridge which links customer needs with company capabilities. It is for this reason that we emphasize *product* planning in the broadest sense to be equivalent to total company planning.

NATURE OF PLANNING

"Planning is the formulation of thoughts and ideas to guide the strategy and tactics of an organization."[1] It is the exercise of foresight to adjust the company and activities in advance to events which will affect them. A business plan is a specification of performance in terms of quality, time and profit.

There are two kinds of planning, strategic and operational. *Strategic Planning* is concerned with top management decisions about the business and its product and marketing competencies; also included would be decisions on asset acquisition or disposal. *Operational Planning* (in contrast to strategic planning, takes the resources available and deploys or utilizes them so as to effectively achieve the near-term objectives and the immediate aspects of strategic decisions.

WHY PLAN?

Planning is not as automatically accepted as a good thing, the way profits are. The attempt to introduce formal periodic planning into a company usually brings objections such as:

"That's for big companies. My company is too small."

"I'm doing all right now. Why should I waste time and money on that?"

"I'm too busy keeping the business alive."

"I do my planning in my head."

"We've had a profitable business for over 50 years and never needed a plan before."

"Things change too fast. If I made a plan today, it would be worthless tomorrow."

The entrepreneur, who has the special talent for launching new products, is apt to be impatient with the careful systematic research and analysis required for long and short range planning. After great initial success with an innovation, lack of subsequent planning may convert a potentially profitable company into a loser. We point out below why and how planning leads to sustained profits and success.

The Need to Adapt

A business must serve a purpose in society by fulfilling a need better than anyone else if it is to exist. The environment of business is continually changing. Consumers' tastes and expectations change. A company must adapt or it will die. Planning provides means for adapting, before it is too late.

Planning as a Framework for Change

New organizational patterns and improved operating systems place stresses on the company. Without planning, such internal changes may be chaotic.

Competition

Aggressive and progressive competitors sharpen their attacks by means of careful planning. Planning must be conducted in self-defense.

Growth

Planning answers the questions, "How fast do we *want* to grow?" and "How fast *can* we grow?"

Product Planning

Planning for a company must begin with the focus on products. We mean that products must be chosen which will fulfill customers' needs on the one hand and be within the company's capability to produce on the other. At the same time, they must be such that they will yield a profit. Planning forces management to think about products in advance.

Gaps

Planning brings up gaps between a company's resources and objectives so that later surprise or disasters are averted.

What, Who, How, When, How Much

Formal planning requires management to specify exactly *what* will be done, *who* will do it, *how* it will be done, *when* it will be done, *how much* it is expected to return, and how much it will cost.

Search for Information

Planning quickly reveals to management information which it needs for more effective operation.

Integration and Coordination of Work

Planning provides the means for integrating all activities into a synchronized operation. Tasks are guided toward the common goals of the firm.

Risk Capital

Great ideas alone are not enough. The entrepreneur needs money to finance his ventures. Investors are more apt to risk money in ventures which are explained and supported by detailed plans.

Values and Beliefs

Nothing paralyzes initiative as much as uncertainty about the values of the top management of a company. Planning requires that values and beliefs be made explicit and conflicting values reconciled.

Basis for Measurement

Plans provide a basis for measuring the company as a whole and the profitability of each product in terms of *expectations*.

Reduces the Squeeze on Profits

Planning isolates projects where profitability is falling. It requires the comparison of alternative projects so that less profitable ones may be dropped.

Shortens the Product Development Cycle

It is very important to minimize the time from the concept of an idea to its entry on the market. The firm which gets a new product on the market first is likely to obtain the major share of the market over the life cycle of the product.

Reduces "Surprises"

Planning, because of its forward look, reduces surprises for management. Surprises generally require quick reaction and a lot of attention by the company. A company which is constantly fighting fires and meeting crises is not effective over the long run.

LONG-RANGE CORPORATE PLANNING

The advantages of long-range corporate planning (LRP) of 5 to 20 years ahead have become well accepted. The influence of companies who adopted it first made its advantages evident to lagging competitors. Generally, there are four major phases in LRP:
1. Establishing proprietary directions for corporate growth and the strategeic mission of the company taking into account the total environment of the business.
2. Establishing criteria for measurement of corporate success and for selection of products to fulfill the strategic mission of the company.
3. Product line and product planning.
4. Programming the business functions to implement product plans.

ESTABLISHING PROPRIETARY DIRECTIONS

The establishment of the strategic objectives is directed towards determining what the company can do best. This is accomplished by analyzing the potential capabilities of the company, by forecasting market opportunities of the future, and then by deciding on the role of the company. We must ask ourselves such broad and basic questions as:
1. What kind of business are we really engaged in now? This requires the company to look below "the surface". For example, IBM asked itself this question and decided its business was not selling computers but selling an information processing service.

2. What business do we want to be in three years from now, five years from now, ten years from now?
3. By what general method do we wish to make our transformations—internal change, acquisition and/or divestment?
4. What factors might affect our strategy?

With respect to developing the answer to question 1, it has always been important to be concerned with marketing the product. However, the company often is too concerned with how it views the product rather than how the *consumer* might view it or perceive it. It is most important to try and understand how the consumer will react, feel and judge the product; not how the company might judge the product. Building a better mouse trap is not enough. If the customer doesn't view it as a better mouse trap and doesn't want to own it for status, utility or some other reason, the product will be a failure. The Edsel automobile is a good example. Almost any kind of an automobile will give us reliable transportation at a cost commensurate to the size of the vehicle, but many other factors affect our purchase decision.

In order to answer all of the above questions especially 2, 3 and 4, the company must first ask itself "What are our major strengths?" and "What are our major weaknesses?" The "profile" analysis of the company should cover the following:
1. Corporate board
2. Executive talent
3. Quality and quantity of general and professional manpower, including special strengths in pertinent areas such as scientific, engineering, skilled craftsman, common labor, etc.
4. Financial position and capabilities
5. Facilities
6. Markets and marketing positions
7. Corporate image and reputation.

The corporate board is made up of individuals. As individuals they will have certain responses to situations which in turn are modified by inter-reactions among the group—the group therefore has another set of reactions. The board must determine the ground rules for risk taking or for "betting the company". Is the experience of the board collectively broad enough to guide the development and marketing of new product lines or the entry of the company into a completely new field? How experienced are they in the area of finance with respect to seeking and securing any required new equity capital and/or loans? These are just a few of the items related to Corporate Board evaluation.

With respect to manpower evaluation, the company must take into account the following:

1. Managerial personnel.
2. Depth of management talent for backup purposes.
3. Engineering and scientific strengths and weaknesses by field, depth in field and specialties.
4. Professional talent other than engineering and scientific with respect to quality and quantity by fields (financial, sales, production, etc.).
5. Supporting personnel by types.
6. Skilled, semi-skilled and unskilled workers with respect to quality and quantity as well as what potential reserves are available in the areas surrounding company plants.
7. Geographical dispersion of plants and employees.
8. Compensation practices.
9. Morale and loyalty of employees.

The evaluation of facilities must include the consideration of items such as the following for each plant, warehouse and/or office.

1. Size, location, type, layout, condition and modernness.
2. Types, kinds, condition, modernness, adaptability of manufacturing and/or material handling equipment.
3. Accessability to transportation, raw materials and markets.
4. Operating and maintenance cost.
5. Ownership and/or leasing arrangements.
6. Excess capacities by classifications.
7. Availability of adequate amounts of water, power, and other required utilities.

The marketing evaluation is going to be extremely important and here the considerations are lengthy and difficult. It should include consideration of the following factors:

1. Total available market for present product lines.

2. Fraction of total market secured for each product.
3. Reasons why a larger market share of the products has not been secured.
4. Market structure. What are the customer characteristics, the geographic locations of markets, price-volume relationships, product substitutes, and life of present products in the market?
5. The replacement parts market for each product line.
6. Seasonal and other important cyclical factors by product line.
7. Competitive position by product, and in total.
8. Channels of distribution (types, number and strengths).
9. Service policies, facilities and organization.
10. Market research capabilities.
11. Brand recognition.
12. Type and cost of advertising and sales promotion as well as effectiveness of same.
13. Service policy.
14. Price and discount structures by markets and/or products.
15. Patent position by product.
16. Scope of corporate charter.

Once the planners have established basic strengths and weaknesses, they are ready to begin the establishment of goals, both for the organization as a whole and with respect to specific new product ventures. New product venture goals cannot successfully be established and implemented without first establishing long-range over-all business goals and objectives. Such over-all goals and objectives include long-range financial, technical, production and marketing objectives. They should be related to anticipated company capabilities and future environmental changes.

The determination of these long-range goals must take into account:

1. Projected technological, economic, sociological, political and market trends.
2. Business prospects and directions.
3. Financial condition and structure of business in view of projected plans.
4. Technical objectives as related to facilities, manpower, organization and finance.

5. Physical facility and manpower requirements taking into account projected new products, materials and markets.

6. Marketing objectives by product line.

In order to take into account the factors in "1" of the above list it is obvious that a company should set up some sort of environmental surveillance—a sort of company CIA with respect to *all* environmental factors. Both the general and the special environments in which they operate must be surveyed regularly.

Product opportunities spring from the nature of society. The best are in the growing areas of society.

The list of six (6) factors will naturally take into account horizontal and vertical diversification of product lines, expansion of present product lines, entry into new related fields as well as unrelated fields and finally any planned entry into frontier fields. The Appendix A at the end of this Chapter provides a checklist for analysis of the company profile and mission.

Determining strengths and weaknesses and determining goals and objectives still will not assure success in new product ventures, but it will increase the odds in our favor.

ESTABLISHING CRITERIA FOR MEASUREMENT

Too many companies set criteria only in terms of what they *want to have* instead of what they *want to be*. Therefore their LRP and criteria for progress are primarily in money terms. While financial criteria are essential, other measures of accomplishment are strongly recommended. For example, General Electric establishes criteria for plans and measurement in eight key result areas:

1. Profitability
2. Market position
3. Productivity (effective utilization of men, capital, and raw materials)
4. Product leadership
5. Personnel developments
6. Public responsibilities

7. Employee attitudes
8. Balance between short-range and long-range goals.

PRODUCT PLANNING AS A FOCUS FOR COMPANY PLANNING

Once broad company goals and criteria for corporate performance have been established, the focus of planning turns to products. If we think about it, not one dollar of profit is made until a product is sold. A profitable set of products does not simply appear upon the scene; it must be planned for. Further, new products must be planned to replace products which must be dropped as they become obsolete.

Product planning is the development of plans for originating, evaluating, developing, and selecting a combination of products which will give the greatest expected profit when marketed. Product planning is a more specific type of planning, and shorter range, than the development of broad company objectives which precedes it. In most companies, the product planning function is a *coordination activity* or staff function which involves the *overseeing* of new product activity and the *resolution* of problems and delays. Line action is often achieved by appointing the functional managers (engineering, marketing, manufacturing) to a Product Planning Committee along with the staff product planner. Product planning *must be assigned as a full-time responsibility* to some individual in order to maintain continuity of effort.

ORGANIZING FOR PRODUCT PLANNING

In very small companies, product planning is usually carried out by the president or the president and some key individual in the company. This key individual may be an "idea" man, the head of marketing, or the chief engineer. The larger the company, the more variations in organization are possible. In large companies, a staff product planner who works with the line managers or with line representatives is common. This man often is the New Products Manager referenced in a later chapter which discusses in detail how to organize the new product function. Having a staff product planner permits coordination of all functional activities and commits the line organization to the support of what plans are developed. Figure 2-1 shows various common organizational arrangements for conducting product planning. Chapter 3 discusses in detail the how-to-do-it side of organizing.

SOME BASIC CONCEPTS FOR PRODUCT PLANNING

The development of the product line and of specific products must always be related to market needs. Yet there are two systematic ways to develop market-oriented products. One method which is particularly suited to development of mass-produced consumer goods is to start with research on evolving (changing preferences) consumers in a changing environment. When specific product needs are identified, the engineering or technical organization is put to work to determine the feasibility of various concepts which will match market needs.

The second systematic approach is one which small companies and industrial-goods producers often adopt. Because of the high cost of rigorous consumer or market research, they depend upon informal information-gathering methods for clues to the market. They invest their resources in the technical development with the hope that they will find a few good commercial possibilities from a large number of technical concepts. Generally in small companies "research" and engineering are directed towards product improvements or closely related products rather than towards major innovations. Further, for many of them the task is simplified because the customers served are often limited in number and each also often has similar characteristics and/or needs.

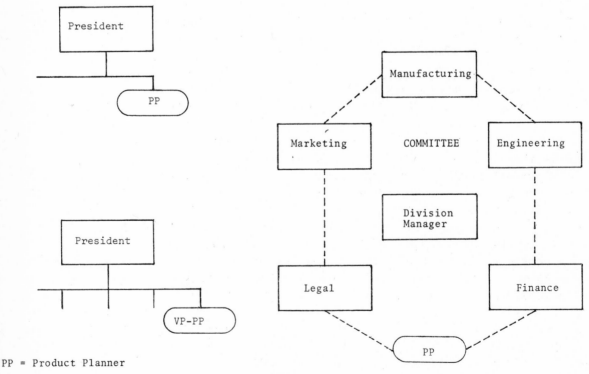

PP = Product Planner

Figure 2-1

Regardless of the simplicity or the sophistication of the new product planning system, it should be a repeated cycle of steps:

1. Compare the ideas available on the basis of (a) marketing, (b) design feasibility, (c) manufacturing feasibility, and (d) profitability and risk.
2. Eliminate from further consideration those product concepts which (1) do not meet minimum criteria or (2) are both low-ranking in terms of profit and risk and would require resources beyond what the company has available after pursuing the higher ranking projects.
3. Conduct further engineering or technical development, further analysis of manufacturing feasibility, further marketing research and profitability analysis, and additional planning for pro-

duct launching until the next screening point is reached.
4. Repeat the cycle, starting with the evaluation of product ideas-in-process as described in Step 1.

The evaluations described in the above steps are more effective if a total evaluation is made at each screening step. When manpower is very limited as in the case of small companies, a serial system of evaluation may be employed. In this method a product is developed (technically or by marketing planning) and then evaluated. If it fails in, say, a technical screening, no simultaneous marketing analysis has been wasted on it. Figure 2-2 illustrates this serial process. Since each step in the new product planning and development process is more costly than the preceding, more effort should

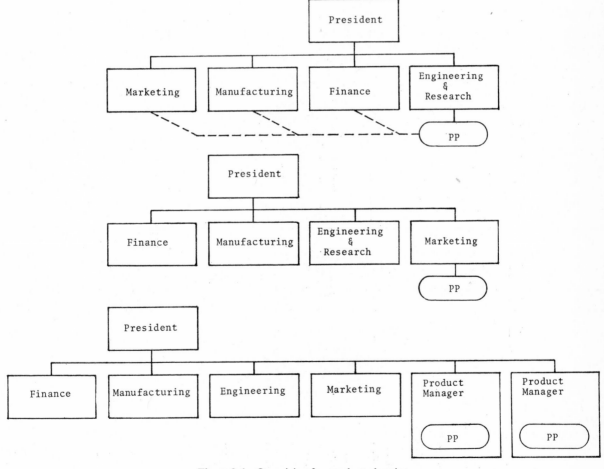

Figure 2-1 Organizing for product planning

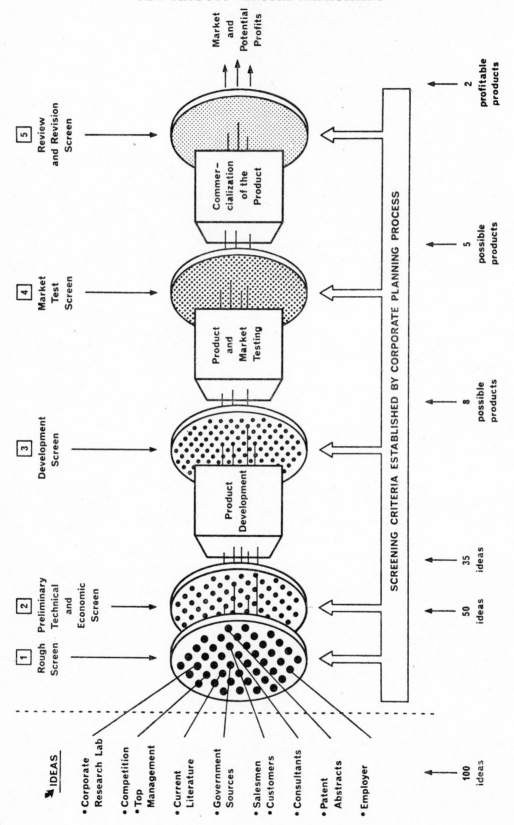

Figure 2-2 The new product screening process

Source: George A. Steiner, *Top Management Planning*, New York: The Macmillan Company, 1969, p. 582

Technique*	'59 or earlier	First year of use									No answer	Total
		'60	'61	'62	'63	'64	'65	'66	'67	'68		
		Number of companies										
Simulation	4	2	0	1	1	0	5†	0	8	1	3	25
Linear programming	5	1	0	0	2	1	1	0	2	2	1	15
Correlation analysis	13	0	0	0	4	0	1	1	2	1	0	22
Mathematical models	10	1	0	0	1	0	5	2	2	2	0	23
Statistical decision making	5	0	0	1	0	1	0	1	1	1	0	10
Decision trees	2	0	0	0	1	0	0	2	3	0	0	8
Bayesian analysis	0	0	0	0	2	0	0	0	1	0	0	3
Exponential smoothing	3	0	0	2	3	1	3	1	6	0	0	19
Delphi technique	0	0	0	0	0	0	0	1	0	0	1	2
Econometric methods	2	0	0	0	1	0	0	0	3	1	1	8
Game theory	0	0	0	0	0	0	0	0	1	0	0	1
PERT	6	2	1	2	2	5	2	5	1	1	0	27
Critical path method	6	2	1	1	4	2	1	3	0	1	0	21
Scenarios	0	0	0	0	0	0	1	0	0	0	0	1
Dynamic programming	0	0	0	0	0	0	0	1	0	0	0	1
Input/output analysis	0	0	0	0	1	0	0	1	4	1	0	7
Risk analysis	1	1	0	0	1	1	0	1	1	3	2	11
Present worth	7	2	0	0	2	2	1	5	3	0	0	22

* Techniques are listed in the order in which they appeared in the questionnaire.

† Indicates the median year of first use when the data were sufficient to make this calculation meaningful. In the absence of other information, those companies that did not report the year the technique was first used were put at the high or the low end of the distribution by the toss of a coin.

Figure 2-3 First year of use of advanced techniques for *operational* planning
Source: Ernest C. Miller, *Advanced Techniques for Strategic Planning*, AMA Research
Study 104, American Management Association, Inc., 1971

be invested in screening at each consecutive stage.

One of the vital functions of product planning is to establish the points at which an evaluation should be made. It may be extremely expensive to develop a product to the prototype stage only to discover that it cannot be produced and sold at a price which makes it commercially feasible. On the other hand, too frequent evaluations may eliminate products which suffer from temporarily unsolved problems. Also, frequent evaluations are cumulatively costly.

The proper emphasis in the evaluations are also very important in product planning. The product planner should distinguish among consumer pro-

ducts, industrial products, and defense products. In the first case, marketing considerations usually surpass technical problems. For industrial products, evaluations vary from balanced marketing-technical considerations to cases where technical considerations predominate almost entirely. Defense products require their own special screenings, since many must be partially developed in order for the company to bid. Bids most frequently involve a winner-take-all gamble. Thus, sophisticated risk analysis and perceptive management intuition must be combined in selecting projects to develop for bids.

Early in this chapter the difference between Operational and Strategic planning was highlighted

Technique*	'59 or earlier	'60	'61	'62	'63	'64	'65	'66	'67	'68	No answer	Total
				First year of use								
				Number of companies								
Simulation	2	1	0	0	1	1	5†	1	7	1	3	22
Linear programming	0	0	0	2	1	0	1	1	2	1	1	9
Correlational analysis	8	0	0	0	3	0	2	2	4	0	0	19
Mathematical models	4	1	0	0	1	0	1	4	3	3	0	17
Statistical decision making	1	1	0	0	0	0	0	1	2	1	0	6
Decision trees	2	0	0	0	1	0	1	0	5	0	0	9
Bayesian analysis	1	0	0	0	1	0	1	0	0	0	0	3
Exponential smoothing	1	1	0	1	1	0	0	1	2	0	0	7
Delphi technique	0	1	0	0	0	0	0	1	0	1	0	3
Econometric methods	1	0	0	0	0	0	0	0	1	0	0	2
Game theory	0	1	0	0	0	0	0	0	0	0	0	1
PERT	1	1	0	0	0	1	0	0	1	1	0	5
Critical path method	0	1	0	0	0	0	0	0	0	3	0	4
Scenarios	0	1	0	0	0	0	0	1	1	1	0	4
Dynamic programming	0	0	0	0	1	0	0	0	1	1	0	3
Input/output analysis	0	0	0	0	1	0	0	0	3	1	0	5
Risk analysis	1	1	0	0	2	2	1	1	4	5	2	19
Present worth	6	1	0	0	3	2	1	3	5	1	0	22

* Techniques are listed in the order in which they appeared in the questionnaire.

† Indicates the median year of first use when the data were sufficient to make this calculation meaningful. In the absence of information, those companies that did not report the year the technique was first used were put at the high or the low end of the distribution by the toss of a coin.

Figure 2-4   First year of use of advanced techniques for *strategic* planning
Source: Ernest C. Miller, *Advanced Techniques for Strategic Planning*, AMA Research
Study 104, American Management Association, Inc., 1971

by defining the activities. More advanced and sophisticated techniques than those mentioned to date (the more common approaches) have been used in connection with each kind of planning. These techniques and their prior application to each kind of planning is given in Figures 2-3 and 2-4 which summarizes the result of a mail survey of 245 companies with interviews of 41 individuals[2].

THE PRODUCT PLANNING PROCEDURE

As we have mentioned, basic corporate planning must precede actual product planning. The product planning procedure covers the following principal responsibilities:

1. Product scope recommendations
2. Product mix recommendations
3. Development of formal procedures for product planning
4. Development of methods for obtaining new-product ideas
5. Preparation of product *performance* specifications
6. Methods for evaluating products-in-development
7. Product timing from launching to the end of the commercial life-cycle

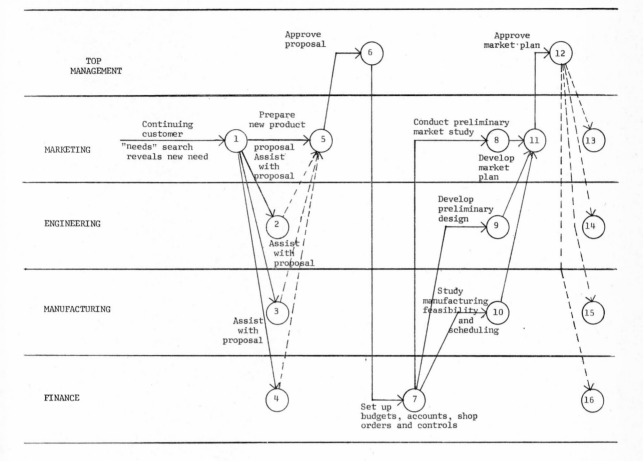

Figure 2-5   (continued on next two pages)

8. Price formulation recommendations
9. Product information for management
10. Monitoring and coordinating the engineering, marketing, and manufacturing activities for each product by the development of management information systems.

The above procedures may be amplified upon in terms of each significant task performed by individuals throughout the company. These may then be arranged in a "network" of activities which shows which activities must immediately precede any particular event. When time estimates are associated with each activity shown in Figure 2-5, the longest time path through the network represents the *minimum* time for completion of the plan. This longest time path is called the *critical path* and the planning method is known variously as PERT (Program Evaluation Review Technique), CPM (Critical Path Method), MP & CT (Management Planning and Control Techniques). The techniques require only simple arithmetic or standard computer programs. Appendix B gives an introduction to network planning and also contains more complete and complex new product critical path charts.

Obviously, the product planner, or even the product planning committee does not have line responsibility for performance and decision-making in each of the above areas. The product planner should, however, have planning, surveillance, and coordinative responsibilities. By a "coordinative" responsibility, we mean that, on the basis of management-approved plans, the product planner keeps line managers aware of all aspects of product development and market performance problems. He at-

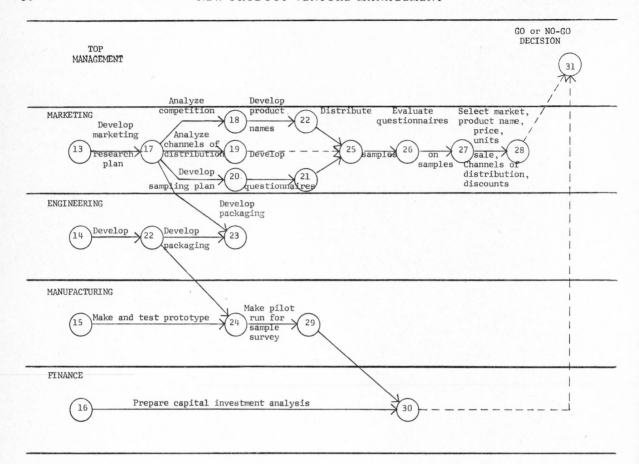

Figure 2-5

tempts to use persuasion to achieve product objectives. By securing the development of management information systems, he keeps top management informed of general product line performance, as well as unexpected opportunities or unexpected reverses.

PROJECT EXPLORATORY PLANNING

The exploration of new products and the critical evaluation at each stage deserve special attention. In later chapters we give specific techniques for finding new product ideas. We also describe the roles of marketing and engineering in evaluating new products. Specific marketing research procedures are described in a special chapter. At this point, we

wish to present the product planner's outlook on exploring new product ideas. This outlook coincides closely with that of top management. It is an integrating, "system" approach. In the following section, we will discuss evaluative techniques in the same light.

We noted earlier that new product ideas tend to appear on the scene as a result of either market studies or engineering/research exploration. In either case, other sources may trigger these studies as suggested by Figure 2-2 and amplified on in Chapter 4. Exploratory planning is the stage at which ideas are originally gathered and evaluated. It offers the chance for great rewards and for tragic foregone opportunities.

Let us look at some examples. Chester B. Carlson

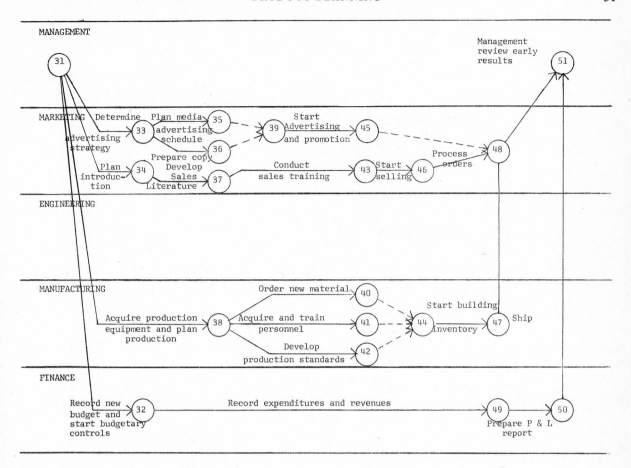

New product diagram *(cont.)*

developed a crude model of the xerographic copy process and finally had to turn over his search for a backer to Battelle Memorial Institute. The growth of the giant Xerox Corporation was based upon its gambling on the future success of this product.

One of the largest textbook publishers turned down a manuscript for a basic economics textbook because the editors didn't like the organization. The text became a best seller when another firm published it.

In 1950 General Electric developed the electronic computer OMIBAC in its Schenectady Aeronautics and Ordinance Systems Division. Lack of management interest let the project die. The small International Business Machines Corporation of 1950 has grown to where it ranks in the top 10 companies in size along with the General Electric Company, largely on the basis of the electronic computer.

One "new product", the push button shift on automobiles, reached the market and died quickly. Since it was only one part of a complex device—the auto itself—it is difficult to estimate the loss from this concept. The total system concept of the Edsel is more easily evaluated as a commercial failure.

In summary, the project exploratory planning is critical for two reasons: Good ideas may be rejected or poor ideas may be accepted. A careful, *thorough*, preliminary study should be made for each idea which could conceivably produce a great commercial success. The product planner could benefit greatly by following the outline for exploratory planning given in Figure 2-6.

MAJOR STEPS

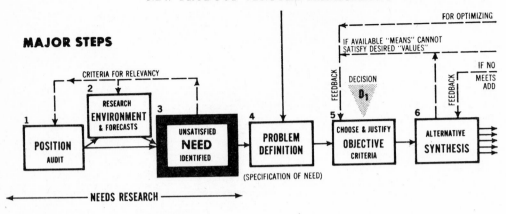

ANALYTICAL COMPONENTS

1. POSITION AUDIT
RESOURCES
CAPACITIES
PROFIT SOURCES
INVESTMENT
FINANCIAL CONSTRAINTS
MARKET SHARE
ATTRIBUTES
    Strengths
    Weaknesses
FLEXIBILITY
MOMENTUM

2. RESEARCH ENVIRONMENT & FORECASTS
SOCIO-ECONOMIC
    FORECASTS
REGULATORY CONSTRAINTS
FUNDAMENTAL SCIENTIFIC
    REVIEW & RESEARCH
TECHNOLOGY FORECASTS
NEEDS-OF-USER STUDY
MARKET POTENTIAL
POSITION OF COMPETITION
    Strengths
    Weaknesses

3. UNSATISFIED NEED IDENTIFIED
POSE CRITICAL QUESTION
    EXAMPLES
        A Business Need
        Problem Requiring Solution
        Goal Desired
        A Marked Demand, Lack,
            or Desire
        A Competitive Threat

An Apparent Opportunity ·
OFFICIALLY INITIATED BY
    "REQUEST-FOR-PROPOSAL"
IDENTIFIED BY FORMALLY
    ORGANIZED SEARCHING

4. PROBLEM DEFINITION
DESCRIBE SITUATION
    Economics
    User Requirements
    Policy
    Input/Output Analysis
LIST BOUNDARY
    CONSTRAINTS
    Tolerance
    User Desires
    "Spillover" Effects
    State-of-the-Art
    Urgency, etc.
MINIMIZE INTERACTION
    WITH OTHER "SYSTEMS"

5. CHOOSE & JUSTIFY OBJECTIVE CRITERIA
LIST VALUES DESIRED (i.e.,
    "ENDS" to be satisfied)
    Economic
    Convenience
    Psychological
    Legal
    Ethical
EVALUATE MERITS &
    SCREEN-OUT
    Assign Measure-of-Value
    Check for Realizability
    Test for Consistency

RANK PREFERENCES IDENTIFY
    DECISION-CRITERIA FOR
    PICKING OPTIMUM
    ALTERNATE
CLEARLY JUSTIFY THE NEED
    "FIT" WITH FIVE YEAR
    GOALS
STATE PREMISES WHERE
    LACKING FACTS
QUANTIFY CRITERIA
    WHEREVER POSSIBLE

6. ALTERNATIVE SYNTHESIS
COMPILE ⎫
INVENT ⎬ ALTERNATIVES
CREATE ⎭
TAKE IDEA CENSUS
APPLIED CREATIVITY
    Check Listing
    Attribute Listing
    Morphological Analysis
    Brainstorming Sessions
LIST AVAILABLE "MEANS"
    Inputs/Outputs
    Boundary Conditions
UNDERTAKE FUNCTIONAL
    SYNTHESIS
    Block Diagram Design
    Construct "Model"

7. ANALYSIS
DEDUCE CONSEQUENCES
    AGAINST OBJECTIVES
    Performance
    Risk
    Quality, etc.

Figure 2-6

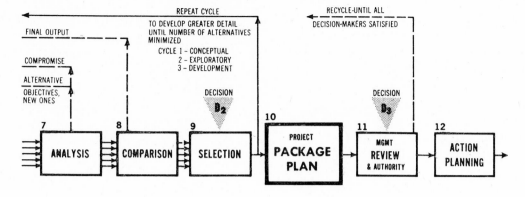

ESTIMATE PROBABILITIES
  OF SUCCESS
      Objectively Established
      Subjectively Judged
              "A Degree of Belief"
PREDICT MOVES BY
  COMPETITION, (USING
  "GAME THEORY")

8. COMPARISON
CONSEQUENCES GROUPED
      Annual Cost
      User Satisfactions
      Goodwill Values
      Legal Constraints
      Safety
ASSIGN "MEASURE-OF-
  VALUE" TO CONSE-
  QUENCES—As Possible
COMPARE AND RANK
IDENTIFY QUALITATIVE PRO
  & CONS

9. SELECTION
EVALUATE AGAINST
      Decision-Criteria
      Objectives
SELECT OPTIMUM USING
  MOST APPLICABLE TYPE OF
  DECISION
      Trial and Error
      Appeal to Authority
          arbitrary power
          intuition
          ethical precepts
      Mathematical
          maximum expectation

          statistical, etc.
      Semi-Automatic

**10. PROJECT PACKAGE
PLAN**
PRECISE DESCRIPTION OF
  ANTICIPATED
      Performance
      Economics
      Schedule
TYPICAL "PROSPECTUS"
  CONTAINS:
WHAT?
      Need to be Satisfied
      Specification of Need
      Goals to be Achieved
      Functional Description
          (Scope) of Chosen
          Alternative
      Premises (if analytical
          depth sacrificed in
          order to expedite
          solution, state
          assumptions)
      Background
          our position at
          present
          significant history
WHY?
      Why Solution Desirable
      "Values" Described &
          Justified
      Project Economic
          Justification
          what replaced
      Chief Environmental
          Factors & Significance

      forecasts
      competitions'
          response
HOW (WHERE)?
      Input/Output Detail
          features
          constraints
          tolerances
      Project "Cradle-to-
          Grave" Costs
      Options & Sequence
      Risk Estimated
      Identification of Critical
          Aspects
      Resource Requirements in
          FIVE YEAR PLAN
      Alternates
          why not chosen
          preference ranking
WHEN (WHO)?
      Preliminary Schedule

**11. MANAGEMENT REVIEW
& AUTHORITY**
PRIORITY AMONG OTHER
  PROJECTS
DESIRED TIMING ESTAB-
  LISHED
LEAD RESPONSIBILITIES
  ASSIGNED
EFFECT OF CHANGE ON
  FIVE YEAR PROGRAM-PLAN

12. ACTION PLANNING
APPLICATION OF PERT
  SCHEDULING AND CON-
  TROL TECHNIQUE

Figure 2-6   Methodology for project exploratory planning (P-E-P)
Source: D. J. Smalter International Minerals and Chemical Co.

We note that because product planning is directed towards developing specific products, an audit of the company's immediate resources is needed rather than a forecast of long-range potential. The long-range environment forecast developed for long-range planning provides a guide for selection of product lines. Item 3 in Figure 2-6 is concerned with current and short-range (1–5 years) marketing needs. Step 4 requires bringing together all information available to define the problem the company faces in developing new products in terms of its limitations and the market situation.

Steps 5–9 deal with the methods for screening exploratory ideas, we will discuss these below. Steps 10 and 11 are procedural steps to insure proper documenting and approval of work. Step 12 is a big one since it requires the development of a complete plan of action for the development of the product by all functional organizations concerned.

PRODUCT SCREENING

In the most simplified view, screening of products at any stage of development consists of:

1. Establishing minimum criteria for acceptance for further development
2. Establishing a method for comparing the relative desirability of products which meet minimum acceptance criteria
3. Selecting for further development *that group of products which together will produce the maximum net benefits* to the company. These benefits may be immediate economic benefits, longer range market position benefits, or non-economic benefits such as meeting goals of the company.

Unfortunately the amplified formulation and the implementation of the above steps have not yet been reduced to a science, as we shall see.

MINIMUM CRITERIA

The basic criteria for a product is the return on investment (ROI) over the life cycle of the product. While this seems easy enough, we run into the prob-

lems of determining actual investment for a single product (because of expenses on capital items shared with other products, for example). Then we must estimate net return over the life cycle to take into account both the time value of money and estimated risk. The cost of capital must also be estimated if we use a present value comparison or if we use cost of capital as a minimum criteria for ROI. Companies often simply set arbitrary criteria such as 15% ROI.

Another, additional, criteria is profit as a per cent of sales. As the ditty goes,

> Count that day lost
> Whose ending sun
> Sees sales at cost
> And business for fun.

Companies which concentrate on growth as a principal criteria may overlook this point. When John W. Dixon took over as President of LTV Electrosystems, he wrote the shareholders (Feb. 9, 1970):

"It is my belief, and I trust one shared by you, that we would be better off doing 80% as much business profitably than 120% at a loss."

Often, competition establishes an industry-wide criteria. In the retail food business, profits of 1–3% on sales are common. However, firms which produce sophisticated specialized integrated circuits and sell directly to users may command 40–60% profit on sales.

Besides basic return and profit criteria, criteria must be established with regard to investment of company resources. A company may set as a policy that not more than 20% of its resources will be tied up in a single product at any one time.

Minimum criteria may also be developed which relate the type of technical talent the company possesses or to its marketing organization and channels of distribution. An example of technical criteria was expressed by President Harry Helzer of Minnesota Mining and Manufacturing.

"We don't do much 'me too' stuff. The emphasis is on products that are new, patentable, and consumable—items that create a heavy volume of business."[3]

Minimum criteria may also be set in terms of risk

PROJECT RATING AND PROFITABILITY STUDY

PROJECT TITLE: _Semi-automatic Overwrap Machine_

OBJECTIVE: _To easily the wrapping and sealing of a wide variety of products by "X" film at 45/min._

EXISTING MARKETS: _Poultry_

POTENTIAL MARKETS: _Produce, Bakeries and supermarkets_

DATE: _May 16, 1961_

BY: _R. S. Phillips_

NO: _058 - 7030_

DATE OF FIRST SALE _1962_

	1960		1961		1962		1963		TOTALS	
	MIN.	MAX.	MIN.	MAX.	MIN.	MAX.	MIN.	MAX.	MIN.	MAX.
1. MACHINERY SALES – UNITS	0	0	0	0	200	400	400	700	600	1100
2. MACHINERY SALES – $M @ 9 $M EACH	0	0	0	0	1800	3600	3600	6300	5400	9900
3. GROSS PROFITS (33 % OF 2) – $M EACH	0	0	0	0	600	1200	1200	2100	1800	3300
4. DEVELOPMENT COSTS – $M	11	11	20	24	6	10	4	6	41	51
5. GROSS PROFITS AFTER DEVELOPMENT – $M	(11)	(11)	(20)	(24)	594	1190	1196	2094	1759	3249
6. CAPITAL INVESTMENT – $M										

7. CHANCES OF TECHNICAL SUCCESS (0 TO 1)	.25
8. CHANCES OF COMMERCIAL SUCCESS (0 TO 1)	.60
9. TOTAL AVG. GROSS PROFIT EXCL. DEVEL. $M	2550
10. TOTAL AVG. DEVEL. COSTS $M	46

SUMMARY

11. MEV (MAX. EXPECTED VALUE)	[7×8(9-10)]	$ 493 M
12. AVERAGE YEARLY RETURN		%
13. PRM (PROJECT RATING NUMBER)		11.1

$$[(7 \times 8 \times 9) + 10]$$

CHANCES OF TECHNICAL SUCCESS

FACTOR	VG	G	A	P	VP	SUB TOTAL
1	24	18	12	✓6	0	6
2	24	18	12	✓6	0	6
3	12	9	6	✓3	0	3
4	16	12	8	✓4	0	4
5	24	18	12	✓6	0	6
TOTAL						.25

CHANCES OF COMMERCIAL SUCCESS

FACTOR	VG	G	A	P	VP	SUB TOTAL
1	✓4	3	2	1	0	4
2	18	✓14	9	4	0	14
3	✓15	11	7	3	0	15
4	14	✓10	7	4	0	10
5	6	✓5	3	1	0	5
6	4	3	✓2	1	0	2
7	16	✓12	8	4	0	12
8	7	✓6	4	2	0	6
9	16	✓12	8	4	0	12
TOTAL						.86

Figure 2-7 Project rating and profitability form

involved in completing technical development or risk involved in market acceptance. One company may take a high risk in terms of achieving completely the technical performance specifications and only accept low risks for successful commercialization, for instance.

Many of the criteria which are used for the "go-no go" screening may be developed further for comparison of projects which meet minimum requirements.

EVALUATION AND SELECTION

Usually only a limited number of projects can be selected for further development from among those which meet minimum criteria. Thus a method for comparison must be developed and a method for

selecting a group of products yielding the best total benefits must be developed. Often, executive committee judgment is employed, but this has many disadvantages. Executives do not have time to study every aspect of a wide variety of products. They also bring prejudices which run counter to available facts. The objective of a good evaluation and comparison system is to express as many of the common characteristics of projects as possible in quantitative terms—which involves executive judgment as well as analysis by the functional specialists. Figure 2-7c[4] illustrates such a Project Rating and Profitability form. It was developed in Harvard Business School case #ICH 9C63. It is designed to be used in conjunction with the evaluation guides presented in Figures 2-7a and 2-7b. MEV in the basic form can take into account the cost of capital and the effect of inflation if the computation takes these factors

CHANCES OF TECHNICAL SUCCESS OF EQUIPMENT - WORKSHEET

FACTOR	VARIANCE FROM ALREADY DEVEL-OPED EQUIPMENT	WGT.	Very Good (100%)	Good (75%)	Average (50%)	Poor (25%)	Very Poor (0)
1	Speed	24	Well below limits already attained - no problem	Same as those now in use	Faster, but still declared attainable by applying principles known to work for others or ourselves	Faster, but a solution is thought to be acceptable	Sufficiently fast to warrant an entirely new solution not now available
2	Versatility	24	Well below limits already attained	Same as those now in use	More versatile, but readily complied with	More versatile than tnat already attained, but a proposed solution is thought to work	Enough more versatile to warrant a new untried and unproven concept
3	Size	12	Required size results in a more simple and workable approach than other commercially acceptable equipment made by us or others	Simply a straightforward application of existing sizes. No size problem	Minor alteration in size which can be readily attained with existing knowledge	Larger (or smaller) than this far reduced to practice but thought to be possible	Enough larger or smaller to warrant extensive development or design work to attain a solution
4	Product to be handled	16	More easily handled than normal or routine products	Simple application of existingly known and proven principles	Awkward, but not enough to handicap a solution in routine fashion	Awkward enough to warrant a new tack, but the proposed solution will work	Sufficiently awkward to warrant a novel approach which is untried and unproven
5	Packaging Material to be used	24	More machinable. than any other material thus far encountered	Very machinable, no problem	Average machinability. Existing methods will work	Poor machinability characteristics necessitating special devices which, when tried, will work.	A new solution must be found to obtain the desired results
		100					

ICH 9C63
BC 245

Figure 2-7a   Guide for use with Figure 2-7c
Source: Case, Harvard Clearing House "Modern Packaging Machinery Corporation" (C). Copyright by President and Fellows of Harvard College, 1962. Reprinted with permission

Chances of Commercial Success – Worksheet

FACTOR		WT.	VERY GOOD (100%)	GOOD (75%)	AVERAGE (50%)	POOR (25%)	VERY POOR (0)
1.	Relation to present distribution channels	4	Can reach major markets by distributing through present channels	Can reach major markets by distributing mostly through present channels and partly through new channels	Will have to distribute equally between new and present channels to reach major markets	Will have to distribute mostly through new channels to reach major markets	Will have to distribute entirely through new channels to reach major markets
2.	Labor savings to customer	18	Very high labor savings in and of itself create a sizeable demand for equipment	Labor savings will be higher than normally realized for similar equipment	Labor will be equal to other types of corresponding equipment	Little or no labor savings will result	The added labor cost to customer will be appreciable
3.	Pkg. material dollar savings to customer.	15	Very significant savings to customer will justify cost of unit	Some savings over other methods	No change in the amount of pkg. material required	New concept adds slightly to the cost in materials	The added cost of materials over and above that of other methods will be a serious objection
4.	Effect on quality of customer's product and/or package	14	A substantial improvement will attract appreciable interest in unit	Some improvement will result	No effect on quality	Quality will have to be lowered	A substantial sacrifice will have to be tolerated
5.	Availability to customer	6	Equipment to be available in plenty of time to satisfy needs	Equipment to be available when needed	Delay in availability of equipment not expected to be harmful	Delay from time needed may be a problem	Delay from time needed will be a problem
6.	Cost of plant changes to customer (beyond that of subject equipment) to utilize this concept	4	New equipment will conserve space and incur no expense and possible savings may result	Cost to utilize unit will be very low	The costs to utilize new approach are in line with those normally required	Cost to convert or utilize this equipment is objectionable, but will be tolerated	Extensive changes to plant and current methods will be a problem
7.	Price	16	Priced below all competing equipment	Priced below most competing equipment	Same price as competing equipment	Priced above most competing products	Priced above all competing products
8.	Exclusiveness to Modern Packaging (patents)	7	Can be protected by a patent with no loopholes	Can be patented, but the patent might be circumvented	Cannot be patented, but has certain salient characteristics that cannot be copied very well	Cannot be patented, and can be copied by larger, more knowledgeable companies	Cannot be patented, and can be copied by anyone or possibly, infringement may result
9.	Place in the market	16	New type of product that will fill a need presently not being filled	Product that will substantially improve on products presently on the market	Product that will have certain new characteristics that will appeal to a substantial segment of the market	Product that will have minor improvements over products presently on the market	Product similar to those presently on the market and which adds nothing new
		100					

Figure 2-7b   Guide for use with Figure 2-7c

Source: Case, Harvard Clearing House "Modern Packaging Machinery Corporation" (C). Copyright by President and Fellows of Harvard College, 1962. Reprinted with permission

- 16 -

ICH 9C63

BC
245

Modern Packaging Machinery Corp.

PROJECT RATING AND PROFITABILITY STUDY

PROJECT TITLE: Semi-automatic Pan Wrapper (Model 41)

OBJECTIVE: To market a unit to accomplish a wide range of package sizes.

EXISTING MARKETS: Bakery goods, Vending Income, Caterers, etc.

POTENTIAL MARKETS: Frozen foods, Meats, Poultry

DATE: March 24, 1961

BY: R. S. Phillips

NO: 077-7051

DATE OF FIRST SALE March 1961	1959-1960 MIN	MAX	1961 MIN	MAX	1962 MIN	MAX	1963-1964 MIN	MAX	TOTALS MIN	MAX
1. MACHINERY SALES - UNITS	0	0	30	40	50	150	800	2500	880	2200
2. MACHINERY SALES - $M @ 5 $M EACH	0	0	150	200	250	750	4000	10000	4400	10950
3. GROSS PROFITS (33 % OF 2) - $M EACH	0	0	50	67	83	250	1333	3333	1466	3650
4. DEVELOPMENT COSTS - $M	23	23	12	16	4	6	0	4	39	49
5. GROSS PROFITS AFTER DEVELOPMENT - $M	(23)	(23)	38	51	79	244	1333	3329	1427	3601
6. CAPITAL INVESTMENT - $M										

7. CHANCES OF TECHNICAL SUCCESS (0 TO 1) .87
8. CHANCES OF COMMERCIAL SUCCESS (0 TO 1) .79
9. TOTAL AVG. GROSS PROFIT EXCL. DEVEL. $M 2558
10. TOTAL AVG. DEVEL. COSTS $M 44

SUMMARY

11. MEV (MAX. EXPECTED VALUE) [7x8(9-10)] $1730 M
12. AVERAGE YEARLY RETURN %
13. PRN (PROJECT RATING NUMBER) [(7x8x9)÷10] 44

CHANCES OF TECHNICAL SUCCESS

FACTOR	VG	G	A	P	VP	SUB TOTAL
1	24 ✓	18	12	6	0	24
2	24	18 ✓	12	6	0	18
3	12	9 ✓	6	3	0	9
4	16	12 ✓	8	4	0	12
5	24 ✓	18	12	6	0	24
TOTAL						.87

CHANCES OF COMMERCIAL SUCCESS

FACTOR	VG	G	A	P	VP	SUB TOTAL
1	4	3 ✓	2	1	0	3
2	18	14 ✓	9	4	0	14
3	15 ✓	11	7	3	0	15
4	14	10 ✓	7	4	0	10
5	6	5	3 ✓	1	0	3
6	4 ✓	3	2	1	0	4
7	16	12 ✓	8	4	0	12
8	7	6 ✓	4	2	0	6
9	16	12 ✓	8	4	0	12
TOTAL						.79

Figure 2-7c Completed project rating and evaluation form

Source: Case, Harvard Clearing House "Modern Packaging Machinery Corporation" (C) Copyright by President and

into account. Figure 2-7c is a completed (fictitious) example.

SUMMARY

Product planning gives more specific definition to general product objectives of long-range planning. It is concerned with the selection, development and launching of specific products and product lines.

Product planning insures a "systems approach" to the company's short range operations by providing a product-oriented anchor point.

Despite its inherent complexity, even the most simple systematic approach to product planning will yield great gains to the small businessman as well as the giant corporation. The use of product selection criteria, comparison methods, risk analysis, network planning and control techniques mean less total risk of disaster and more profit in general.

APPENDIX A

BASIC PROGRAM FOR PRODUCT PLANNING AND DEVELOPMENT

I. Evaluate the Corporate Strength

A. Financial Position

1. Capital structure
2. Retained income and credit
3. Profit ratios
4. Availability and sources of capital
5. Contingent liabilities
6. Flexibility of fiscal policies

B. Quantity, Quality and Mix of Manpower

1. Numbers of people classified by field they are working in and background in other fields
2. Classifications of people in each field according to quality or level and potential
3. Managerial personnel according to age, present stature, special talents, and potential growth
4. Geographical dispersion of employees
5. Compensation practices
6. Morale and loyalty of employees

C. Facilities of All Kinds

1. The number, size, location, layout, moderness (including mechanization and automation) of manufacturing plants, warehouses, and offices

2. Accessability of facilities to transportation, raw materials, markets
3. Operating and maintenance costs of facilities
4. Own-lease arrangements

D. Market and Marketing Positions

1. The total market for present products
2. Market participation by product
3. Market penetration by product
4. Market structure—customer characteristics and geographic locations, price-volume relationships, product substitutes, life of market
5. Life of market
6. Replacement parts market
7. Seasonal factors
8. Competitive position by product and in total
9. Channels of distribution—their number and strength
10. Brand recognition
11. Type and cost of advertising and sales promotion
12. Service policy
13. Price and discount structure
14. Sales compensation policies
15. Patent position

E. Corporate Charter—Its Scope

II. Determine the Long-Range over-all Business Objectives and the Long-Range Financial, Technical, Production and Marketing Objectives

A. *In what business are we now engaged?*

1. Electronic, electrical, mechanical, chemical, or other field
2. Systems, equipment, component or element
3. Specific types of products such as computers, instruments, ethical drugs, office equipment, OEM, etc.

B. *In what business do we want to be and should we be engaged in the next ten years? Consider such things as:*

1. Projected technological, economic, and market trends
2. Horizontal and vertical diversification of product lines
3. Filling out present product lines
4. Entry into new related fields and unrelated fields
5. Do we want to enter frontier fields? (atomic energy, space flight, solar energy)

C. *What should be the financial condition and structure of the business?*

D. *What are our technical objectives as related to manpower, organization, facilities and scope of programs?*

E. *What plants, locations, facilities, and manpower, will be required for our products in relation to raw materials and markets? What will be our production and control policies to insure steady output and maximum utilization of facilities?*

F. *What should be our marketing objectives?*

1. Type of market
2. Size of market and our share
3. Advertising
4. Methods of distribution
5. Service and replacement parts
6. Seasonal and cyclical stability

III. Organize and Establish Policies for Product Planning and Development

A. *Organization*

1. Establish objectives and organization for product planning and define the scope of responsibilities. The organization of the product planning organization and its place in the company organization.
2. Establish accountability and authority of individuals charged with product planning functions.
3. Establish reporting and relationship responsibilities of personnel.

B. *New Product Planning Policies*

1. Improvement, expansion of lines, diversification of products
2. Internal technical development, subcontract, or acquisition.
3. Marketing—including advertising and sales promotion, forecasting sales methods, channels of distribution, brand development, etc.
4. Technical policies—quality of product, extent of development and research work, technical leadership.
5. Manufacturing policies—make or buy, make or assemble, stable production, suppliers, inventory control, manufacturing process development, extent of automation and mechanization, standards and quality control, packaging, storing, and shipping.
6. Facilities policies—geographical location, buy or lease, build or buy, buy now or over a period of time, buy for expansion, liberal or conservative office area per individual. Fiscal policies—(See items IA 1-6) include customer credit, vendor payments, financial budgeting, and control of operations and capital expenditures.
8. Personnel policies—(See items IB 1-6).

C. *Over-all Timing of A and B above*

IV. Develop and Find New Product Ideas

A. *Sources for Ideas—Internal*
1. Market researchers
2. Salesmen aware of market needs
3. Purchasing agents knowing market requirements
4. Scientists and engineers
5. Manufacturing personnel
6. Patent attorneys
7. Management committees
8. "Brainstorming" groups
9. Employee suggestion systems

B. *Sources for Ideas—External*
1. Venture-capital organizations
2. Trade journals
3. Patent searches
4. Technical societies
5. Customers
6. Vendors and suppliers
7. Independent inventers
8. Business friends
9. Government publications
10. Competitors

C. *Creative Approach in Finding New Ideas*

V. Select and Develop Selected New-Product Ideas

A. *Standards for Measurement of Proposed Ideas in Terms of—*
1. Objectives of company
2. Policies of company
3. Capabilities of company

B. *Selection of New Product Ideas*
1. Responsibility fixed for careful evaluation of each idea by the best qualified people
2. General industry background for new product
3. Characteristics of the product, including consumer benefits, costs, servicing
4. Legal situation with regard to corporate charter and patents
5. Effect on related products of the company
6. Market structure, size, and future
7. Methods of distribution

8. Competition now and in the future
9. Rate of technical obsolescence
10. Profit potential

C. *Establishment of Specifications*

D. *Developing New Product Ideas*
1. Organizing for R & D
2. R & D defensive and aggressive
3. Engineering and creativity
4. Subcontracting
5. Use of consultants
6. Scheduling priority of projects and scheduling the development of each project
7. Models, pilot plants, prototypes
8. Testing

VI. Conduct Manufacturing, Marketing, and Product Service Activities Required to Introduce New Products

A. *Manufacturing Activities*
1. Make or buy
2. Facilities
3. Geographical location
4. Personnel
5. Production plan
6. Total investment

B. *Marketing Activities*
1. Short and long range market forecasts
2. Advertising and sales promotion
3. Channels and methods of distribution
4. Development of new markets and consumers
5. Pricing policies
6. Sales compensation methods
7. Customer service and warrantees
8. Replacement parts program

VIII. Standards and Measurements

A. *Profit (financial return)*
1. Total dollars of profit
2. Profit as percent return on investment
3. Profit as percent of sales
4. Percent profit to contributed value (capital and work)

5. Percent profit to value added

6. Percent profit to total employee costs

7. Residual dollar profit ratios (net book profit after deduction of Federal taxes less a capital charge equivalent to a specified percentage of net investment)

B. *Market Position*

1. Ratio of sales to total market

2. Customer satisfaction with quality of products and services

C. *Productivity (effective and balanced utilization of men, capital, and materials in present and future product planning)*

Output	versus	Input
Sales billed	,,	Man-hours worked
Units sold	,,	Payroll dollars
Value added	,,	Equivalent man-hours

Manufacturing cost		Floor area
Units produced	,,	First cost of plant and equipment

D. *Product Leadership*

1. Comparison of products with competitors' products

2. Source of research on which the products are based

3. Whether basic product and subsequent improvements were first introduced by own company or competition

E. *Personnel development for product and profitability leadership*

F. *Employee attitudes*

G. *Public responsibility*

H. *Balance between short-range and long-range goals*

APPENDIX B

CRITICAL PATH SCHEDULING OF THE PRODUCT PLANNING AND NEW PRODUCT ACTIVITIES

In the final analysis, planning involves a consideration of detail, many details. Every step that must be accomplished from birth of the idea to the eventual placing on the market of a new product must be encompassed within a new product plan. Within the past decade the use of network management techniques for planning almost any kind of effort has become commonplace for the simple reason that it provides benefits unachievable by almost any means. Such network management techniques are known as Program Evaluation Review Technique (PERT), the Critical Path Method (CPM), program evaluation review techniques with a consideration of cost (PERT/COST). All of these are network management techniques (NMT).

NMT require the identification of every step in the process and the relating of these steps to each other and to time. CPM was developed in the construc-

tion industry and PERT was developed by the Navy and Booz, Allen and Hamilton to guide the development of the Polaris missile which is used on our atomic submarines. Figure 2-5 in the Product Planning Chapter shows a network diagram for new product planning that is probably a little more abbreviated than what is actually required. However, it does illustrate what a network plan looks like and how it relates to new product planning. A more detailed and complex version will be found at the end of this appendix.

A network requires the accomplishment of a few fundamental steps that seem deceptively easy.

The First Step: *Establish the Objective.* If you don't know where you're going, *no* road map can help. The destination must be identified, not just the direction of desired progress.

The Second Step: *List all the tasks or activities*

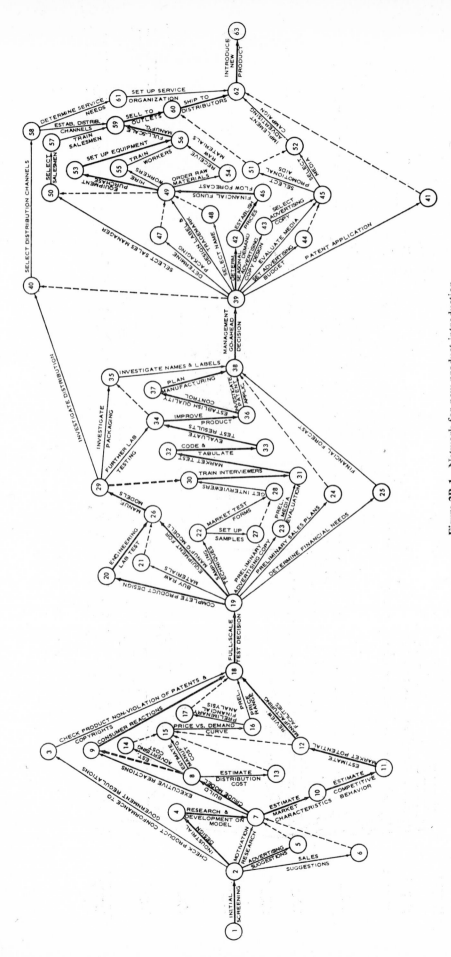

Figure 2B-1 Network for new product introduction

Source: Yung Wong, "Critical Path Analysis for New Product Planning", Reprinted from *Journal of Marketing,* October, 1964, published by the American Marketing Association

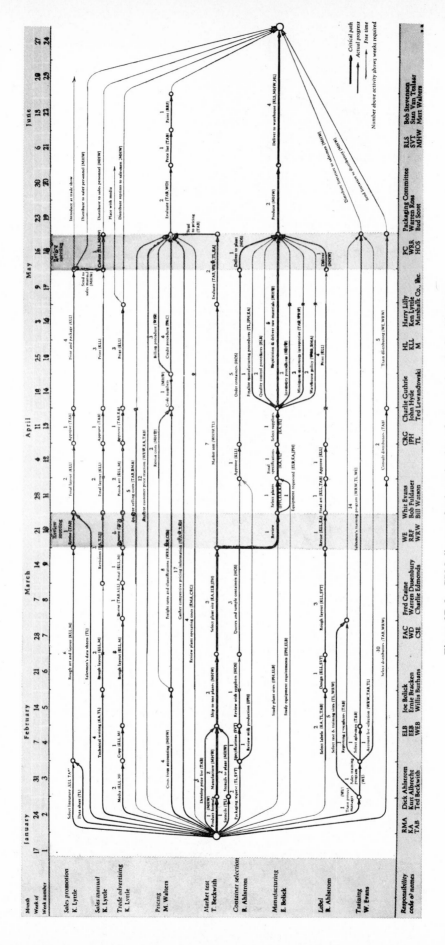

Figure 2B-2 CPM diagram for introduction of new product in food industry

Source: W. Dusenbury, "CPM for New Product Introductions", *Harvard Business Review*, July–August, 1967

that must be accomplished. Include everything. How much detail? Enough to give the degree of control desired. The steps or events must be carefully defined and agreed upon. There must be concensus by those involved regarding the meaning of each of the events or steps.

The Third Step: *Arrange the activities in some reasonable sequence.* Convention says to start with the concluding step and to work backward toward the beginning. However, there is no reason why one cannot start at any familiar point and work in both directions.

Except for the first and last events each activity must have a preceding and a following event. No activity can start until all the activities on which it depends are completed. There can be no looping—that is no activity can be followed by a sequence that leads back to that activity.

Sometimes "dummy arrows" are needed to preserve the logic of the network when two or more activities begin and end at the same events.

The Fourth Step: *Establish time estimates for each activity or event in the network.* Dummy events are assigned zero time. If the critical path method is used, the establishment of time schedules calls for one estimate. PERT is designed to deal a bit more with uncertainty and therefore calls for three estimates.

The three PERT estimates required for each activity are:
1. The "most likely" time.
2. The most optimistic time (the "100 to 1 shot").
3. The most pessimistic time (the "100 to 1 shot").

The three estimates are then averaged to come up with an "expected" time for the activity.

Once all activities are estimated, the critical path (the longest direct sequence of events in the network from the beginning to the end) and the estimated completion time can be found.

The inherent limitations of network management techniques is that it creates an illusion of certainty. While it permits trade-off or reallocation of resources, the impact of these upon later performance or quality is not always evident. Another limitation is that time-cost trade-offs are deceptive in that time and cost can vary independently. Obviously there are many other things that need to be considered in the full utilization of network techniques, but it is well to consider using such techniques for product planning.

REFERENCES

1. D. W. Karger and R. G. Murdick, *Managing Engineering and Research*, The Industrial Press, New York, N.Y., 1969.
2. Ernest C. Miller, *Advanced Techniques for Strategic Planning*, AMA Research Study 104, American Management Association, Inc., 1971.
3. Reprinted from the November 23, 1968, issue of *Business Week* by special permission. Copyrighted (C) 1968 by McGraw-Hill, Inc.
4. See D. W. Karger and R. G. Murdick, *Managing Engineering and Research*, Industrial Press, 1969, for discussion of a variety of evaluation methods.

BIBLIOGRAPHY

Aguilar, F. J., *Scanning the Business Environment*, New York: The Macmillan Company, 1967.

Bass, F. M. *et al.* (eds.), *Mathematical Models and Methods in Marketing*. Homewood, Ill.: Richard D. Irwin, Inc., 1961.

Berg, Thomas and Shuckman, Abe, *Product Strategy and Management*, Holt, Rinehart and Winston, New York, 1963.

Branch, M. C., *The Corporate Planning Process*, New York: American Management Association, 1962.

Buck, C. H., *Problems of Product Design and Development*, New York: The Macmillan Company, 1963.

"Business Response to Consumerism", *Business Week*, September 6, 1969.

Cannon, J. T., *Business Strategy and Policy*, New York: Harcourt, Brace & World, Inc., 1968.

Chorafas, D., *An Introduction to Product Planning and Reliability Management* Cassels, London, 1967.

Collier, J. R., *Effective Long-Range Business Planning*, Englewood Cliffs, New Jersey, Prentice-Hall, Inc., 1968.

Dusenbury, W., "CPM for New Product Introductions", *Harvard Business Review*, July–August, 1967.

Evans, G. H., *The Product Manager's Job*, AMA Research Study 69, New York: American Management Association, 1964.

Ewing, D. W., ed., *Long-Range Planning for Mamagenent*, New York: Harper & Row, 1958; a revised edition of this book was published in 1964.

Ewing, D. W. *The Human Side of Planning*, New York: The Macmillan Company, 1969.

Ewing, D. W., *The Practice of Planning*, New York: Harper & Row, 1968.

Fendrich, C. W., Jr., *The Industrial Product Management System*, American Management Association Bulletin 80, 1966.

Ferrell, R. W., *Customer-Oriented Planning*, New York: American Management Association, 1964.

Flaks, M., Olsen, D. R., and Lund, H. F., "Network Management Techniques", *Factory*, McGraw-Hill, Inc., New York, March 1964.

Goslin, Lewis, *The Product Planning System*, Homewood, Ill.: Richard D. Irwin, Inc., 1967.

Haas, R., *Long Range View of Product Planning in Business*, Morgantown, W.V.: West Virginia University Library, 1965.

Hastings, D. C., *The Place of Forecasting in Basic Planning for Small Business*. Minneapolis: University of Minnesota Press, 1961.

Henry, H. W., *Long-Range Planning Practices in 45 Industrial Companies*. Englewood Cliffs, N.J.: Prentice-Hall, Inc., 1967.

Hilton, P., *Handbook of New Product Development*. Englewood Cliffs, N.J.: Prentice-Hall, Inc., 1961.

Hilton, Peter, *New Product Introduction for Small Business Owners*, Washington, D.C.: Small Business Administration, 1961.

Karger, D. W. and A. B. Jack, *Problems of Small Business in Developing and Exploiting New Products*. Troy, N.Y.: Rensselaer Polytechnic Institute, 1963.

Karger, D. W. and R. G. Murdick, *Managing Engineering and Research* (1st and 2nd eds.) New York: The Industrial Press, 1963 and 1969.

King, E. B., "A Control System of Profitability of New Products" *Management Accounting*, July, 1968.

Konopa, L. J., *New Products: Assessing Commercial Potential*, AMA Management Bulletin 88. New York: American Management Association, 1966.

Kotler, P., *Marketing Management*, Englewood Cliffs, N.J.: Prentice-Hall, Inc., 1967.

LeBreton, P. P. and D. A. Henning, *Planning Theory*, Englewood Cliffs, N.J.: Prentice-Hall, Inc., 1961.

Management of New Products. Booz, Allen & Hamilton, Inc., 1968.

Miller, Ernest C., *Advanced Techniques for Strategic Planning*, AMA Research Study 104, American Management Association, Inc., 1971.

Marting, E. (ed.), *New Products, New Profits and Companies Experience in New Product Planning*, New York: American Management Association, 1964.

Newell, W. T., *Long-Range Planning Policies and Practices: Selected Companies Operating in Texas*. Austin, Texas: The University of Texas, Bureau of Business Research, 1963.

Payne, Bruce, *Planning for Company Growth*. New York: McGraw-Hill Book Company, 1963.

Pessemier, E. A., *New Product Decisions*, New York: McGraw Hill Book Company, Inc., 1966.

Planning for Future Company Growth: A Small Company Must, Research Institute Staff Recommendations, File 32, New York: The Research Institute of America, 1967.

Roberts, E., "What it takes to be an Entrepreneur ... And to Hang on to One", *Innovation*, New York, N.Y., 1969.

Scott, B. W., *Long-Range Planning in American Industry*, New York: American Management Association, 1965.

Scrase, R. R., (ed.), "New Products: Concepts, Development, and Strategy", Sixth Annual New Products Marketing Conference, 1966, University of Michigan, Graduate School of Business Administration, 1967.

Smith, D. M. K., *How to Avoid Mistakes When Introducing New Products*, New York: Vantage Press, 1964.

Steiner, G. A. and Cannon, W. M., editors, *Multinational Corporate Planning*, New York: The Macmillan Company, 1966.

Steiner, G. A., *Strategic Factors in Business Success*, New York: Financial Executives Research Foundation, 1969.

Steiner, G. A., *Top Management Planning*, New York: The Macmillan Company, 1969.

St. Thomas, C. E., *Practical Business Planning*, New York: American Management Association, 1965.

Wallenstein, G. D., *Concept and Practice of Product Planning*, New York: American Management Association, Inc., 1968.

Warren, E. K., *Long-Range Planning: The Executive Viewpoint*, Englewood Cliffs, New Jersey, Prentice-Hall, Inc., 1966.

Warshaw, M. R., and Murphy, G. P., editors, *New Product Planning for Changing Markets:* Seventh Annual New Products Marketing Conference, 1967, University of Michigan, Graduate School of Business Administration, 1968.

Watton, H., *New Product Planning: A Practical Guide for Diversification*, Prentice Hall, New Jersey, 1969.

Wong, Yung, "Critical Path Analysis for New Product Planning", *Journal of Marketing*, October 1964.

CHAPTER 3

ORGANIZING FOR PRODUCT PLANNING
AND DEVELOPMENT

NEED TO ASSIGN RESPONSIBILITY

It requires more than defining objectives and asking people in the organization to be new-product conscious in order to get the new product program implemented. *Responsibility for implementing the planning and development of new products must be assigned.*

A warning flag should be hoisted at this point. Merely having assigned the responsibility to someone does not get the work done. The organization must be structured to give the responsible individuals both the freedom and the authority to take the necessary risks involved in new product development. Second, the right people must be found to staff this element of the organization. Third, proper provision must be made for their interaction with the rest of the organization. If these three requirements are not recognized and taken into account in setting up the new product organization, the entire activity will bog down in the typical bureaucratic morass.

Booz, Allen & Hamilton tried to identify through

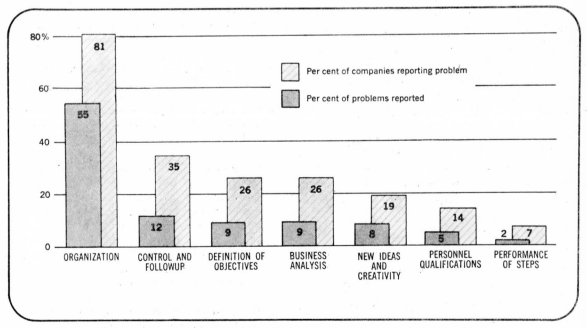

Figure 3-1 Opportunities for improvement (Problems reported by leading companies)
Source: *Management of New Products*, New York: Booz, Allen and Hamilton, Management Consultants, 1968

research the opportunities for improvement in new product management problems as reported by leading companies. The results indicated that the largest opportunity and also the largest problem area was that of organization. The various areas defined in this research by Booz, Allen & Hamilton are illustrated in Figure 3-1.

Our own survey of presidents who head companies active in new product development confirmed that organization still is a major problem with respect to new product projects. This survey disclosed that the need to assign responsibility for product planning and development was a major concern. Almost as important, the respondents believed, was the problem of creating a climate for venture managers who should take risks without fear of severe penalties for occasional failures. At the same time, the need for some control to prevent ventures of *disaster* magnitude was desired.

Apparently there is a need for an organizational structure which fixes responsibility on specific individuals for entrepreneurial performance. Unfortunately, in most organizations, responsibility for product development is so diffused that it is not identifiable. Also, the penalty to the individual for a single failure is usually severe. The risky, highly differentiated, novel products are killed off by committees and accountants. The consequences are that only "safe" products, those which any firm would likely produce, are accepted. Since other firms also feel that such products are safe, competition is intense upon their introduction and profit margins are low.

The assignment of new product responsibility requires careful consideration of the company's size, products, and outlook. In companies just starting up or in small growing companies, the new product responsibility usually remains with the founding owner or president. In some cases, the chief engineer or the marketing executive is a co-founder of the company and provides the spark for new product development. As the operating duties of such individuals increase with company growth, they find less and less time to devote to product innovation. This represents a slow trip to going out of business unless action is taken to counteract the situation.

In larger companies, new product responsibilities are often so dispersed that no one has the prime responsibility. The need in such companies is to organize in some way so that one individual has the responsibility for integrating all new product effort and provide the necessary leadership. Since these activities cut across numerous "empires" or spheres of control (organizational segments), setting up an effective organization requires careful consideration in devising and operating the new product organization.

---

1. Many people come forward to claim credit for new ideas that work out, but nobody can be identified with flops.

2. Executives keep throwing new ideas into the hopper, but nobody knows which ones to develop.

3. The company hasn't had a new product idea in two years.

4. Marketing people proposing ideas but the engineers are working on other ideas.

5. Idea men who don't seem to be producing ideas.

6. A steady stream of funds flows into pet projects of executives over the years with no concrete results.

7. Many products are introduced, but few are making a profit.

8. The product that got to the market was inferior, higher priced, and later than the competitors' products.

9. The product is returned by 20,000 consumers.

10. The product floats around the company for a year until a competitor introduces a similar product which becomes a big success.

11. The sales force takes advance orders for a product which engineering can't debug, and if they could, manufacturing couldn't produce it.

12. The product that was engineered until the price was too high and the appearance was poor.

Figure 3-2 Symptoms of organizational problems

The nature of the products exerts an influence on the urgency of product development and organization. Consumer products face constant change from old competitive companies and from new companies entering the market on the basis of a new advance in function or style. Technologically, most of these consumer products are relatively simple. Many industrial products, on the other hand, change more slowly because of the high engineering content involved.

Symptoms of the need to review new product responsibilities are listed in Figure 3-2.

GENERAL CONSIDERATIONS FOR ORGANIZING NEW PRODUCT DEVELOPMENT

Since product development is directly and vitally concerned with implementing a company's plans for survival and growth, the key individuals must have free access to top management. Too often the product development function reports to a do-nothing executive who forms a barrier blocking off new money-making ideas. In some cases the new-product executive has been given an office and more or less told, "Close the door and think." This approach will *not* work. The new product executive must be given the management responsibility for development through initial market introduction of new product concepts. Unless this is done, people concerned with product planning become frustrated and dissatisfied. The good men leave, the company stagnates, and the president wakes up some day to wonder what got this company in such a hole.

Since product development is so critical to the company, projects often must be reviewed by the board of directors as well as the president. The proper allocation of the company's money to plant, personnel, and activities is at stake. It does not appear reasonable to have the executive with product development know-how and responsibility report to an intermediate or middle level executive. It will also be found that many unnecessary moves can be eliminated if the access to top management is real. For example, one product manager practically concluded a licensing agreement to exploit various patents only to have the idea killed at the

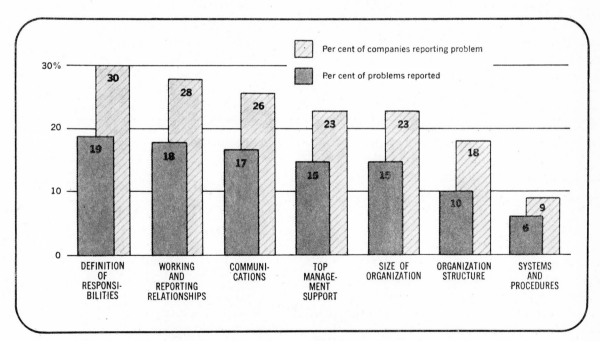

Figure 3-3 Organizational improvement opportunities
Source: *Management of New Products*, New York: Booz, Allen and Hamilton, Management Consultants, 1968

last minute by the top executive—not because it wasn't sound, but because relations were considered undesirable with the other firm by the person capable of enforcing his views. All the time and money spent in developing the agreement was lost because the development function was insulated from the top executive.

The product development function will ordinarily represent the company to inventors, trade associations, attorneys, top executives of other firms, etc. This cannot be successfully accomplished unless they have the status to speak and negotiate with authority. Also, the new-product executives will, of necessity, have frequent and intimate contacts with the other major company executives in sales, finance, production, engineering, etc. Freedom to move effectively both inside and outside the company cannot be achieved without proper organizational placement.

In order to make the organizing of the new product function more likely to be a success, the results of the previously referenced Booz, Allen & Hamilton Research Department survey should be studied. These results include a delineation of the problem areas of organization and their approximate frequency of occurrence—the idea is to anticipate them and *design them out* of the organization. These results are given in Figure 3-3.

As a company becomes large enough so that the top management cannot handle the product development, *the responsibility should not be assigned to the financial or the production managers*, although each should definitely contribute to the planning and participate in new product ventures. Manufacturing managers have their hands full getting the product produced at low cost and hence do not enthusiastically welcome product innovations! "Who needs another headache" is too often their plaint Financial managers tend to be ultra conservative, even if they try not to be. Imagination, daring (within reason) and practical optimism are needed—and these are not characteristics often found in financial managers. Financial managers want to be right *all* of the time. Venture managers of necessity as risk takers can be right only part of the time.

New product development is a coordinative func-

tion and as such the function should be located either at a *high corporate staff level*, or it should report to the top marketing or engineering executive. In small companies, the high corporate staff level would mean the company president. In fact, this is exactly where a very large number of new product departments report.

A word of explanation is needed here. New product development *must* be basically marketing oriented. Today, however, there are numerous R&D oriented companies which essentially sell research or designs or very highly engineered and complex products to the government and/or other firms. The marketing aspects are highly technological so that many of the "marketing" specialists are within the engineering organization or else act as if they are an integral part of the technical function organization. In such a company the new product function would often logically report to the engineering vice president.

In a consumer product company, a similar rationale can be easily developed for having the new product function report to the marketing vice president. In consumer-market companies, the marketing function must dominate the activities of the firm.

In very large companies, a new product organization is often required for each division, assuming these divisions are largely autonomous and highly decentralized. In such an organization, a division that is oriented toward highly technical products, the function could report to the division president or to the engineering manager. In another division that is oriented toward consumer products, it could report to its president or to the marketing manager.

ORGANIZATIONAL STRUCTURES FOR NEW PRODUCT DEVELOPMENT

There are six basic methods of organizing to provide the company with at least some kind of systematic approach to getting new products to the market. Some of these succeed in working in spite of themselves. The structures are:
1. Personal staff assistant
2. The management committee

3. Task force or new-product venture team
4. Product and project manager organizations
5. New product department
6. Corporate coordinator for product development carried out through new product organizations in the line divisions or company profit centers.

Personal Staff Assistant

The relatively inexperienced organizer might be tempted to try *the personal staff assistant approach* to handling the new product management problem. Such an assistant does not have any *official* authority over line organization. However, because of his close and personal relationship with his superior he does wield undelegated authority. It is a difficult and potentially dangerous approach and the modern trend is away from personal staff assistants. At best, this is a temporary organizational expedient that deteriorates over time.

The Management Committee

The Management Committee for new product development often consists of the marketing manager, the engineering manager, and the manufacturing and/or the financial manager. In small firms, the general manager or the president also sits on the committee. Such a top-level committee may work very well in small companies with close relationships among the top officers.

The committee is at its worst in large companies. Its principal advantage in large firms is that it permits an interchange of ideas and group deliberation on problems considered too important, too difficult, or too broad for any one individual.

While there are many objections to using committees, the following are considered most significant, the first two being particularly cogent reasons for not using this approach to new product organization.
1. Diffusion of responsibility and lack of accountability of the individual members.
2. Committee recommendations and actions represent the lowest common dominator (in terms of ideas, concepts, or recommended action) that the group will agree to—it is therefore likely that good ideas are discarded. *Committees are not risk-takers!*

Unfortunately, committees are often used because the top manager believes that he can thereby avoid making a personal decision. While he may think he escapes responsibility, it is a short-run illusion. In reality he must still bear the responsibility for the growth or the decline of the firm.

Management rarely evaluates the cost incurred in committee deliberations and associated activities. If such evaluation were done realistically and recognition given to the fact that the salary-time charges are actual cost, then far fewer committees would exist. Admittedly, committees represent one approach to organizing new product management, but they are not action-oriented and in general will prove to be a failure. A summary of committee fundamentals is given in Figure 3-4.

Task Force or New Product Venture Team

An outgrowth of a committee concept which overcomes many of their disadvantages, is the "task force" or the new product venture team. A task force is basically a group charged with a very specific mission, usually to be completed in a specific time. The task force is disbanded at the end of the project. Normally, the men constituting the group are those involved in accomplishing the mission, or men reporting to them whom they have nominated to the task force. The task force emphasizes the mission and forces action. It is responsible for a specific mission in the case of each product. It is one of the successful methods of organizing for, and managing, the finding, developing, manufacturing and successful introduction of new products.

The task force may consist of all managers, all key specialists, or a mixture of these. It must have a representative from each of the major functional components of the company, however, to be successful. For example, a new product team in small or medium size companies, in addition to having a chairman from the new products department or from the product manager's staff, logically includes the heads of marketing, manufacturing, engineering, and a re-

The real functions of a committee are to:

1. Interchange ideas.
2. Secure a meeting of minds.
3. Supply important information to the members or through them to the departments and the organization.
4. Receive and act on reports from committee members or from departments which have been asked for data or information.
5. Secure facts from many sources and assemble them into a combined plan.
6. Assay the results of operations, arrive at conclusions, and formulate reports or suggestions.
7. Make intelligent and expert studies of important factors, activities, or problems.
8. Develop and recommend procedures of operation.
9. Coordinate or set up time relationships between the operations or different departments.
10. Correlate or combine the activities of different departments.
11. Provide cooperation or special efforts in performance between the different departments.
12. Formulate and establish standards of various kinds.
13. Act as a clearing house for matters for which no other channel has been provided.

Advantages of Committee Organizations:

1. Under a strong executive chairman, a committee may quickly marshal many valuable points of view, since "two heads are better than one."
2. In conducting investigations, the several phases of the various questions may be quickly assigned to responsible members with a reasonable assurance of speedy action if a time schedule and proper follow-up are instituted.
3. Decisions arrived at are impersonal, leaving the chairman free from the personal criticisms so often leveled at a managing executive.
4. There is a stimulus toward cooperative action.
5. The members of the committee know better what is happening in the plant so that they can disseminate the information and team up with other individuals or departments.

Disadvantages of Committee Organizations:

1. Committees may be too large for constructive action since the number should seldom exceed three.
2. Committees are time-consuming and usually have to be prodded or prevent delays.
3. Important executives may be called so frequently from their work for meetings that the operations of the enterprise lag.
4. The members of the committee often are unfamiliar with important details of questions at issue and therefore may make wrong or ineffective decisions.
5. Action may often be superficial because of lack of time or interest of committee members.
6. Committees weaken individual responsibility resulting in compromise instead of clear-cut decisions.
7. The decisions often are made to conform to some executive's wants or to enable the members to avoid direct responsibility for unfavorable results.
8. Aggressive and outspoken members may dominate committee meetings and unduly influence the action, often adversely.

Figure 3-4 Committee fundamentals

Source: D.W.Karger and R.G.Murdick, *Managing Engineering and Research*, New York: The Industrial Press, 1969

presentative from finance. In larger firms, representatives of the heads of the functional departments will compose the team's membership. The successful new product team usually reports in a staff relationship to the general manager or president.

The nucleus of a new product team for a specific product can be formed at the business analysis stage. While the major emphasis within the work of the team will shift from one department or function to another as the product evolves, the team approach assures maintenance of continuity of thought and action. Essentially the team should be viewed as a venture team which will assume significant risks.

Product and Project Manager Organizations

The term "Product Manager" appears primarily in consumer goods firms. These companies are heavily marketing oriented. The term "Project Manager" is used primarily in industrial firms which design and produce highly technical products. We will use the two terms interchangeably here, since the organizational structures are similar. Indications are that the use of Product Managers and Project Managers as the basis for organizing new product development is increasing.

Project management is a form of organization and a philosophy of action that focuses responsibility on a project manager for attainment of project objectives. The goals of the project are specific, the time limitations for the project are defined, and the resources to be employed are negotiated by the pro-ject manager with his superiors. Projects usually cut across many disciplines and draw upon many resources within the company. They are concerned with "systems" or complex products so that project management is sometimes referred to as "systems management", "program management", or "product management". In the case of consumer products, the complexity is due mainly to the marketing aspects.

There are two subclassifications of project organizations that are distinctly different. The first type, and the least common, is the line project management organization. In line project management, complete responsibility for all line activities is vested in the project manager. There is no dual reporting by subordinates. The project manager has cost, technical, marketing, and personnel responsibilities. Usually, only manufacturing is "contracted" for. Such a system obviously provides tight time/cost/performance planning and control. The product manager or project manager is free to take such risks as he wishes; responsibility is clear. Problems

	ACTIVITY	CONSUMER GOODS COMPANY	INDUSTRIAL GOODS COMPANY
1.	Planning	Key duty	Key duty
2.	Advertising	Creates plan	Limited role
3.	Sales promotion	Originates, may manage	Suggests technical material
4.	Merchandising	Recommends policies and plans	Limited role
5.	Packaging, branding, labeling	Makes recommendations	Limited role
6.	Pricing	Studies and makes recommendations	Bid pricing, estimating, volume pricing
7.	Product development, new products	Studies and makes recommendations	Works with laboratories and may approve modifications
8.	Product line planning	Recommends changes	Recommends and may have authority over mix
9.	Market research	Makes requests for studies	May do his own research
10.	Production planning	Forecasts sales volume	Establishes mix and schedule
11.	Inventories and warehousing	Estimates inventory needs	Estimates inventory needs
12.	Field sales and distribution	Recommends channels of distribution	May be primary technical advisor to field

Figure 3-5 Comparison of the roles of the product manager in consumer goods firms and industrial goods firms
Source: Reprinted by permission of the publisher from *The Product Manager's Job*, AMA Research Study No. 69, New York: American Management Association, 1964

arise because of the growth and decline of multiple projects requiring shifting of personnel from old to new projects.

The second type of project management organization is the staff or "matrix" form. The product or project managers are each responsible for one or more projects. The project manager may report to the manager of engineering and the product manager may report to the manager of marketing. It is possible to have a product or project manager with all others reporting both to him and to line managers. These project managers "contract" with line managers for the services of line people. Since the line specialists report both to line managers and project managers, the term matrix is used to represent the idea of cross communications and dual reporting.

A possible serious weakness of product or project-type organizations is that they are not oriented towards searching for new ideas. They are set up develop new ideas, *once the performance specifications have been provided*. Provided by whom? That is the question. The strength of such an organization is its single purpose and clear-cut responsibility. The duties and responsibilities of product managers are shown in Figure 3-5.

New Product Department

A popular and successful approach to handling the new product responsibility is *a separate new products department* (staff type and subject to the previous comments concerning organizational placement) which reports to a chief executive.

The new product department usually contains only a very few people—in a smaller company only one man. When several men are involved, the department includes men with experience in marketing, marketing research, R & D, and general administration. Marketing research is a key requirement because very key questions regarding all new products relate to the identification of markets and the marketability of the products. R & D is necessary because development and engineering are always involved. The finance area is represented because reports must be developed, budgets must be watched and controlled, cost estimates are always involved and paper work cannot be allowed to "bog down". A combination of these skills is needed for the one man department and this makes the staffing of the one man operation extremely difficult.

The administrative function is entirely internal and involves maintenance of critical path schedules

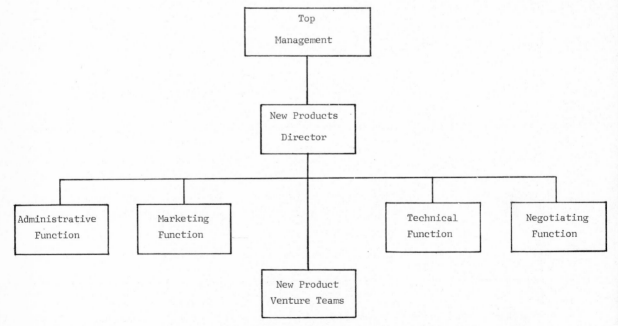

Figure 3-6 Typical new product departmental organization

and reports, monitoring other schedules, etc. The function of market research and analysis is included because close liaison with existing sales and marketing personnel must be maintained.

The negotiating function, when it is present, is concerned with acquisitions, negotiations, patents, export licenses, etc. (see Figure 3-6).

Corporate Coordinator

The sixth approach to organizing for new products is only suitable for the large organization. It identifies *a corporate coordinator* who could work through new product departments and/or teams in divisional organizations. The coordinator in the very large organization undoubtedly would have his own new product department.

PROFILE OF THE NEW PRODUCT MANAGER—THE NEW ENTREPRENEURS

Much of what will follow will apply equally well to the staff of the new product department as to its manager. The company body will eventually become a corpse if the organizational box(es) for new product managers and their staff are allowed to become caskets for warm motionless bodies! The nature of new product development requires people with high creativity, drive, and persistence. We say people, we don't say "men", because women constitute a great source of unused, creative talent.

Such people must use imagination and good business judgment in:
1. Identifying and recommending opportunities for exploitation and growth
2. Establishing a basis for evaluating product opportunities
3. Coordinating people and other resources to develop such opportunities
4. Developing measures of achievement and methods for moving out of low-profit, no-growth situations
5. Managing the new products from "the cradle to manhood".

The nature of the work is such that strict supervision and control over the *activities*, not the end achievements, is unthinkable. The new product developers must have freedom to do what others consider foolish until success proves otherwise.

The new product managers in a "go-go company" should be recognized as *entrepreneurs* operating loosely within an organizational framework that in the past has not been able to accommodate them. Entrepreneurs are the risk-takers. As such, they must be allowed occasional and costly mistakes. These must be compensated for by the successful projects which they bring off.

The new product managers should also be venture managers because they coordinate the product development from conception to eventual marketing. Thus while imagination and dreams are requirements for the position, business practicality is the ultimate test. Such a man must have broad company experience and yet not be a prisoner of his background, but rather a man who thrives in a world of constant change.

The new product manager is the communication center of product projects and operations. On request he makes available any detail of the product program so that marketing, financial, engineering, and production people have a single source of information. Therefore, he should be able to speak the language of the various functions and know where to go to get the answers he doesn't have himself.

In general, new product managers need to be at least partially technically competent. While expert help can be obtained, either from staff associated with the new product manager or from engineering and/or R & D, they still must be able to evaluate data and formulate valid opinions. While this can be successfully accomplished by non-technical people, such ability only is developed after a long exposure to the industry and to the products involved.

A successful new product manager must essentially be the equivalent of a small company president. Such personnel must understand and feel almost equally at home in sales, engineering, production, finance, accounting, etc. This is a most difficult requirement to find in combination with the others required.

Since the new product manager is usually in a staff position, he must be accepted by the line people. He must be capable of arousing their enthusiasm, motivating them to action, and serving them cheerfully. If such a man seems hard to find, it beomes apparent that every effort should be made to retain one when he is found! They tend to be mobile upward in the company.

INFORMAL ORGANIZATION

New product managers and their staff will constantly make use of the so-called informal organization. Under optimum conditions, a company's informal organization supplements and is compatible with the formal organization. It permits rapid communication and the cutting of red tape. However, it is an ever-shifting and undefined structure; hence, it is vulnerable to expediency, manipulation and opportunism.

The informal organization line tends to be short and this is one of its advantages and appeals. The problem is that when a person high in the organization makes contact far down the line of authority by skipping the intervening layers, the intermediate individuals who actually have authority may not even know what has been transmitted in the way of information.

While it is certainly acceptable to have contact between a superior and a subordinate who does not occupy adjacent organizational levels, it should occur only when the information passed down is of significance *only* to the subordinate and concerns a task previously assigned to him through formal channels.

Applying pressure across the organization between two components not in the same vertical line of authority represents a horizontal abuse of the informal organization. Such abuse is not highly visible and may masquerade as a legitimate application of a basic advantage of informal organization. The advantage *is* significant when the people involved are qualified to make the decision involved and especially if top management has issued policy guide lines to cover this kind of situation.

LINEAR RESPONSIBILITY CHARTING—AN ORGANIZATIONAL AID

The Linear Responsibility Chart (LRC) was developed by Ernest Hijmans and simplified by Serge A. Birn, Management Consultant. The preparation of the chart and the chart itself will show or uncover answers to questions such as the following:

1. Who has direct responsibility for performing specific tasks?
2. Who has supervision over the work and to what degree?
3. Who must be consulted?
4. What persons must be notified of specific acts?
5. To whom does a man report?
6. Are key men being bypassed?
7. Are work loads unbalanced?

An LRC Chart describes how new products can be handled in a somewhat typical industrial organization. It is recommended that a techniques such as an LRC Chart be used in devising the new product organization in order to insure its correct design and that it takes into account all of the concerned problems.[1]

SOME POSSIBLE PROBLEMS WITH UPPER LEVEL MANAGEMENT

Even though a company has long and continuous experience in a new product development, and even in some of the firms where new product development has been successfully carried out, there often exists various sets of internal barriers to success in new product development.

One might be the attitude of management toward innovation. People propose ideas and management disposes of almost anything that is proposed. The rejecting of an employee's idea cannot be a light matter. A careful review of the idea should be made and a report sent to the employee.

In other firms, it is virtually impossible to discuss anything in an informal manner. No one will consider a matter except on a formal basis. Only major proposals will be given any weight and here there is always the danger that enough data are not available to make a serious risky proposal.

In still other firms, the head of the company may have no background for judging a project's worth on the basis of content. The unfortunate result is that he immediately challenges any new idea. To make it worse, he often tends to reject the idea and say, "The issues involved cannot be discussed".

A new product development manager needs to receive clarification on all of these points and a firm understanding with management concerning them before he even begins to try to function in an effective manner.

SUMMARY OF KEY IDEAS

New product planning and development only yield optimum results when the activities and organization are tailored to meet the specific needs of each company. Don't make the mistake of literally lifting someone else's organization or product program. While it is appropriate to examine and study the organizational forms of other firms for guidance, *do not copy.* The American Management Association and the National Industrial Conference Board have published special reports or books showing dozens of examples of company organization in some detail. Texts on organization are another source.

We have attempted to provide general guides which can be developed in detail according to company needs. The key ideas are:

1. Top management must recognize that new product development is their responsibility.
2. Organization for new product planning and development depends upon the size and type of company, the nature of the products, the outlook of top management, the experience represented by management, and the capabilities of *all* parties involved.

3. New product development should be a staff function reporting to top management.
4. The new product venture teams or manager forms of organization are gaining in numbers because they offer freedom of creative activity, cross-functional coordination, expeditions communication, and "cradle-to-the-grave" responsibility assignment.
5. The new product manager must be treated as an entrepreneur and venture manager. This means he must be accepted as a risk-maker for the company (actually top managers are the risk-*takers*) and allowed to operate on his overall percentage results.
6. The organization for new product planning and development must be market-oriented. The only basis for the company to exist is to fill a need which nobody else fills.
7. A company in organizing for new product development must be careful not to over-balance the organization so as to weaken their exploitation of existing products. There should be organization "balance" suitable to the company involved.

REFERENCES

1. More information on Linear Responsibility Charting can be obtained from D.W.Karger and R.G.Murdick, *Managing Engineering and Research*, New York: Industrial Press, Inc., 1969, also Alfred G.Larke, "Linear Responsibility Chart—New Tool for Executive Control", *Dunn's Review and Modern Industry*, September, 1954, "Linear Responsibility Charting", *Manufacturing and Industrial Engineering*, February, 1957, and George A.Steiner and L.Eugene Root, "Linear Organization Charts", *California Management Review*, winter, 1959.

BIBLIOGRAPHY

Gerlach, J.T. and C.A.Wainwright, *Successful Management of New Products*. New York: Hastings House Publishers, Inc., 1968.

Hilton, Peter, *Handbook of New Product Development*. Englewood Cliffs, N.J.: Prentice-Hall, Inc., 1961.

–, *New Product Introduction for Small Business Owners*. Washington, D.C.: Small Business Administration, 1961.

Organization for New Product Development. New York: National Industrial Conference Board, 1966.

Organizing for Product Development. New York: American Management Association, 1959.

Lorsch, Jay W., *Product Innovation and Organization*. New York: The Macmillan Co., 1965.

Roberts, E., "What it Takes to be an Entrepreneur ... And to Hang on to One", *Innovation*, No. 7, St. Louis, 110, 1969.

Schon, D.A., "Six Ways to Strangle Innovation", *Think*, July–August, 1963.

Scrase, R.R. (ed.), "New Products: Concepts, Development and Strategy", Sixth Annual New Products Marketing Conference, 1966, University of Michigan, Graduate School of Business Administration, 1967.

Sherman, R., "The Two-and-a-Half Year Man: With New Products, Everyone is an Amateur", *Innovation*, No. 7, St. Louis, 110, 1969.

Simons, W.W., "Organizing the Commercial Development of New Products", American Management Association, Products, Design and Development Forum, December 17, 1959.

Tietjen, Karl, *Organizing the Product Planning Function*, American Management Association. New York: The Macmillan Company, 1963.

Wallenstein, G.D., *Concept and Practice of Product Planning*, American Management Association. New York: The Macmillan Company, 1968.

Warshaw, M.R., and G.P. Murphy (eds.), *New Product Planning for Changing Markets*. Seventh Annual New Products Marketing Conference, 1967, University of Michigan, Graduate School of Business Administration, 1968.

CHAPTER 4

TECHNOLOGICAL INNOVATION

THE RISK RANGE OF INNOVATION

In our technology-oriented society, many enthusiastic experts claim that a firm must innovate or die. Despite the theme of this book, we point out that for many firms the strategy of innovation leads to death. To illustrate the potential risks of technical innovation, let us look at the experiences of a small company and a huge company. Talley Corp. of Seattle, a manufacturer of computer equipment and data communications systems was obsessed with technological development. For 11 consecutive years it increased sales, but it lost money in each of the last few years. "It spent more time developing glamorous new products than making a buck." A new president, James A. Navarre, has now turned the company around to a marketing-oriented profit-seeking firm.[1]

A major innovation in recent years was the "breathable" man-made leather product, Corfam, introduced by E.I. du Pont de Nemours & Co. After eight years of production, du Pont has lost $80 to $100 million dollars on this once-promising innovation.[2]

The small company may be far better off to adopt a policy of small innovations over the years, or even a policy of imitative innovations. There are many small firms which are very successful with the latter strategy. They follow closely the research and new products of large competitors. As soon as a large competitor comes out with a new product in quantity, or even before, the small firm "designs around it", or copies, it if it is not patentable. The small firm can move more rapidly into the market with its small sales force. By doing no advertising and no research and by selling on the basis of lower price, these small firms have been very successful as well as thorns in the sides of the large companies.

It is apparent that great innovations are often costly in terms of research. The high cost must be recovered, and this in turn endangers the ability of the company to price competitively and still make a profit. This concept is often overlooked by overly optimistic venture managers.

CONCEPTS OF TECHNOLOGICAL INNOVATION

While innovation has broad economic implications for the economy of a country as a whole, the businessman is more interested in innovation as a profitable strategy.[3] The development of a conceptual understanding of innovation will aid the executive in making wiser strategy decisions.

An operational definition of technological innovation is *any changed form of a product that has become available in a specified market within a specified recent time.* Thus minor modifications or completely new products introduced to a certain geographic region is an innovation for that region. The specified recent time may be amplified to mean "a product which has achieved less than 10% (say) of market penetration and has only been on the market one year or less". In other words, the product is "new" to the market as a whole if only 10% of the market is using it. This must be modified by the time element to exclude dying products, however, as indicated by the time limitation of one year (or other

Classification	Degree of innovation	Impact on the market	Examples
1. Minor change	Evolutionary small steps which represent annual model changes	No change in market penetration	Noiseless typewriter, new model automobiles and TV's
2. Major change	Application of the state of the art knowledge to produce a new "generation"	Obsoletes previous products and, if competitors do not match, leads to a significant increase in market penetration	New models of computers, color TV, video-telephones
3. Step change	Extension of the state of the art to produce a completely different product to perform the same function as previous products, often an "ingenious" device	Disrupts market patterns and modifies customer behavior patterns	IBM Selectric typewriter, turbine-powered automobiles, ball point pen, Teflon pans
4. Nascency	New product with a completely new function, often "ingenious" product also	Establishes new behavior patterns	Radio, TV, computers, numerical controlled machine tools, vitamin pills, antibiotics, electrocardiograph, heart pacer
5. Breakthrough	New product which incoporates a solution to a technical problem which (a) has long defied solution, or (b) is a completely unanticipated solution	Revolutionizes an industry or consumer behavior patterns	Communication satellites, transistors

Figure 4-1   Classification of Technological Innovation

such limit). (An invention is not a technological innovation under this concept until it is commercialized.)

A classification system to identify degrees of innovation for risk evaluation purposes is given in Figure 4-1 (somewhat similar data is given in Figures 1-7 und 1-8). Others less extensive have been proposed.[4] From a risk viewpoint, it is apparent that less money is risked for a Minor Change than for attempting to obtain a Breakthrough Product. The rewards are potentially far greater for the Breakthrough Product, but are by no means guaranteed to the innovator. Imitators or government regulation of monopolies may undercut profits.

SOURCES OF INNOVATION

The three sources of technological innovation in a company are:
1. Creativity of individuals

2. Search for, and identification of, an idea which requires primarily development and exploitation. Chapter 5 deals with this concept in detail

3. Massive research and engineering directed towards a known goal. This is a broad group approach in which often progress is made by many individuals solving many small problems to make many small advances.

In this chapter we are concerned with the close tie between significant advances in innovation and individual creativity. For difficult conceptual problems requiring creative solutions, one highly creative person may perform what a dozen well-trained but unimaginative people may never accomplish.

WHAT IS CREATIVE THINKING IN BUSINESS?

Creative thinking extends beyond "original thinking; it produces ideas or problem solutions which are both *novel* and *of value*. The novelty is represented by a new organization of the components of the problem. For an Eskimo who never heard of the telephone, to invent it would represent original thinking but not creative thinking since the solution has no value in the current techno-economic world. Creativity is illustrated in simple form by the innovations produced by Henry A. Sherwood. He designs toys by substituting "geometry" for parts. He designed a phonograph to retail for $5. He examined an amplifier (designed by a low-cost competitor) which used 36 parts and designed one with 12 parts. He designed a tape drive with a rotating part which serves as an idler, two different cams, and a transfer wheel during the playing cycle.[5]

HOW TO PREDICT CREATIVE PERFORMANCE

Every individual possesses some creativity in problem solving. Companies, however, need to identify candidates who have considerably more creative power than the average population. It is not that firms should be fully stocked with such people; disaster might result. However, firms need to seed their organizational components with one or two creative individuals. Creative people are not easy to identify except by past performance. Unfortunately, many applicants come from environments where their creativity was stifled or they have not been previously employed.

It has been suggested by Meehl that one of the difficulties in identifying the creative person through tests is the fact that creativity is difficult to correlate with any single characteristic. Meehl suggests six dimensions or characteristics that effect creativity and indicates that all of these are involved. His list of characteristics are as follows:

"1. The creative person is independent and idiosyncratic, but not to the point of meaningless eccentricity.

2. He is thoughtful and inward-looking, but not to the point of psychotic autism.

3. He is persistent, but does not hang on to inappropriate approaches to a problem.

4. He puts together ideas from different fields, but the relationships are not so incoherent as to be unintelligible to other people.

5. He needs a well-stocked mind, but should not suffer from a "trained incapacity" which makes it impossible for him to question time-honored hypotheses.

6. Finally, he needs physical energy, but should not dissipate it in rushing about and spinning his wheels."[6]

It seems to be easier to identify the uncreative, than the creative person. Creative persons tend to be non-conformists and good tests are available for measuring conformity since the conformist tends to be less intelligent, less motivated, represses impulses, seems to be more anxious, tends to feel inferior, passive and/or dependent, rigid, authoritarian, and often moralistic. However, just because a person is not a strong conformist, does not mean he is a creative individual. Creative people tend to be sensitive to problems, have a fluency of ideas and associations, they are adaptive and flexible, tend to have a source of spontaneous flexibility. It can also be said that a creative person is original and has an evaluative capacity.

Using standardized psychological tests which were validated against management evaluations of the creativity of Engineers and Scientists. Francis E. Jones (a deceased Rensselaer Polytechnic Professor and Researcher) derived or identified predictors of creativity. The tests used disclosed the following data:

Low score description	High score description
Reserved, detached, critical, cool (*Sizothymia*)	Outgoing, warmhearted, easy-going, participating (*Cyclothymia*)
Less intelligent, concrete-thinking (*Lower scholastic mental capacity*)	More intelligent, abstract-thinking, bright (*Higher scholastic mental capacity*)
Affected by feelings, emotionally less stable, easily upset (*Lower ego strength*)	Emotionally stable, faces reality, calm (*Higher ego strength*)
Humble, mild, obedient, conforming (*Submissiveness*)	Assertive, independent, aggressive, stubborn (*Dominance*)

(Cont. from page 61)

Low score description	High score description
Sober, prudent, serious, taciturn *(Desurgency)*	Happy-go-lucky, heedless, gay, enthusiastic *(Surgency)*
Expedient, a law to himself, by-passes obligations *(Weaker superego strength)*	Conscientious, persevering, staid, rule-bound *(Stronger superego strength)*
Shy, restrained, diffident, timid *(Threctia)*	Venturesome, socially bold, uninhibited, spontaneous *(Parmia)*
Tough-minded, self-reliant, realistic, no-nonsense *(Harria)*	Tender-minded, dependent, over-protected, sensitive *(Premsia)*
Trusting, adaptable, free of jealousy, easy to get on with *(Alaxia)*	Suspictous, self-opinionated hard to pool *(Protension)*
Practical, careful, conventional, regulated by external realities, proper *(Praxernia)*	Imaginative, wrapped up in inner urgencies, careless of practical matters, Bohemian *(Autia)*
Forthright, natural, artless, sentimental *(Artlessness)*	Shrewd, calculating, world-ly, penetrating *(Shrewdness)*
Placid, self-assured, confident, serene *(Untroubled adequacy)*	Apprehensive, worrying, depressive, troubled *(Guilt proneness)*
Conservative, respecting established ideas, tolerant of traditional difficulties *(Conservatism)*	Experimenting, critical, liberal, analytical, free-thinking *(Radicalism)*
Group-dependent, a "joiner" and sound follower *(Group adherence)*	Self-sufficient, prefers own decisions, resourceful *(Self-sufficiency)*
Casual, careless of protocol, untidy, follows own urges *(Low integration)*	Controlled, socially-precise, self-disciplined, compulsive *(High self-concept control)*
Relaxed, tranquil, torpid, unfrustrated *(Low ergic tension)*	Temse, driven, overwrought, fretful *(High ergic tension)*

The original work was concerned with Chemical Engineers and Scientists working in a chemical laboratory. Later this work was expanded to cover other kinds of Engineers and Scientists.

It was found to be especially important for creative scientists to have relatively high scores on Dominance, Parmia and Radicalism. Creative Engineers seemed to have relatively high scores on Emotional Stability, Radicalism and Self Sufficiency.

Creative Thinking Techniques

It has been noted that one highly creative person is far more productive than a number of averagely endowed individuals. Many companies, however, are not able to find or afford such talented people. The alternative is to use group creative techniques or other systematic approaches to obtain new product concepts. We will describe very briefly the nature of some of these techniques below and refer the reader to the bibliography for publications which treat these methods fully.

Brainstorming

Brainstorming is a technique that enjoyed considerable popularity in the fifties. It consists of bringing together persons concerned with the problem and some who are not. This is done in a completely permissive way with no criticism permitted. Each person is encouraged to throw out as many ideas as possible, no matter how wild or implausable, that might contribute to a solution to the problem. Notes are taken by a recorder and the solutions proposed are reviewed *after* the session. The rationale is that the group atmosphere will cause one idea to bring out another and that more ideas will be generated than if each person simply sat alone and recorded any ideas that came to mind.

The sessions are exhilarating and the participants become extraordinarily fluent in the production of ideas. Some people believe that the difficulty is that fluency of ideas is the only dimension of creativity tapped. Other critics say that it is a waste of time, that it cannot be used to solve a complex problem, or that most ideas come from a few individuals in the group who would generate them any way if left alone.

It seems that brainstorming is most useful in solving what some people call "single-node" problems. These are problems calling for a single answer, such as the naming of a product. More difficult problems with many interrelationships require long hours of patient thought and experimentation and are not solvable through brainstorming, at least not in detail. Conceptualizations may be possible.

Reverse Brainstorming

Another group procedure is that of Reverse Brainstorming. Here the group is asked to think of as many things wrong with a product as they possibly can.

Catalog Technique

This is the idea of listing catalogs and other sources of printed information that might contain the germ of an idea. This concept can be used with the Forced Relationship Technique discussed further on.

Check List Technique

In the check list technique, the items on a prepared list are checked against the product or idea. The purpose is to obtain some further ideas for development and follow-up.

Free Association

In free association an attempt is made to stimulate the imagination to produce ideas *relative to some desired concept* or purpose—i.e., to produce intangible ideas, advertising slogans, designs, or names.

The procedure is to:
1. Jot down something related to an important aspect of the subject or problem. Examples are sketches, symbols, words, number, picture, etc.
2. Jot down things suggested by the first action
3. Continue the procedure until useable ideas or concepts emerge.

Disparate Thinking Technique

In disparate thinking for problem solving, the idea is to think of some product completely dissimilar from the product you are most concerned with, and then try to find a relationship between the two. It can be utilized with the group approach, such as in a brainstorming session.

Induced Disassociation

Induced disassociation consists of looking or staring at a product, while trying to keep your mind as blank as possible. It sometimes produces a new view of the product—as if it had never been seen before.

Another approach that can be used in a group is that of Attribute Listing. Here one simply tries to describe a product in as complete a detail as possible so as to find ways to improve it.

Synectics

Another approach is Synectics, developed by the Cambridge Synectics Group. Here the approach is to bring together the findings from different fields to solve a problem. It brings together different and apparently irrelevant elements. A team of highly trained people from different fields is set up to attack the problem and by working together and cross-fertilizing each other, original and often creative solutions are often found. Synectics is almost the opposite of brainstorming. The group is smaller, not especially permissive and the group is composed of specialists. The objective sought is not fluency, but an increase in the probability in new combinations. Sometimes the participants are often not told immediately of the exact nature of the problem they are expected to solve. For example if the object is to develop an improved paint, the group might be asked to think about the concept of covering rather than to think about the concept of paint. While synectics can be applied in a formal manner, it is almost an automatic by-product of a well constructed product planning and development group. Figure 4-2 shows the process in detail.

Attribute Listing

Attribute listing is a technique used principally for improving tangible items already in existence. First-some object is chosen for improvement. The parts of the object are then listed. Next, the procedure calls for the listing of the essential basic qualities, features or attributes of the object and its parts. Finally a sytematic attempt is made to change or

Problem Definition Is Critical

It is important to recognize that problem statement significantly influences the way the problem will be approached. Consequently, following the PAG (Problem-As-Given) statement, there is an analytical phase leading the group to decide on which formulation of the problem is going to be the first subject of attack. This statement is called the PAU (Problem-As-Understood).

The analytical stage from PAG to PAU usually accomplishes a number of purposes: it makes the strange familiar to those participants in the group who are not familiar with the problem and its background; it is used to elicit and nullify those immediate solution possibilities which inevitably occur to group members but which rarely prove adequate. It is held essential that all members of the group purge themselves of the "premature" solutions as they arise, for an indivual's constructive participation in the session is lost as long as he dwells on his first solution possibility.

The first PAU serves merely as a common starting point, judged be the group as a potentially fruitful topic to concentrate upon. The PAU is frequently restated, and it is not uncommon for the group to discover that the real heart of the problem lies elsewhere than in the first definition by the PAG.

In the Synetics process, thinking oscillates in an orderly fashion between analysis and analogy, between making-the-strange-familiar, and making-the-familiar-strange. Analogies permit the group to deliberately distort the "image" of the problem, to gain a new look at it, after which it is allowed to come back into focus.

The Group Leader's Role

The important decision of which analogical route the group is to take rests on the leader. He makes this decision by the criterion of "constructive psychological strain". With a mechanical problem, for example, he would look for biological models. With people-oriented problems, he might seek analogies from the exact sciences. The Synectics groups have found that the more concrete the problem, the greater is the likelihood that symbolic analogy will be fruitful.

It is the leader's responsibility to evoke analogical responses by means of so-called Evocative Questions, which form the bridge between the analysis and analogy. The leader specifies which type of analogy he wants (direct, personal, or symbolic), and he usually singles out the response from one particular group member. A good leader soon learns that each group member usually has greater facility with one kind of analogy than the others, and the leader capitalizes on that knowledge.

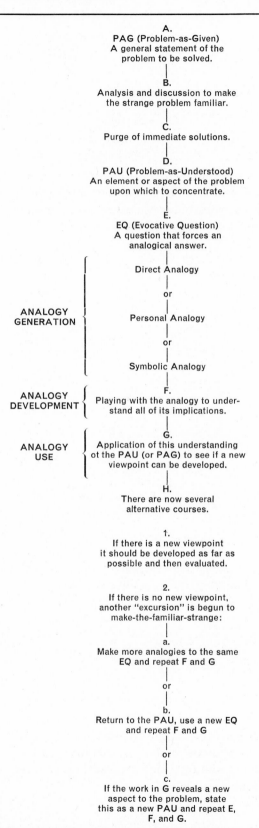

Figure 4-2 Synectics Flow Chart. Sessions should be constructed according to this plan
Source: Eugene Raudsepp, "Forcing Ideas with Synectics", *Machine Design*, Oct. 16, 1969

the subject and it is not felt appropriate to go into detail. Primarily the following questions are asked of each part involved with a particular item:

> What is it?
> What must it do?
> What does it do?
> What did it cost?
> How else can the job be done?
> How much will that cost?

Actually, it is a far more complex process, but this questioning represents the essential idea of the process.

Alex Osborn developed a rather well-known check-list which is to be applied in questioning an existing product. It includes the following suggestive questions, ideas, or concepts:

1. Can it be put to other uses? Are there new ways to use it as it is? Would there be other uses if it is modified?
2. Can it be adapted? What else is like this? What other ideas does this product suggest? Does the past offer parallels that suggest adaptations? What could I copy in order to adapt it to a new use or market. Whom or what could I emulate?
3. Modify it? Give it a new twist? Can one change meaning, color, motion, odor, form, and/or shape? What other desirable changes could be made?
4. Can one magnify it? What can one add? Would more time to perform help? Does greater frequency, strong, larger, thicker, extra-value, plus ingredients, duplicate, multiply and/or exaggerate suggest ways to magnify it in a desirable manner?
5. Would minification help? What can one substitute to accomplish it or anything else? Condense it? Miniaturize it? Lower it? Shorten it? Lighten it? Can one omit something or split it up? Would understanding it help?
6. What of substitution? Examples include: who else, what else? Other ingredients, materials, process, power, place, and/or approaches are also substitution possibilities. Does another tone of voice suggest anything?
7. Can one rearrange it? Would interchange of components help? Can one advantageously use other patterns, layout, and/or sequence?

Would transposition of cause and effect help? How about change of pace or schedule?

8. Does the idea "reverse" suggest anything? Can one transpose positive and negative? How about transposition through the concept of opposites? Can it be turned backward? Would turning it upside down help? What of reversal of roles? Change its shoes? What of concept "Turn tables?"
9. What of the concept of combining? Would it help to blend or alloy the product? Does assortment suggest anything? What of an ensemble? Can one advantageously combine units, purpose, appeals, or ideas?[8]

Trial and Error

Trial and error was the backbone of many of Edison's inventions. This method involves trying out one solution after another with very little reliance on preliminary analysis and science. Edison, however, always had a conceptual idea he was exploring *before* he began the trial and error process. Today the trial and error approach is belittled as being unscientific and costly. However, if a systematic approach does not work, and the results are needed, do not laugh off the trial and error or experimental approach. It still is of considerable value if applied with imagination and tenacity.

Kepner-Tregoe Method

The Kepner-Tregoe method is to isolate or find the problem and then decide what to do about it. This method calls for making a systematic outline which precisely describes both the problem and what lies outside of it (but closely related to it) in order to find possible causes of the problem and to facilitate decision making.

Scientific Method

Many of today's planned innovations are developed following the scientific method which involves defining the problem, analyzing it, gathering data, analyzing the data, arriving at a solution, and testing the solution in practice.

- Gain better knowledge of creative people. Understand their personalities, their powers and foibles, their needs and motives, their fears, and their enthusiasms.

- Improve understanding of the nature of creativity and the difficulties implicit in the creative process.

- Adopt selection procedures capable of "screening in" genuinely creative people. Do not hire people primarily on the basis of getting along with others. Encourage constructive nonconformity and individual differences.

- Learn the internal and external incentives to creative effort. Spell out carefully and demonstrate incentives for success.

- Allow creative departments to have an important part in management's long-term plans and keep creative people informed about important aspects of company operations, policies, and goals.

- Place a high value on creative effort. Provide the inspirational beginning for a creative project. Show faith that creative people will be creative in their solution to problems. Show interest in projects at hand and recognize progress made. Realize that creativity thrives on recognition, praise, and understanding.

- Encourage in both word and deed. Provide moral support and respect. Have a genuine desire to see creative people succeed. Establish a receptive and co-operative climate.

- Recognize accomplishment and deliver adequate rewards for accomplishment. Honestly evaluate creative ideas and see to it that individuals receive proper recognition for their ideas.

- Develop an open-minded, receptive, "let's-go-further" attitude. Have respect for creative people's opinions. Give creative people a chance to try out ideas without prejudicial criticism.

- Convince technical people that they individually are expected to take responsibility for initiating new work and new ideas, and that management will back them up. Allow them to guide their own work. Provide everybody with areas of freedom and self-direction. Keep the organizational structure flexible.

- Recognize technical people's dedication to their field of specialty. Accept the long-range goals and objectives of creative work.

- Provide funds and facilities for creative work.

- Constantly and consistently reflect the sincerity of published objectives and policies.

- Bring people together who stimulate each other. With the more creative, see to it that group work is on a strictly voluntary basis, that is, let them determine when to be alone and when to seek each other out. Realize that the team approach will solve problems but that the real advances in creative work are made by men who enjoy the freedom of selecting their own challenging problems and solving them without the restriction of unrealistic time-schedules.

- Avoid over-regimentation and gearing of efforts to a too-rigid time-table. Recognize that a good group can supply its own brakes without stifling creativity. Realize that pressure and push for a desired result often hamper creativity. Minimize deadline pressures, trivial routines, and administrative details. Know that informality and freedom are necessary to spontaneity of creative thought.

- Consider individual personalities in making assignments. Actively seek out, develop, and encourage those with creative ability.

- Be willing to take calculated risks. Recognize that the attitude of no-risk-taking, this-has-gotta-pay-off is inhibiting of true creative thought.

- Maintain open communication channels up and down.

- Provide parallel paths of advancement with management. See to it that salaries of top creative personnel are on a par with management.

- Give prestige to creative people. Provide personal recognition. Establish honors and distinctions of the purely professional sort. Provide opportunities for social and professional recognition of creative talent.

- Provide leadership which will press for the development of a creative environment not only in tangible things, but in the nature of creativity. Strive for an atmosphere of encouragement.

Figure 4-4   Tips to Management for Improving Creative Climates
Source: Eugene Raudsepp, "Climate For Creativity", *Machine Design*, July 21, 1960

THE MANAGER AND INNOVATION

Not only must the manager plan, organize and control in today's world, he must also innovate. This means that a manager must continually extend his capacity to monitor innovations in order to keep abreast with the world.

The past view of the manager has been that he is both entrepreneur and owner. In our modern society the manager is a hired professional who controls the substance of the business enterprise.

The hired professional manager is responsible and accountable for the success or failure of his company. If he innovates, he risks his position in the company hierarchy. Second, since he is part of a larger group of managers, any innovation he has brought about or encouraged will usually require the cooperation of other managers. Seldom will today's manager go it alone.

Today's manager is different from his older counterpart in another respect. Previously, the extent of the risks taken were largely determined by

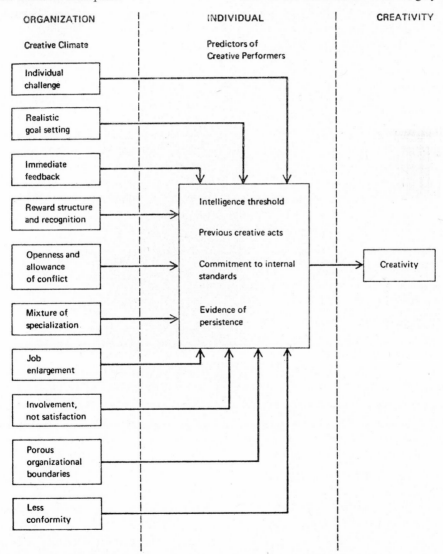

Figure 4-5   The Creative Individual in A Creative Climate
Source: Arthur Gestenfeld, *Effective Management of Research and Development*, Reading, Massachusetts, Addison-Wesley Publishing Company, 1970

whether the economy was in a boom or in a recession. Today the general view is that the great booms or depressions are past, and the great focus of attention is on rate of growth. The government, industry and the financial community all focus on growth—growth of national product and growth of every other variety. Therefore, a manager today does not wait until signs of recovery to introduce innovations. There is a tendency to disregard the level of business activity as a critical factor in encouraging or implementing innovations. This kind of decision tends to restrict the extreme economic fluctuations of the past.

Not only must the professional manager continue his caretaking role, but he must add to it the role of managing innovation. He must fully understand that for innovation to be a success it must produce a profit. He should also understand, as outlined in Chapter 1, that risks are multiplied as the innovation passes through the stages from conception to actual manufacturing and sale of the product.

Successful management of innovation is achieved by stimulating the creativity of the idea-producers in the organization. Each manager should create a climate for creativity. Carl J. Ally summarized the entire concept of establishing such a climate by observing that a good creative person provides his own discipline, that he does not respond to any kind of "You must" directive. Also he observed that the way to keep him happy and creative is to give him interesting things to do and leave him alone.

A more detailed set of explicit suggestions for establishing and maintaining a climate for creativity is given in Figure 4-4.

Conceptually, the relationship between the organization climate and the creative individual may be seen from Figure 4-5.

SOCIAL VALUES AND INNOVATION

Our social values have a pervasive influence in innovations. For example, the men and women of today have a high regard for the individual as a person.

There is optimism about the future and what it has in store for us. Finally, there is a strong experimental attitude. The regard for the individual and his rights should continue into the future, and this, plus the experimental attitude, should all tend to provide encouragement of innovation.

Another view of our society is provided by Reisman and his associates in *The Lonely Crowd*.[10] The essence of their views is that people can be divided into essentially three groups. The first is the tradition-directed type of person who is devoid of initiative. The second type has been labeled as the "inner-directed" person who is more of an independent soul. He is portrayed as the pioneer of frontier days and the entrepreneur of our industrial expansion. The last character type was identified as the "other-directed" type and has been popularized as "the organization man" who lives in strict conformity. This latter character certainly is not good for innovation. However, it appears that a revival of the independent spirit is gaining over the "organization man" type.

One of the more significant effects of the current emphasis upon innovation is that corporations of today tend to stress, more and more, the need for individual creativity and initiative.

GOVERNMENT IMPACT ON INNOVATION

The Federal Government encourages innovation in two ways. One is by direct commitment, the other is by indirect means.

Direct commitment first involves that of economic incentives. In former times, government made direct grants to companies cush as to railroads, in order to spur them on to extend their lines. Today direct grants are not generally used, but there are subsidies awarded to such industry groups as farm, maritime, and airline industries. Secondly, there *are* direct grants for specific research endeavors. Third, the government permits faster depreciation in order to spur investment and innovation. Fourth, the government has used tax reform as a spur. This was done in 1964 when the levels of corporate and personal taxes are reduced. There are other government aids to innovation such as patent protection and retraining of people due to dislocation resulting from technological progress.

Indirectly, there is a form of pressure put on vendors to the government to innovate. Also, anti-trust law is designed to prevent restraints on competition. Ours and other governments also often resort to emphasizing patriotism in order to spur certain kinds of innovation and economic investment. Occassionally they almost legislate when innovation is to occur. An example of this might be the time (May, 1965) when the FCC required that all television receivers be able to receive UHF as well as VHF broadcasts. State and local governments also look favorably upon innovation.

THE COMPANY AND INNOVATION

J. B. Weiner examined 13 top growth companies in the United States and isolated those ingredients which he thought had a direct bearing on their success. He identified six basic factors which lay beneath the successful innovating characteristic of these companies:

1. The difficult task of starting long-range planning at the grass roots level of management and the involvement of even lower level employees in the job of looking into the future.
2. A truly dynamic corporate structure that enables the company to seize a profit opportunity whenever or wherever one appears.
3. An active, viable program to encourage employee innovation and creativity.
4. An infallible sense of timing, of being equally adept at knowing when to launch a new product or close down an old plant.
5. Above-average investment acumen, a particularly challenging capability that few corporations can really master.
6. An integrated line, with a program of product development and acquisition designed to avoid both risk and merely temporary gain.[11]

It seems that the heart of the message is that growth is dependent on an innovative attitude among the company's managers.

Proceeding with the company's view of management with respect to innovation, we might well look at Drucker's thoughts as to the directions in which innovation opportunities should lie:

1. New products and services that are needed to attain marketing objectives.
2. New products or services that will be needed because of technological changes that may make present products obsolete.
3. Product improvements needed both to attain market objectives and to anticipate expected technological changes.
4. New processes and improvements in old processes needed to satisfy market goals—for instance, manufacturing improvements to make possible the attainment of pricing objectives.
5. Innovations and improvements in all major areas of activity—in accounting, design, office management, or labor relations—so as to keep up with advances in knowledge and skills.[12]

It should be emphasized that innovation should always keep a customer orientation. There is a continual danger that it will veer away from customer needs and thereby fail in its purpose to create more profit.

SUMMARY

Technological innovation is a high risk but high profit strategy. Not all companies should or can pursue such a strategy. For those which do, the means for success lies in selecting and hiring a few highly creative people. The problem of identifying such people is a difficult one. Often they are buried in the organizational bureaucracy, their creative talents stifled by unimaginative plodding managers.

Identifying creative people is only the first step. They must be given the opportunity to perform and the backing of management in their risk-taking. In other words, management must actively and continuously create a climate for creativity.

If there are few or no highly creative people in the company, a number of systematic approaches to stimulating the imagination of the key individuals are covered in this chapter.

REFERENCES

1. For a more complete writeup, see "Talley Forgets About Glamour", *Business Week*, June, 20, 1970, pp. 59, 61.
2. See "Corfam's Last Mile", *Business Week*, March 20, 1971, p. 34.
3. For papers on many phases of innovation such as knowledge-production, economic development, effects of antitrust and patent laws on innovation, and tax treatment of innovative investment, see "Papers and Proceedings of the 78th Annual Meeting of American Economic Association", *American Economic Review*, May, 1966.
4. For a reference to other classifications, see James E. Engle, David T. Kollat, and Roger D. Blackwell, *Consumer Behavior*, New York: Holt, Rinehart and Winston, Inc., 1968, pp. 544–546.
5. "How Toying About Led to a Discovery", *Business Week*, Oct. 31, 1970, p. 68.
6. B. E. Meehl, "The Creative Individual: Why it is Hard to Identify Him", in Garry A. Steiner (ed.), *The Creative Organization*, Chicago, Ill.: University of Chicago Press, 1965.
7. Francis E. Jones, "Predictor Variables for Creativity in Industrial Science", *J. of Applied Psychology*, April, 1964.
8. A. F. Osborn, *Applied Imagination*, New York: Charles Scribners & Sons, 1958.
9. Donald W. Taylor *et al.*, "How to Manage Creative People", *Business Management*, April, 1967, p. 43.
10. David Riesman, with N. Glazer and R. Denny, *The Lonely Crowd*, New Haven, Conn.: Yale University Press, 1950.
11. J. B. Weiner, "What Makes a Growth Company", *Dun's Review*, Nov., 1964.
12. P. F. Drucker, *Practice of Management*, New York: Harper & Row Publishers, Inc., 1954.

BIBLIOGRAPHY

Alger, John R. M. and Carl V. Hays, *Creative Synthesis in Design*. Englewood Cliffs, N.J.: Prentice-Hall, Inc., 1964.

Barron, Frank, *Creative Person and Creative Process*. New York: Holt, Rinehart & Winston, Inc., 1969.

–, *Creativity and Psychological Health*. Princeton, N.J.: D. Van Nostrand Co., Inc., 1963.

Bennis, W. G., K. D. Benne, and R. Chin (eds.), *The Planning of Change*. New York: Holt, Rinehart & Winston, Inc., 1962.

Clarke, Arthur C., *Profiles of the Future: An Inquiry Into the Limits of the Possible*. New York: Harper & Row Publishers, Inc., 1962.

"Corfam's Last Mile", *Business Week*, March 20, 1971.

Drucker, Peter F., *Landmarks of Tomorrow*. New York: Harper & Row Publishers, Inc., 1957.

–, *Practice of Management*. New York: Harper & Row Publishers, Inc., 1954.

Eels, R. and C. Walton, *Conceptual Foundation of Business*. Homewood, Ill.: Richard D. Irwin, Inc., 1961.

Eco, Umberto, and G. B. Zorzoli, *The Picture History of Inventions*. New York: The Macmillan Co., 1963.

Engle, James E., David T. Kollat, and Roger D. Blackwell, *Consumer Behavior*. New York: Holt, Rinehart & Winston, Inc., 1968.

Gerstenfeld, Arthur, *Effective Management of Research and Development*. Reading, Mass.: Addison-Wesley Publishing Co., 1970.

Ghiselin, B. (ed.), *The Creative Process*. Berkeley, Cal.: University of California Press, 1954.

Gordon, William J., Jr. *Synthetics: The Development of Creative Capacity*. New York: Harper and Brothers, 1961,

Haefele, John W., *Creativity and Innovation*. New York: Reinhold Publishing Co., 1962.

"How Toying About Led to a Discovery", *Business Week*, Oct. 31, 1970.

Jones, Francis E., "Predictor Variables for Creativity in Industrial Science", *J. of Applied Psychology*, April, 1964.

Levitt, Theodore, *Innovation in Marketing*. New York: McGraw-Hill Book Co., 1962.

Mansfield, Edwin, *Industrial Research and Technological Innovation: An Econometric Analysis*. New York: W. W. Norton & Co., Inc., 1968.

Meehl, P. E., "The Creative Individual: Why It is Hard to Identify Him", in Gary A. Steiner (ed.). *The Creative Organization*. Chicago, Ill.: University of Chicago Press, 1965.

Miller, Ben, *Managing Innovation for Growth and Profit*. Homewood, Ill.: Richard D. Irwin, Inc., 1970.

Moore, A. D., *Invention, Discovery and Creativity*. Garden City, N.Y.: Doubleday & Co., Inc., 1969.

Osborn, A. F., *Applied Imagination*. New York: Charles Scribner's Sons, 1958.

"Papers and Proceedings of the 78th Annual Meeting of American Economic Association", *American Economic Review*, May, 1966.

Prince, George M., *The Practice of Creativity*. New York: Harper and Row Publishers, Inc., 1970.

Raudssepp, Eugene, "Forcing Ideas With Synectics", *Machine Design*, Oct. 16, 1969.

Riesman, David, N. Glazer, and R. Denny, *The Lonely Crowd*, New Haven, Conn.: Yale University Press, 1950.

Reynolds, W. H., *Products and Markets*. New York: Appleton-Century-Crofts, Educational Division, Meredith Corp., 1969.

Rugg, H., *Imagination*. New York: Harper and Row Publishers, Inc., 1963.

Simon, Herbert, "Proverbs of Administration", *Public Administration Review*, Jan.–March, 1946.

Steiner, G. A. (ed.), *The Creative Organization*. Chicago, Ill.: University of Chicago Press, 1965.

"Talley Forgets About Glamour", *Business Week*, June 20, 1970.

Taylor, Donald W., *et al.*, "How To Manage Creative People", *Business Management*, April, 1967.

Wall Street Journal Staff. *The Innovators*. Princeton, N.J.: Dow Jones Books, 1968.

Weiner, J. B., "What Makes a Growth Company". *Dun's Review*, Nov., 1964.

Whiting, C. S., *Creative Thinking*. New York: Reinhold Publishing Co., 1968.

CHAPTER 5

OBTAINING NEW PRODUCT IDEAS

The start of a new venture begins with finding an original idea, or an idea that others have overlooked. Ideas are passed over because they appear technically risky or commercially risky. The venture manager seeks ways to reduce the risk and take the new remaining risk when the opportunity and payoffs are large. In essence, he finds creative ways to convert the improbable to the probable. A systematic search for new product ideas offers the venture manager a greater chance of identifying good venture situations.

Before starting the search, a company should
1. Determine its weaknesses and strengths.
2. Identify the social, business and technological areas that will likely progress at the fastest rate.
3. Establish a policy which defines its product areas of interest.

Only then start your search for ideas and direct the search to those areas where company strengths are strongest and which are in accord with the above criteria.

OPPORTUNITIES FROM NEW IDEAS

Finding the good new product idea is the foundation of successful product development. There can be no successful new product development unless there are good ideas to build upon. Further, the search for new product ideas should not be kept secret as many firms do. The advantage lies with the firm that does this work openly and welcomes suggestions.

In the medium and large sized companies there always seems to be ideas around to consider; how-ever, their quality may well be questioned based upon the number of rejections during the development and introduction process. In the small company one often finds a dearth of ideas. Therefore, for the small company, the discovery of its next new idea for a product may be critical to its survival.

It will be the objective of this chapter to help new product managers find new product ideas. In creating or finding ideas the emphasis must be on number and variety. The determination of quality *then* follows.

Companies have been built and have survived on the successes of simple things such as high intensity reading lamps, plastic fold-up raincoats, skate boards, dolls that tan in the sun, bar accessories, magnetic cases for hiding automobile keys, etc. You don't need to find or develop such complex things as picture frame color TV, automatic pin setters, or a numerical controlled multiple spindle machine. The individual who thinks he has a good idea should take heart from this. If his product survives some of the evaluations outlined further on in this book, he may well have a winner.

In Chapter 1 it was explained how it is possible to have varying degrees of product newness, market newness, and manufacturing newness. Each approach, for all practical purposes of new product development, can serve to bring in additional sales and profits. This approach considerably widens the idea search and is exactly why new product risk managers should take this broader approach in the search for ideas.

Another concept that should not be ignored is

that another company's product(s) can be utilized in connection with successful new product ideas. Modern examples of this approach are the companies making and selling peripheral (input and output) devices for computers as well as those developing and marketing software (computer programs). These are two of the fastest growing markets in today's world and the successful companies have some of the highest profit and growth rates to be found anywhere. Another similar example are the companies offering data processing services, including time sharing services—many of these successful companies succeeded by using computers manufactured by others. The new technical areas are the best bets for this approach. The use and application of lasers is another example of this approach.

Technological forecasting is the approach to use for identifying *early* these new areas in order to have time to prepare to take advantage of them. Confirmation of the correctness of the forecast, at about the time they begin to become commercially important can often be found in the opinions of security analysts and/or the knowledgeable equity investor.

Old technological areas are not as productive and it is also much more difficult to succeed, and especially to secure high profits. Yet one firm even succeeded by developing a light-weight highly reliable motorcycle to fulfill a specific market need.

Another area of possibilities for some very small companies with manufacturing and marketing flexibility and know-how is to identify fads early in their brief lives and jump in and out of the market quickly. It is a very dangerous way to live because of the short lives of fad items.

The two key formulas for the small entrepreneur are:

1. *Find a need* and develop a product to fill it.
2. *Find a new product idea* and *then determine if it fills a need* before developing the product.

Most companies are to a large degree locked in to their product lines and markets in the short run. They must seek long in advance the kinds of products they will make. For this reason, technological forecasts for five or ten years ahead are usually required for major successes in product development

in technologically oriented companies. Large companies such as General Electric and TRW, Inc. forecast technological changes 20 years into the future New ideas for products are sought which will suit the forecasted socio-economic and technical *environments*. Many of the products will utilize forecasted technological advances. Naturally, all must fit the socio-economic environment.

BASIC SOURCES OF NEW IDEAS

In Chapter 1 we discussed the three types of innovation: product design, marketing, and manufacturing. Most new product development efforts largely ignore the possible opportunities in manufacturing newness and many of the benefits possible from marketing innovation. Sources of new product ideas from either internal sources (within the company) or external sources (outside the company) may apply to any of these forms of innovation. The new product risk manager should maintain records of the sources of new ideas so as to better exploit opportunities in the future. A yearly tabulation, with comparison to prior years, should be produced for the larger operations.

No individual, or even groups of individuals, within the company can alone be depended on for the production of new product ideas. Rather, such individuals or groups must find ways to uncover ideas of others, both recorded and unrecorded. This search should be a systematic search among company employees *and* sources outside the company.

IN-COMPANY SOURCES OF NEWIDEAS

Direct Creation of Ideas

Direct creation of new product ideas may occur through three processes:

1. The analytical approach consisting of observing things in the company and outside; remembering past facts, processes, and circumstances; reasoning based upon such data; and using judgment to

evaluate alternative approaches to the problem of development. This is typical of programmed research and engineering.

2. Trial-and-error methods to develop new combinations or a solution to some specified need. Thomas Edison's development of the electric light bulb filament is a classic example.

3. Inspiration is the sudden unplanned recognition of a potential idea. For example, Dr. Edward Benedictus dropped a chemical flask which he had neglected to clean. Instead of pieces flying all over the lab, the plastic film coating the interior held the broken pieces together Several days later, he witnessed an auto accident in which one occupant was severely injured. Benedictus related the two events and the result is today's safety glass.

4. The creative approach which involves formulation of the problem; reformulation of the problem over and over; intensive concentration over a period during which critical judgment is suspended; intermission periods, since creative solutions cannot be forced; and finally, illumination or inspiration in which pieces of the solution fall into place with relative swiftness.

Methods 1, 3, and 4 will yield the largest number of ideas if each is properly exploited, both inside and outside of the organization.

The analytical approach is the method pursued by Engineering and Research. The "bug" here is that an idea or problem leading to an idea has to be identified prior to applying the approach. How to organize and operate Engineering and Research activities is not to be covered in this text since other available modern books deal with the subject; two examples of these are *Managing Engineering and Research* (2nd Edition) by Karger and Murdick and *Handbook of Industrial Research Management* (2nd Edition) by Heyel. It should also be mentioned that such books are complementary and supplementary to a book such as this one.

With respect to methods 3 and 4, one prolific idea generator can keep a host of people busy evaluating and developing. The real problem is to identify these people and assiduously cultivate their output. More will be said later as to where to look for such people

and how to keep them producing ideas at near peak output.

The third and fourth methods are apt to yield the biggest dividends. Therefore, the company, particularly the small company without large resources for programmed research, should provide a climate for creativity. Creative people, and this includes *everyone* should be allowed to develop ideas free from such inhibiting views as:

> It won't work.
> We tried that before.
> It will never get by the Underwriters.
> We can't pay for the tools.
> We haven't had a failure in fifty years; why change it?
> There's no other source of supply.
> It can't be done.
> It's a government job.
> We can't help it—that's the policy.
> We don't have enough time.
> Our business is different.
> We'll come back to it later.
> It leaves me cold.
> Let's think about it some more.
> This isn't the right time for it.
> We don't do it that way.
> We can't hold up production for that.
> It costs too much.
> That's not my responsibility.
> No one else knows as much about it as we do.

Figure 5-1 shows a list of idea stimulators which will be helpful to people trying to generate new product ideas or product improvements.

How to Seek In-Company Sources of New Ideas. Very few companies make a systematic effort to seek new product ideas from all employees in the company. It is true that suggestion systems are common, but these are not directed at uncovering new product ideas and hence few turn up. If anything, companies *discourage* employees from making the extra effort of consciously thinking about possible new products. The employee is usually required to sign a pre-employment agreement turning over all inventions to the company for nothing or for some trivial monetary amount. Consider the possibilities

1. Have I pinpointed the problem?
2. Have I searched books, reports, the trade magazines, patents?
3. How would I design it if I were to build it in my workshop at home?
4. Have I considered the physical, thermal, electrical, chemical, and mechanical properties of this material?
5. What other materials have the same properties required?
6. Have I looked for electrical, electronic, optical, hydraulic, mechanical, or magnetic ways of doing this?
7. Have I followed tradition, custom, authority, opinion blindly?
8. Have I looked at analogs for parallel problems?
9. Is this function really necessary?
10. How would other experts look at this problem?
11. Have I made this design accomplish its purpose?
12. Could I alter something already available to do the job?
13. Have I analyzed this in several ways?
14. Could I construct a model?
15. Why must it have this shape?
16. Could it be speeded up or slowed down?
17. Could this be turned inside out, upside down, or reversed?
18. Could this be changed to more of a three dimensional object, or could it be flattened out?
19. Could this be made cheaper, or should it be made more expensive?
20. What if this were made larger, higher, longer, wider, thicker, or lower?
21. What could be substituted? For what?
22. How could I rearrange or alter the parts, the subassemblies?
23. Has it been simplified as much as possible?
24. What new ways could it be used as it is?
25. What other forms of power would make it work better?
26. Where else can this be done?
27. Would this work better in the day, in the night, intermittently, or continuously?
28. Could this be put to other uses if it were modified?
29. Could several parts be combined?
30. Could standard components be substituted?
31. Could this be made easier to operate?
32. What if the order of the process were changed?
33. Can materials be salvaged or reclaimed?
34. Suppose this were left out?
35. How can this be made to appeal to the senses? Appearance improved?
36. Can it be made safer?
37. Can it be made more compact?
38. Should it be made more symmetrical or more asymmetrical?
39. Can I forget the specifications and get a better performance?
40. How about extra value?
41. Can this be multiplied, reduced, blown up, or carried to extremes?
42. What form could this be in—liquid, powder, paste, or solid? Rod, tube, polyhedron, cube, or sphere?
43. Can motion be added to it?
44. Will it be better standing still?
45. Can it be made better or cheaper for another production process?
46. Can cause and effect be reversed? Which is cause and which is effect?
47. Should it be put on the other end or in the middle?
48. Should it rotate instead of slide?
49. Should it slide instead of roll?
50. Could the package be used for something else afterwards?
51. What other method is there for separating the variables?
52. What if the speed were increased or decreased?
53. What if it were heat-treated, hardened, alloyed, cured, frozen, plated?
54. What if color were added or changed or it were made transparent or translucent?
55. What if it were twisted, streamlined, condensed?
56. How about blending or adding an assortment?
57. What if it were crushed, distilled, or compressed?
58. Would it be internally braced or externally braced?

Figure 5-1 Idea Stimulators
Source: D.W. Karger and R.G. Murdick, Managing Engineering and Research, New York: The Industrial Press, 1963, p. 142

if a company offered individuals a 20% share of the net profits!

This sounds big and it is from one viewpoint. But consider a profit margin of 10% which *is* big. Twenty per cent of 10% (as stated) would only amount to 2% of the selling price—a very common royalty for an invention. When employees observe cases of products making thousands of dollars of profit for the company, the motivation could be tremendous. Yet, companies forego this great opportunity because of the traditional way of viewing employees as legal servants of the owners rather than partners in enterprise. The New Product Suggestion System could be set up despite some difficulties in evaluating ideas for development.

An alternative to the New Product Suggestion System would be the systematic soliciting of ideas from technical, marketing, and manufacturing personnel by the new product organization. Only a few people can *successfully* play the role of a solicitor of new product ideas. He must have the necessary technical *and* business background and have a personality that commands the confidence of others. He must be able to act as a catalyst on many occasions. On others he must make a contribution. He cannot be "negative" in any respect. Certainly he cannot "sit in judgement" as the ideas are given. It is much easier to dry up an idea source than keep it flowing. If he ridicules or even mildly discourages a contributor at any time, he will not be likely to obtain the free-wheeling thoughts on new products.

Typical general approaches to querying individuals in the technical function are:

1. A direct and unrestricted request for a new product idea.
2. A request for the other person to describe any unusual features of equipment being designed. This is followed by questions as to why or how this portion of the project could be converted into a new product.
3. A direct question as to which components, subsystems, or mechanisms developed in the past were unusual, and then following up again with questions as to why or how such items could be converted into new products.

4. As a last resort (if the previous approaches did not dredge up any ideas), ask them to describe the equipment they are now engineering. Here, skill in posing the proper follow-up questions is of paramount importance. In other words, the idea searcher must act as a catalyst, and perhaps even, on his own, synthesize ideas.

Some specific questions which might be asked for a wide variety of company personnel are:

1. What products can they see as a real need that the *industry* should develop and offer for sale? (If they are consumers of the product, ask them to consider it as a consumer rather than as a producer).
2. What new equipment, gadget, or mechanism would they like to see developed to help them in their work? What is needed to help someone else on the job?
3. What safety device is needed?
4. What have they heard others say was needed as a new product?
5. What operation(s) on their or someone else's job seems unnecessarily difficult? Such situations can often lead to a new product idea.
6. What would help them reduce costs in their particular function of the business? (Some people need the dollar concept to trigger their thoughts).
7. What job have their friends complained or talked about as being most difficult or expensive?
8. What piece of equipment is not performing correctly? Why?
9. What new technology is affecting the products presently being produced? How?
10. What could be done to improve product performance and/or salability?

Employee Invention Records

Well-organized companies record ideas which are patentable and file for patent coverage on many of these. These records should be regularly scanned for new product ideas by *both* the engineering management and the new product function to see if new product ideas are involved. More will be said later in this chapter about the availability of these ideas from other companies.

Reports

Salesmen reports can be a fruitful source of ideas, particularly if the salesmen are encouraged to both listen and search for new product ideas. It is surprising how rarely this request is made of salesmen; nevertheless, they can be a most fruitful source if efforts are made to develop them.

Any company engaged in engineering, research and/or development usually requires regular submission of technical notebooks to management. These reports should be carefully screened for new product ideas, not merely for the presence of engineering problems. This means a review, not by the typical sub-engineering manager who hasn't thought about a new product idea in the last five years!

Make-Buy Decisions

Every company continuously screens the parts and materials which it makes and which it purchases on either a formal or informal basis to determine whether to make or purchase the item in the future. Obviously, this must be done for the entire parts list of a new product to be produced, and old product part list's are usually regularly reviewed relative to the make-buy decision.

If one can make an item at less cost than the money required to buy it, there certainly exists the possibility of making and selling this item or something *similar* to someone else's product, at least from many of the parts or subsystems. The company already has an internal market and apparently can be competitive in the external market, providing an outside market does exist for the item. It does not always follow that one can be competitive in the external market if one can make a product at less cost than it takes to buy it, but at least there is a good possibility that this may be so. The advantages of having a captive market, one's own company, is always attractive. In fact, large companies sometimes acquire another firm primarily to ensure that the latter will use their product, thereby resulting in increased profits through expansion of the product's volume which usually permits manufacturing economies.

Credit and Collection Departments

A percentage of almost any firm's delinquent accounts stems from deficiencies in the company's products. Collection personnel should be trained to notify Product Planning of complaints encountered, especially if numerous complaints are received about a particular defect. Better yet, the new product risk manager should ensure the analysis of such reports. A pattern of complaints might very well reflect a basic widespread need that a new product could satisfy.

In smaller companies, the company president often looks at samples of letters from complaining and/or delinquent customers to learn about product performance. Similarly, these should be seen by the product planner, regardless of the company's size, in order to obtain clues for new products.

Service Department

Company servicemen have intimate contacts with the final users, which enables the servicemen to fill four "new product" roles. First, a portion of the service calls stem from weaknesses in existing products. In a similar manner to the complaints previously mentioned regarding credit and collection delinquencies, the serviceman when he finds weaknesses in the product can often give suggestions as to how an improved product could be built. Most engineering departments do not consistently and *deliberately* utilize the service personnel for fulfilling this role.

The second new product role of the servicemen is perhaps of even greater importance. He often is in the position to observe an adaption of the company's equipment by some ingenious mechanic to fit a peculiar operating condition or job requirement. Such adaptions may well reflect a need that exists among other prospective customers for a new kind of equipment.

Third, it is suggested that a special place on the serviceman's report be provided to list unusual successful applications or uses for the company equipment. This could open an entire new market for an existing product, the equivalent of a new product.

Fourth, another approach would be to have him prepare a special report on breakdowns resulting from attempts to use the machine in both illegitimate or legitimate applications. Illegitimate usage would be usage in ways for which it was not intended. These illegitimate uses often point the way to a new product that would fill the observed need.

Some people have even suggested establishing a bonus system for any such ideas that are converted into new or improved products in a manner similar to the suggested new product suggestion system.

Sales Department

As previously mentioned, salesmen as well as other company personnel should be approached for new product ideas. They have many opportunities for talking with the customer about new applications for existing equipment, modifications that the customer feels should be made on the equipment, and, in fact, new product suggestions.

Some companies ask each salesman annually to visit a specified number of customers, and work through a simple questionnaire aimed at discovering new product ideas. They will find that customers are eager to express their ideas if they feel that the salesman is genuinely interested in their point of view and not simply looking for phrases which can be used as testimonials in selling products.

Other companies have used sales meetings to staff brainstorming sessions (the technique was described in chapter 4) aimed at developing new product ideas. Out of one such session came 226 ideas, ten per cent of which received careful study and six of which were put into production.

It is suggested that there be a specific place on the salesman report form for new ideas, suggestions, reports on competitors' new products, and on customers' complaints. New products and new product ideas should be stressed; in fact, one could even run special new product contests among salesmen.

Purchasing

Vendors are continually bringing the attention of your purchasing agents to new products which they are trying to introduce. Some of these might be produced by your company with a distinct advantage over the competing firm because of peculiar facilities or abilities which you have within the plant. In other cases, vendors often mention to the purchasing agent that a great need exists for a product having certain characteristics; therefore, the help of the purchasing department should be secured. In a similar manner, your advertising agency can sometimes suggest possible new product ideas.

Company Acquisition

This is a route that many companies take in acquiring new products in parallel with internal development efforts. There is little difference in the end result obtained. The advantages in company acquisition are great since company growth is achieved in the shortest possible time. Not only does the purchaser obtain new products, he also secures facilities to produce, personnel to research, engineer, market and manage the operation. New distribution channels and/or classes of customers are often also obtained via an acquisition. It would seem logical that an immediate survey of the new personnel in an acquired company to identify new product ideas would be an appropriate action by the firm who engineered the take-over. However, these authors have never encountered an actual example of such practical action.

EXTERNAL SOURCES OF IDEAS

Solicited and Unsolicited Ideas

It is possible to actively solicit suggestions from outside sources. However, great care should be taken in inviting suggestions. Otherwise, many difficulties will be encountered including that of being swamped with a thousand old ideas that have been previously reviewed and discarded. Moreover, as will be shown in Chapter 6, it is dangerous to consider ideas from the outside especially if they are not covered by a patent which is still in force and owned by the discloser. If the patent has expired, the company still is involved in a hazardous procedure if it uses the idea—provided it was called to the company's attention through a suggestion from outside in such a manner that could be classified as a confidential disclosure. Great care must be taken in even considering such an idea. Otherwise, the company may incur major liabilities for something that is either unpatentable or even for something that has been patented but on which the patent has expired or which has been "dedicated to the public".

Practically all companies receive unsolicited new product ideas. Chapter 7 presents ways in which such ideas must be handled if the company is to protect itself from major damage or liability claims.

Other Companies

It does make sense to look to other industrial firms which may have patented certain products or processes that are outside of the area of their normal operation. Such patents are filed away and only brought out if they are needed to defend the company from a patent litigation or to use as trading assets if they are attacked; or if they want access to a patent right owned by another company. Companies holding such protective (but unused) patents often are perfectly willing to license others to use them; furthermore, such companies are often interested in supplying basic materials needed to make the end item. An example of this latter situation was the Fansteel Metallurgical Corporation which was interested in expanding the use of tantalum. Since electrolytic capacitor manufacturers were slow in exploiting the properties of this metal, Fansteel was producing capacitors, yet they were more than interested in having other firms join in the production of such capacitors and were perfectly willing to license responsible firms.

The principal difficulty encountered in soliciting other industrial firms is that the company often insists that the prospective client disclose rather specifically what product or type of product or technical area he is interested and why. Also, unless you are affiliated with a well-known firm, they will want some reasonable proof that your company is both capable and desirous of manufacturing and selling any product that shows good potential and which falls in the desired product line or category.

Clues as to the research activities of companies and thereby possible available developments might be offered by the research facilities of a company. One source of such information can be obtained from a directory, *Industrial Research Laboratories of the United States*, available from the National Research Council, Washington, 25, D.C.

Better clues, however, are the parts and/or subsystems they make for their own products, what their technical people say at conventions and what they write in journals.

Research Laboratories

If new product ideas are to be solicited and/or developed, one should be sure to include in the consideration the various industrial research laboratories—both nonprofit and profit organizations. They will develop products for you on a contract basis and they also often have ideas to sell or license. Examples of profit organizations are:

Arthur D. Little, Inc., Cambridge, Massachusetts
Foster, D. Snell, Inc., New York
Research Corporation, New York

Examples of nonprofit organizations are:

Battelle Memorial Institute, Columbus, Ohio
Stanford Research Institute, Menlo Park, California
Cornell Aeronautical Laboratory, Buffalo
I.I.T. Research Institute, Chicago, Illinois
Mellon Institute Research Foundation, Pittsburgh, Pa.
Southwest Research Institute, San Antonio, Texas
Franklin Research Institute, Philadelphia
Midwest Research Institute, Kansas City, Missouri
Southern Research Institute, Birmingham, Alabama
Research Triangle Institute, Durham, N. Carolina

In addition to the institutes listed above, there are some nonprofit organizations that began as essentially captive R & D organizations of one or more government agencies or departments. Examples of these are:

Aerospace Corporation, El Segundo, California

Institute for Defense Analysis, Washington, D.C.

Mitre Corporation, Bedford, Massachusetts

Rand Corporation, Santa Monica, California

System Development Corporation, Santa Monica, California

Listings of these and a host of others can be found in *Research Centers Directory*, Archie N. Palmer and Anthony P. Kruzas (eds.), Gale Research Company, Detroit, 1965, and *New Research Centers* (Quarterly supplement), Archie N. Palmer. Gale Research Company, Detroit.

Many of these laboratories often have developments they are willing to license to others. Battelle, for example, has a sizable development budget of its own and helped start xerography on its way to success.

In a similar manner, most of the country's educational institutions providing degrees in engineering and/or science are possible sources of new product ideas and therefore should be solicited; in fact, many of them have separate research institutes similar to the not-for-profit institutions mentioned before. Educational institutions, with or without research institutes, often have patented ideas which represent potentially profitable new products. In fact, many universities are deriving substantial income from royalties collected on ideas that have become profitable products for one or more companies. Some universities have tried to simplify licensing their patented ideas by cooperating with the Research Corporation of New York City.

Many research institutes and research laboratories, in addition to being sources of already developed or defined new product ideas, will also find and/or develop new products for you on a contractual basis. This is especially true of the non-university affiliated laboratories. The independent-research laboratories or institutes, which are established to do research, have this kind of work as one of their major objectives. The institutes affiliated with colleges and universities usually have other kinds of primary goals, such as promoting the university, providing part-time employment for professors and/or students, etc. Such university laboratories or institutes will have a less commercial orientation, which may be good or bad depending upon the project involved.

Almost every major college or university that offers a technical curriculum will accept some outside research projects. One major problem with university affiliated laboratories is that they generally reserve the right to publish all findings.

All of these research laboratories or institutes do work on a contract basis, and it is advantageous to define the work to be done as precisely as possible if costs are to be minimized. If merely the product category is specified, maximum expense will be incurred; at the same time it could well be worth the cost. The reasons for going to such research institutes, laboratories, or university research activities for a service are quite numerous; some of the more usual reasons are:

1. The firm's engineering or research staff is loaded and cannot accept additional work without expansion.
2. The staff cannot be expanded to accomplish the desired work in the time available.
3. The existing engineering and/or research skills in the company are not well suited to the desired product or product category.
4. Facilities are needed which would necessitate a large and undesirable capital expenditure.
5. The laboratory or institute has the required specialized personnel and/or facilities.
6. The company has a partially developed idea that apparently has great potential but which the firms' own designers have been unable to make work satisfactorily or production engineer the idea so that it can be produced at a competitive cost.
7. The company desires to see the results from scientists who are not as rigidly controlled as those within the company.
8. The company's technical function is not succeeding in accomplishing a particular development.

Middlemen

The Research Corporation of New York City was mentioned earlier as being used by universities to find outlets for their inventions. Private inventors also use this source.

There are other companies in this field. Others are the Resources and Facilities Corporation (Refac) of New York and Dr. Dvorkovitz & Associates of Ormond Beach, Fla. This latter organization will accept retainers for finding an invention.

Another inventor or patent development agency is NAVAN Products, an affiliate of North American Aviation. NAVAN purchases, licenses or markets promising new products submitted by individuals. The products bear the NAVAN trademark.

The National Patent Development Corporation which has offices in New York, Chicago, Washington, and Zurich offers inventors ideas to clients.

University Patents, Inc. of Illinois is an affiliate of the University of Illinois Foundation and acts as a middle man for the University's scientists.

The *International Intertrade Index* is published by I.I.I. Publishers, 744 Broad Street, Suite 3400, Newark, N.J. 07101. Its stated purpose is to inform the business community what new products will soon be available from foreign manufacturers. It therefore is a source for new product ideas, licenses, and patents.

INPC International New Products Center, 680 Fifth Avenue, New York City, 10019, publishes monthly the *New Product Preview Report*, *Product Licensing News* and *The New Product Managers Letter*. In addition, an annual *INPC New Product Directory* and other interim reports are published.

Outside Individuals

Exactly the same approaches and practically all of the questions used for company employees will work equally well for almost any individual. The principal change is that one must recognize that non-plant personnel may have a moral or actual obligation not to disclose certain information because of their employment. This is especially true for military personnel, for civilians working on military projects, and for company personnel working for a company producing competing products.

Government Sources

There are many government sources of new product ideas. Since the United States Government sponsors a major portion of the research and development conducted in this country, obviously it controls an increasingly large number of patents. A vast majority of these patents are available for license to the general public; however, it must be understood that an exclusive license cannot be obtained. The National Aeronautics and Space Administration and the U.S. Atomic Energy Commission supply brochures and assistance to management on product innovation.

Types of patents available and useful as a source of ideas for new products are shown in Figure 5-2.

Ideas from Abroad

American manufacturers in many cases have increased their U.S. sales and profits by introducing European products, processes and engineering techniques. Successful U.S. firms have found three types of items existing in Europe which sometimes fit into their American programs.

1. Products on the European market and processes in European plants which are successful in Europe, but which have never been introduced in the United States.
2. Products and processes which were never successful in Europe due to the condition of their market, but could succeed in the U.S. market. Often such product and processes are fully developed.
3. Products and processes under development in European laboratories and plants which would be successful in the U.S. when they are ready.

One way of securing possible ideas from abroad is to utilize a firm to do your searching for you. One of these is IRCONSO—International Research Consultants who have offices in many European cities and whose U.S. office is in Detroit, Michigan.

Another approach is to do it yourself. Many U.S. firms have their own agents abroad working at this job fulltime. However, if you haven't been able to do it (successfully search and find new

Types of patents	Terms of use	Are lists of patents available?	Are abstracts available?	Review copy of patent at—	Purchase copy of patent from—	Make application for use to—
Expired	Free	Numerical only; see Gazette.[2]	No; see selected claim in Gazette.	Patent Office and some public libraries.[3]	Patent Office, Washington 25, D.C., or photocopy from some libraries.	None required.
Dedicated	do.	No; see Gazette	do.	do.	do.	do.
Available for license or sale	By royalty or outright purchase.	Yes; in Gazette	No; see Gazette prior to June 30, 1954; otherwise see patent.	do.	do.	Patent owner.
Foreign-owned (United States patents issued to nationals of other countries).	do.	No; see Gazette	No; see Gazette or patent.	do.	do.	do.
Design	Same as other patents above.	do.	do.	do.	do.	do
Government-owned	Ordinarily free	Yes; Superintendent of Documents, Washington 25, D.C.	Yes; at Commerce field offices, SBA field offices, or Government Patents Board, Washington 25, D.C.	Patent Office or Government, Patents Board, Washington 25, D.C.	Patent Office, Washington 25, D.C.	Government agency having jurisdiction.
Government-licensed	Dependent upon terms of license accorded to Government.	Yes; Government Patents Board, Washington 25, D.C.	Yes; Government Patents Board, Washington 25, D.C.	do.	do.	do.
Acquired from enemies	Licensed upon application.	Yes; Office of Alien Property, Washington 25, D.C.	Yes; Office of Alien Property, Washington 25, D.C.	Commerce field offices and some public libraries	do.	Office of Alien Property, Washington 25, D.C.
Foreign (issued by countries other than United States).	([4])	Some lists available: Write to Patent Office, Washington 25, D.C.	Generally, not in the United States.	New York Public Library or Patent Office.[5]	Photostat from New York Public Library or Patent Office.	Patent owner.

[1] Any expired patent for invention is available to the public for use; provided, however, there are no later patents applicable to the original invention.

[2] Official Gazette (Selected Reference No. 1): A weekly publication of the Patent Office. Copies are available in many public libraries and from the Superintendent of Documents, Government Printing Office, Washington 25, D.C.

[3] Public libraries which have patents for public inspection:

Albany, N.Y., University of State of New York.
Atlanta, Ga., Georgia Tech. Library.[a]
Boston, Mass., Public Library.
Buffalo, N.Y., Grosvenor Library.
Chicago, Ill., Public Library.
Cincinnati, Ohio, Public Library.
Cleveland, Ohio, Public Library.
Columbus, Ohio, Ohio State University Library.
Detroit, Mich., Public Library.
Kansas City, Mo., Linda Hall Library.[a]
Los Angeles, Calif., Public Library.

Madison, Wis., State Historical Society of Wisconsin.
Milwaukee, Wis., Public Library.[a]
Minneapolis, Minn., Public Library.[a]
Newark, N.J., Public Library.
New York, N.Y., Public Library,
Philadelphia, Pa., Franklin Institute.
Pittsburgh, Pa., Carnegie Library.
Providence, R.I., Public Library.
S. Louis, Mo., Public Library.
Toledo, Ohio, Public Library.
[a] Collections incomplete but copies of patents issued subsequent to July 1, 1946, should be available.

[4] No general statement possible except that foreign patents protect only in country of issuance. Their use in United States restricted only if United States patent has been issued.

[5] Copies in classified order at Patent Office only. Copies in numerical order at Patent Office and New York Public Library.

Figure 5-2 Types of patents available and useful in new-product development
Source: *Ibid*, p. 182

product ideas) in the U.S., you certainly can't expect to succeed in Europe. Also, you almost need local contacts. If you have a foreign subsidiary, this would be a starting point.

In the reverse, old and new ideas from the U.S. often will be successful in another country. Particular attention here must be paid to the size of the market and the sophistication of the culture into which you want to introduce the idea.

Printed and Published Sources of Ideas

There are a large number of places to look for sources of published new product ideas. Since the number of sources are great and they vary from time to time, the authors will only endeavor to indicate classes or types of such sources leaving it to the reader to identify the specific sources he would want to use.

Often, you will find in the Wall Street Journal, the financial section of the Sunday New York Times, and in similar publications, advertisements offering new product ideas. Other companies advertise that they are seeking new product ideas.

In England, the Financial Times, the Times, and the Daily Telegraph, all of London, often carry such advertisements. It is also understood that the "Product Licensing Index" and the "NRDC Bulletin", both of London, list products and/or patents available to industry under license. Further, additional foreign sources will be found in the material associated with Section 4 of the conference on "New Product Development Proceedings" as edited by D. Roxborgh, dated March 1966 and published by the University of Strathclyde, Glasgow, Scotland. Section 5 of the above referenced new products conference at the University of Strathclyde also contains a substantial number of published suggestions of sources of new product ideas. Many of the sources mentioned are reproduced in Appendix A of this chapter.

There are a large number of publications such as *Industrial Equipment News* and *Product Digest* which list new products offered by companies. These kinds of publications are usually directed to specific segments of industry or to specific classes of technical specialists. This is one way to "keep tabs on the activities of competitors".

Foreign (ideas from abroad) new product ideas can sometimes be found in publications dealing with the problems of international trade

COMMUNIFAX WESTPORT publishes every other Friday an interpretive report on new products entitled "Fax Forecast". Its services were originally confined and directed to the securities investor to give him information on important new product developments at the earliest possible moment, developments which might be important enough to affect the prices of the stocks of the company involved. Some of the ideas listed might possibly be available for licensing. The ideas are classified under the following headings: New-General, New-Consumer, New-Entering Markets, Moving in Markets, Developments from Overseas, and Pointers and Predictions.

Another investor oriented service is the weekly *New Venture Reports* published by *New Venture Reports*, Fifth Avenue Financial Center, San Diego, California 92103. It features companies implementing an important project which appears to have the potential to significantly affect the company's future.

BIBLIOGRAPHY

Berton, L., "The Innovators' Firms Trying to Profit from Inventions Often Face Many Obstacles", *The Wall Street Journal*, June 6, 1968.

Bishop, J.E., "The Innovators ... Despite Much Scoffing an Army of Inventors Pursues Way-Out Ideas", *The Wall Street Journal*, July 30, 1968.

Blood, J., ed., *Utilizing Research and Development By-Products*, American Management Association, N.Y., 1967.

de Bono, E., "The Virtues of ZigZag Thinking", *Think*, May–June, 1969.

Hilton, Peter, *Handbook of New Product Development*, Englewood Cliffs, N.J.: Prentice Hall, 1961.

Hilton, Peter, *New Product Introduction for Small Business Owners*, Small Business Administration, Washington D.C., 1961.

Jackson, M., *The President's Involvement in the Development, of New Products*, American Management Association, N.Y., 1966.

Karger, D.W. and Jack, E.B., *Problems of Small Business Developing and Exploiting New Products*, Rensselaer Polytechnic Institute, Troy, New York, 1963.

Karger, D.W. and Jack, E.B., "New Product Development" (Proceedings of the seminar presented on March 29, 1963 at the Royal York Hotel, Toronto, Southern Ontario Chapter American Institute of Industrial Engineers).

Kranzberg, M., "Men, Myths and Inventions", *The President's Forum*, summer 1968, pp. 10–15.

Miller, Stanley, *The Management Problems of Diversification*, New York, John Wiley and Sons, 1963.

Prestbo, J.A., "The Innovators", *The Wall Street Journal*, July 18, 1968.

Roxborgh, D., *New Product Development*, University of Strathclyde, Glasgow, Scotland.

"Science Scouts", *The Wall Street Journal*, May 12, 1960.

Tangerman, E.J., "The Facts Behind the Fad", *Product Engineering*, August 24, 1959.

"Tap Your Customer's Thinking ... A Gold Mine of Low-Cost Sources for New Product Ideas", *The Prentice Hall Management Letter*, April 6, 1964.

"*Technology and Your New Products*", Small Business Administration, Washington, 1967.

"The Inventor's Best Friend", *Business Week*, September 20, 1969.

"The Riches in Dormant Patents", *Business Week*, April 15, 1961.

Wilke, G., "Practical Uses of Patents Lag", *New York Times*, October 9, 1966.

APPENDIX A

Sources of New Product Idea Information developed in a New Product Conference at the University of Strathclyde held under the chairmanship of Professor T.T. Paterson, Department of Industrial Administration.

A. Reference Books for Choosing Technical Journals

1. E.C. Greves, Editor, "Ulrich's Periodicals Directory", 10th Edition, 1963, R.R. Barker & Co., New York.
2. M. Trase, Editor, "Guide to Current British Periodicals", 1962, The Library Association, London.

B. Reference Books for Choosing Abstract Sources

3. "A Guide to the World's Abstracting and Indexing Services in Science and Technology", Report No. 102 (1963)—National Federation of Science Abstracting and Indexing Service, Washington, D.C.
4. "Index Bibliographies Vol. 1", 4th Edition, 1959—Fédération Internationale de Documentation. The Hague, Netherlands.
5. "Technological Abstracts Originating in the British Commonwealth", D.S.I.R., London, 1963.

C. Universities, Research Stations and Associations

6. "Scientific Research in British Universities and Colleges, 1964–65, Volume I—Physical Sciences"—H.M.S.O., London.
7. "Technical Services for Industry", September 1964—Department of Scientific and Industrial Research, London.
8. "Industrial Research in Britain", 4th Edition, 1962—Harrap Research Publications, London.
9. "Guide to European Sources of Technical Information", 1965—O.E.C.D., available from H.M.S.O.

D. Private Research Organisations carrying out Sponsored Research

10. Arthur D. Little Research Institute, Inveresk, Midlothian, Scotland.
11. International Research & Development Co., Ltd., Fossway, Newcastle-upon-Tyne 6.
12. Sondes Place Research Institute, Dorking, Surrey.
13. The Fulmer Research Institute, Stoke Poges, Buckinghamshire.
14. Ellis Research and Testing Laboratories Ltd., Albury, Guildford, Surrey.
15. Yarsley Research Laboratories Limited, Clayton Road, Chessington, Surrey.
16. Battelle Institute Ltd., 46 Bryanston Street, London, W. 1.

E. Some Bodies issuing Publications Specialising in New Products

17. National Research and Development Corporation, 1 Tilney Street, London, W. 1.
18. United Kingdom Atomic Energy Authority, 11 Charles II Street, London, S.W. 1.
19. Scottish Council (Development and Industry), 1 Castle Street, Edinburgh.
20. New Products Centre, Radnor House, London Road, Norbury, London, S.W. 16.
21. Technological Digests—O.E.C.D.—available from H.M.S.O. (Discontinued during 1965).
22. Product List Circular, Small Business Administration, Washington 25, D.C.
23. Patent Abstract Series, Office of Technical Services, Washington 25, D.C.
24. Patents Lists of Agricultural Research Service, Department of Agriculture, Washington 25, D.C.
25. The Institute of New Products, Ardsley on Hudson, New York.
26. Industrial Bulletin, 450 Ohio Street, Chicago 11, Illinois.
27. New Equipment Digest, Penton Building, Cleveland Ohio.
28. Industrial Equipment News, A. Thomas Publishing Co., 461 Eightieth Avenue, New York 1, N.Y.
29. Industrial Equipment News, Tothill Press Ltd., London.

F. Some Bodies having some Interest in New Products

30. Institute of Inventors, President M.V.Rodrigues, 7 Wimberne Gardens, London, W.13.
31. Ideas Marketing Pool, 6 Old Bond Street, London, W.1.
32. Scientific Development Corporation (G.B.) Ltd., 47 Victoria Street, London, S.W.1.
33. Market Research Office, 'Industrial Intelligence", 67 Clerkenwell Road, London, E.C.1.
34. European Enterprises Development S.A., c/o S.Montague & Co., 114 Old Broad Street, London, E.C.2.

G. Some Licensing Brokers

35. Anglo-Austrian Trading Co. Ltd., 1–11 Hay Hill, London, W.1.
36. Buckingham, Bailey & Associates Ltd., 21 College Road, Harrow, Middlesex.
37. James Buckley & Co., Hyrons Manor, Hyrons Lane, Amersham, Bucks.
38. Cox & Gillpesie, Chemists & Chemical Engineers, 2 East Main Street, Richmond 19, Virginia, U.S.A.
39. Cryden Industrial Services Ltd., 27 Chancery Lane, London, W.C.2.
40. Dixon International Projects Ltd., Cross Keys House, 56 Moorgate, London, E.C.2.
41. Economic Research Corporation Ltd., 1255 University Street, Montreal 2, Canada.
42. E.R.Friedlaender, 102 Ealing Road, Wembley, Middlesex.
43. Euramco, 367 Winchester House, Old Broad Street, London, E.C.2.
44. Greenwood, Kaye & Co. Ltd., 64 Aldermanbury, London, E.C.2.
45. Industrial Management Services, Suite 46, 427 Bloomfield Avenue, Montclair, N.J., U.S.A., P.O. Box 515, Zurich, Switzerland.
46. International Patents Trust Ltd., 128 Ebury Street, London, S.W.1.
47. LIMEX, Außenhandelsgesellschaft mbH, Berlin C 2.
48. R.M.Maud, 68 Taunton Road, Pietermaritzburg, Natal.
49. Metropolitan Industrial and Commercial Co. Ltd., 125 High Holborn, London, W.C.1.

50. Patent- und Lizenz-Verwaltungs-GmbH., Karlsruhe, Hans-Thoma-Straße 3, Germany.
51. Storey, Keir Watson & Co. Ltd., 3 Emperor's Gate, London, S.W.7.
52. Clark, King, Poynter & Co. Ltd., 2 Trafford Road, Reading, Berks.
53. Cooperator A.A., Tyvangs Alle 28, Hellerup, Copenhagen, Denmark.
54. Reeve Angel International Ltd., 9 Bridewell Place, London, E.C.4.
55. I.Bier & Son (Iron & Steel) Ltd., Roman House, Wood Street, London, E.C.2.
56. Resources and Facilities Limited, 142 Sloane Street, London, S.W.1.
57. Kapazitätenvermittlung, Usinger Straße, 6 Frankfurt/M. 14, Germany.
58. Richard E.Dupont & Associates Ltd., 19 Hanover Square, London, W.1.
59. Glomb Products Company, P.O. Box 6636, El Paso, Texas, U.S.A.
60. International Consultants Associates, Via Settembrini 17, Milano, Italy.
61. Hivag, Vaduz, Liechtenstein.
62. Patents and Licences (Pty.) Ltd., 68 Taunton Road, Pietermaritzburg, South Africa.

H. Some Consultants dealing in New Product Planning

63. Product Planning Ltd., Carolyn House, Dingwall Road, Croydon, Surrey.
64. Arthur D.Little Ltd., Berkeley Square House, Berkeley Square, London, W.1.
65. Production Engineering Research Association (Management Economics Division), Melton Mowbray, Leicestershire.
66. O.W.Roskill Ltd., 14 Great College Street, Westminster, London, S.W.1.
67. Colin Melver Associates Ltd., 17 Manchester Street, London, W.1.
68. P-E Consulting Group Limited, Scottish Area, 140 West George Street, Glasgow, C.2.
69. Personnel Administration Limited, 2 Albert Gate, Knightsbridge, London, S.W.1.
70. Industrial Administration Ltd., 18 Thurloe Place, London, S.W.7.

CHAPTER 6

RESEARCH AND ENGINEERING

IMPACT AND BACKGROUND

In the 150 year period from 1776 to 1926, the total expenditure for research and developmental engineering in the U.S. was less than 2 billion dollars. Expenditures *per year* now exceed 27 billion dollars! The rapid growth of national research and development expenditures shown in Figure 6-1, even though the major amount is for weapons and space, is evidence that technological innovation has become a way of life for the nation and for business. If the population expansion has been the primary force behind America's economic growth, technology has been the second great force.

Government believes R & D to be important to the nation's welfare and gives evidence of this by providing an estimated 52% of the supporting funds in 1971 (Industry will provide about 42% and our colleges about 3.7%). However, the government only performs about 13% of the R & D, colleges 12%, and industry performs 72% of the work involved. More importantly, in 1968 dollars the actual real support has already begun to decline (see Figure 6-2), an effect of inflation and a change in administration. Industry is already beginning to provide some of the support dropped by the government.

The effect of inflation is also seen in the index of the cost professional man as shown in Figure 6-3. The table in Figure 6-3 can be of great practical value when estimating the cost of the engineering and research associated with new products.

Criteria for Spending the Engineering and Research Dollar

Simply spending money on research and engineering projects does not guarantee profits. The rate of commercial successes for product development projects in industry is *less than 15%*. (See Figure 6-4.)

The picture for products actually introduced may be much blacker. A study by *Machine Design* of 27,000 consumer and industrial products introduced in 1964 showed that four out of five failed to go over the break even point. How many were dropped and how many later produced profits is not known.

In attempting to determine criteria for expenditures on research, development, and engineering, management must seek answers to two questions:

1. What should be the total amount spent each year on technical effort?
2. How should this money be allocated among the different stages of effort, i.e., research, development, and engineering?

One strategy is for the company to spend a certain percentage of forecasted sales on its technical development work. Industry percentages vary from about 1% to 6% of sales, with the fast-developing glamour industries at the high end. Unless sales remain steady or grow evenly, however, such a policy results in erratic ups and downs in technical effort. In fact, it might be advisable in the face of steadily declining sales to *increase* expenditures for research and engineering.

Trade associations and publications usually provide information regarding the amounts that

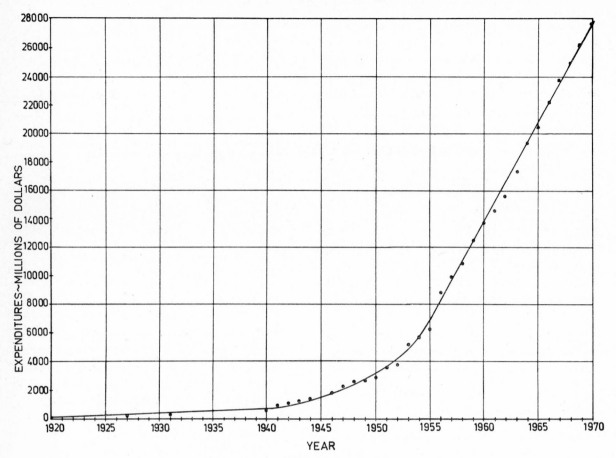

TOTAL U.S. RESEARCH AND DEVELOPMENT EXPENDITURES
MILLIONS OF DOLLARS

Figure 6-1 Growth of R & D Expenditures
Source: National Science Foundation

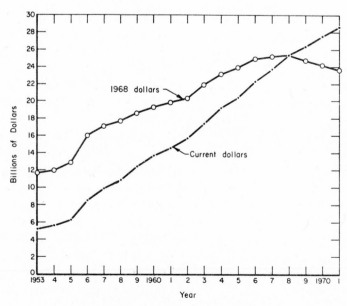

Figure 6-2 U.S. R & D Activity, 1953–71
Source: "Probable Levels of R & D Expenditures in 1971, Forecast and Analysis", Battelle Memorial Institute,
Columbus Laboratories, December 1970

industries and/or companies classified by type and/ or size are spending on technical development. Such data does provide a kind of general target. The smaller company is thereby often able to pinpoint its deficiencies. If the sales organization is strong but the company has few or inferior products, then more emphasis is needed on product development. On the other hand, if the engineering organization is

	New product ideas	Product development projects	New products introduced
	Success percentages		
All industry groups	1.7%	14.5%	62.5%
Chemical	2%	18%	59%
Consumer packaged goods	2%	11%	63%
Electrical machinery	1%	13%	63%
Metal fabricators	3%	11%	71%
Non-electrical machinery	2%	21%	59%
Raw material processors	5%	14%	59%

Figure 6-4 Rate of Commercial Success
Source: Booz Allen & Hamilton, Inc., *Management of New Products*, 1968

Year	(1) 1958 = 100.0	(2) 1968 = 100.0	(3) Current dollars	(4) 1968 dollars
	Index of costs of R & D inputs		Total R & D activity, millions of dollars	
1953	72.4	44.5	5,207	11,701
1954	77.6	47.7	5,738	12,029
1955	79.3	48.8	6,279	12,867
1956	86.2	53.0	8,483	16,006
1957	94.3	58.0	9,912	17,090
1958	100.0	61.5	10,870	17,675
1959	109.8	67.5	12,540	18,578
1960	115.5	71.0	13,730	19,338
1961	119.5	73.5	14,552	19,799
1962	125.3	77.1	15,665	20,318
1963	128.7	79.2	17,371	21,933
1964	135.1	83.1	19,215	23,123
1965	139.1	85.5	20,449	23,917
1966	145.7	89.6	22,285	24,872
1967	152.8	94.0	23,680	25,191
1968	162.6	100.0	25,330	25,330
1969	173.0	106.4	26,250	24,671
1970	184.6	113.5	27,469	24,202
1971	195.8	120.4	28,461	23,639

Sources and Notes:
* See Table 3 and related text, *Probable Levels of R & D Expenditures in 1970*, Batelle-Columbus.
(1) 1953–65 based on Helen S. Milton, "Cost-of-Research Index 1920–65", *Operations Research, 14*, 977–91 (1966).
1966–71 estimated by Batelle-Columbus, Technical and Business Planning Section. Also see Technical Appendix.
(2) Derived from Column 1.
(3) From Tables 2 and 3.
(4) Column 3 deflated by Column 2. These are dollars of average 1968 research purchasing power. See text.

Figure 6-3 Revised provisional index of the cost of R & D inputs per professional man, U.S., 1953–71
Source: *Ibid.*

producing prototypes and new product models faster than the rest of the company can produce and distribute them, then more resources should be devoted to expansion of these other functions.

It has been proposed by Mr. R. C. Dale, an executive of the successful Nashua Corporation, that
1. The first research dollar increment be spent because you are in business
2. Spend the second dollar to improve the existing product
3. Spend the third dollar to round out the product line
4. Spend the fourth dollar to diversify while still maintaining a thread of continuity
5. Spend the fifth dollar in pure exploratory research
6. Spend the sixth dollar to diversify into new fields— fields having no thread of continuity with present products.

Dale merely is trying to show a rationale for constructing a research and engineering budget i.e. the reasons behind the expenditures. The point being made regarding the first dollar increment is that the company has a direct responsibility to both stockholders and consumers to maintain product position and to keep ahead of market requirements. It amounts to virtually "standing still" which is practically impossible since one normally either goes forward or slips back.

In spending the second dollar increment to improve the product, management moves one step beyond the bare minimum. It is not the hallmark of a progressive company.

Spending the third dollar increment to round out the product line is the beginning of the establishment of objectives based upon other assets of the company. The objective usually is to take advantage of the company's distribution system which provides for or demands another compatible product or else to take advantage of production facilities and skills which are adaptable to the efficient production of a compatible product.

The fourth increment mentioned by Mr. Dale is of utmost importance—diversification with a "thread of continuity". A prime example of such diversification is the successful and profitable expansion of the Minnesota Mining and Manufacturing Company (3 M). From product to product runs a golden thread of continuity. Through a knowledge of markets and abrasive materials it moved into sandpaper. Through a knowledge of resins used in bonding abrasive wheels, the sandpaper was made waterproof so as to expand its applications. The sandpaper was soon adopted by the automotive body trade where the 3M organization learned of the need for masking materials. The first masking tape produced had a thermoplastic adhesive making necessary the use of a hot iron in applying the tape. In spite of this handicap, it was widely used. Recognizing the need for a better product, 3M developed a tape with a pressure sensitive adhesive. From here, they extended the pressure sensitive adhesive into other areas. From product to product within the 3 M organization the continuity can be traced.

This undoubtedly has been a major plus factor in the company's success. The continuity is present mainly because the 3M organization did a good job of what has previously been recommended—that management appraise their strengths and weaknesses and then capitalize on their strengths.

It has been recommended that the fifth dollar increment of the research effort be expended in pure exploratory research of an undefined nature. This is how the Minnesota Mining and Manufacturing Company developed the Thermofax process, which

is today used in thousands of offices to make reproductions of documents. It has been said that vastly more important scientific advances have been made in undirected research than in research with a specific objective. The degree to which a company can or should follow this path is dependent upon many factors and a decision should only be reached after serious study and analysis *by top management*. If top management isn't able to, or doens't want to take advantage of the results of such research, then it should not be started.

Spending research dollars to diversify into new fields with no thread of continuity is both extremely difficult and dangerous. This is why Dale listed this as the last dollar increment in his hierarchy of expenditures. *In the usual case it might be well to spend available dollars in one of the previous categories.* Corporate management might better be served to achieve this kind of diversification through purchase of another company or through the merger route.

SOME LESSONS LEARNED FROM NASA PROJECTS

According to Dr. Philip Marvin, consultant to NASA, the lessons or situations described under this subtitle stand out as important with respect to any research or engineering project.

No matter whether a research project is large or small, the *first* thing that should be done is to define *what* must be done. Secondly, find what must be done in terms of (a) performance, (b) schedule, (c) costs. *Third*, establish *priorities for a, b, and c*.

Without really knowing what is wanted when it is needed and how much we are willing to pay—the job cannot really be done.

Another important idea (subscribed to by most experienced scientific managers) is to bring both the scientists and the engineers together at the concept stage. Do not wait until the concept is established by the work of the scientists and then plan on turning it over to the engineers. *Both* are needed at the beginning. The engineering ideas are needed in the conceptual stage and throughout the project.

The ability to make decisions as work progresses

is important. In making such decisions, we must consider the cost and value of additional information at each step. We must also determine whether it is information or whether it is "noise" (unwanted signal or information) that is being received. The information must be isolated from the noise.

With respect to information, we must ask whether it is (a) necessary, (b) desirable or (c) diagnostically helpful. Data is not the same as information; information is data which is useful to our operation of the firm.

Finally, there is always a time-cost delay in decision making. To some degree this also should bring forth the question or the concept of time-frame distortion. What is meant by time-frame distortion? Let us use Apollo as an example.

A recent Apollo mission had to be aborted due to the explosion of an oxygen tank. The oxygen tank was a rather complex device; it had in it an electric heater and also a fan to circulate the air. The heater was used to keep up pressure and it did have a manual switch that could have been operated. About two to three seconds before the explosion, perhaps even more, a signal was transmitted over the telemetering circuitry that a runaway condition was developing.

Unfortunately, transmission at the distance involved was not instantaneous. It took about a second and a half just to transmit the information. Next it took some time to interpret and display the information for action. A computer is used to analyze incoming data and it only displays that information that requires action. So again another second or so was involved. Next, it required some time to decide how to act. Once the decision as to how to act was determined, it still would take another second and a half to get the information back to the Apollo ship on the way to the moon. Further time would then be involved in any action required.

If one would take the trouble to add up the seconds involved it is quite obvious that by the time anything could have been decided and sent back, the oxygen tank had already exploded.

Do not think that this time-frame distortion only occurs on Apollo missions. It occurs in even the simplest testing procedure.

A rather interesting lesson for computer buffs is contained in NASA use of computers on the Apollo program. First, they determined what data was really needed. Secondly, they had to determine what to do with the data when they had it. Third, if they had the data and knew what to do with it, then they decided to by all means have the computer perform the necessary work. They only have the computer print out abnormalities with which it cannot deal. This is precisely how NASA uses three IBM 360 computers in the Apollo program.

TIMING

The importance of timing and tackling the problem at the right *time*—cannot be overemphasized. Dr. Guy Suits, former GE Vicepresident and Director of Research and Development, in a paper presented at the Industrial Research Institute of 15 May, 1962, at Colorado Springs, Colorado, provided some excellent guide lines from a technical viewpoint. Below are paraphrased his most important and timely observations at this meeting:

A key technical problem should be identified as early as possible.

If there is a key or pivotal problem and if you can identify it, economy of effort and therefore dollars favors concentration on the solution of this essential problem first. If you can't solve the pivotal problem, don't mount a massive attack on the project.

If you can't do it today and the problem is still important, don't forget the problem—take it out and look at it from time to time and even try to solve it.

Be alert to progress in other fields. New knowledge in a related field may help you solve a key problem in another.

When the pivotal problem can be solved, then attack the project if the output is still of sufficient value.

THE STRATEGIC CONCEPT OF EFFECTIVE RESEARCH

Approximately 85 per cent of companies employing between 2000 and 5000 employees maintain research organizations, in larger firms the proportion is even larger. The true research organization is one that is insulated from the pressures of the day-to-day operating problems. The proper technical strategy is for technical operating problems to be transmitted to the research lab only for the purpose of being considered annually when the objectives of the laboratory are reviewed and the following year's plans are formulated.

Misunderstanding of the research function accounts for the unnecessary loss of vast sums *presumably* being spent to promote product development. Research is not product development, and new products are therefore not the immediate result. Yet research departments are often sidetracked by specific product development assignments.

While such sidetracking is often the fault of management decrees, it is also often the result of engineering's rejecting its proper responsibility. Research staffs are usually competent in many areas; hence, without proper direction their main function becomes a secondary one.

Product development and engineering should be conducted by engineering groups within the operating divisions or organization. Engineers in these groups should have full responsibility for developing and improving the technological side of the company's products.

Research should point the way to new products, processes and lowered costs. Once the opportunities are revealed, it should be the engineer's job of developing the most promising of the opportunities disclosed. Such action, previously mentioned, leaves the research group free for further exploratory studies.

Research is costly, especially if it is mismanaged at any level. Also, any good research group can think up ways to spend money faster than it can be accumulated. This makes it necessary to utilize the best possible judgment in grappling with the problem of research administration. Do not rely on percentage control. Just because the Jones Corporation spends 6 per cent of their gross sales in research does not mean that another somewhat similar firm can or should do the same thing. Incidentally, such

figures always include research, development and all engineering.

Research productivity depends upon many features—selection of projects, the planning of investigational programs, staffing, etc. The old adage "Don't put all your eggs in one basket" shouldn't be overlooked as applied to research projects. Multiple project programs will allow performance and result averaging.

The cost of the actual research program can't be the only consideration. It is equally costly to turn research results into commercial products. One can't therefore spend all of his money on research.

Project selection is of prime importance. Here is where experienced judgment is of vital importance. The best is none too good. Penny pinching at this point can be the most expensive action that could be taken. Marketing, engineering, and the head of new product development should have equal responsibility for making the selection of projects. The manufacturing organization should usually be consulted as well in order to determine the "producibility" of proposed products.

Investigation of broad areas in the sciences can uncover opportunities. Analysis of the company's products also often provides leads for research projects. Analysis of consumer needs can provide important additional leads. Do *not* spend research and development money in areas where the market is dying, because the service or product is no longer needed—put the research into *new and growing* areas.

Research must be planned if maximum results are to be attained. Without planning, research tends to wander from company objectives and projects never seem to get completed. The coordination of technical development and research requires advanced management techniques.

Flexibility is needed to optimize new developments because of the following:

1. Management of research itself requires the use of techniques that vary widely from normal practice. Flexibility to tolerate variance from normal is therefore needed to extract maximum creative effort from research personnel.

2. Management must have among its members men of science who can understand what is being done and can see the potentialities.

3. Flexibility of the general management to accept these new ideas and to learn to use them is vital.

The management of a research function is most difficult. Creative problem-solving results in uncertainties, unexpected by-products, time lags, etc., all of which make almost unreasonable demands on the administrator who is asked to show visible signs that the research investment is paying off. Company administrative needs and requirements are often diametrically opposed to the freedom required by the research department.

It is not at all unusual to find an R & D manager who sincerely believes that this function cannot really be managed and that managing is beneath the dignity of a research oriented professional. He extends the concept of freedom of investigation to freedom from responsibility. If close examination shows that this is the case within a particular company, a new manager had better be installed.

Research programs, even more so than other kinds, can't be turned off and on as sales fluctuate. It requires a continuous effort. Once the effort is stopped, one needs to go back to the beginning to start again. When the time cycles, the kinds of personnel involved, etc. are considered, it becomes obvious that it would be sheer folly to try to make the research effort fluctuate.

Before starting a research program it is necessary to know what kind of research is going to be undertaken. Surprisingly it happens too often that management doesn't really know what is to be done or what has been started. Without this knowledge, it is likely that they won't know where to look for their returns.

Finally, research alone will not produce a jackpot. It can only provide the resultant big money if management knows how to take advantage of the opportunity through executive decisions, skillful engineering, good plant operation, excellent marketing, etc. Payoff even then is not guaranteed and it takes time and the combined efforts of the entire enterprise to win.

The formal organization of a research department must be tailored to the company and the research personnel involved.[2]

It would normally take a large organization to require both a scientific director and an administrator director. Usually, these responsibilities are vested in the top director of research. When possible, especially in larger organizations, it has been found advantageous to segregate the technical side of research from its business and general administrative requirements. This has also been a trend in engineering organizations.

CONSIDERATIONS INVOLVING ALL THREE

Relationships Among Research, Development and Engineering

For most companies, the development of new products is based nearer to the engineering than the research end of the spectrum. From a policy viewpoint, it is important that each company clearly establish its position so that it can define its technical objectives. By doing so, the small company will not fritter away its meager resources on basic research, and the large company will not let its large competitors pull ahead through long-range research.

Figure 6-5 not only presents this spectrum to some degree, but it also indicates the flow of dollars and the relationship to the elements of the organizations to new product development, including relationships to top management.

Technical management bears a heavy responsibility in support of new product development and major company objectives such as:

1. Ensuring that the corporation will operate in areas of rapidly advancing technology

2. Assuring maximum uses of the company's resources

3. Exploiting fully available as well as potential markets

4. Providing diversification of the company's products

5. Ensuring an increasing profit potential.

To fulfill these prime responsibilities, the engineering organization must:

1. Recognize:

a. Problems of determining the product such as design problems, manufacturing problems, marketing and product planning problems, known or anticipated customer wants, long-range business plans, industry trends, technical advances, and competitors' activities.

b. Oportunities now resulting or expected to result from the availability of new knowledge from basic research, new materials, new processes, and advances in the industry which will permit developing and demonstrating the technical feasibility of new and improved products.

2. Define:

Problems arising in the development of new products by determining the data required, methods for obtaining data, laboratory and prototype facilities required, models needed, and the creative and analytical technical skills required.

3. Conceive:

a. Solutions to problems of applied research, advance engineering, and improved product design.

b. New modifications of products through additional sizes, capacities, colors, models, etc.

c. New combinations and applications of existing products.

4. Establish

a. Standards and specifications for designs, materials, and equipment which may be produced within the company or purchased by any division of the company.

b. Laboratory and prototype-manufacturing facilities.

c. An adequate system of patent protection within the engineering division with the assistance and advice of the Patent Counsel.

d. A climate which stimulates self-development and creativity on the part of the engineers and scientists in the company.

5. Evaluate:

a. Products of competitors.

b. Products which the company does not presently manufacture, but which it might market.

c. Products of the company on a continuing basis.

d. Companies which may possibly be acquired through purchase or merger.

6. Communicate with proper documentation :

a. Work and results.

b. Adequate product specifications to the manufacturing organization.

c. Technical advice to other sections and to management.

d. Technical advice to customers and to vendors when appropriate.

The vital roles of engineering, research, and marketing in product development is typified by the responsibilities shown in Figure 6-6.

Because of the size and inherent bureaucratic control structure of large companies, special efforts must be made to create a climate for creativity in both the engineering and research organizations. This requires both enlightened technical leadership and general management. Control aspects required by company objectives should be minimized by employing administrative and financial people *in support* of technical activities *rather than in control* of technical activities.

Another major requirement for a successful engineering and research contribution is the maintenance of a good mix of ability, knowledge and experience. This goal is more nearly achieved if it is first recognized, then defined, and then consciously sought after. By proper mix of people with the above-mentioned characteristics, we mean that the company should staff up in terms of its technical objectives and its related capabilities. For example, a company should not hire all technical geniuses even if it could, since a lot of technical work requires less or a different type of intellectual effort. At the other extreme, no company should be staffed up with 100 per cent nincompoops. A few may possibly be absorbed in routine work, but generally a company requires a range of talents. Not only should a variety of knowledge be "on board", people of different

Code:

1—Responsible   3—Must be advised
2—Must be consulted   4—May contribute

Typical Functional Responsibility	Top Management	Marketing	E & R	Manufacturing	Finance
SIZE UP					
Market Position	3	1	2	4	3
Product Leadership	3	2	1	4	3
Manufacturing Capability	3		4	1	3
LOOK AHEAD					
Customer Needs & Wants	3	1	2	3	
Business Conditions		1	3	3	4
New Technologies	3	3	1	2	
DEFINE OBJECTIVES					
Company	1	4	4	4	4
Product	2	2	1	2	3
Marketing	2	1	2	2	3
Manufacturing	2	2	2	1	3
DEVELOP NEW PRODUCTS					
Product Concept	------------ Anybody ------------				
Preliminary Appraisal and Assignment of Priority	New Product Department or Product-Planning Department				
Literature and Patent Search	Same as above in conjunction with Engineering				
Project Authorization	1				
Preliminary Technical-Economic Survey	Same as above if company has a New Product				
Appraisal and Final Screening	Department or Product-Planning Department in conjunction with product teams as men-				
Project Scheduling	tioned in Chapter 1.				
Research			1		
Advance Engineering			1		
Design Engineering			1		
Design Review	4	4	1	4	
Marketing Review	4	1*	2	4	
Prototype Model			1	4	
Engineering Tests			1		
Field Tests			1	4	
Redesign			1	4	
Production Planning			4	1	
Pilot Run			4	1	
Initial Market Test		1**			
Final Marketing Plan	2	1**			
Production Tooling			4	1	
Production				1	
Marketing		1	4		

* New Product or Product-Planning Department if it exists.
** Will involve the product team mentioned in this chapter, if it exists.

Figure 6-6 Linear Chart of Responsibility
Source: D.W. Karger and R.G. Murdick, *Managing Engineering and Research*, New York: The Industrial Press, 1969

disciplines or specialties, but also usually a mixture of young and old. Experience and lack of experience each have their advantages and disadvantages. The young inexperienced man is usually willing to perform less complex tasks and also try more original things. The experienced engineer provides balance, but he is often the prisoner of his own background.

NEW PRODUCT CONSIDERATIONS
RE TECHNOLOGICAL FORECASTING

In the material presented earlier it was indicated that engineering and research have a responsibility to keep the company abreast of new technological developments. Also involved should be the idea that research projects should be originated in the areas of new knowledge that are likely to prove profitable. This means that the firm must take advantage of the techniques of technological forecasting to guide research and development programs to the most fruitful areas of future technology.

Today we can't imagine how the New England textile mills turned down Arthur Dehon Little when he presented them with the chance to get in on the ground floor of the viscose rayon process. They refused with the comment: "Do you mean to say that man can ever produce fibres as good as those God has provided us with?" Similar opportunities are being brushed aside every day in today's business world. It was difficult 60 years ago for the New Englanders to see ahead. It's much more difficult to do so today. It therefore should be clear that one element crucial to successful research is the ability to see ahead.

Large modern up-to-date research and engineering departments make use of technological forecasting techniques. TRW Inc. call their technique "PROBE". General Electric has a forecasting procedure identified as "TEMPO" which is a sort of think tank. Westinghouse is another firm who has moved into technological forecasting. These are just a few of the larger firms.

A technological forecast is an attempt to look into the future in such a manner as to try to estimate the technological conditions which are likely to exist, to make reasonable evaluations of the probability of their occurrence and to some degree to try and identify the significance of the development and/or its associated developments. Quite simply, it is a planning tool for managers that is particularly invaluable to marketing managers and research and development managers.

The real pioneer in technological forecasting has been the United States Government and in particular the Department of Defense. DOD long ago decided this was a very important activity.

In a fundamental sort of way the existing techniques can be divided into five categories, i.e. intuition, trend extrapolation, trend correlation, growth analogy and dynamic modeling.

Whole books have been written on technological forecasting so it would obviously be impossible to cover the subject in this one chapter.[3] We are sure that the readers of this text will have read of the results of such forecasts and seen some of the material in the form of graphs. The graphs usually come from trend extrapolation.

Probably the best known of the techniques is an intuitive one called the Delphi method. It was developed several years ago by the Rand Corporation. Basically it utilizes a series of questionnaires to men who really are not supposed to be in touch with each other except through the written questionnaires. This is to eliminate the influence of one or two strong individuals and to avoid what may be an embarrassment to an individual who has had to reconsider a previously expressed firm opinion. Obviously, the men polled are specialists (experts in one or more fields). A modification of the Delphi technique was developed as part of a research project by Professor Gene Simons of Rensselaer Polytechnic Institute.[4] This modified method is faster and has *the advantage of securing a consensus among both forecasters and the concerned decision makers.* It can be applied in a large corporation.

The smaller firm obviously does not have the qualified men to do technological forecasting. Their approach should be to try and find the results of other technological forecasts and appropriate to their use those portions which are valuable to them.

What are the guides or uses of technological forecasting? Some of these can be enumerated as follows:

1. To guide R & D into the most fruitful areas of future technology.
2. To pinpoint new markets for the future.
3. To assess the strength of present and future competition.
4. To direct the firm's short-run and long-term marketing programs.
5. To identify major threats to the organization.
6. To help identify possible new products and materials.

Before leaving the topic of forecasting we probably should also state that other kinds of forecasts should not be ignored i.e. sociological forecasts, population forecasts, political forecasts, etc. All of these can help in the planning effort and in developing the strategy and tactics of the organization for its future survival and development.

SOURCES OF TECHNICAL INFORMATION

There are three major sources of research and development information on new technological areas (not to be confused with technological forecasts) available from the U.S. government. These are (1) the Clearing House for Federal Scientific and Technical Information (CFSTI), (2) the Defense Documentation Center (DDC), and (3) the National Aeronautics and Space Administration (NASA). The information offered ranges from the highly abstruse to the down-to-earth.

In addition to the above, more secondary government sources would be (1) National Academy of Sciences, National Resource Council, (2) National Bureau of Standards (U.S. Department of Commerce), (3) National Referral Center for Science and Technology, (4) National Science Foundation and (5) Science Information Exchange.

Almost every one of these sources have several types of publications and information and it is necessary to write to find out what is available or to use the indexes in one of the libraries which serve as government depositories.

The problem with the information obtained from these sources, and many others, is (really) what to do with it. There is so much information available that merely providing it to everyone is a waste of time and effort. Some kind of internal evaluation must be set up and one of its functions should be to distribute the information to only those in the company who can probably use it. Another method or procedure is to provide information on a given subject when a specific request is received.

Engineering and Research activities are not going to make much of a contribution if creativity and new approaches are not encouraged. Every aspect of the design must be questioned and new approaches welcomed. Figure 5-1 (Chapter 5) has given you some idea of the manner in which existing design concepts could be questioned.

With respect to projects aimed at product development, if financial information and general yardsticks for measurement are available, a group of projects could be compared in a manner similar to Figure 6-7.

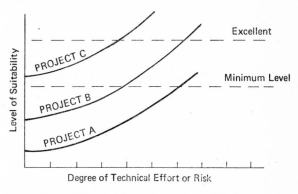

Figure 6-7 Model for Comparison of Projects
Source: *Ibid.*

Project "A" starts out poorly, and even if technical efforts succeed, it barely meets the minimum standard. Project C is a far superior choice from a business view. What is lost in this particular view of the situation is that of total return, unless this is the basis of the vertical scale.

An over-view of new product or product planning is the relationship expressed between engineering, marketing, manufacturing and top management in Figure 6-8.

	Manager	Marketing	Engineering	Manufacturing
PHASE I—STUDY				
1. Establish Business Objectives, Timing and Strategy	R			
2. Define Responsibilities and Relationships	R			
3. Establish Customer Requirements		R		
4. Establish Specific Product Requirements and Schedules	R			
5. Establish Product Design Philosophy			R	
6. Establish Manufacturing Philosophy				R
7. Establish Marketing Philosophy		R		
8. Select Preliminary Product Design Approach			R	
9. Identify Critical Problems and Alternate Approaches			R	R
10. Plan Feasibility Program Including Resource Requirements		R	R	R
11. Estimate Design and Production Program Resource Requirements		R	R	R
12. Review and Authorize Feasibility Program	R			
PHASE II—FEASIBILITY PROGRAM				
13. Establish Subsystem and Component Functional Design Requirements			R	
14. Establish Component Design Approaches			R	
15. Make Electrical Schematics and Mechanical Layouts			R	
16. Preliminary Product Design Review			R	
17. Propose Possible Manufacturing Methods for Critical Components			R	R
18. Determine Design Alternatives for Critical Components			R	
19. Producibility Review for Critical Components				R
20. Establish Design Specifications for Critical Components			R	
21. Determine Design Alternatives for Critical Manufacturing Processes			R	
22. Prove Feasibility of Critical Manufacturing Processes				R
23. Establish Design of Critical Manufacturing Processes				R
24. Plan Design Program Including Resource Requirements			R	R
25. Re-estimate Production Program Requirements		R	R	R
26. Review and Authorize Design Program	R			
PHASE III—DESIGN PROGRAM (PRODUCT AND PROCESS)				
27. Review Product Design Approach			R	
28. Revise Electrical Schematics and Mechanical Layouts			R	
29. Product Design Review			R	
30. Propose Possible Manufacturing Methods			R	R
31. Determine Product Design Alternatives			R	
32. Producibility Review				R
33. Complete Product Design Evaluation			R	
34. Finalize Product Design Specifications for Initial Production			R	
35. Complete Production Process Design				R

Figure 6-8

	Manager	Market-ing	Engineer-ing	Manufac-turing
36. Establish Market Plan for Distribution and Service		R		
37. Prepare Production Program Plan Including Resource Requirements		R	R	R
38. Review and Authorize Production Program Plan	R			
PHASE IV—INITIAL PRODUCTION				
39. Release Product Design to Manufacturing			R	
40. Interpret Product Design Specifications			R	
41. Establish Production Equipment Methods and Procedures				R
42. Build Products to Established Product Design Specifications				R
43. Establish Product Installation, Maintenance and Operating Procedures		R		
44. Distribute and Service Products		R		
45. Evaluate Adequacy of Product Design Specifications			R	
46. Evaluate Production Samples			R	
47. Evaluate Manufacturing Process from Product Viewpoint			R	
48. Evaluate Manufacturing Process from Capability and Productivity Viewpoint				R
49. Evaluate Distribution and Service System		R		
50. Evaluate Customer Satisfaction		R		
51. Evaluate Business Performance of Initial Production	R			
PHASE V—CONTINUING PRODUCTION				
52. Propose Design Changes to Improve "Quality" or Reduce Costs			R	R
53. Propose Process Changes to Improve "Quality"			R	R
54. Propose Process Changes to Reduce Cost				R
55. Evaluate Proposed Design and Process Changes from Product Viewpoint			R	
56. Evaluate Required Process Changes from Productivity Viewpoint				R
57. Evaluate Proposed Design and Process Changes from Marketing Viewpoint		R		
58. Propose Design Change Program		R	R	R
59. Review and Authorize Design Change Program	R			
60. Establish Revised Product Design Specifications			R	
61. Establish Necessary Process Changes				R
62. Produce Redesigned Products				R
63. Evaluate Redesigned Products			R	
64. Distribute Redesigned Products, Spare Parts, and Service Information		R		
65. Evaluate Productivity of Redesigned Manufacturing Process				R
66. Evaluate Business Performance	R			

R—Primary Responsibility for Result

Figure 6-8 Integrated Program Plan
Source: "An Integrated Approach to Product Quality and Producibility", Engineering Services (Schenectady, N.Y.: General Electric Company)

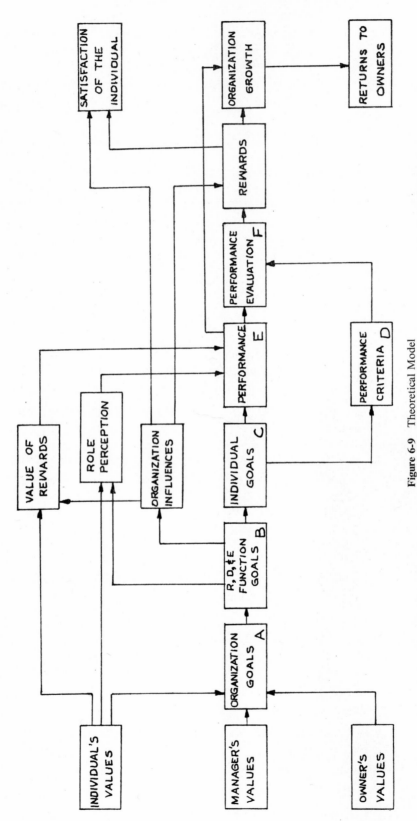

Figure 6-9 Theoretical Model

Source: Paul Croke, "Research on Research: (1) The Management Planning and Control of Research and (2) The Attitudes of Industrial Research Scientists", *Doctoral Thesis*, Rensselaer Polytechnic Institute, Troy, New York, 1969

With respect to new product development, it is important that technical functional management keep in mind that engineering must also be involved with standardization, variety control, producibility, reliability and maintainability. Marketing is involved with variety control and engineering should assist in keeping the number of models to a minimum consistent with the requirements of the market.

Manufacturing is involved with producibility concepts. However the engineering department produces the design and this in turn locks manufacturing into using certain manufacturing processes and thereby engineering design largely determines the relative cost of the product. The best manufacturing engineering function in the world cannot overcome poor design engineering with respect to producibility.

With the current emphasis on consumerism, designing for high reliability and maintainability is an absolute must. In fact, legal considerations are beginning to force this matter.

It is inevitable that one or more of the company's new products will run into sales problems. Typically, under such situations the engineering department and/or the marketing department suggests a product modification. A big change is quickly launched —and it flops. Everyone is subject to the resulting pressure. It is suggested that when this occurs that engineering does not take such action as (1) doing nothing, or (2) recommending a drastic action. Rather it is necessary to go back to the basics and ask why the product is failing. This should be done honestly, analytically, and objectively. This question could be asked either by engineering, marketing or by the new product department's top management. If a mistake in selection has been made, the product should be dropped rather than trying expensive heroic efforts to save it.

Finally, there is one other new-product consideration which has been getting a lot of attention. This is the legal liability for potential injury to people who will use the product.

There is almost no product which, under certain circumstances, could not cause an injury. Therefore, companies should be prepared to receive a products liability suit—sooner or later. It is suggested that the company and, in particular, the engineering group take the following two steps:

1. Take steps to reduce the probable frequency and severity of product liability claims by designing and manufacturing safer products and be sure to include instruction warnings with the product and the advertising.
2. Maintain very complete design records.

HOW TO EVALUATE ENGINEERING AND RESEARCH DEPARTMENTS

Its not enough to plan, staff and operate an Engineering and Research Department, its performance collectively and by individuals must be evaluated for corrective action and for reward of good performance. An approach to evaluation is herewith presented based on Figure 6-9.

Figure 6-9 illustrates a description of performance evaluation developed in a research project by Dr. Paul Croke while a doctoral student at Rensselaer

Company goals		Research, development and engineering goals			Individual goals	
Goals indirectly related to R, D, E	Goals directly related to R, D, E	Fulfillment of a specific need	Project mile-stones	Project profit-ability	Goals directly related to R, D, E	Goals indirectly related to R, D, E
1	2	3	4	5	6	7

Figure 6-10 Breakdown of Goals to Categories
Source: D. D. Albrecht, "The Evaluation of Research, Development and Engineering Through Goal Establishment", *Master's Thesis*, Rensselaer Polytechnic Institute, Troy, New York, 1970

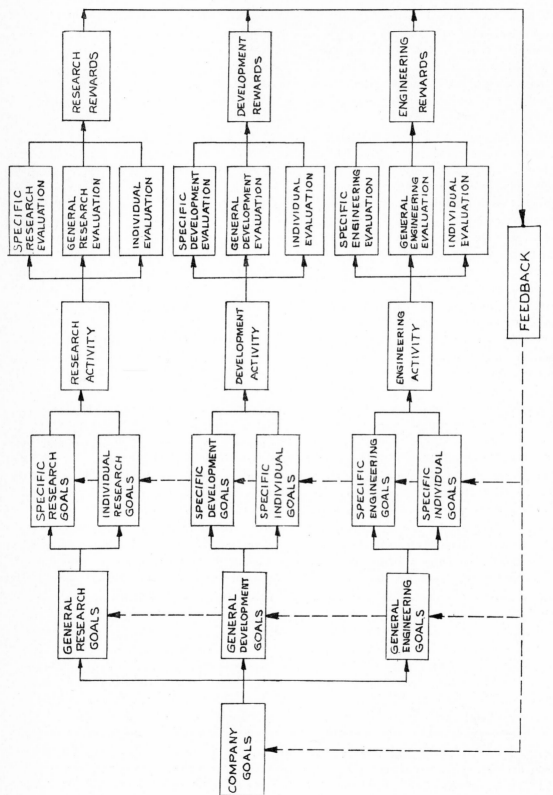

Figure 6-11 Parallel Departmental Actions
Source: *Ibid.*

Polytechnic Institute. It shows the various goal setting and evaluation interrelationships involved in the functioning of a typical engineering and/or research department or division, the idea in its simplest concept is that if one can set goals, performance can be measured by measuring the degree of attainment of the goals.

Company goals, research goals and individual goals each can be broken down into various categories.

It will simplify any measuring or evaluation process if such goals are broken down into categories such as illustrated in Figure 6-10 titled Breakdow of Goals to Categories.

If the company is of substantial size, the engineering and research activity will have projects which could be classified as research, others that could be classified as development engineering and finally there would be a large group of activities carried on that could largely be classified as design or product engineering. It needs to be understood that each of these activities would have their own goals and that the men in the activities would also have their own individual goals. This idea or concept is brought forth in Figure 6-11 entitled "Parallel Departmental Actions".

It will be noted that Project Milestones were referenced in Figure 6-10, the idea is that the PERT technique should be applied to engineering projects for both internal control purposes and to permit evaluation of the activity.

Mr. Albrecht in his study of Engineering and Research Evaluation Through Goal Measurement developed the concept that an engineering or research activity should establish some method oriented goals in addition to its specific goals. These method oriented goals were to reflect the kind of activity or concern that management should have if its technical function management was to be in accord with the views of experts in the field. For example, experts generally believe that technological forecasting is useful in setting the proper engineering an research goals for the future. Again experts believe that participative management techniques are especially applicable to the management of engineering and research departments or activities.

His thought was therefore expressed in his thesis that one could measure the degree to which such recognized methods were being utilized by the management of the engineering and/or research functions and thereby attain a further measure of the effectiveness of engineering and research management within a given company. In his thesis he cited that some nine major method oriented goals be established and indicated how they would bear a relationship to company goals, engineering and research goals, and individual goals. This is illustrated in Figure 6-12 which is titled "Output Goals Versus Method Goal Matrix".

Mr. Albrecht goes on to state that where an intersection of the method goal and company goal occurs that has a specific relationship, i.e., the methods goal will help attain the type of specific goal, the matrix designation will have been indicated. He further goes on to state that some of these have stronger relationships than others and finally he indicates that while the existence of such relationships has not been proven, that it is a reasonable assumption that they do exist. It is our opinion that such a relationship does exist and this would be an excellent manner in which to review the activities of the management of a technical activity such as engineering or research. Anyone attempting this goal approach to evaluation should, of course, review the thesis for further information.

There are many other approaches to the evaluation of the technical function. Some commonly cited, but not very practical approaches are counting patents obtained, publications, speeches, etc.

Work activity sampling (determining percentage of time spent on various work and non-work activities) is useful, but only provides clues as to some possible trouble spots. It is a worthwhile partial approach to consider.

Comparing money spent with profits made is extremely difficult because of the time lag between research and the full marketing of the idea. Because of this and the general difficulties encountered in trying to measure or evaluate research; the goal setting-evaluation approach is recommended and/or some combination of approaches to evalu-

Specific goals / Method oriented goals	G/M	Company goals		Research, development, and engineering goals			Individual goals	
		Goals indirectly related to R, D, and E	Goals directly related to R, D, and E	Fulfillment of a specific need	Project milestones	Project profitability	Goals directly related to R, D, and E	Goals indirectly related to R, D, and E
		1.	2.	3.	4.	5.	6.	7.
Utilize technological forecasting	1.	$R_{1,1}$	$R_{1,2}$	$R_{1,3}$		$R_{1,5}$		
Secure and maintain executive support	2.		$R_{2,2}$	$R_{2,3}$		$R_{2,5}$		
Utilize participative management techniques	3.		$R_{3,2}$				$R_{3,6}$	$R_{3,7}$
Encourage, promote, and provide continuing education and training opportunities	4.			$R_{4,3}$	$R_{4,4}$	$R_{4,5}$	$R_{4,6}$	$R_{4,7}$
Encourage creative thinking	5.	$R_{5,1}$	$R_{5,2}$		$R_{5,4}$	$R_{5,5}$	$R_{5,6}$	
Utilize company "system" for personal advancement	6.						$R_{6,6}$	$R_{6,7}$
Managerial participation in goal establishment	7.			$R_{7,3}$	$R_{7,4}$		$R_{7,6}$	
Assist individual in alignment of personal goals with department and company goals	8.		$R_{8,2}$	$R_{8,3}$			$R_{8,6}$	
Establishment of reasonable goals for new employees	9.			$R_{9,3}$			$R_{9,6}$	$R_{9,7}$

Figure 6-12   Output Goals vs. Method Goal Matrix
Source: *Ibid.*

ation based on measuring performance against one or more of the following criteria:

1. Was the work performed on time and was the budget kept?
2. The degree of difficulty or complexness of the work performed.
3. Was solution the result of using existing techniques and equipment or did it require a really creative approach?
4. Was the project handed to manufacturing in such a manner as to minimize difficulties and conflicts?
5. Is adequate and timely support engineering service provided on a continuing basis?
6. How effectively was equipment and technical personnel utilized?
7. Were the needed accurate, dated records kept for legal purposes, liability suits, patents, future research, manufacturing needs, etc.?
8. Was upper management properly kept aware of progress during the programs life?
9. The effectiveness of the presentation of results, written and oral.

THE SMALL COMPANY

The very small company cannot afford to drift along with its original products; it must continually improve its products or come up with new ones. How can it do this on a very limited budget? If its sales are $1,000,000 per year, 5% set aside for technical development barely supports one engineer and modest shop and test expenses. It is apparent that the company should carefully limit the scope of activities of its technical organization, even if it can afford several engineers and technicians and a modest laboratory. Development must be extremely short range and basic or even applied research represent a very risky venture.

The strategy of the very small company should be to:

1. Conduct "bird-dogging" of scientific developments, new products suitable for the company to manufacture, and products which appear to be easily susceptible to improvement by the company's engineers. "Bird-dogging" consists of following reports in trade publications, visiting trade shows, talking with people in the industry, observing products on the market related to the company's line. Seeking untapped markets or new applications would be joint searches conducted with marketing personnel.

. Staff the R & D team with *competent* generalists. Small firms should emphasize quality and versatility except where "the product" represents a new technological breakthrough.

3. Limit its technical development to one, or a very few products at one time; do not get spread too thin.

4. Make sure the R & D team is fully aware of the company's operations, markets, customer needs, etc.

5. Use outside consulting assistance if it runs into a difficult technical problem in an important development. The reasons for this are (1) that even if the company's engineers are very competent, they may be tied up for a long time on such a problem, and (2) highly specialized outside assistance may be cheaper in the long run.

A large company can afford to hire a wide variety of generalists and specialists in engineering, but what about the small company? If a small firm can afford only one or two technical people, should it hire a broad-gage engineer or a highly specialized individual? The answer lies in the nature of the firm's business. Suppose a firm has a single narrow product line such as ball bearing lubricants. Its innovations are apt to depend upon depth of knowledge in this field. Contrast this with a firm which makes, say, electromechanical toys. Here breadth of knowledge and creativity rather than great theoretical depth in a single discipline are necessary. These are the two extremes, of course, and companies which fall between the extremes should hire men which suit stated company technical objectives.

Slightly larger companies may face the choice of hiring, say, five average engineers or one highly creative, productive, engineer and, perhaps, a technician. Generally, we would recommend hiring the outstanding man. Innovation is more a function of individual creativity than the number of manhours applied to a problem.

THE MEDIUM AND LARGE SIZE COMPANY

The medium and large size companies will have a substantial technical function existing within them and it would seem inappropriate to spend much time on the organization of engineering in a book dealing with new products. There are complete books dealing with the management of the technical function as referenced in the bibliography.

VALUE DESIGN AND VALUE ANALYSIS

The engineer or engineering organization has two chances to substantially reduce the risk in new product venture management. In the first instance, the engineers may give full attention to product value, from a customer systems viewpoint during the design process. The components of the product value system are shown in Figure 6-13. Tables have also been published, based upon research at General Electric Co., which guide the engineering designer towards minimum cost in terms of process, component size and shape, materials, and the size of the production run.[5]

Value analysis, often called value engineering or

post-design, offers the engineer an opportunity to review critically every aspect of design. In particular, he examines the cost-function relationship. What materials and what design changes will yield equivalent performance at lower cost? Often, the greatest cost reduction are achieved by design changes which simplify the manufacturing process. The

10. Is it made on proper tooling considering the quantities made?
11. Do material, reasonable labor, overhead, and profit total to its costs?
12. Will another dependable supplier provide it for less?
13. Is anyone buying it for less?

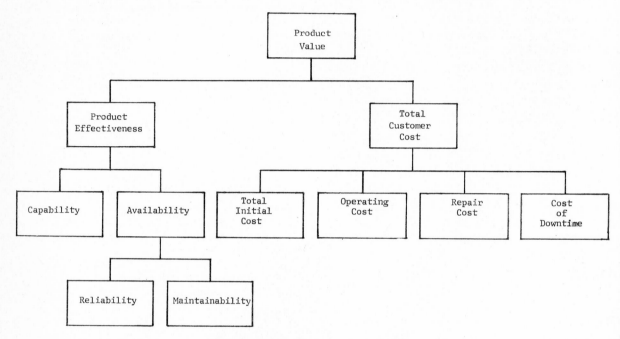

Figure 6-13   Components of Product Value
Source: Frank M. Gryna, Jr., "Product Effectiveness Concepts in Design", permission of McGraw-Hill Book Company, Automotive Engineering Congress, Detroit, Michigan, Jan. 10–14, 1966, Society of Automative Engineers, Inc.

process of value analysis is based upon examining each function and each part and asking such questions as:
1. What is it?
2. What does it cost per year?
3. What does it do?
4. Does its use contribute value?
5. Is its cost proportionate to its usefulness?
6. Does it need all of its features?
7. Is there anything better for the intended use?
8. Can a usable part be made by a lower cost method?
9. Can a standard product be found which will be usable?

PRODUCT AND INDUSTRIAL DESIGN

Since the product is in one respect the desired end result it needs a little more attention, especially the industrial design aspects which are slighted in most such discussions.

Realize that the techniques and requirements of building a product image are well known, and be sure it is understood that the design of the product is at the heart of the matter.

Fashion and trends should not be ignored. Take advantage of them in the design.

With respect to function, the businessman should realize that he doesn't know whether a control knob should protrude an inch or whether it should be knurled. Leave such matters to the engineers.

Usually the aesthetics should be left to professionals, few businessmen (top managers) have the skill and feel to comment meaningfully. If in doubt, resort to market research.

While the top manager may not have had the answers to the two foregoing aspects of the product, he does have *much better* judgment as to whether the product will sell. Here his judgment is not based on aesthetics, but on marketing to the consumer.

Different designs communicate different messages relative to the value of the product. Here again the businessman (top manager) is in a position to make a major contribution.

A consumer's image of a product (as he sees it) is the result of a complex process. He receives bits and pieces of the flood of information directed at him and from these constructs his image. The designer, engineer and manufacturer all must be concerned with how the consumer builds his image and how the process can be controlled. It is the image or belief of the customer that is important, not the facts (if they are not being communicated).

SUMMARY

We have covered the roles of research and engineering in new product venture management. The emphasis has been on the relationship of research and engineering contributions to company plans and profits. Their roles must first be viewed as both economic and technical. The engineering organization must be a continuous and dynamic factor in the new product venture. The risk of technical failure should constantly be objectively evaluated in terms of the potential for profit.

REFERENCES

1. "New Products Called Risky But Necessary", *Machine Design*, Dec. 22, 1966.
2. Examples of a wide variety of industrial research, development and engineering organizations can be found in Alexander O. Stanley and K. K. White's *Organizing the R & D Function*, AMA Research Study 72, American Management Association, 1965.
3. One rather complete review of forecasting techniques is James B. Bright's, *Technological Forecasting for Industry and Government*, Englewood Cliffs, N.J.: Prentice-Hall, 1968.
4. G. R. Simons, *Technological Forecasting: The Identification and Selection of High Priority Solutions*, (doctorial thesis), Rensselaer Polytechnic Institute, Troy, New York, June, 1969.
5. See the series "Design Guide to Value" in *Product Engineering*, October 28, 1963, March 2, 1964, and March 30, 1964.

BIBLIOGRAPHY

Albrecht, D. D., *The Evaluation of Research Development and Engineering trough Goal Establishment*, (masters thesis), Rensselaer Polytechnic Institute, Tro, N. Y., 1970.

Bass, L. W., *Management of Technical Programs*, (Arthur D. Little) Praeger, N.Y., 1965.

Baumgarten, *Project Management*, Irwin Co., Illinois, 1963.

Blood, J. ed., *Utilizing Research and Development By-Products*, American Management Association, N.Y., 1967.

Buck, C., *Problems of Product Design and Development*, New York: Pergamon Press (Macmillan), 1963.

Dean, B., *Evaluating, Selecting and Controlling R & D Projects*, American Management Association, N.Y., 1968.

Clarke, E., "Government Information Sources", *Machine Design*, October 30, 1969.

Hainer, R., ed., *Uncertainty in Research, Management and New Product Development*, New York: Reinhold Publishing Corp., 1967.

Halcomb, J. L., PERT in Product Design, *Mechanical Engineering*, May 1963.

Hanan, M., *The Marked Orientation of Research and Development, A Recommendation for Minimizing New Product Risk*, American Management Association, N.Y., 1965.

Hilton, P., *Handbook of New Product Development*, Englewood Cliffs, N.J.: Prentice Hall, 1961.

Hilton, P., *New Product Introduction for Small Business Owners*, Small Business Administration, Washington, 1961.

"How the Law is Affecting Product Design", *Machine Design*, January 8, 1970.

Katazenstein, H. S., "Designing for Reliability", *Mechanical Engineering*, May 1963.

Jackson, M., *New Product Development as a Normal Part of General Management Activity*, American Management Association, N.Y., 1966.

McCory, R. J., "The Design Method", *Mechanical Engineering*, May 1963.

Rogers, J. R., "The Closed Loop of Design", *Mechanical Engineering*, May 1963.

Simons, W.W., "*Organizing the Commercial Development of New Products*", American Management Association, Products, Design and Development Forum, December 17, 1959.

Stedfeld, R., "Flop Sweat", *Machine Design*, October, 1969.

Cetron, M.J., *Technological Forecasting: A Practical Approach*, New York: Gordon and Breach, 1969.

Wells, Gordon, *et al.*, *Technological Forecasting and Corporate Strategy*, New York: American Elsevier, 1969.

Ayres, R.U., *Technological Forecasting and Long-Range Planning*, New York: McGraw-Hill, 1969.

Organization for Economic cooperation and Development, *Technological Forecasting in Perspective*, Paris, 1967.

Bright, J.D., *Technological Forecasting for Industry and Government*, Englewood Cliffs, N.J.: Prentice-Hall, 1968.

Bright, J.D., "Can We Forecast Technology?", *Industrial Research*, March, 1968.

Isenson, R.S., "Technological Forecasting in Perspective", *Management Science*, October, 1966.

Cetron, M.J., "Technological Forecasting: A Prescription for the Military R & D Manager", *Naval War College Review*, April, 1969.

Cetron, M.J., *Technological Forecasting*, A Practical Approach, New York: Gordon and Breach, Science Publishers, Inc., 1969.

Vantage Point 2000 A.D. (A Report on a Conference on the "Influence of Technological Innovation on the Future of Connecticut"), Connecticut Research Commission, Hartford, Connecticut, 1968.

"TRW Finds Mapping Technology May be the Only Way to Go", *Industry Week*, January 12, 1970.

CHAPTER 7

LEGAL RISKS

The businessman who is about to launch a new product faces a wide variety of legal hazards. Since in many cases the interpretation of the law cannot, or will not, be made until the new product is on the market, the legal aspects of new products require a risk-management approach. That is, a considerable cost is required to put a new product on the market and legal hazards jeopardize the potential profits. When we think that a product must first overcome the risks of development, manufacture and market failure, we see that new products are truly in multiple jeopardy.

There are three basic types of legal risk the venture manager faces:

1. The risk that his product is not protected against partial or even complete copying (outright adoption by copying) by competitors.

2. The risk of consumer suits because of injury or loss the consumers suffered by using the manufacturer's product.

3. The risk of government charges that he has violated some legal statute or a regulation of some government agency.

The risk of competitors' adopting and marketing our new idea may be reduced by patenting or by non-disclosure methods. We will cover these methods in some length in this chapter. The second risk is one that is not at all clearly defined but is being developed by court decisions. We will discuss the nature of these legal hazards and suggest some precautions. The third risk covers a wide variety of activities which have been classified as shown below:

I. *Regulation of Monopolistic Methods*
   A. Market Control
   B. Collusive Practices
   C. Market Exclusion Tactics
II. *Regulation of Product Characteristics*
   A. Product Standards
   B. Product Quality
   C. Packaging and Conditions of Sale
   D. Safety
III. *Regulation of Price Competition*
   A. Price Discrimination
   B. Resale Price Maintenance
   C. Price Control (Minimum and Maximum)
IV. *Regulation of Channels of Distribution*
   A. Operating Features of Marketing Institutions
   B. Relations Between Buyers and Sellers: Exclusive Dealing Arrangements, etc.
V. *Regulation of Unfair Competition*
   A. Advertising
   B. Nonadvertising Promotional Methods
   C. Trademarks and Trade Names
VI. *Procedural and Miscellaneous Developments*[1]

For the venture manager or entrepreneur who wishes to reduce his risks in this area, we offer only two suggestions. First, act in all business transactions as fairly as you know how. Second, subscribe to some service which provides brief, easily understandable summaries of legal developments. Third, secure as good legal advice as you can make available. Two information services are:

Journal of Marketing (regular feature is "Legal Developments in Marketing"), quarterly,
American Marketing Association
230 North Michigan Avenue
Chicago, Illinois 60601

Marketing and the Law, twice-a-month news letter,
Man and Manager, Inc.
87 Terminal Drive
Plainview, New York 11803

MECHANICAL (BASIC) PATENTS

The types of patents issued to protect inventions of mechanical and other physical devices, electrical circuits, chemical compounds, various types of processes are known as *mechanical* or *utility patents*. Utility patents having very broad claims are referred to as *basic patents*. We need to answer such questions as: What is invention? When can invention be patented? What protection and risks are involved in the patent activities of business operations?

We assume that recognition of an unfulfilled need for a product and identification of an associated profit opportunity has led us to develop a new product or at least make a significant change in an old one. We suspect we have made an invention which we can protect by patenting. However, since we have many ideas in the shop, we don't want to waste our people's time and our money for patent lawyers unless there is a likely prospect of protection for a money-making idea. What, then, is an invention?

The Basic Patent Issued by the U.S. Patent Office

Invention is the creation of something which did not exist before, something *new*. If it existed before but was simply unknown, like a law of nature or scientific principle, it is not an invention. Other requirements are that an invention must be useful, must be fully disclosed, and must never have been dropped or given up during its development.

Ideas come before an invention occurs, so that ideas alone are not patentable. The legally issued documents which claim and describe inventions are called patents. The patent is a *contract* and therefore requires an exchange of value, in legal terms there must be a consideration. In exchange for a public disclosure of the invention by the inventor, the government promises exclusive rights to the inventor to:

1. Manufacture, use, and sell the invention and exclude all others from doing any one or all of these.
2. Sell his patent.
3. License others to do any or all of the above.

The inventor has exclusive rights to his invention until 17 years after the date the patent is issued. The contract then terminates and anyone may use the invention.

A patent, just like any other business contract, may not hold up if there is fraud in its creation, failure to disclose completely, or a mistake in fact. Even a very minor occurrence of any one of these is all it takes to make a patent worthless. Despite the fact that the inventor expects his patent (contract with the government) to be valid, patents are often proven to be invalid when challenged by another party.

This fault in the patent contract arises naturally because businessmen, like everyone else, when faced with an obstacle look for a way around it. Thus, if someone else holds a patent that stands in his way, he may question its validity on legal grounds or try to avoid the patent by "designing around it". By designing around it, he tries to achieve the same end result by using a similar construction which is different enough so that it won't infringe (violate the rights of) the patent. This is explained in more detail later in the chapter.

A patent owner can enforce his exclusive rights against infringers by suing them in federal courts. He may recover money damages and also obtain a court order barring current infringements. He may even obtain an injunction to restrain a threatened infringement.

The patent owner can mortgage his patent by using it as collateral for a loan. He may also rent it by licensing it to others or sell the rights completely for cash, for licenses to use other patents he wishes to use (called cross-licensing), or for anything else of value. He may bequeath it in his will; otherwise, on his death it passes to his heirs as personal property. He may also give the patent away to anyone else or to the public at large.

The rights of co-ownership of a patent are somewhat unusual. Any owner of a fractional interest in a patent, in the absence of a limiting agreement, has unrestricted power to sell or license the entire invention without consent of other co-owners. He has the right to all profits and royalties without accounting to other co-owners.

What is a Patentable Invention?

The line dividing invention and non-invention is not a clear one. Generally, if a device produces a new result, or an old result in a new or more efficient manner, it is an invention and may be patented. Congress and the courts have not defined what invention is, but rather what it is *not*.

For example, a new result is *not* invention if anyone would think of it, given the problem if it is obvious. In a particular situation and at a particular time, something might be obvious which would not have been obvious ten years ago.

If anyone skilled in the art could have readily designed it, the result is not an invention.

Substitution of equivalents, such as copper for silver, or one motor for another motor, is not invention. If, however, substitution accomplishes the same result in a different manner, or performs a different function to arrive at the same ultimate result, it can be classified as invention.

A *new combination* of old elements (electrical circuits, chemicals, subassemblies, materials) can be invention if it produces a new result or an old result in a different manner.

Changing the size, shape, speed, or range of some other characteristic is not invention unless the result is different or the manner of obtaining the result is different.

Mere *addition* or *omission* of parts is not invention. The parts which make up the whole must cooperate with each other and must produce a new result or an old result in a new manner.

The parts or elements cannot be mere aggregation, they must coact or cooperate with each other. The combination of a pencil and eraser do not coact and the combination, therefore, cannot be potented.

The fact that "invention" is present does not mean that a patent is possible. Other requirements must be met. These are summarized in Exhibit 7-1.

Broad Claims or Narrow Claims?

The claims in a patent application are by far the most important items in this document since they are the *only basis* of patent protection. The allowed claims, of course, have this same importance in the issued patent. Claims should be stated in as broad terms as possible so that it will be impossible, or at least very difficult, for someone else to design around the patent. If another person is able to produce a comparable device by eliminating one part of each claim, he will not be infringing the patent. This is known as designing around the patent. The risk involved in broad claims is that the patent may infringe on a previous patent and be disallowed.

A patent is infringed when every element of one claim is included in the so-called infringing structure. It is for this reason that long and detailed claims are said to have a narrow scope since they tend to be easily avoided by omitting one of the claimed elements.

The question of what is an equivalent element is a troublesome problem in infringement. The courts have ruled that an equivalent not only must perform the same function, but that it must do so in the same mode of operation.

Will the Real Inventor Please Step Forward?

In modern companies where products are complex and many teams or many individuals work on a problem, pinning down the individuals who actually conceived the invention is often difficult. The law is very clear. The patent application must be filed in the names of the individuals who contributed to the conception of ideas embodied in the invention. The courts will find a patent to be invalid if *all* the inventors and *only* the inventors are not given in the application. The courts have established both negative and positive guides as to inventorship. However, this is a confusing area and a competent patent attorney should make the decision. Do not try to convince the attorney that it was a team or an individual

Here are 10 basic requirements for patentability which must be met in addition to invention.

1. The person (or persons, jointly) must be the original inventor and state so under oath. This means that not only must the applicant(s) believe he originated the invention, but no "free-loaders" can be joined with him. If it turns out that a patent is granted to two supposed coinventors when actually only one of them invented the device, the patent is void.

2. The invention must be useful, not frivolous, not contrary to public policy, and not harmful to public welfare. "Usefulness" covers even toys such as "bouncing putty". New species of roses have been patented. Other coverable items, by statute, are chemical compositions, processes of all kinds, mechanical devices, electrical circuits, and medical drugs. Not patentable are mental processes, mathematical systems, methods of doing business, printed matter, or products of nature.

3. The invention must not have been previously known or used in the U.S. or described in *any* printed publication anywhere in the world prior to the inventing by the applicant. "Prior knowledge" in the legal sense is knowledge of a completed operable device. Mere knowledge of the idea of someone else's is not enough to prevent the obtaining of a patent by the true "first inventor" who makes the invention in operable form.

4. The invention must not have been patented or described in any printed publication, anywhere, more than a year before the *filing date* of the patent application. Many foreign countries require that there be no prior publications anywhere before the application is filed in those countries. Once an inventor notes that someone else is claiming the same invention, he should not delay in filing himself if he believes he may have a prior claim.

5. The invention must not have been in public use or on sale in the U.S. by others before the applicant made the invention. Also, it must not have been placed in use or on public sale *by the applicant* more than one year before his filing. Using experimental models to test the invention is not considered public use. Use by the government or contractors to the government in "classified" work is considered as use.

6. Work on the invention cannot have been stopped and then later started up again: the inventor must be legally "diligent". This does not bar part-time inventors from securing a patent since such a person is able to work only part of the time. However, he can't abandon work for several months and still prove diligence in working on it.

7. The inventor may not, prior to filing in this country, obtain a patent in a foreign country on any foreign application filed more than twelve months before the U.S. filing date.

8. The invention must not have been described in a U.S. patent. An issued patent is a bar to the granting of a patent to a second applicant. The bar can only be overcome by proof that the second applicant completed the invention first.

9. The invention cannot be something that is obvious to anyone having ordinary skill in the art or field of the invention. It is, of course, not possible to define "ordinary skill" so that patent protection is often sought and obtained when experts believed the invention to be obvious.

10. The first person to *conceive* of an invention, and make an operable model, providing he doesn't abandon it at any time is entitled to the patent. Although the relative time which two patent claimants make an operable model is important, the time of conception is even more important. Therefore, as soon as the inventor conceives of an invention, he should write out a description and sketches. The description should be immediately shown to someone who can understand it and will sign and date the material and acknowledge the explanation as a witness.

Reduction to practice means completion and satisfactory operation of a working model. Where the expense of building such a model is too high. the inventor may make a "constructive reduction to practice". This involves making and filing a patent application and detailed specification so complete that one could build an operable device in accordance with the patent specification and that it would work or perform as described.

Diligence related to the effort put forth from the time of conception to the reduction to practice of filing of the patent application—any lack of continuing effort might be in favor of a second inventor working on the same idea.

Figure 7-1   What is a patentible invention?

effort when it was not and therefore cite the wrong inventor(s). The authors have seen this happen.

How a Fair Peek at the Patent Office File May Unblock the Way

Suppose that an inventor in applying for a patent has been required to define the meaning of certain points in the patent claim to such an extent that only a restricted interpretation results—and this often happens. This information is put into the Patent Office records which are maintained in a "file wrapper". The patent is issued as applied for, but it is subject to the narrow interpretation in the records. Since he is "stopped" from using any but the restricted interpretation of the claims, lawyers call this "file-wrapper estoppel". If we find that a patent is blocking our use of a process or product, it is worth while looking at the complete filing folder of that patent in the Patent Office for such restricted interpretations which may enable one to use it without causing infringement.

HOW TO PROTECT YOUNG VENTURES WITH A COMPANY PATENT PROGRAM

Patent protection does not just happen; it must be planned and implemented by a formal organizational procedure. Someone within the company should be appointed to coordinate the patent program. The program should consist of three main activities, (1) education about company patent protection procedures, (2) educating the necessary key people to recognize invention as defined for patenting purposes and (3) stimulating people to follow the procedures.

Get it on Paper with Witnesses

Good records are a necessity to win patent contests and they also help to identify inventions and/or new products. Therefore, notebooks should be supplied to engineers, scientists, or other key personnel concerned with product development and manufacture.

Employees should be instructed to record their ideas and experimental results as they occur and have the pages of the notebook dated, witnessed, and signed by someone who can understand what has been written. Notebooks with stitched-in pages do not need to have every page witnessed. While the individual-page (loose-leaf) notebook does, it also has its advantage. In a patent contest, only selected pages need to be brought into court so that the company may keep other parts of the notebook confidential.

The second security step in the patent program is to have a patent committee select the promising inventions for patenting and possible exploitation.

The company should have available a patent disclosure form for recording potential inventions. Disclosure forms usually provide space for dates, a verbal description of the invention, required drawings, the inventor's comments regarding known prior or related "art" (knowledge), and provision of space for the oaths and signature of witnesses.

Usually two witnesses sign the patent disclosure. The inventor describes his invention to witnesses who have the technical knowledge and ability needed to understand his explanations so that they can swear to the explanations and make an attestation similar to that in a typical witness oath as shown in Figure 7-2.

Where each page of the engineer's (or other potential inventor's) notebook is signed, a separate patent disclosure form is not needed from a technical view if notebook pages can be removed from the binder and reproduced. Such pages should have

The invention was first explained to me by the above identified inventor(s) on_____ , 19_____ .

_____   _____

Signature of Witness   Date of Signature

Figure 7-2   Witness oath

space provided to add other information which the patent attorney requires. Most firms, however, require both signed and witnessed notebook pages *and* separate disclosure forms.

The need for a witness is often misunderstood. This is illustrated by the misbelief that the inventor obtains protection for his invention by sending a registered letter to himself in which his invention is described and his signature has been notarized. Such a letter is generally meaningless since the inventor has not proved, by explanation to witnesses, that he himself really understands the invention. Such a letter can only help to prove the date claimed for originally "thinking up" the invention.

The New Product Manager and the Patent Attorney

The new product venture manager should stay in close touch with the company's patent department or patent attorney. Once the patent attorney has specialized in the area of the company's product line, he can provide valuable suggestions with regard to product development. He may suggest ideas where current patents have indicated trends or he may forestall work where the field is dense with patent coverage by other firms and is therefore not likely to be of advantage to the company. Also, remember that patenting activity is closely aligned with economic opportunities.

Courts have generally upheld the view that inventions made on the job are company property. However, most companies play safe by having new employees sign agreements to assign their inventions to the company and to protect company trade secrets. Identification of possible inventions is therefore important, and managers, in particular, should be *trained* to recognize them and as to what should be done about them. Annual refresher sessions on both these topics are advisable. *If invention is not recognized, it will be lost to the company.*

In order to maintain "patent awareness", many companies form a Patent Committee of product managers, the patent attorney, engineering and research managers, and a Patent Coordinator, who can be the New Products Manager. The Patent Coordinator works on a continuing basis to establish

procedures, stimulate patent awareness through educational and communication programs, and acts as chairman of the Patent Committee.

The Patent Committee reviews disclosures of inventions in terms of commercial possibilities and patentability, but with primary emphasis on patentability since its function is not the exploitation of invention. The group only needs to decide that an invention has possible commercial application, before it proceeds with the patenting considerations. It may recommend a "novelty search" of Patent Office files to determine the likelihood that an invention is new and worth attempted patenting.

WATCH OUT FOR OUTSIDE OFFERS OF INVENTIONS

Ideas from outsiders can be dangerous. If such ideas are incorrectly handled, an unasked-for brainstorm can easily cost tens of thousands of dollars in legal costs. Damage claims have often exceeded one million dollars. The number of such offers from outsiders is growing every year. Everyone in the company from board chairman down should know what action to take when they receive a letter that begins, "Dear Sir: I have an idea that will make a million dollars for your company..."

If a company receives a would-be inventor's secret, in confidence, then we neither disclose it to anyone else or use it ourselves without the permission of the inventor. In fact, we must not disclose or use the secret even if it is not valuable or not patentable, or if it is patented later by the inventor and not licensed to us for use. The courts have consistently upheld this confidential relationship. There are even cases on record in favor of the person disclosing an expired patent which automatically is available for use by anyone from the viewpoint of patent law. Such solicitors therefore may or may not be inventors.

The formulation of the company's policy on handling ideas submitted from outsiders should take into account:
1. The possible values of outside ideas
2. The loss of competitive advantage if the man goes to another company

3. The risk in considering ideas for adoption because of possible damage suits

4. The possible risk that the procedures may aleniate customers (since only a few people are involved this is seldom a major issue).

On the above basis, one of the following alternative policies might be adopted:

1. Refuse to accept the idea in confidence

2. Return all material and letters with a statement that no copies have been made

3. Keep all papers in a closed file until the solicitor signs an agreement with the company (as outlined below).

4. Cite references if the idea is already known

5. Refuse to admit that the information is new or novel, even through no refeences can be cited.

6. Send an agreement form if the idea is believed worth consideration

7. Request that the information be resubmitted in the form of a patent application or as a witnessed full disclosure.

8. Request that the inventor meet with company officials if it wants to negotiate.

Policies 2 and 3 are used effectively by many companies; however there is conflicting opinion in legal circles as to which of the above minimizes risk.

The disclosure statements which outside solicitors are asked to sign usually contain some or all of the following ideas:

1. The submitted information must be in writing, preferably a copy of a patent application that has been submitted to the patent office or, at least, a dated and witnessed full disclosure.

2. The company does not have to agree to hold a correspondent's information in confidence.

3. The sender is requested to keep an exact duplicate of all materials submitted.

4. The company is not obligated to reveal its own knowledge on the subject.

5. The company is allowed to reserve the right to negotiate for payments after it sees the correspondent's full information; in fact, maximum payment may even be specified.

6. The company is not bound either by contract or by a confidential relationship if a patent issues except under the term of future agreements on licenses.

7. The company is under no obligation to consider the information other than to say whether it is interested.

8. The company is not asked to admit that the idea is new, novel, and concrete.

If this kind of case gets into a court of law, the court will examine the facts in every case to determine:

1. What was submitted and was the inventive idea the outsider's property?

2. How the idea was submitted and was a contract made or implied or was a confidential relationship established?

3. Who received the idea? Did an "agent" of the company commit the firm?

4. What may be recovered as compensation?

DESIGN PATENTS

The U.S. patent law also provides for issuance of *design patents* for certain types of new designs. Unique and aesthetically pleasing design of a product is an important factor in its commercial success and deserves this protection from copying. Design patents only cover the exterior appearance of an article, not its internal structure, workings, functions or functioning. Because of the limited scope of design patents, they are usually less valuable than mechanical patents.

Design patents are obtainable for periods of three and one-half, seven, or fourteen years, depending upon the fee paid by the applicant and the time period for which he requests or elects to apply. It is only possible to cover one part in a design patent. If two or more parts are to be protected, separate design patents must be obtained for each part.

Design patents are usually obtained to protect items such as wallpaper patterns, chinaware, cabinets, bathroom fixtures, etc. While they can be used to cover parts such as machine screws, here one normally can and should obtain a utility patent unless only an ornamental design is involved. When an item can be covered by either a utility patent or a design patent, the utility patent protection is usually the kind to obtain, if for no other reason than the utility patent is issued for a longer period of time. Sometimes both kinds of patents are needed to properly cover a given item. However, this is "treading on dangerous ground" and should only be done under the guidance of a knowledgeable patent attorney.

Even without a design patent, the law does provide some protection against copying products by competitors. Such protection stems from the sweeping monopoly granted by the law of unfair competition. Unfortunately, the layman is faced with a difficult task in trying to interpret or predict just what is protected by this sweeping monopoly; in fact, attorneys have a difficult time doing so. Sometimes, an identical copy is legal whereas in other cases the mere similarity in appearance of a competitor's product may be ruled illegal.

GOVERNMENT CONTRACTS AND PATENTS

Since some new ideas for new products stem from government contracts (or at least are related to the results achieved by contractors to the government), it is believed important to at least discuss this subject with respect to new product ventures.

The procurement policies of federal agencies affect the patent rights of industry and the basic structure of E & R organizations. This problem is highlighted by the fact that the Government is sponsoring the major portion of our country's research and development and by the fact that the Government does not operate under one uniform policy. At present the Atomic Energy Commission (AEC), the National Aeronautics and Space Administration (NASA), and the Federal Aviation Agency (FAA) take title to inventions associated with their contracts, whereas the Department of Defense (DOD) takes a free license.

There is a difference of opinion, both in and out of the Government, as to the most desirable ownership policy regarding Government-sponsored inventions. One group proposes that title to inventions

made under the Government contract should be in the Government to assure that the public does not pay twice for such inventions (once in taxes and again in monopoly). The opposite view is that the Government should take only a free license, thereby leaving the inventor which the right of commercial exploitation since this will serve as a very powerful incentive for future technological advancement.

In connection with government contracts, three big classes of property rights must be considered. They are:
1. Patents on inventions
2. Trade secrets
3. Industry know-how.

Patents on Inventions

Patents on inventions pose no particular problem if the invention is made using private funds. The problem arises in the Patent Rights Clause used in government contracts which says that the Government shall have title (AEC, NASA, FAA) or a free license (DOD) in inventions "first actually reduced to practice" in the performance of contract. It therefore makes no difference whether the invention actually had been conceived prior to the receipt of the contract, the government gets whole or partial ownership in all inventions reduced to practice in performance of the contract regardless as to when, where, or how they were conceived. While industry can object, Government procurement agencies, however, require it as a condition of obtaining a research contract. It is the inclusion of the "first actually reduced to practice" provision in the government contracts that poses a very serious problem to industry.

A second problem regarding patents is that concerning security. A patent may be withheld from issue because of security classification or considerations; therefore, the company is prevented from exploiting it commercially. The delays caused by security clearance can cause the invention to become obsolete and in some cases the term of the patent has seven expired. A second problem concerning security, involves the inventor's right to obtain foreign patents for exploitation. An inventor is not permitted to file applications abroad until the subject matter has been declassified. Consequently, the opportunity to obtain a valid foreign patent has often passed. The only relief offered him is that he may petition the government for a modification of secrecy to permit him to file in a specified country or countries. Such a petition is not ordinarily greated unless the government has disclosed the invention to the foreign government. Even if the subject matter is not classified, security measures often make it difficult to obtain valid patents abroad since the patent application cannot be sent to a foreign government within six months after filing in the United States unless a Commerce Department permit is obtained ; moreover, delays in obtaining such permits are quite usual.

NON-PATENT PROTECTION

Trade Secrets

Another problem concerns itself with trade secrets. A trade secret is "know-how" held confidential in a company, of which a good example is the formula for Coca-Cola. If the company maintains a trade secret, it can through court action enjoin any individual who obtains knowledge of the trade secret in confidence from improperly using said knowledge, as well as anyone else or any company which obtains said knowledge from said individual. The right to protect trade secrets, which arises in common law, is recognized by all of our courts. The Department of Defense includes in its procurement regulations a provision for obtaining trade secret data from contractors in return for a reasonable compensation. The problem arises, however, from the fact that no company wishes to part with trade secret data even if compensated; yet it must do so if it wishes to bid on certain government contracts.

Know-How

"Know-how" encompasses other items in addition to trade secrets. Such items range from the skills of workmen to detailed manufacturing specifications.

Know-how is unpatentable and inherently cannot be kept secret. It can only be protected by restricting its dissemination. The problem arises under a Department of Defense ruling which makes it a requirement in certain contracts that manufacturing drawings, supporting specifications, and much other generally considered private know-how be released with the product.

While industry must and should cooperate with the government procurement agencies, even though the situation is confused, it nevertheless needs to take those measures still left to it to protect its own property rights in its designs, inventions, know-how, and trade secrets.

There is little that can be done by the sales department of any company to help the situation as it presently exists. While sales may object to a particular clause, their proposal runs the danger of being classed as being in noncompliance with the invitation to bid unless the clause is previously removed. The government agencies generally do not remove such clauses, and most sales departments therefore do not wish to run this danger since their bid can be and often is rejected if it does not comply with all of the requirements indicated by the invitation.

The only place where remedy can be achieved at least to a degree is in engineering. Some companies have taken the position that when manufacturing drawings are required, a minimum of drawings should be supplied—only enough to comply with the contract.

FOREIGN LICENSING FOR PROFIT

International Problems and Opportunities

Foreign licensing of U.S. developed inventions earns the companies involved more than $800,000,000 annually. A large number of firms earn over $500,000, with many reaping $5,000,000 or more. However, *before you can take advantage of the opportunities, it is necessary to patent your inventions abroad*—a U.S. patent is essentially worthless in this situation.

Since foreign patents are the first requirement, this

topic needs discussion. First there is *no* world-wide or area system to which U.S. companies can apply for a patent and expect protection from copying. Without being able to stop copying *in the countries involved*, no license can be negotiated.

One requirement for the granting of a foreign patent is that there be *no* publication or public use of the invention anywhere at any time prior to application, Canada is the one important exception where the grace period is two years. Since applying for a patent in some countries creates a public notice of invention, an International Convention for the Protection of Industrial Property was created (the U.S. is a signatory) to solve this and other problems. With respect to filing, the agreement provides that one filing for an application for patent in any member country may file in any other member countries and have the date of first filing be regarded as the date of subsequent filing during the initial 12 months period. This means one has only 12 months to file in all the countries in which protection is desired. If one thinks about the time required to get legal representation in each, write the applications and prepare drawings so as to meet each country's requirements (they do vary—simple translations of U.S. applications rarely work) is very short.

Claims allowed in the U.S. are not necessarily allowed in a foreign country since *their* view of the "state of the art" may be vastly different than ours. Therefore an investigation in each country involved would be appropriate in order to be able to request as many claims as might be arguable.

Most foreign countries assess an annual charge against patent holders which usually increases each year, total charges over patent life range from about $200 to over $2500. Also, some countries (France for example) requires the patent holder to either use the invention himself, license its use, or forfeit rights to the patent.

All these different problems and consideration make it difficult to decide upon the countries in which patents will be sought. The company should primarily keep its attention on the size of the potential market and the probability of being able to exploit it, either directly or through licensing.

Since it might be helpful to know where other U.S. companies are going with patent applications, Figure 7-3 presents such data for 1968. The other industrialized nations show essentially the same interests. Also, the number of their foreign patents exceed local patents, as does the U.S. (US 149 %— see Figure 1). It is believed that 1970 data would present the same general facts, but with increased patenting activity.

In spite of potentially large licensing profits for companies with a significant patent portfolio, most international managers do not aggressively set out to exploit it—many merely look on such income as windfall profits.

It makes sense to analyze carefully each foreign license with regard to at least the following items as related to each product involved:

1. Potential market now and in the future.
2. Must the product based upon the patent be redesigned for successful sale in the foreign country?
3. Is it best exploited by a U.S. owned subsidiary or by a licensed foreign national company?
4. What resources (men and financial) are required for direct exploitation?
5. Do we have or can we acquire the needed resources?
6. What costs and what profits based on present value of money are involved for both licensing and for direct exploitation?
7. Is there a better way to utilize scarce resources than direct exploitation, or even exploitation by licensing?

With regard to licensing one must consider licensing, not only from a direct cost–income view, but also as a possibility of acquiring access to possibly valuable foreign inventions. Licensing sometimes makes it possible to send back to the US funds earned abroad. It can be used to acquire an equity position in a foreign firm—and if properly handled the IRS may view it as a capital gain.

As mentioned previously, many companies pay little attention to analyzing foreign licenses because they often are all-too-glad to reap some benefits from R & D activity. Some firms reason that the expenses attached to foreign litigation to defend a foreign patent probably would outweigh a favorable court decision—hence license almost anyone who asks and seems to guarantee costs plus a slight profit.

"Licensing has a risk which large companies have only recently become aware of. At the end of the licensing period, they find that they have a competitor instead of a partner. Therefore, the risks of

joint ventures with foreign companies may be preferable when possible."

The analysis of possible profits should consider the time value of money. For example, other things being equal, an agreement projecting royalties of $30,000 per year for five (5) years is more valuable in absolute terms than one projected to yield $15,000 per year for ten (10) years. A license cost and income check list to aid the risk manager is shown in Figure 7-4.

In conclusion, the possible money involved is substantial and as much care and management know-how should be exercised here as in any other part of the business.

One final word, there seems to be some tendency today for some companies to prefer joint ventures, with foreign firms over setting up a licensing agreement.

LEGAL ACTIONS CONCERNING PATENTS

Companies and their new product venture managers at times will become involved in litigation (suits and counter suits in the country's courts) concerning patents.

If this happens and there is an opportunity for influencing the selection of the attorney, then by all means get the most experience and successful (from the view cases won vs. cases lost) TRIAL attorney that can be located. The total cost of a litigation involving patents is so great that the attorney's fees should never be the overriding consideration. Just as in criminal law, trial attorneys accumulate different records of success and those who have been really successful tend to continue to win far more often than they lose.

Expert witnesses are usually required in a patent litigation—the problem here is to locate and use expert testifiers rather than expert engineers and scientists who have no real experience in testifying before a court of law. The difference between winning and losing the case often rests upon the witnesses and the expert testifier at times can swing the balance in your favor, so says one of the country's successful trial attorneys specializing in patent cases.

Licensing cost and income checklist

Benefits

1. Cash and/or equity down payments
2. Cash and/or equity lump sum payments
3. Periodic cash royalties
4. Sales to licensee of components, prototypes, and equipment
5. Dividends front license when investment follows licensing agreement
6. Fees from extra technical or managerial service
7. Patents, trademarks, and know-how from licensee
8. Increased export sales of other products where licensee also serves as a distributor
9. Lower cost supply of licensee products to licensee affiliates

Costs

1. In-house and field evaluation of prospective licensee
2. Legal, technical, managerial time in negotiations
3. Adapting licenser's products and processes to local requirements
4. Transmission of technical data (blueprints, specs, etc.)
5. Assistance in use of licensed process
6. Periodic retraining of licensee's staff
7. Policing the license: testing, auditing, field customer surveys, on-spot inspection
8. Correspondence with licensee on technical, legal, managerial questions
9. Advertising
10. Full range of legal expenses: contract advice, filling and maintaining foreign patents, litigation against foreign infringement, arbitration and renegotiation
11. R & D activities to upgrade and modify licenser's product and processes

Figure 7-4 "Licensing Cost and Income Checklist" Copyrighted 1968 by The Reuben H. Donnelley Corporation. Reprinted by special permission from the December issue of BUSINESS ABROAD

Patents and Anti-trust Actions

The patent is a monopoly which is granted for public disclosure and is a just reward for invention. However, a patent monopoly must be managed with finesse in order to avoid anti-trust violations. The Justice Department, from time to time, has attacked major companies who hold many patents such as E.I. du Pont de Nemours and Company and American Telephone & Telegraph Company. It seems that anti-trusters generally look with disfavor at patent holders or licensees if they do, among other things, the following:

Fix prices

Set territories for using the patents

Limit types of business in which the patent can be used

Limit sales volume

Let a licensee sell a product only if he buys it from the patent holder

Require buying other products from the patent holder

Insist on cross-licensing of patents.

In simple language, the monopoly granted the inventor has some "strings attached" by the grantor.

It would be advisable for the new product manager who is concerned with the legalities associated with patents, to keep an eye on business publications such as *Business Week*, the Financial and Business section of the *New York Times*, etc., for articles dealing with patent problems and anti-trust actions associated with patents. What is under attack today, is not always under attack the following year. Also, each year usually sees anti-trust action aimed at a new area.

In a somewhat similar manner, the new product manager should keep abreast of likely patent law changes so as to adjust his organization to be in accord with them before they become law.

COPYRIGHTS

The design of certain articles can be protected by copyright registration rather than by means of a mechanical or a design patent if such articles are clas-sified as works of art. Examples include artistic jewelry, enameled glassware, etc. Copyright registration offers some advantages since it provides protection for a longer period, namely twenty-eight years, and it may be renewed for a like period. In addition, the work of art need not be novel or inventive although it must be original with the artist or author who claimed the copyright.

There are two kinds of basic copyrights—common-law and statutory. Common-law copyright is a fundamental right which stems from the common-law and will be upheld by the courts even without a certificate of copyright registration. This kind of copyright covers the results of an individual's personal efforts and intellectual labor. Everyone has an inherent common-law copyright on his private correspondence, speeches, etc. However, if such writing or speeches are published without restriction, then the common-law right is lost.

Statutory copyright has the same origin as the U.S. patent laws. Registration of copyrights is the responsibility of the Library of Congress instead of the U.S. Patent Office. The register of copyrights is empowered to issue certificates of copyright registration to anyone who complies with the regulations. The application for copyright can be made by the original author, his legal representative, or by the company that publishes the work. There is no examination for novelty or originality.

The copyright is valid only if the work is original. The statutory notice—that is, "Copyright, (year), by (name of author)" must appear on the book or other material at the time it is printed and distributed; in fact, it must so appear before registration. All printed and distributed material becomes dedicated to the public unless the above action is taken.

Trade-Marks and Service Marks

The philosophy of trade-mark law is based on protection of the public, whereas the patent law was created to protect the inventory. Since the "public interest" is involved in all legal cases dealing with trade-marks, the courts tend to be much stricter in the filings on trade-mark infringement.

Trade-marks are used to identify goods. They are

considered by many to be indispensable in sales promotion and advertising and offer many benefits. Registered trade-marks do not expire; however, they may be lost through nonuse or misuse.

The right to trade-mark protection, which stems from common law, is acquired by priority of adoption in use rather than by registration. Congress has, however, passed a number of federal laws which provide for registration in the U.S. Patent Office of trade-marks, which are used in interstate or foreign commerce.

Service marks are similar to trade-marks, the only difference being that service marks are used to identify services rendered rather than a tangible and useable product. They have the same purpose as trade-marks and are acquired and protected in exactly the same manner. They normally appear on literature, brochures, stationary, advertisements, etc., since no physical product is normally involved and service is the thing being offered.

THE LAWS OF AGENCY AND CONTRACTS

Understanding the Basics of Contract and Agency Law

Without understanding the rudimentary basics of contract and agency law, the venture manager is at a severe disadvantage in many of his dealings. Involvement in both kinds of legal acts in inevitable. For example, if an agreement with a consulting engineer is negotiated and he performs the desired services as a result of a manager's *action*, the manager has acted as an agent of the corporation (which is a legal entity) and has thereby committed the company to an employment contract.

No one can escape contact with the agency device, since it happens when one buys a loaf of bread or deposits money in a bank. Business could not exist without it. Basically, an agency is a relationship where one party acts for and under the control of the other; however, the control does not have to be exercised to ensure or create an agency relation-ship. An agent can do practically anything business-wide that a principal can do.

An agency can be created by (1) agreement (compensation is not necessary), (2) creating an impression of agency and if a third party reasonably relies on it, the principal may be stopped denying an agency, (3) ratification (where a person acts for another without authority and the other confirms the act by work or conduct, he has ratified), and (4) by operation of law (an example would be a wife and/or child authorized to act as agent of husband and/or father who has failed to support them.

The principal has a duty:

1. Not a breach agency contract
2. To compensate except where agent acts gratuitously.
3. To reimburse for sums spent on behalf of principal
4. To exonerate agent and save him harmless from liabilities incurred while acting as directed.
5. To comply with statutory duties such as to maintain safe and healthful working conditions, pay minimum wages, recognize qualified unions, etc.

Practically all managerial employees and hordes of others will occasionally or regularly act as agents. Be assured that the specific laws and principles are complex and should be studied.

In a similar vein, the law of contracts (of which agency law is a special case) also deeply affects the venture manager. One definition of a contract is that it is an agreement between two or more competent (sane and of legal age) persons, having for its purpose an object that is considered lawful, wherein both persons agree to act or refrain from acting in a certain manner, and where such agreement is supported by a consideration (an exchange of money or other item of value which could be an action). There are five, and sometimes six, essentials that must be present to have established a contract. They are the following:

1. There must have been an offer that was intended as an offer, and it must have been communicated.
2. The offer must be accepted, and the acceptance must be communicated—except where it is accepted by completion of the action requested.

3. The promises or actions must be supported by a consideration; however, the consideration cannot be something given gratuitously. It must be the thing bargained for. Adequacy is not important in court except in cases of fraud. Also, past consideration will not support a contract.
4. Parties must have legal capacity to contract; for example: infants, the insane, or intoxicated persons cannot form a binding contract.
5. The objective of the contract must be legal.
6. In general, contracts can be oral; however, some must be in writing such as the contracts covering the sale of real estate.

Many special rules and conditions attach to each of the six points, and the venture manager is advised to read a good text on business law so as to be able to recognize danger areas. He should then consult the company attorney when they are encountered.

THE RISK IN WARRANTIES

Warranties pose both a consumer's risk and a seller's/manufacturer's risk. In the long run, for a firm which wishes to establish a good reputation, all risk falls eventually on the firm. The principal policies of a company which reduce the loss from making good on products which fail are:
1. The length of the warranty period
2. The "mix" of warranty in terms of length of warranty, parts, and labor
3. Choice of pro rata rebate (allowance based on proportion of warranty period left) or lump sum rebate
4. Portion of sales revenue set aside to build a warranty reserved fund
5. Quality of design and manufacture as measured by the average time the product is used before it fails (based on many units used up to failure time).

In view of the current move to "consumer protection", venture managers may call forth considerable ingenuity in developing a formula which will yield customer satisfaction and still maintain a competitive price and adequate warranty reserve. Figure 7-5 shows the proportion of cost per unit of a product which should be added on to the selling price for various values of warranty time as a multiple of average time to failure of the product.

This is for the pro rata policy. For example, if the warranty were 12 months and the average time to failure was 24 months, we would find 12/24 or 0.5 on the horizontal scale. If we read vertically up to the curve and then over to the left vertical scale, we would note that an amount of about 23% of the cost of the product should be added on for the warranty reserve.

We advise strongly against avoiding warranty responsibilities as one piano manufacturer did by stating that he agreed to promptly repair or replace without charge any part which was found to be defective, provided that the piano was delivered to their factory (or other place designated by them), and that the transportation costs be borne by the purchaser.[3]

PRODUCTS LIABILITY AND RELIABILITY

When we say we are "liable", we generally mean we're worried about the risk of one big loss or of many small losses. Some aerospace companies carry liability insurance up to $15 million. Liability for damage or injury can be reduced by improving the *reliability* of our products and by using some "legal wisdom". The degree to which a company is successful in controling the spiraling liability costs is directly proportional to the effort it expends in designing and manufacturing defect free products, identifying and warning of dangers in using the products *and* in developing defenses against claims and lawsuits.

In the past, the liability of the manufacturer to the consumers of his product primarily arose from (1) negligence in the design or manufacture of the product and (2) warrantly. The recognization of negligence has increased. However, the liability associated with warranty is increasing at a fast pace.

Today a new trend appears to be beginning—the imposing of liability regardless of whose fault it is! One immediate and direct result is that insurance

r/c vs W/M

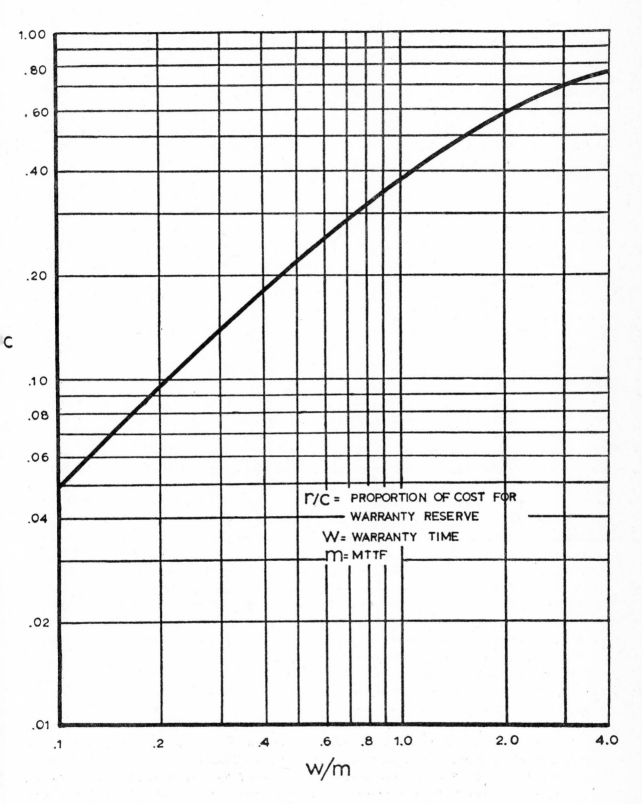

Figure 7-5 Proportion of cost per unit of product which should be added to the selling price for various values of warranty time expressed as a fraction of average time to failure of the product

Source: Warren W. Menke, "Determination of Warranty Reserves", *Management Science*, June, 1969

rates have gone up substantially in the last two years and will continue to rise for some time. If the company carries its own insurance, raise the allowance for claims.

The law is also changing in other respects. In the past the manufacturer was *usually* only liable to those with whom he dealt directly who were parties to a transaction (sale, lease, exchange, etc.). According to one source the courts have used 29 fictions, subterfuges and theories to avoid this limitation and to extend the liability to persons who were directly involved in the transaction. This means that the manufacturer is now often liable to a customer with whom he had no direct dealings, i.e., the customer bought from an independent dealer (a dealer doing business as an individual, partnership or as an independent corporation), or even from a used equipment dealer.

Another primary reason why the new products manager be increasingly concerned with this general subject is the fact that the verdicts are increasing in size as well as in number.

The old disclaimers and "hold harmless" agreements to limit the liability are now largely ineffective and the danger is real.

One way the courts have gotten around the old privity concepts of a contract is by finding that an obligation runs from the manufacturer to a remote purchaser on the basis of an express warranty. Law in the past recognized express warranties, but had limited them to an affirmation of fact as to the quality of the goods. Anything other than this was called "sales talk". Now the courts appear to be saying that what is said on advertising labels and sales literature are an express warranty on which an injured party can base a legal action.

If we limit our consideration of liability under warranties as being between a manufacturer and the buyer (not liability to third party), it appears that reasonable warranties that are freely negotiated between the manufacturer and the buyer will be recognized for what they say. Here we are not considering a third party, i.e. a man who later buys the product, perhaps as a used piece of equipment. In this case, (freely negotiated warranties) however, it is extremely important that the bar gaining position of the buyer be about equal to the bargaining position of the seller from all viewpoints.

Another point. It appears that the desire and philosophy of the courts, and perhaps of society in general, to place the burden of liability on the manufacturer since he is far more financially capable of paying the judgment. As to liability to third parties, there seems to be a tendency to bite the biggest fish, the manufacturer, rather than the sub-manufacturer.

A manufacturer's responsibility in the product liability arena has moved so as to fall within the scope of strict liability doctrine—simply put this doctrine holds that a manufacturer is liable without fault if he sells a defective product.

Under strict liability in tort doctrine (where warranty of fitness or merchant ability is involved) proof of a manufacturer's negligence is *not* required. If the article is defective—not reasonably fit for its designated or expected use, if defects arose from design *or* manufacture, or while the article was in control of the manufacturer, and if the defect approximately (reasonably in the eyes of the judge or jury) caused the injury or damage to the purchaser or reasonably expected consumer—then liability ensues.

In recognition of the above, there is now a national commission on product safety and "a buyer's bill of rights" has been requested of commerce. This all in addition to new muscle provided to the FTC and the Food and Drug Administration.

The whole organization must be made more aware of the problems in this area. Key personnel, engineers, etc. must not only keep in mind that the device must work well and must be economically feasible, but they also must take into account that human beings will operate the device and will be in contact with it. The possible backgrounds of the user of a product must be considered in this process. In particular, from a non-legal view, the following actions will reduce the risk:

—The firm's response to the problems of a product's liability and reliability (these are closely related) must involve every department or function of the business; i.e., Engineering, Manufacturing, Advertising, Sales, Insurance, Service, and Legal.

—Engineering must produce better designs from a

LEGAL RISKS 127

safety view for manufactured products so that they can be produced at a reasonable cost and yet meet new criteria for safety and reliability.

—The elimination of products liability hazards in the manufacturing cycle must be aided by Engineering, *beyond the mere specification of design* since the company is expected to perform reasonable tests and inspections to discover *hazards*, not just to see that the product words. Also, engineering should help Quality Control by assisting in producing production test guides which are effective and still permit keeping costs within reasonable limits. This may require the design of special equipment for the testing procedures since a failure to perform a necessary test can bring about liability.

—Research and Engineering must work with the insurance carriers in order that claims can be properly handled and thereby minimize liability on claims. They do this, in part, by educating legal counsel, investigating complaints, performing extra tests, providing expert witnesses, etc. Also, working with insurance carriers will clue them as to needed design changes.

—Service and operating instructions are usually written by engineers since they are in a good position to reduce risk or equipment hazards by carefully written manuals. Thus they have a unique opportunity to minimize hazards by writing good and understandable instructions. Also, if a hazard cannot be eliminated, the proper statements concerning a hazard can often minimize future damage claims—don't fail to be truthful.

It is inevitable that a company will eventually receive a products liability suit. The resultant problem can be minimized if engineering records are complete, the product was properly designed to reduce frequency of accidents, the sales literature and instructions included proper warnings of possible injury (and are as specific as possible) and if the receipt of the suit is handled with dispatch, initiative and imagination. In many cases, a firm may be contracted about an accident before the initiation of a suit. Here it is even more important to handle the problem with dispatch and imagination. Do not stick your head in the sand as the proverbial ostrich.

Whenever a claim reaches company counsel, a review by counsel is instigated and it encompasses at a minimum the following:

1. Sampling procedures, including all tests and inspection in both engineering and the factory.
2. Labeling as to clarity, warnings, instructions, etc.
3. A review of the entire production process, especially quality control.
4. Packaging, including facts regarding the package if it is involved.
5. Records—perhaps the most important part. Without good records the case is essentially lost.

The new product venture manager who is on his toes will check to see that the responsible people in the company are "liability conscious". Also, he will make sure to get adequate legal guidance.

CONCLUDING REMARKS

Between the problem of patents, labor laws, government rules and regulations, contract law, the law of agency and the problem of products liability and reliability, it would seem rather obvious that the new product manager cannot afford to ignore legal problems and must in fact become reasonably familiar with the legal aspects of the business—enough so to know when he needs to turn to an expert, the company's legal department or attorney. Also, here he will often find that attorneys tend to provide the pro's and con's of a situation and leave the final decision up to management.

REFERENCES

1. This classification covers new legal developments found as a regular feature in the *Journal of Marketing* under the heading, "Legal Developments in Marketing".
2. Jacob Schmookler, *Invention and Economic Growth*, Harvard University Press, Cambridge, Massachusetts, 1966.
3. "How much is that Guarantee Worth?", condensed from *Changing Times, Reader's Digest*, November 1969, Vol. 95, No. 571.

BIBLIOGRAPHY

"A poke at the Power of Patent Holders", *Business Week*, February 18, 1967.
Alderson, W., Terpstra, V. and Shapiro, S.J., *Patents and Progress*, Homewood, Illinois, Richard B. Irwin, Inc., 1965.

Anderson, R.A., "Social Forces and the Law", Cincinnati, Ohio; Southwestern Publishing Co., 1969.

Black, H.C., "Black's Law Dictionary", West Publishing Co., 1968.

Brainerd, A.W., "Protecting Patents, Know-How and Trademarks Abroad", *Management Review*, December, 1964.

Buckles, R.A., *Ideas, Inventions and Patents*, New York; John Wiley and Sons, Inc., 1957.

Business Week, "The Riches in Dormant Patents", April 15, 1961.

Calvert, R., Ed., "Encyclopedia of Patent Practices and Invention Management", Van Nostrand-Reinhold, 1964.

Catallo, B.F. et al., *Introduction to Law and the Legal Process*, New York; John Wiley and Sons, Inc., 1965.

Corley, R.N. and Black, R.L., *The Legal Environment of Business*, N.Y.; McGraw-Hill Book Co., 1968.

Dalrymple, D.J., "Patent Monopolies and the Law", *California Management Review*, Spring, 1967.

Dalrymple, D.J., "Do You Know the Law? Implied Warranty", *Business Management*, July, 1966, 30: 8.

Eaton, W.W., "Patent Problem: Who Owns the Rights", *Harvard Business Review*, July–August, 1967.

"Employee Patent and Secrecy Agreements", National Industrial Conference Board.

"Environmental Law", Research and Documentation Corporation, Greenville, N.Y., 1970.

Eshelman, R.H., "Patent Searches Pay Their Way in Design and Development", *Iron Age*, September 3, 1959.

Fot, S., *Management and the Law*, New York; Appleton-Century-Crofts, 1966.

"General Information Concerning Patents", U.S. Department of Commerce/Patent Office, Supt. of Documents, U.S. Government Printing Office, Wahington, D.C. Reprinted September, 1967.

"General Information Concerning Trademarks", U.S. Department of Commerce/Patent Office, Supt. of Documents, U.S. Government Printing Office, Washington, D.C. 20402. Reprinted August, 1968.

Gray, A.W., "How to Handle a Breach of Warranty", *Purchasing*, October 5, 1967, 63: 60–62.

Gray, A.W., "What Are Company Rights... When An Employee Gets a Patent?" *American Machinist*, August 10, 1959.

Harris, L.J., Ed., "Nurturing New Ideas", Bureau of National Affairs, 1969.

"How Much is that Guarantee Worth?" (condensed from Changing Times, *The Kiplinger Magazine*), *The Reader's Digest*, November, 1969.

"How the Law is Affecting Product Design", *Machine Design*, January 8, 1970.

Karger, D.W., "Patent Fundamentals", *Machine Design*, August 20, 1959.

Kintner, Earl W., *A Primer on the Law of Deceptive Practices*, New York; The Macmillan Company, 1971.

Kintner, Earl W., "Licensing Handbook", Advance House, 1965.

Lusk, H.F., Hewitt, C.M., Donell, J.D., and Barnes, A.J., *Business Law*, Homewood, Ill., Richard D. Irwin, Inc., 1970.

Legal Problems of Contractors, Architects and Engineers, Greenville, N.Y., Research and Documentation Corporation, 1970.

Legal Problems of the Technically Oriented Company, Greenville, N.Y., Research and Documentation Corporation, 1970.

Menke, Warren W., "Determination of Warranty Reserves", *Management Science*, June, 1969.

"Patents and Inventions: An Information Aid for Inventors", U.S. Department of Commerce/Patent Office, Supt. of Documents, U.S. Government Printing Office, Washington, D.C. Revised April, 1968.

"Products, Liability and Reliability: Some Management Considerations", Machinery and Allied Products Institute and Council for Technological Advancement, Washington, D.C., 20036, 1967.

"Q and A About Patents", U.S. Department of Commerce/Patent Office, Supt. of Documents, U.S. Government Printing Office, Washington, D.C., 20402.

Quinn, H., "Warranty is Name of the (ad) Game in Detroit, Auto Makers Find; but U.S. is taking hard look at some nebulous wording", *Advertising Age*, Dec. 19, 1966, 37: 3.

Redmond, W.H. and F.M. Webster, "How Chrysler Communicates Data on its Warranty Program", *Office*, August, 1966, 64: 69–72.

"Rules of Practice in Patent Cases", U.S. Department of Commerce/Patent Office, Supt. of Documents, U.S. Government Printing Office, Washington, D.C. 20402. Jan., 1968.

Scher, V.Y., "Protecting Your New Ideas", *Textile World*, Vol. 110, No. 6, pp. 38–39, June, 1960.

Schmookler, Jacob, *Invention and Economic Growth*, Cambridge, Mass., Harvard University Press, 1966.

Shipman, John R., "International Patent Planning", *Harvard Business Review*, March–April, 1967.

Smith, L.Y. and Roberson, G.G., *Business Law*, West Publishing Co., 1971.

Spangenberg, C., "You, Your Product and the Law", *Mechanical Engineering*, pp. 18–24, June, 1968.

"The Lines Are Drawn for a Patent Law Fight", *Business Week*, January 28, 1967.

"The Inventors Best Friend", *Business Week*, Sep. 20, 1969.

Vaughn, R.C., *Legal Aspects of Engineering*, Englewood Cliffs, New Jersey, Prentice-Hall, Inc., 1962.

Wade, W., "Patent Guide for the Research Director", Ardmore, Pennsylvania, Advance House Publishers, 1964.

Wilcke, G., "Practical Uses of Patents Lag", *The New York Times*, October 9, 1966.

White, W.W., and Ravenscroft, R.C., *Patents Throughout the World*, Trade Activities, Inc., New York 17, 1963.

Winter, E.L., *A Complete Guide to Making Public Stock Offering*, Prentice-Hall, Inc., Englewood Cliffs, N.J., 1962.

Zenoff, D.B., Jepson, J.A., "How to Boost Profits from your Foreign Licensing Agreement", *Marketing Insights*, March, 1969.

CHAPTER 8

THE ROLE OF MARKETING
IN THE NEW PRODUCT PROCESS

INTRODUCTION

It is obvious that this chapter cannot serve as a text on how to set up the marketing organization and how to operate all its elements. As in other chapters, concentration will be on those elements of the marketing organization most concerned with new products. Separate chapters will be found on market research, pricing, and selling.

It must also be understood that this discussion of marketing is directed at the responsibilities or tasks that must be carried out by what is ordinarily identified as the marketing organization. It may be that the new product development activity is so organized that the marketing responsibilities for a new product are vested in a new product venture team, organization, or department. If so, then it must be understood that this discussion of marketing is still valid and that the various tasks and considerations discussed must become those of the new product venture team or similar organizational element in their discharge of their marketing responsibilities.

In other cases, this may be a shared responsibility where the new product venture team carries some of it and the regular marketing organization carries other portions of the responsibility.

THE MARKETING CONCEPT

The marketing concept is a way of life most marketing experts urge upon their companies[1]. In their view the really important consideration is the con-

sumer and all the major effort should be placed in building on this concept. In terms of development or organizational elements, top management cannot afford to ignore the firm's complex of resources and consequently must therefore properly evaluate the resources and determine where the priorities are to be placed—and these priorities and related development areas vary with time. However, the general concepts of marketing as expressed in this book do *apply at all times*.

The *marketing concept* recognizes that a product's success depends upon what the customer thinks about the product, not what the manufacturer thinks. In the marketing concept, the entire company is essentially devoted to identifying and satisfying needs of people. The focus must be on the consumer or customer.

In order to translate the marketing concept into action the company must adopt a systematic approach to matching the company's capabilities to market opportunities. This requires careful forecasting and product planning (as discussed in Chapters I and II). Secondly, everyone in the company must be educated to understand that the customer is *the most important factor in company profits*—not inventory control, not brilliant engineering design, not manufacturing tolerances, not advertising, or not any other function of the business.

Finally, the marketing concept includes planned risk-taking and the evaluation of foregone opportunities. For each new product that a company introduces, it has foregone the opportunity of launching some other product at that time. In other words, it should consider the alternatives and their associated risks rather than evaluating only the opportunity at the end of its nose.

SOME FUNCTIONS OF MARKETING AS RELATED TO NEW PRODUCTS

Marketing shares responsibilities with engineering and manufacturing for a number of tasks in the developing and launching of new products as shown earlier. However, the specialized knowledge of marketing is critical to the selection of new products and the commercial success of new products.

With respect to the conventional approach to marketing it is usual to include in marketing discussions or considerations the categories (the 4 P's of marketing) of product, price, promotion and place (distribution). These are all involved in the development of a marketing strategy which is really a system of decisions into which all of the 4 P's are taken into account.

In a slightly more restricted sense marketing and/ or the New Product Department must:

1. Ascertain needs and wants of customers. These are *different* and the difference is important. A want is a desire which the customer has largely defined for himself. A need is something the customer would like to have if he knew it existed or if he could conceive it (the want). For example, a customer may feel a vague dissatisfaction because her arm tires after ironing the laundry. She has an unexpressed need for some product which will prevent this. The product might be a lighter iron, a mechanical ironer, or an iron which rests on a cushion of air until pressed down, etc.

2. Specify who the potential customers are—identifying the market or markets if the customers fall into different categories or classifications.

3. Determine the proper relationship of price to the customers *and* the product so as to maximize total return on investment.

4. Supplying the marketing services relative to getting the right product in the right place at the right time. This involves both planning of strategy and implementation of plans.

This requires some amplification. *Consider why customers buy.* They buy because a product fills a basic need or want in terms of its function and its form or appearance. It is Marketing's responsibility to see that the new product meets these needs or wants by identifying and communicating them to Engineering.

The customer, even though he has a need or want, sometimes does not have a desire to purchase a product, or even to go out and look for it. Therefore, an associated marketing must is to create an awareness of and a desire for the product. This awareness and desire is created by both the selling element of the marketing organization and through advertising. Separate chapters have been written on each of these, emphasizing again the elements of these that relate to new products.

In 1968, 9450 supermarket lines were introduced to the market. Less than 20 percent of these met sales goals according to a study by New Products Action Team Incorporated, a company specializing in new product services for consumer package goods manufacturers. Their overriding conclusion was that the major reason for new product failure was unquestionably a lack of real consumer point of difference. The companies may have thought there was a point of difference but this was more in the eyes of the manufacturer than in the eyes of the consumer where it really counts.

If there is a product difference which is real to the consumer, advertising will fall into its place naturally and there will be no difficulty in knowing what to advertise or what the advertisement and the salesman are to say.

This whole process is made more complicated by the fact that sometimes one needs to start with a product that came unexpectedly on the scene out of the laboratory and in others a customer need is identified in the more classical sense and then developed in the lab.

MARKETING FUNCTIONS

Customers buy a new product, even if similar ones are on the market, if it is readily available or can

				Product				
	Function	Form	Place	Price	Time	Promotion	Possession	Service
Marketing	x	x	x	x	x	x	x	x
Engineering	x	x			x			x
Manufacturing	x		x		x			x

Figure 8-1 Responsibilities for Getting the Right Product in the Right Place at the Right Time

be made available. Marketing must see that the product is more readily available to potential customers (if possible) than competing products directed at meeting the same customer needs or wants. To the extent that Manufacturing locates its plants near the customers, it also contributes to satisfying the availability of the product.

Although there are many ways of pricing a product, Marketing must have the responsibility for pricing. Price is an important factor influencing sales and profits. It must be set in the light of many considerations, one of which is the market demand at various prices.

While pricing is a prime responsibility of marketing, also involved to a very major degree are engineering, manufacturing, and finance. Prices are affected by cost and cost in turn is affected by the functions and attributes designed into the product by engineering, as well as the associated manufacturing cost. It is marketing's responsibility to see to it that functions and attributes are not included in the product that will not help make it sell. Providing the customer with something he does not want or need, will not help sell the product. It merely raises the cost and thereby increases the price and/or reduces the profit margin.

Timing of the product's introduction is the primary responsibility of Marketing, although Engineering and Manufacturing affect the timing as to when it *could* be introduced. There is usually a right time for a new product to be made available. If a product appears on the market late, other better products may already have appeared. If it appears too early, it may not have any purpose. For example, TV sets in certain African countries would have been premature in the 1950's, but there will be some time in the future which will be just right to start the introductions.

Marketing is responsible for the transfer of ownership to the customer. For some products, this means that Marketing may develop credit and/or collection policies and procedures. Such services may well make a new product a success, despite highly competitive substitute products selling in the market on a cash only basis.

The product is not complete without service, in many cases. Marketing is responsible for service policies (or counsels top management), and also for proper implementation of service procedures.

Figure 8-1 is a summary chart which shows the responsibilities (and how they overlap) of each of the three major functional groups involved offering a new product.

NEEDS RESEARCH AND MARKET IDENTIFICATION

Wherever an analysis of the people and environment outside of the company is involved, Marketing bears the responsibility. Marketing conducts the research and makes its recommendations to top management with regard to needs to be filled and characteristics of the potential customers.

PRODUCT EVALUATION AND SCREENING

In the first two chapters one of the things emphasized was to determine early a product's possibility of success so as to kill it off before major costs were incurred if it did not appear to have good potentiality or chance for success.

The first step in the new product process was identified as business screening or analysis which was shown to occur immediately after a new product idea came into being. This process is a "rough" analysis considering *probable* price, cost, market size, product life cycle, probable sales and profits. It will vary as to the amount of work with the difficulty of obtaining answers to these questions. In some cases, knowledgeable people will be able to establish the minimums and maximums for each of these items in a rough sort of way. Once these are put down, the answer is quite often obvious as to what should be done, i.e. discard the idea or develop it further so as to define the parameters better. What is important is that this information be recorded, even though the values may be arrived at through subjective opinion of one or more people.

SCREENING CHECK LIST

Both the preliminary and subsequent more thorough study and analysis of new product ideas should consider (as a minimum) the following factors:

1. Performance
2. Market size
3. Marketability of product
4. Growth of sales and profits
5. Legal aspects
6. Development and engineering
7. Production
8. Cost
9. Distribution

If the idea is retained for further investigation, then another analysis usually occurs as soon as some kind of engineering sketches have been made as well as a possible list of the major parts and/or subsystems making up the total product. Such data permits making a better estimate of the costs to develop and manufacture the product. This analysis may also include a more detailed look at the probable market parameters.

If the product is retained after the second analysis than a continuing series of detailed economic and/or market analysis including detailed business analyses should be made regularly as the product is developed and does into manufacturing. This does not mean doing it once, but many times. These business analyses in the later stages are quite detailed.

Again it must be understood that once it is virtually positive that the product has little or no profit potential, the product should be dropped. Do not try to beat a dead horse to try and get it to move. It is not wise to invest in hopeless projects simply because you have previously made an investment in them. Losing money on some new product ventures is inevitable.

More detail is provided elsewhere in this book on costing, pricing and business analysis.

There are several stages in evaluating and screening new products where Marketing and/or the New Product Department plays a key role. When an idea for a product is first conceived, Marketing must make some rough analysis regarding price, costs, market size, product life cycle, and profits. At a later stage, perhaps after engineering sketches have been made and more cost data are available, Marketing usually makes another economic and market analysis. In some cases, after design has been completed and some preproduction prototypes are available, Marketing may make a very thorough study and analysis of the situation. Although heavy engineering costs have been incurred up to this point, these are small compared to manufacturing and marketing costs involved in getting a new product on the market.

COSTING

Marketing's role is an integrative one with respect to estimating costs for a new product. With the aid of Accounting, Marketing gathers the data on development costs, production costs, and marketing costs in order to determine profit margins.

PRICING

One of the most important objectives of Marketing is to establish a price for the new product which will fulfill short- and long-range objectives. Pricing depends more upon market conditions than cost. If the cost cannot be reconciled with the desired price, the product should be abandoned. However, it should be realized that forecast cost in the early estimations will usually be high unless the experience factor and a suitable adjustment for little engineering information is made.

At each stage of new product development from conception of the idea to launching the product, the selling price must be estimated and evaluated. The many factors which are important in pricing are covered in a later chapter.

CHOOSING A NAME

A good name for a product is a strong promotional advantage. A salesman has an easier time explaining Frigid Air refrigerators than Hot Spot refrigerators. Steelcase furniture, Rainbird sprinklers, Toro lawnmowers, Whirlpool clothes washers, Disposall garbage disposal units, and Hush Puppies are all protected names which are designed to suggest and reinforce the qualities of the respective products. Some consulting organizations are available to help in naming a product, one example is Lippincott & Margulies, Inc. of New York City. This organization also handles industrial design problems—i.e., the form or appearance of the product.

LAUNCHING THE NEW PRODUCT

Once the decision has been made definitely to put the new product on the market, Marketing must prepare and carry out detailed plans. Because of the complexities of the launching, charts are very helpful in synchronizing this major effort. The first step in preparing such a chart is to list key activities such as:

1. Conduct the market analysis or test market study
2. Set the price
3. Establish the advertising and sales promotion plan

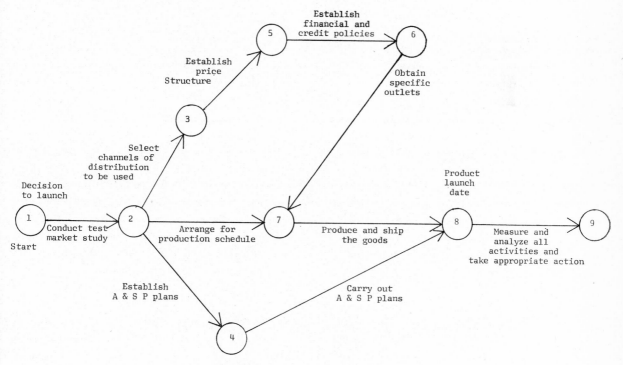

Figure 8-2 Product Launching Network

4. Select the channels of distribution
5. Establish actual outlets for the products
6. Establish financing and credit policies
7. Arrange with Manufacturing for production of products to meet the introductory data and forecasted needs
8. Initiate the advertising and promotion
9. Get the products into the channels of distribution
10. Measure the sales and modify activities as required

Some of these activities should be carried on in parallel to reduce the time from the decision to launch to the time of actual launching. Other activities cannot be started until certain preceding activities have been completed. The critical path charting technique covered in an earlier chapter is what is often needed at this point. A generalized view of a New Product introduction on a critical path chart is shown in Figure 8-2.

Figure 8-2 is simply an example. Each company must work out the principal activities and the order in which they must be completed for each product.

In launching a new product, Marketing's primary goal is to build sales quickly and iron out problems later. Marketing's orientation is therefore different from that of other groups such as Engineering, Production and Finance. Each group has different goals which are conflicting until a balance is struck which leads to achievement of the best interests of the company. Figure 8-3 shows the emphasis of various company departments relative to Marketing. The action to optimize total company performance is also indicated. The optimizing action in many cases will vary from company to company. The important thing is that management recognizes that trade-offs between departments are necessary. Domination of company activities by a single department means that the goals of other departments are subordinated. This imbalance reduces the effectiveness and profitability of the company.

ORGANIZING FOR MARKETING

There are certain functions which must be performed by Marketing, and each company must organize to perform these. The size of the company, the nature of the products, the type and geographical dispersion of customers, and the nature of the product management desired all exert an influence on organizational form. Generally, the following processes are involved in marketing:

1. Product planning and management
2. Marketing research
3. Selling
4. Advertising and sales promotion
5. Customer service
6. Staff services (long-range research, policy and information dissemination, personnel development).
7. Financing the product (where necessary)
8. Product standardization and grading (where appropriate)
9. Transportation and storage (a responsibility of marketing in some companies)

Although credit and collections as well as financing are sometimes found in marketing organizations, their emphasis is such that it is not usually advisable to include them.

In a small company, all marketing activities except field selling may be performed by the sales manager and, perhaps, an assistant sales manager. Obviously, marketing research and sales forecasting must be relatively simple and minimum in such a case. The sales manager may work with a small budget. The sales manager is his own product manager.

At the other extreme, all functions may appear individually within the organization. There are, of course, many variations in terms of decentralized selling organizations. That is, there may be regional and district sales managers for geographical dispersions or there may be division and department sales managers for diversified product lines. In some cases the marketing operations of sales, advertising and sales promotions, and customer services may report to a marketing operations manager while marketing research is under the Manager of Marketing Services. The advantage of this is to locate staff planning, research, and coordinating activities separate from the pressures of day-to-day problems.

Other departments	Their emphasis	Marketing emphasis	Action to optimize company performance
Engineering	Long design lead time	Short design lead time	Market introduction controls lead time
	Functional features	Functional and style features	Style designers work with functional designers
	Overdesign for long life	Limited life and style obsolescence	Style predominates for consumer goods and operational life predominates for producers' goods
	Custom components for each model	Standard components interchangeable for all models	Market strategy with regard to price and quality dictates action
Production	Long production lead time	Short production lead time	Long range gross estimates and regular revision of estimates right up to final lead time sign-off
	Long runs with few models, no model changes	Short runs with many models	Interchangeable parts, modular design, sophisticated inventory and production control to permit model variety and/or change at reasonable cost
	Level demand	Immediate delivery even in peak periods	Optimise within the limits of the market carrying costs and costs of production. Subcontract work during peak periods if at all possible
	Standard components	Standard components of good quality	Quality of components selected on basis of marketing strategy with regard to quality and price
	Ease of fabrication	Style predominates	Design and style developed with concern for fabrication
	Low inventories of finished goods	High inventories	Optimize inventories in terms of market (not marketing's) requirements, carrying costs and stockout costs
	Low quality control requirements	High quality	Set quality level in terms of company policy, price, and cost of service
Finance	Rationalized budgets	Intuitive budgets	Budgets based on realizable opportunities
	Rigid budgets	Flexible budgets	Flexible budgets where justification can be made
	Return on investment	Sales and profits	Multiple goals relating sales, profits, and return on investment
Accounting	Uniform transactions	Special terms and discounts	Policies for special terms and discounts changing with major changes in marketing conditions
	Many expense reports	Few expense reports and frequent sales reports	Few expense reports as long as expenses are controlled. Frequent sales reports
Credit	Full financial information from customers	Minimum credit information	Key-factors credit check
	Low credit risk	High credit based on character	Risks established so as to assure protection from excess bad debt losses and loss of potential sales
	High interest rates	Low interest terms	Low interest for short term and high interest for long term
	Tough collection procedures	Easy collection policies	Collection procedures based on each individual case

Figure 8-3   Balanced Action for Marketing

THE SALESMAN

There is a stereotype of the salesman as the hard-driving, aggressive, tall, strong, smooth-talking individual. Large companies recognize the falsity of such an image and use very careful selection procedures based on studies of successful salesmen and their background as related to the industry involved. Selling today is a profession, so that many men who have the basic persistence and technical knowledge may be trained to become good salesmen. While for some types of selling, aggressive and dominant behavior may be appropriate, generally products are sold by technically competent men who are self-disciplined, who know their own products well, who have studied the needs of their customers, and who have analyzed the weaknesses of competitors' products.

The ultimate test of the salesman, of course, is the amount of his sales. Despite the professional approach to selling, there is usually a star performer on the sales force whose success cannot seem to be duplicated by selection and training. The sales manager should be skilled in recognizing such stars before they develop fully and exploit them to their limit. Since they often sell two or three times the quantity of the next best salesman, the company should reward them generously in both economic and non-economic ways in order to retain them.

SOME MARKETING NO-NO'S

Some typical actions that prevent the effective application of modern marketing techniques are the following:

1. Do not engage in bloody, knock-down-and-drag-out fights with entrenched competitors.
2. Do not haphazardly or sophomorically apply marketing strategies—even though they are individually theoretically sound.
3. Do not try to market products having no truly demonstrable points of difference meaningful to the consumer.
4. Do not stick to a policy just because it has worked in the past.
5. Do not form emotional attachments to products which have outlived their viability, i.e. or are in the declining phase of their life cycle.
6. Do not get so entranced by building volume that proper recognition of the cost of attaining the volume is not taken into account.
7. Just because you have only been dealing with one class of customers or with one geographical area, do not fail to consider the advantages of change.

MARKETING VERSUS R & D

The material which follows could almost be labeled "some don'ts". It is all right to be a believer in the marketing concept, but do not over emphasize the role of marketing to the detriment of R & D. People in R & D have a normal amount of pride and will become defensive with respect to marketing if this policy is pursued too vigorously.

R & D is likely to give equal priority to new products for all customer groups unless given guidance. Don't make it a secret as to why marketing favors certain groups of customers. Bring R & D into the total picture.

If there is a product rejection or a market failure, bring it out on the table early to keep production and R & D from wasting good money in an area where there is going to be little return.

Do let R & D know marketing's current sales problems. They need to have this information in order for them to do a good job for marketing.

It is difficult to handle the situation where R & D is not generating new products. However, this problem should be discussed in a confidential manner between the heads of marketing and R & D. Then if this tactic does not resolve the problem, there is only one solution—go to the top.

It is important for marketing to follow new product development. Do not wait until the last minute to get involved. Such a problem will not happen if there is a new product department as described in an earlier chapter.

Some marketing people have the opinion that Research and Development men should be kept away from the customer, i.e., "out of the field".

Actually it is usually well for the marketing people to take R & D men along into the field. This is the only way R & D personnel can actually get a true feeling for customer reactions and customer needs.

Marketing should not pick fights with R & D. Battles between R & D and marketing make absolutely no sense. The company is damaged, new product development will not succeed and heads are sure to roll in the long run.

When there are production problems with a new product, marketing should be careful not to promote a fight between R & D and production or vice versa. Rather, marketing should try to help resolve the problems.

If a product is in trouble, put the best man on it that you can, in order to try and clear up the problem. However, make sure it is a person who can work with R & D.

Post mortems can be painful. However, while every product weakness should be brought to the fore, there had better be concurrent exhibition of the fact that marketing did and was participating in the development effort. Certainly a failure should not be blamed on R & D unless they went completely contrary to what was recommended by marketing and/or the new product department.

GOALS

It is vital to have marketing goals. The establishment of goals provides a focus. In addition, goals provide an indication of fiscal manpower and other needs. They furnish an instrument to control and channel the efforts of marketing. Finally, they erect a standard against which to measure marketing performance.

One danger in setting goals is to block broader thinking or a consideration of alternatives. For example, goals might be set as building brand X's share of the market from 19% to 25% within two years. This goal may so occupy the thoughts and efforts of marketing that they fail to consider the launching of another brand in the market or to consider franchising to broaden the market, or for that matter to

consider the introduction of a new product which may make brand X completely obsolete.

DEFINING THE COMPANY'S BUSINESS

Too many organizations consider their business to be an obvious fact and too few marketing managers and/or new product managers concern themselves with this question.

Companies which have set out to either define or redefine their business usually perceive that the core of their business is a concept, a philosophy, a policy, a talent, an orientation toward a market, a capacity to fill certain customer needs, or some similar aspect. They will find that their business is not properly identified as a particular product, or process, or set of procedures, or as a business primarily oriented to exploiting a particular supply of raw materials.

Space does not permit giving examples of all of the ways one can define a company's business. However, one example might be Proctor and Gamble which obviously manufactures soaps and detergents. To limit their business to this area, however, is not what the company does and it certainly does not view itself (based upon its actions) as being in just specific product lines. By its actions it seems to view itself as an organization capable of marketing a wide variety of consumer products through careful market testing, the assurance of product quality, application of merchandising skills, and through the guidance of well supported brand managers.

Another example would be the Carborundum Company which has changed itself from merely viewing its business as selling abrasives. It decided to look at its business through the eyes of its customers, which meant that it had to see how abrasives fited into metal polishing, cleaning and/or removal systems. They also realized that the emphasis had to be on "the system". As a result, it overhauled its entire company. In fact, it even went into machine tool building through various acquisitions.

Other examples could be shown. Keuffel & Esser make products for engineers and draftsmen and could view this as their business. However, the company slogan is "Creative Products for Creative Engineers".

How do we identify the parameters of the company's business and decide on what should be done? We should search for vision. Such vision springs from several sources.

1. Identification on unique talents and skills within the company.
2. Identification of competitive pressures.
3. Identification of the areas in which the company is truly expert.
4. Knowing what the customers want you to define your business as being.
5. Realizing what a customer is *really* buying.

One can define one's business either narrowly or broadly. For example, Hertz originally developed its reputation in renting cars and many still have this as a vision of Hertz. However, they did not constrain their activities and now one can rent practically anything from Hertz. Steamship companies, for example, do not view themselves as merely providing transportation; more and more of them now also view themselves as providing floating resort and recreational centers.

By contrast, airlines have chosen to define their universe rather narrowly. They seem to be viewing their business as furnishing air carriage from one runway to another. This means that there are many subsidiary commercially successful firms riding their coat tails.

In defining the company's purpose or business it would be wise to make sure the definition is in accord with the following:

1. Take into account existing company strengths and weaknesses
2. Be capable of continued application and usefulness in spite of anticipated changes in the social, political, and business environments
3. Be sure that it will embrace or include a large number of products with many directed toward growth markets
4. Not be limited to a single market, market area, or industry—in other words, that it have sufficient breadth
5. Be simple of definition and easily understood

6. Be at least partially (preferably to a major degree) directed toward growth areas that take into account the changing social, political and business environments
7. Not ignore the existing company image
8. Relate, at least in part, to the markets the company presently serves.

SPECIFIC MARKETING STRATEGIES THAT COULD ACCELERATE GROWTH AND PROFITS

Strategies which accelerate growth and profits require careful analysis, a search for opportunities and prompt action. Whatever strategies are selected must be tailored specifically for the company in question. The following represent possible strategies:

1. *Special product—total industry strategy*—Rather than seeking a full line and meeting competition head-on, define the customer-industry as broad as possible and seek a single special product which is not being provided well, or at all, by your competitors.

2. *Roving strike force*—Rather than disperse your resources uniformly across a broad front (industry or geographical area), concentrate them heavily in one spot until significant market share gains have been made. Then move to another area to concentrate them, etc.

3. *Target industry strategy*—Select a new industry for your market for a product; concentrate your selling effort on this narrow front in order to dominate this market.

4. *Truncated life-cycle strategy*—Seek initial entry (or rapid imitation) with new products, and withdraw them from the market as soon as total market sales appears to reach near a peak. This means all your resources are devoted to new, high-profit, products rather than to competing in a diminishing market against toughening competition.

5. *Brand manipulation*—Use multibrand entries, or extend a strong brand name to other models or products, or switch to private brands.

6. *Import items* or components you can't make as

well or as cheaply. When tariffs are not prohibitive or production in certain protectorates of the U.S. is possible, import items to be sold under your brand name. In some cases, the fact that the item is made abroad enhances its value so that a special brand name should be used.

7. *Blockout strategy*—Where your product is used in conjunction with another, try to make your product a universal fit to competitors', but block competitors by your design. An example is the razor blade and razor. Design your razor so that only your blade fits, but try to develop a universal blade that fits all competitors' razors.

8. *ABC account strategy*—It is likely that 80% of your sales comes from about 15% of your customers, the "A group". At the other end, perhaps 60% of your customers are small and yield only 10% of your sales, the "C group". The B group of customers lie in between. By concentrating on the A group and key accounts in the B group, and eliminating some of the C group which represent losses instead of profits, you may increase overall profits greatly.

9. *Segment the market*—Divide the market according to psychological, sociological, or economic wants and match models and styles of your product to each segment.

10. *Find substitute products for established applications*—The introduction of plastic trash cans for metal cans, the Disposal unit in the sink as a substitute for other garbage disposal methods, the electronic desk computer as a substitute for mechanical calculators, and video lectures with programmed texts as a substitute for teachers are examples.

11. *Look for new distribution methods*—Evaluate traditional channels of distribution and try to find methods which will save time, cut middleman costs, or provide more effective promotion and service.

MARKED CONDITIONS MAKING IT RIGHT FOR NEW PRODUCT EXPANSION

1. Insignificant differences in products offered by the various brands.

2. Very high profit returns.
3. Low advertising to sales ratio.
4. No real innovations introduced over the past several years.
5. High gross profits.
6. Innovations in related fields that could be applied in other product categories.
7. New uses which have not really been exploited.
8. Much brand switching due to low consumer loyalty.

HOW SOME PROS PICK NEW PRODUCT WINNERS

Business Week long ago began identifying new products that were likely to succeed by having a panel of experts review the major new products introduced in a given year and decide which would succeed. Over a number of years, their identified new products succeeded nine times out of ten. In general, the men examining the products consisted of an approximately equal mixture of technical experts and marketing experts. In general, these men were looking for a soundly engineered answer to a well studied market need. They gave about as much weight to the way the inside of the product worked as to the way the outside looked and how it might appeal to the customer.

They tended to concentrate on products that reflected a system approach and that were a part of a family of uses.

They were particularly concerned with how well the product was engineered from a human-use viewpoint. "Was it engineered for humans?", was placed rather high on their list of importance.

Some products were rejected because the judges often concluded that while the product was good, the field was changing and soon would eliminate the operation or service function offered by the product.

CONCLUSION

It is quite obvious that the responsibilities of marketing as related to new products is extremely important. It is also obvious that many "hands" need to be involved in handling the multitude of duties and responsibilities that must be fulfilled. Therefore, even though there is a separate New Products Department with its own marketing responsibilities, it obviously needs to take advantage of the services of and know-how offered by the existing marketing organization. Too often these two groups try to compete with each other rather than cooperate. It is a very real danger that must not be ignored.

Finally, the marketing function should take such actions as to assure the company's products and/or services be of social, economic, and technological change.

REFERENCES

1. Discussed in detail in many texts, some of which are included in the bibliography.

BIBLIOGRAPHY

Adler, L., *Handbook of Modern Marketing*, New York: McGraw-Hill, 1969.

Adler, L., *Plotting Marketing Strategy*, New York: Simon and Schuster, 1967.

Angelus, T. L., "Why Most New Products Fail", *Marketing Insights*, May 12, 1969.

Harris, J. S., "New Products Profile Chart", *Chemical and Engineering News*, April 17, 1961.

Linowes, D. F., *Managing Growth through Acquisition*, American Management Association, New York City, 1968.

Marting, E., editor, "New Products/New Profits", American Management Association, Inc., New York City, 1964.

"Why New Products Fail", *The Conference Board Record*, October, 1964.

Berg, T. and A. Shuckman, *Product Strategy and Management*, New York: Holt, Rinehart and Winston, 1963.

Enrick, L. N., *Market and Sales Forecasting*, San Francisco: Chandler Publishers, 1969.

Evans, G., *The Product Manager's Job*, American Management Association, New York, 1964.

Hanan, M., *The Market Orientation of Research and Development. A Recommendation for Minimizing New Product Risk*, AMA, N.Y., 1965.

Hilton, P., *New Product Introduction for Small Business Owners*, Washington, D.C.: Small Business Administration, 1961.

Larson, G., *Developing and Selling New Products*, Small Business Administration, Washington, 1955.

Leduc, R., *How to Launch a New Product*, Albert J. Phiebig Books, 1966.

New Products Marketing, editors of "Printers Ink", Duell, Sloan and Pearce Pearce, 1964.

Maintaining the Product Portfolio, American Management Association, (R & D) New York, 1960.

Marting, E., ed., *The Commercialization of Research Results*, AMA, New York: 1957.

Reynold, W., *Products and Markets*, Appleton-Century-Crofts, N.Y., 1969.

Scrase, R. R., (ed.), *"New Products: Concepts, Development, and Strategy"*: Sixth Annual New Products Marketing Conference, 1966, University of Michigan, Graduate School of Business Administration, 1967.

Smith, D., *How to Avoid Mistakes When Introducing New Products*, New York: Vantage Press, 1964.

Talley, W., Jr., *The Profitable Product—Its Planning, Launching and Management*, Englewood Cliffs, N. J.: Prentice Hall, 1965.

Wallenstein, G., *Concept and Practice of Product Planning*, AMA, New York, 1965.

Warshaw, M. R. and Murphy, G. P., Editors, *New Product Planning for Changing Markets:* Seventh Annual New Products Marketing Conference, 1967.

Watton, H., *New New Product Planning: A Practical Guide for Diversification*, Englewood Cliffs, N.J.: Prentice Hall, 1969.

Engle, James, F., David T. Kollat, and Roger D. Blackwall, *Consumer Behavior*, New York: Holt, Rinehart and Winston, 1966.

Cannon, J.T., *Business Strategy and Policy*, New York: Harcourt, Brace & World, 1968.

Kotler, Philip, *Marketing Management: Analysis, Planning and Control*, Englewood Cliffs, N.J.: Prentice-Hall, 1967.

Alderson, Wroe, and Green, Paul E., *Planning and Problem Solving*, Homewood, Ill., 1964.

Lazer, William and Kelley, Eugene J., *Managerial Marketing: Perspectives and Viewpoints:* Richard D. Irwin, Inc. 1962.

Beckman, Theodore N. and Davidson, William R., *Marketing*, New York: Ronald Press, 1962.

CHAPTER 9

MARKETING RESEARCH FOR DECISION MAKING

REDUCING RISK

Putting out a new product can be analogous to rolling dice. If you make the throw in ignorance, the dice may be loaded against you. If you gather some data and reason with it, you may be able to load them in your favor.

If you merely put the product on the market without thorough knowledgeable investigation, the odds will be greatly in favor of "the house", i.e., your product is likely to fail in the market place. Marketing research is the application of systematic formal procedures for providing information and recommendations which will *reduce the risk* of making wrong and poor decisions concerning new products. Marketing research is a means of immediate feedback from the potential customers regarding a prospective product. Its cost is almost always a fraction of the total cost of product introduction, and if the money for some market research is not available, then maybe the product is too much for the company to handle. Judgment is not eliminated because of marketing research, but is sharpened.

Hardly any money is spent in rough screening (see Figure 1-12) and not much more in early research. Internal review which usually follows is only a little more costly. The amount spent on evaluation increases sequentially. The ideas which get through the above steps should get the full market research treatment.

Any time there is a decision to be made concerning the future, there is risk. By studying the forces at work and using predictive methods that appear to have good reliability, we can reduce the area of the unknown and aid the decision maker.

Highly formalized mathematical procedures and sophisticated behavioral research techniques have been developed. The small businessman usually does not have the resources to conduct such research in great detail, and in most cases, he cannot afford to buy them.

The larger manufacturer, as the smaller firm, needs to minimize the costs in order to maximize the profits. Also, he will more likely want to do the market research "in house". This chapter should be beneficial to firms of all sizes, but especially to the smaller and/or relatively inexperienced firms.

There are various approaches to gathering data and solving marketing problems. Research is finding an answer to a question, and inelegant techniques combined with skilled imaginative judgment may surpass elegant techniques combined with timid unimaginative judgment.

Market researchers have a professional bias against the "quick and dirty" study. The bias is easily understood since pride in craftsmanship is involved as well as the fact that the researcher's reputation is "on the line". Moreover, once management learns that a researcher (or market research department) is willing to produce a cheap and quick study, they are likely to continue to press for such results unless they are "burned" badly. Gresham's Law applies to this situation: bad research tends to drive out good research.

Internal review was mentioned. Here there is *great* danger that responsible departments commit themselves prematurely to a position which they later feel they must defend.

Another danger with early research and evaluation is that the techniques used are often too powerful for application to the merger data available and will therefore lead to false conclusions that seem absolutely correct.

In trying to establish why a design is liked, it should be understood that large majority of consumers tend to reject "the way-out". Liking and familiarity tend to have a coefficient of correlation of $+0.50$. Designs that "look like money" tend to find favor. However, in the final analysis consumers find it difficult to verbalize why they like something

This chapter surveys the key decision points in new product planning and launching. It indicates basic data sources and simple techniques. At the same time, a reference is provided for corresponding sophisticated techniques.

THE MARKET RESEARCH LIBRARY

The large company is likely to have a good sized room or group of rooms, a librarian, and catalog files. The small firm should also have a library which may be maintained on a self service basis at a very low annual cost. The basic materials may consist of as little as the following:

1. Several books on marketing research methods
2. A few trade reference books
3. Relevant government publications giving statistical information on the United States and the particular industry
4. Trade magazines
5. Certain government periodicals
6. General business publications, such as *Business Week, the Wall Street Journal, Fortune* and *Forbes.*

The entire annual cost of such a library could be under $200 and be worth many times its cost. In addition to the suggestions above and those which follow below, the chapter bibliography will contain additional material suggestions which could be valuable.

In many respects, one of the best sources of market research data is the U.S. Government. While specific references will be cited, it is impossible to list even a small portion of the data available by

specific items. The following are just a few of the U.S. government agencies and departments which compile data useful to the businessman in market research:

Social Security Administration
Bureau of Census
Office of Business Economics
National Resources Board
Office of Educations
Food and Drug Administration
Office of Industry and Commerce
Office of International Trade
The Bureau of Mines
The Bureau of Labor Statistics
U.S. Employment Service
The U.S. Post Office
Federal Trade Commission
Interstate Commerce Commission
Bureau of Internal Revenue
The Fish and Wildlife Service

The Library of Congress publishes a "Monthly Check List of State Publications". This list only accounts for the announced type of state publications. It is difficult to keep up with the birth of new magazines, and therefore it is suggested that a book such as the *Annual Standard Rate and Data Service* which is published by the Standard Rate and Data Service Inc. of Chicago, Illinois be consulted to determine what trade and new product announcement type journals should be ordered for the library.

The founder of such a market research library should consider including among the business publications several of the magazines and publications produced by large brokerage houses such as Merrill Lynch, Pierce, Fenner and Smith, Inc., Bache, Inc., etc. In a similar manner, a general advisory service on stocks and investments, such as Value Line often contains information concerning industry trends and on competing companies that is valuable to the market researcher.

If you are involved in foreign markets, the governments of the countries in which you operate or will usually have publications of interest to businessmen of their country. The drawback of these and any foreign journals is the fact that they will not be in

English (in most cases) unless they are from an English speaking country. U.S. government publications such as *Foreign Commerce Weekly* and *Quarterly Summary of Foreign Commerce* may be helpful. The *Checklist of Bureau of Foreign Commerce Publications* provides a guide to government literature.

SOME BASIC QUESTIONS FOR THE NEW PRODUCT

Market research must be a continuing kind of activity since at frequent stages in the development of a new product, a decision must be made as to whether to continue or drop the product. Basic marketing questions must be answered each time. The initial screening usually only involves a rough estimate, but thereafter, the market answers publications made known to the Library of Congress, however, it covers a majority of such publications.

The various state departments of commerce as well as city planning and development commissions provide data, much of it without cost. If a product is to be sold, for example, to owners of automobiles, automobile registration data is available from all state governments.

The *Marketing Information Guide* published monthly by the Business and Defense Services Administration, U.S. Department of Commerce, is a valuable guide to marketing information; it is a continuation of the former *Distribution Data Guide*. Also, it is helpful to contact the local field offices of the U.S. Department of Commerce and the Small Business Administration to obtain additional information.

Bulletins 9 and 10 of the Department of Commerce will be of interest to market researchers since No. 9 provides some information sources regarding market research and No. 18 provides statistics and maps for use in national market analysis. In a similar manner, No. 42 provides basic information on new product development and sales. These are just a few of the government publications of value to a market researcher.

Many direct mail advertising specialists have lists of names and addresses broken down to various characteristics such as education, income, profession, etc. Other firms can supply lists of companies plus the names and titles of certain kinds of officers and/or managers by Standard Industrial Classification (SIC) number (An example: Thomas Publishing Company of New York City). Lists such as these are equally valuable for the sales and advertising functions.

Many of the trade magazines are free for the asking. Others require a paid subscription. The library certainly should contain as many of the data sources as possible since answers must come with ever-increasing precision. The questions include:

1. What is the total number of potential buyers available for the next five years by year at several selected prices?
2. What proportion of the market could be reached (contacted) by advertising and/or sales for various assumed levels of expenditures for advertising and selling efforts?
3. If there were no competition, what are estimated annual sales by year (probably by quarter for the first few years) for the next five years?
4. If competitors enter the market, what would annual sales be for the next five years by year (assume different entry points in order to thoroughly explore this problem)?
5. What is the "next-nearest-product", not other market?
6. What is the probable product life cycle?
7. What changes in the product would increase sales? Which should be sought, market segmentation or more mass distribution?
8. If there are various classes of customers and applications for the product, then questions 3, 4, 5 and 6 need further delineation (subdivided answers) with regard to this problem.
9. What channels of distribution would be most effective?
10. Should initial distribution start locally and expand, open regionally, or open nationally? In most cases the question will also involve breakdown to classes of customers and multiple channels of distribution.

Answering these and other questions involves

answering related questions (in some cases unrelated ones) as follows:

1. Are the potential buyers men, women, children or all of these or some of these?
2. What are the age groups?
3. Must they be engaged in specific occupations? If so, what are they?
4. Must they participate in certain forms of recreation or sports? If so, what are they?
5. Are they members of a particular religious group? If so, what is the group (or groups)?
6. Are they likely to be of a particular ethnic group? Which ones?
7. Will they likely read certain magazines? If so, which ones?
8. Must they be in a particular economic bracket? If so, which one?
9. Would they have certain styling expectations for the product as evidenced by their present purchases of similar or related products? If so, what are they?
10. How do they usually buy similar or related products?

Many other questions of a similar nature could be listed.

The second set of questions apply primarily to a consumer product market. In a similar manner, a market research effort for an industrial product involves asking and answering similar questions. Many of the questions already posed apply equally well to industrial products. However, in order to provide the reader with maximum information, the questions which follow apply very directly to market research concerning industrial products. The questions that logically should be investigated concerning potential customers for such products include:

1. Are the potential customers manufacturers of specific products? If so, what are they and what are their industry or product classifications? (More will be said later about classifications.)
2. Are they located in particular sections of the country? If so, what are they?
3. What members of the industrial organizations are the principal buying influences? What are their titles? Who are the individuals holding such titles, or how can lists of such individuals be obtained?

4. How and from whom are similar products purchased?
5. Are the buyers generally members of a particular trade association? If so, who are they and what association do they belong to?
6. Are the buyers readers of particular magazines or trade journals? If so, what are they?
7. Do the prospective buyers attend conventions and trade shows? If so, what are they and where are they held? What does it cost to exhibit?
8. Do the prospective customers have defined or undefined expectations concerning service to be associated with the product as based upon that experienced with similar or competing products? If so, what are they?
9. Do they have styling expectations as evidenced by present purchases of similar or related products? If so, what are they?
10. What loyalty might they have concerning existing brands or products offering a similar utility? How much?

The kinds of research conducted will depend upon whether the new product is a consumer item, an industrial product, or a product to be sold to a government or military organization.

CUSTOMER RESEARCH

Determining Market Potential by Identifying Consumers

It is extremely difficult and costly to change preferences and attitudes towards products, as many firms have learned to their sorrow. If a major change is required to sell a product, it probably should not be attempted by the very small firm. Therefore, the first step in consumer market research is to attempt to determine, from basic needs of people, current needs (conscious or subconscious) and *trends*. We must then try in some way to estimate the total number of people who form the arm-ket for the product, and how the potential customers view products similar to those being explored.

Figure 9-1 is an attempt to provide examples of how markets can be segmented and the segments identified. While the majority of examples relate mostly to consumer products, the classifications of individuals also have some relevance to industrial products and markets. Furthermore, some examples of the segmentation of industrial products are provided. Does *your* proposed new product satisfy one or more of these market classes as they presently exist? How will they change with time? For example, at various periods of historical crisis, a need to identify with conservatism may take a back seat relative to other needs.

New products may be related to or involved in a company strategy to pursue sales expansion through *product* differentiation. This is based on *market* differentiation or *segmentation*. Market segmentation consists of viewing the market as consisting of segments, each of which demands special features in a product and often different channels of distribution. The automobile company does not simply introduce a new car each year, it introduces one or more cars for the low income, middle income, and upper income families. It also segments by sports car lovers, 2-car families, prestige groups, etc. While its new products are not only differentiated from competitors' products by class of automobile, they are also aimed at the various *different* classes of customers (segments of the market). By these actions the automobile companies have expanded and sharpened their sales approach and will likely achieve greater total sales and profits.

Market segmentation is of obvious importance to not only the market research function, but also to the selling and advertising functions of marketing. The idea is that each segment has its own set of needs, tastes, and way of life and that a product, its advertising, its method of selling, its servicing, etc. can be designed to appeal to the market segment.

Some segments are obvious. Examples of these are denture wearers and the hard of hearing. Sex is a broad, but definite method of segmentation.

There are other reasons for segmentation than profit maximization or because of the functional needs of the firm. If a company has limited capital,

it may be forced into restricting its approach to a particular segment. Another reason may involve trying not to draw sales from another brand of the company. Still another is the belief (real or imagined) that wide appeals (those directed to the broad market) are weaker than appeals to segments which tend to be narrow appeals.

Marketing segmentation can be approached from both the product side or the market side.

Segmentation, to be worthwhile, must be relevant—there must be an identifiable tie between the product and the market segment.

For years, demographic and income segmentation were the principal modes. Today many are beginning to believe that psychological segmentation (an example would be by personality characteristics) is becoming of greater importance.

Once the idea of appealing to a certain market segment has been proposed on the basis of the type of need the product fulfills, the sizes and location of the market segments (classes or types of buyers) must be determined. Also, the best channel of distribution for each segment must be identified. It has been found that many consumer needs are closely related to:

1. Socio-economic characteristics
2. Age
3. Sex
4. Geographical region (in some cases)

For example, college-educated mothers between 30 and 35 years old, whose husbands earn from $20,000–$25,000 per year, and who live in northeastern U.S. suburban areas may be expected to have similar needs and to desire similar products. A few classifications of characteristics used to segment the consumer market are given in Figure 9-2. These classifications are helpful in guiding the market researcher in test market studies or in simple searches or statistical information already available.

In the early stages of product conception and development, the market researcher must establish the characteristics of the potential customers. He may then estimate market potential by referring to statistical sources such as those given in the annotated bibliography at the end of this chapter.

I Dividing the market on the need to economize. Here one can break it down to people who either need to or wish to be identified as having or being:

1. Thrifty
2. Frugal
3. Modest

4. Efficient
5. Saving
6. Minimizing expenses

7. Conservative
8. Simple tastes
9. Utilization in orientation

Related segmentation might be by:

1. Income Class ($5000–$7000)
2. Automobile owned (Volkswagen vs. Cadillac & Continental)
3. Housing type (assessed valuation $3000–$8000)
5. Savings accounts, savings bonds held

II Divide the market and/or appeal on the basis of personal vanity as evidenced by the need to be identified as:

1. Affluent
2. Wealthy
3. Social Leader
4. Successful
5. Wise
6. Influential
7. Artistic

8. Healthy
9. Powerful
10. Beautiful
11. Strong
12. Rugged
13. Witty
14. Fashionable

15. Athletic
16. Musical
17. Intellectual
18. Innovators or early
    adopters of new ideas
    and new products

Related segmentation might be by means of one or more identifiers such as the following:

1. Income level (e.g. $50,000 and up)
2. Housing type (e.g. assessed valuation over $30,000)
3. Primary living area (e.g. by neighborhood)
4. Reading Habits (e.g. magazines such as Vogue, Yachting, Holiday, Saturday Review, Fortune, etc.)
5. Recreation
6. Automobile owned (e.g. Cadillac, Continental, etc.)
7. Club membership (e.g. country clubs, yacht clubs)
8. Yacht ownership
9. Job (e.g. president, vice president, treasurer)
10. Church membership (e.g. many cities have churches identified as "wealthy congregation")
11. Listing in Who's Who, American Men of Science, or in one of the numerous other such rosters
12. Social registers, "best-dressed" lists

III Possible Segmentation based on the desire to be identified as a conservative could be related to the personal characteristics of:

1. Safety orientation
2. Moderation

3. Law and order
4. Unostentatious

5. Dependability
6. Tradition

People of these orientations could be identified by such as the following:

1. Political party membership (e.g. Republican)
2. Publications read (e.g. Daily Observer)
3. Association membership

4. Military rank (e.g. above Lieutenant)
5. Church membership (e.g. Mormon)
6. Civic action group membership

Figure 9-1

IV Market segmentation could be on the basis of appealing to those oriented toward:

1. Independence	5. Enjoyment	9. Permissiveness
2. Unconventionality	6. Being "a Christian"	10. Worrying
3. Sensuality	7. Dependence	11. Religious
4. Cleanliness	8. Loving	12. Sports

People possessing one of these characteristics might be identified by:

1. Church membership (Jehovah's Witnesses)
2. Club membership (Playboy Club, Nudist)
3. Magazine subscriber (Field & Stream, Sport Digest, etc.)
4. Resort attenders
5. Television viewing habits (for sports)

V Individuals can be market segmented by one or more of such general classification as:

1. Race	6. Age
2. Ethnic grouping	7. Education
3. Income	8. Political Views
4. Geographic Area	9. Socio-economic class
5. Family Status	10. Profession or occupation

These can be identified by:

1. Magazines read (Ebony, The Episcopalian, Field & Stream)
2. Income Level ($10,000 to $15,000 which in turn might be identified by position, trade)
3. Home retirement community resident, valuation of home)

VI On a more prosaic level, industrial markets can be segmentized by one or more classes such as the following:

1. Industry groups	7. Distribution channels
2. Products	8. Classes of materials purchased
3. Value of assets	9. Professions
4. Plant processes used	10. Managerial positions
5. Number of employees	11. Geographic area
6. Equipment utilized	

These in turn can be identified by means of such devices as:

1. Industrial Directories	4. Trade Shows and Fairs
2. Association Memberships	5. Professional institute memberships
3. Journals subscribed to	6. Licences held

Some possible approaches to market segmentation

Age—Years

1. Under 5
2. 5–9
3. 10–14
4. 15–19
5. 20–24

6. 25–34
7. 35–44
8. 45–54
9. 55–64
10. 65 and over

Dollars:

1. Under 1000
2. 1000–1999
3. 2000–2999
4. 3000–3999
5. 4000–4999

6. 5000–5999
7. 6000–7999
8. 8000–9999
9. 10,000–11,999
10. 12,000–14,999

11. 15,000–19,999
12. 20,000–29,999
13. 30,000–49,999
14. Over 50,000

Monthly Rent Dollars:

1. Less than 40
2. 40–49
3. 50–59
4. 60–69

5. 70–79
6. 80–99
7. 100–119
8. 120–139

9. 140–159
10. 160–179
11. 180–199
12. 200 or more

Values of Owner-Occupied Nonfarm Housing Units (Dollars)

1. Less than 5000
2. 5000–7499
3. 7500–9999
4. 10,000–12,499
5. 13,000–14,999

6. 15,000–17,499
7. 17,500–19,999
8. 20,000–24,999
9. 25,000–34,999
10. 35,000 or more

Socio-Economic Strata[1]

Class	Description
Upper upper	Families with old wealth: certainly Henry Cabot Lodge, probably Henry Ford II, possibly Jack Kennedy prior to election
Lower upper	Old families with declining wealth, the newer wealthy, some persons with prestigious jobs: J. Paul Getty, Sam Goldwyn, Barry Goldwater, possibly the local millionaire
Upper middle	Well off, well educated with respected job or profession: the doctor, the bank officer, the corporation executive, the newspaper editor
Lower middle	Salaried, probably high-school education: the proprietor of the small store, the clerical worker, the superviser, the fireman
Upper lower	The hourly wage earner, grammar-school education: the retail sales clerk, the carpenter, the small farmer
Lower lower	Little education, irregular job: the migrant laborer, the tenant farmer, the slum dweller

Education (completed)

1. 8th grade or less
2. 9–12 grade
3. Some college

4. Bachelor's degree
5. Master's degree
6. Doctoral degree

Marital Status

1. Single (never married)
2. Married

3. Divorced or separated
4. Widowed

Other Characteristics

1. Sex
2. Ethnic origin or language group (Italian, Spanish, Polish, etc.)
3. Race

4. Religion
5. Urban, suburban, farm and rural
6. Occupation or occupational group

Figure 9-2   Consumer Characteristics
Source: W. T. Tucker, *The Social Context Economic Behavior*, Holt-Rinehart and Winston, Inc., 1964

As the company invests more money in the development of the new product, more refined estimates of market potential are necessary. A probability or sample survey to determine the market potential may be advisable if the value of the information is estimated to exceed the cost of obtaining it. Actually, a relatively small sample making use of probability or statistical theory, say about 1200 respondents, may give good precision for the entire country. The precision of the estimate of buyers (from a statistical viewpoint) depends only on the sample size and not the population.

The small-business manager may be able to purchase information on market potential for products similar to his own from trade associations. If his product is completely new and different and a large investment will be required, he should consider purchasing market research.[1] Some of the market research organizations maintain national panels which can be used to test the marketability of a consumer product.

Identifying the customers for an industrial product, not only as to type but also as to quantity is usually far more simple. Many industrial products are aimed at solving a particular industry's problem. The companies making up the given industry are relatively easy to identify from the kinds of sources already indicated.

If the industrial product solves a particular kinds or class of problems, it sometimes is necessary to determine what kind of industry would contain or present such problems. If there are far more classes of industries that contain the problem than do not contain it, then try to identify the ones who do not contain the problem.

The economic considerations, in other words, does the purchase of an industrial product offer an economic advantage to the purchasing company, are always the overriding question. Not only must the new product provide this advantage, but it also must be *provable*. In some cases, the proving of the economic advantage ranges from very difficult to impossible due to such things as lack of enough detailed data as it exists in the involved industries, the great variability in costing techniques (many of which are discussed in a later chapter), prejudices for or against a particular kind of problem or approach, etc.

DETERMINING MARKET POTENTIAL BY INDENTIFYING RELATED PRODUCT AND REPLACEMENT MARKET

If the new product will be sold in conjunction with an item whose sales are known or which could be closely estimated, then the potential for the new product may be determined with relative ease. Some representative primary items, on which quarterly production data exist are houses, batteries, automobiles, computers, boats, etc.

Let us suppose that we have developed a new and more efficient type of hot water heater. Then almost every house represents a potential "customer". This market could logically be segmented into (1) new construction, (2) the replacement market represented by "in service heaters that failed", and (3) installed heaters that have not yet failed in service. For the replacement market and the "good, but in service" market; one must first determine the number of

homes in existence; then one must determine the average life of hot water heaters. Suppose the average life is 10 years; then a rough estimate is that 10 per cent of hot water heaters will need to be replaced each year. At the end of a year the "good, but in service" market will be total homes minus 10 per cent. This is a rather "simple minded" approach. The new construction market can be approached in a similar manner. Since data on the number of new homes constructed is available from the U.S. government; these new homes minus the units sold to the new housing market, should be added to the remainder from the above replacement market calculation to establish the third market category mentioned above. Of course, the "$64 question" is, how many heaters can be sold to each market?

With respect to the new house market for water heaters, the actual purchaser may be the contractor, the purchaser of the home, or original equipment manufacturer in the case of homes built by an industrial firm. The new home market for water heaters is therefore logically segmented into three classifications. One of these classes, the purchaser of the home, is a direct consumer. The same promotion material will serve for such customers, the replacement market customer and the home owner operating a more inefficient water heater.

When the consumer may either specify the product or purchase it himself, it may be viewed as a consumer good. This means that the design and promotion are directed to the consumer.

SALES FORECASTING

The above methods were concerned with how to estimate and predict the total sales potential. Here we are to be concerned with predicting the portion of the market or markets that the company can sell each year over the product's life cycle. The factors which must be considered are:
1. Price
2. Quality (design and manufacturing)
3. Merchandising effort (what is spent on selling and advertising)

4. Competitors' efforts (quality and quantity of merchandising efforts)

It should be remembered that costs decrease with volume and experience in producing and marketing a product. Further, the new product developer must be concerned with the interrelationships among (1) business and market conditions, (2) our efforts and those of competitors, and (3) cost, price, and profit as shown in Figure 9-3.

In order to forecast sales a trial and error search process is usually used (unless it is possible to go to very sophisticated mathematical and/or computer techniques) to find how much one should spend to maximize profits. The steps needed to accomplish this task would normally be approximately as follows:

1. Forecast general business conditions. A simple forecasted index is the Gross National Product. However, forecast for the specific industry involved or for a closely related industry usually yields more accurate results.

2. Estimate the market potential for the new product or by market segment and/or channel of distribution.

3. Assume a certain product quality, degree of newness, ruggedness, output or rate of output, projected life, etc.

4. Assume a selling price.

5. Assume a specified level of sales. This is a best-guess estimate based on the assumed selling price.

6. Estimate average variable cost (defined in detail in the chapter on costing) per unit for the sales level. Remember that unit variable cost will decrease. The greater the total sales, the less the unit variable cost for the last unit (see chapter X for a discussion of the effect of the "experience factor" on costs).

7. Check unit price against unit variable cost to make sure there is a "reasonable" margin (discussed in the chapters on costing and on pricing).

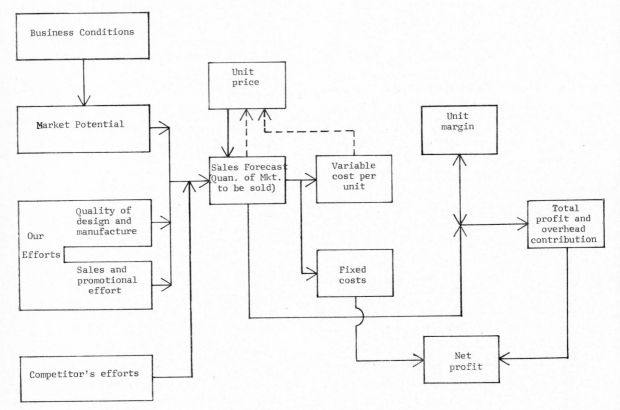

Figure 9-3   Interrelationships

8. Estimate the impact of competitors' efforts on sales as forecasted at the assumed price. This may be negligible or serious; in any event sales should then be re-forecast and a new unit margin computed.

9. Find total gross profit and overhead contribution by multiplying unit margin by sales volume. Deduct fixed costs to find net profit (see the chapters on costing and pricing for more detail).

10. Assume another price and repeat calculation of new product profit. Try several other prices and repeat in order to find an appropriate optimum price.

11. Change the quality of design and manufacture and try several prices for the net profit computation.

12. Try various values for expenditures on sales and promotional effort with various prices to obtain the resulting net profits.

13. Select the combination of efforts and unit price which appears to achieve the best net profit.

Ideally, the company should conduct an experiment in the market place to derive an estimate of total sales for various combinations of price, effort, and competitors' efforts. Practically, this is not always possible. It is sometimes possible to conduct limited experiments to increase the information required to reduce the risk of the decision to launch a product.

Theoretically most texts tell the market researcher to plot the price-volume relationship and then find the price which will yield maximum revenue. Obtaining the necessary data is *extremely* difficult in most cases.

In the past researchers asked consumers what they would be willing to pay. Here the respondents tended to substantially overstate what they would pay. Also, respondents who named a low price often wouldn't buy at any price.

Another approach is to present a range of prices. Here respondents usually pick a price in the middle regardless of the range used.

Still another tactic is to present a range of prices, i.e. Would you pay $1.98 (if yes), how about $2.49? etc. Respondents tend to keep on say-

ing yes or no, once having started on a given track.

A more modern approach is to (1) make sure that the respondent understands the product, if possible he should see and handle it and taste it (if taste is involved). He should have literature to read (and time to read it). Advantages *and* disadvantages should be presented realistically.

(2) No respondent should be quoted more than one price. This means that mutli-cell samples are required. Respondents in each cell are quoted a different price.

(3) As a control measure, some similar product currently on the market about which the firm has some information should be presented to each respondent.

The above procedures can produce reasonably accurate demand curves and a measure of the price elasticity of a new product.

The cost of reliable and valid information regarding the entire system of Figure 9-3 is likely to be expensive and even impossible. The strategy should therefore be to obtain those *bits* of information which will be most useful to the management in making necessary estimates.

The large sophisticated company will employ probability sampling techniques as described in Leslie Kish, *Survey Sampling* (New York: John Wiley & Sons, 1965), or experimental design research as described in Seymour Banks, *Experimentation in Marketing* (New York: McGraw-Hill, 1965).

Statistical techniques such as Monte Carlo simulation, decision trees, Bayesian estimates, and modeling with computers are used. Edgar A. Pessemier, *New Product Decisions: An Analytical Approach* (New York: McGraw-Hill, 1966) gives a lucid practical description of many of these techniques. A model which has been field-tested is described in A. Charnes, et al., Demon: "A Management Model for Marketing New Products", *California Management Review*, Fall 1968. This network, developed for computerized analysis, integrates financial, marketing, and production considerations into a comprehensive practical plan for action.

The small business firm will likely use judgmental forecasting techniques such as:

1. One-man judgment. This works best when there is an extremely intuitive individual in the company with considerable knowledge and "feel" for the market.
2. Executive group judgment. The combined views of E & R, Marketing, and Production are reconciled to yield a forecast.
3. Sales force composite. Salesmen after being given base parameters are requested to submit sales estimates to their managers. These are reviewed and set to the company's top management after they have been combined into a total forecast.[2]

FIELD TESTS

Field tests or checks can be made before and after development. Regardless of when it is done, in making a field check in order to determine probable sales it is advisable to have some way of detecting when one has contacted enough people to obtain a reasonably firm estimate of sales potential. One way of accomplishing this task is to determine the trend of one's questioning and/or sales effort by means of graphical analysis of data. This is relatively easy to do and can, for example, be applied to the analysis to any one or all (on an individual or group basis) of the answers to questions being recorded in a custom-

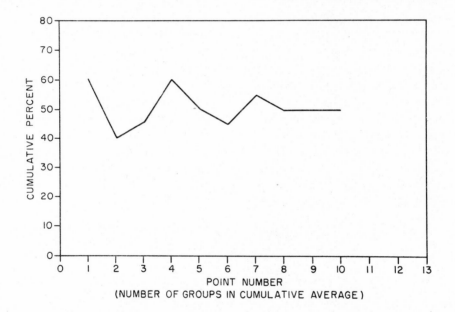

The question posed for the plotting of Figure 9-4 was "would you buy this product if it were available at a price of $150.00 by the XLZ Company and sold through manufacturing engineering sales representatives?" Obviously, there had to be a prior explanation of the product, how it was to be marketed, etc. Answers from groups made up of 5 potential cusmoters were averaged.

The detailed procedure of doing this is as follows:

Computation for Determining Point No. 1 (Includes Group 1 only)	Computation for Determining Point No. 2 (Includes Groups 1 and 2)
Yes 3	1 etc.
No $\frac{2}{5}$	$\frac{4}{5}$
$\frac{3}{5} = 60\%$	$\frac{4}{10} = 40\%$

This procedure can be expressed by the formula:

$$\text{Cummulative average in percent of yes replies} = \frac{\text{yes replies}}{\text{total queries}} \times 100$$

Figure 9-4 Graph showing typical method of plotting cumulative average
Source: D. W. Karger, *The New Product*, The Industrial Press, 1960

er survey. It can also be applied to a test marketing or sales effort.

The basic technique is to plot the cumulative average of the answers or other results and visually determine when a reasonably correct average has been attained. This is done by noting when the wide fluctuations in variance cease and when the plot begins to approach a straight line. Remember that this technique can be applied to answers to questions or to a sample sales effort—the basic procedure is the same. What follows for illustrative purposes involves the answers to a question.

In order to be able to plot an average of the answers to any one question, it will be necessary to so phrase the question that a yes or no answer will be received—or at least something approximating this. One can then plot the cumulative average of the yes's and no's.

In order to make the job a little easier, also to make it come out better; users of this technique usually plot cumulative averages of 5, 10, 25, or 50 answers. The size of the group chosen depends at least partially upon the number of potential customers and how many can be contacted each day or week. A practical group number would be the answers from those contacted during the average day. The graph will usually have an appearance similar to that shown in Figure 9-4.

TEST MARKETING

When the new product is completely developed or when several versions of it are completely developed, the manufacturer can estimate its market reception by making a limited quantity and marketing these units in one or several typical limited market areas. This is the last step in the evaluation process.

As an example, consider the case of the company which developed two shampoos which might have been marketed as liquid-cream shampoos. One was white and creamy; the other contained a perfume or fragrance which made it slightly brownish in color. Which should the company market, or should it market both? Two groups of markets (one for each product) were selected so that the groups were matched with respect to major marketing characteristics. A panel of stores was set up in each market and each store audited to determine the relative rate of movement and share of the total shampoo market each shampoo would achieve in its group of markets. On the basis of this test marketing, the white-creamy product was selected alone and later achieved considerable success.

Sounds like an easy and sure process? Don't bet on it. Test marketing is one of the most frustrating and difficult exercises. The market used usually is not representative of "the" market and often funds are not available for tests in several markets. Snowstorms, strikes and other acts of God, and the competition can and often do confuse the results.

The product should be introduced in a natural manner, no different than the ultimate plan calls for. Do not tell *anyone* it is a test or they will invariably do things to confuse the results. The administrative detail required is of significant magnitude.

Don't draw too quick a conclusion. Competition almost always develops and changes the result from what was experienced. The reader should *not* conclude from this remark that market research should not be pursued.

INDUSTRIAL PRODUCT RESEARCH

Determining Market Potential

It is usually far easier to determine the market potential of a product which is to be sold to industrial or service companies. Most of what has been said relative to a consumer product can be applied to an industrial product. The main reason it is easier to market research an industrial product is that there are almost always a relatively limited number of such companies likely to consider purchasing such a product as compared with the total number of people making up consumer product markets. Further, various financial, product, and statistical information is usually available on business firms. Often an industrial product is directed only at a particular industry, or to a particular application. In addition, the basic need which a new industrial product must

The SIC system (available from the Superintendent of Documents, U.S. Government Printing Office) provides a classification of business establishments by tape of activity. It is employed for the purpose of facilitating collection, tabulators, presentation, and analysis of data and for promoting uniformity and comparability in the presentation of statistical data collected by various public and private agencies. Although there are subclassifications up to 7 digits, the two-digit code structure provides the primary activity of establishments. Two-digit classifications are:

Division A—Agriculture, forestry and fisheries

01 commercial farms
02 noncommercial farms
07 agricultural services, hunting and trapping
08 forestry
09 fisheries

Division B—Mining

10 metal mining
11 anthracite mining
12 bituminous coal and lignite mining
13 crude petroleum and natural gas
14 mining and quarrying of non-metallic minerals except gas

Division C—Contract construction

15 building construction—general contractors
16 construction other than building construction—general contractors
17 construction—special trade contractors

Division D—Manufacturing

19 ordinance and accessories
20 food and kindred products
21 tobacco manufacturers
22 textile mill products
23 apparel and other finished products made from fabrics and other similar materials
24 lumber and wood products except furniture
25 furniture and fixtures
26 paper and allied products
27 printing, publishing, and allied industries
28 chemicals and allied industries
29 petroleum refining and related industries
30 rubber and miscellaneous plastic products
31 leather and leather products
32 stone, clay and glass products
33 primary metal industries
34 fabricated metal products, except ordinance, machinery and transportation equipment
35 machinery, except electrical
36 electrical machinery, equipment
37 transportation equipment
38 professional, scientific, and controlling instruments—photographic, optical, watches and clocks
39 miscellaneous manufacturing industries

Division E—Transportation, communication, electric, gas and sanitary services

40 railroad transportation

41 local and suburban transit and interurban passenger transportation
42 motor freight transportation and warehousing
44 water transportation
45 transportation by air
46 pipeline transportation
47 transportation services
48 communication
49 electric, gas, and sanitary services

Division F—Wholesale and retail trade

52 retail trade—building materials, hardware, and farm equipment
53 retail trade—general merchandise
54 retail trade—food
55 automotive dealers and gas service stations
56 retail trade—apparel and accessories
57 retail trade—furniture, home furnishings and equipment
58 retail trade—eating and drinking places
59 retail trade—miscellaneous retail stores

Division G—Finance, insurance and real estate

60 banking
61 credit agencies other than banks
62 security and commodity brokers, dealers exchanges and services
63 insurance carriers
64 insurance agents, brokers and services
65 real estate
66 combinations of real estate, insurance, loans and law offices
67 holding and other investment companies

Division H—Services

70 hotels, rooming houses, camps and other lodging places
72 personal services
73 miscellaneous bus services
74 automobile repair, services and garages
76 miscellaneous repair services
78 motion pictures
79 amusement and recreation services except motion pictures
80 medical and other health services
81 legal services
82 educational services
84 museums, art galleries, botanical and zoological gardens
86 nonprofit membership organizations
88 private households
89 miscellaneous services

Division I—Government

91 Federal government
92 state government
93 local government
94 international

Division J—Nonclassifiable establishments

99 nonclassifiable establishments.

Figure 9-5 SIC List

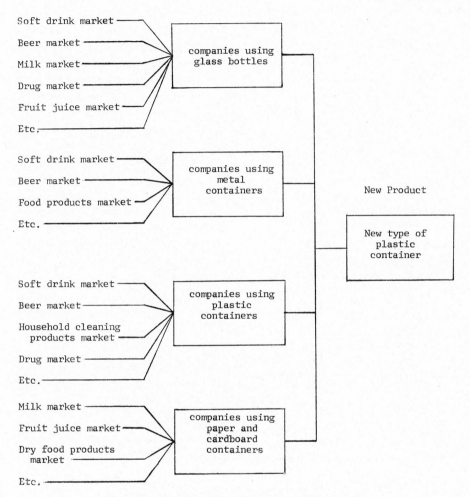

1. Determine trends
   for companies
   such as these

2. Determine container
   needs and trends
   for these companies

3. Determine market
   potential in
   terms of likely
   substitution for
   our new product

Soft drink market

Beer market

Milk market

Drug market

Fruit juice market

Etc.

companies using
glass bottles

Soft drink market

Beer market

Food products market

Etc.

companies using
metal
containers

New Product

New type of
plastic
container

Soft drink market

Beer market

Household cleaning
products market

Drug market

Etc.

companies using
plastic
containers

Milk market

Fruit juice market

Dry food products
market

Etc.

companies using
paper and
cardboard
containers

Figure 9-6   Market analysis for an industrial product

fulfill is usually an economic one. That is, it must lower the cost of the customer's production or improve the quality of his product or fill a previously unfilled need.

If the product is suitable only for a particular industry, there is very likely a trade association which can supply information about the firms in the industry. (See list of references at the end of this chapter for directories.) If the product is suitable for a number of industries, the market researcher should try to identify these from the Standard In-

dustrial Classification list in Figure 9-5. Considerable government and trade association information is available on SIC-identified industries. States publish industrial directories which list companies in the state, their products, their SIC members, their sizes, and often additional information. An increasing number of states are now offering such listings on computer tapes to facilitate analysis.

It is not enough simply to determine what firms would be able to benefit by the product today. Too often, mail surveys are carried which yield only this limited information. What is important are trends. For example, suppose that we develop a new type of glass container. Next it is discovered that companies presently use X glass containers per year, Y metal containers, and Z plastic containers. Suppose that we then studied the trends in sales of each of these three types of containers and discovered that companies have been rapidly shifting away from glass containers. Then before we introduce our new container we obviously should find out the reason for the trend to other types before preparing to sell to a rapidly de-creasing market. However, many companies fail to conduct such elementary market research or analysis.

Another way we can sharpen up the market potential determination is to identify potential customers and then examine the *economic activity trends of our customers' customers*. We can then forecast the expansion or contraction of purchases we might expect to be placed with us. Figure 9-6 clarifies this point.

Let us take an example of how market potential may be estimated from available data.

CASE A[3]

Corrugated Boxes Inc.

Objective:

To estimate the total market potential for corrugated and solid fibre boxes in a given area
Kind of Business:
Manufacturer of corrugated and solid fibre boxes

Problem:

The sales manager of a company manufacturing corrugated and solid fibre boxes in one of the Mountain States decided that he wanted to intensify the company's States efforts in Arizona, one of the States which the firm served. In the Phoenix Standard Metropolitan Statistical Area (coextensive with Maricopa County), for example, the firm's sales totaled $250,000 in 1963—$200,000, or 80 percent, to firms within the food and kindred products industry, and the remaining $50,000, or 20 percent, to firms manufacturing electrical machinery, equipment, and supplies. The sales manager felt this was a very poor sales record considering the diversity of industry in the Phoenix area.

In view of this preliminary analysis, he decided to determine the market potential for fibre boxes in the Phoenix area as the first step in establishing the firm's sales potential (or market share) and setting a realistic sales quota for the area.

Source of Data:

(1) *County Business Patterns, First Quarter 1962.*
(2) *1962 Annual Survey of Manufactures: General Statistics for Industry Groups and Industries.*
(3) *Fibre Box Statistics 1963.*

Procedure:

In order to estimate the total market potential for corrugated and solid-fibre boxes on an industry-by-industry basis, it was concluded that the initial ana-lysis should be based on "end use" or consumption statistics as a means of determining the extent to which various industry groups use such products.[1] Consumption per employee was determined by applying national employment data of each 2-digit SIC industry to the level or corrugated and solid fibre boxes used by each industry. The potential for Maricopa County was then determined by applying county employment data to arrive at the market potential for each using industry in the county. The 5-step procedure is shown below. The results appear in Table A-1.

(1) Value of fibre container shipments by industry was arrived at by applying end-use percentage data from source 3 to total U.S. shipments of the fibre box industry from Source 2. The resulting dollar values appear in column 1 of Table A-1.

(2) Total U.S. and Maricopa County employment in each of the using industries were determined from Source 1. Columns 2 and 4 of Table A-1 shows these data.

(3) Consumption per employee in each of the using industries were calculated by dividing data in column 1 by column 2. The results appear in column 3.

(4) An estimate of the value of fibre box use by each industry in Maricopa County was then obtained by multiplying the consumption per employee data in column 3 by county employment in column 4. The resulting dollar estimate for each 2-digit industry in Maricopa County appears in column 5.

(5) Total market potential in Maricopa County was obtained by adding the potential for individual industries.

---

[1] Although the distribution of the fibre box industry among using industries could have been based with some modefication upon the input-output analysis of the Office of Business Economics, it was decided to use a classification of corrugated and fibre box shipments by end use published by the Fibre Box Association. See: U.S. Office of Business Economics, *Survey of Current Business,* November 1964, pp. 10–29; and Fibre Box Association, *Fibre Box Industry Statistics 1963,* p. 15.

Table A-1   Estimated Market for Corrugated and Solid Fibre Box by Industry Groups, Phoenix, Arizona
Standard Metropolitan Statistical Area, 1962

SIC Major Group Code	Using Industry	Value of Box Shipments by End Use ($ 000)[1]	Employment by Industry Groups[3]	Consumption per Employee by Industry Groups (1 + 2) (Dollars)	Maricoya County	
					Employment by Industry Groups[3]	Estimated Share of the Market (3 × 4) ($ 000)
		1	2	3	4	5
20	Food & Kindred Products	586,164	1,578,305	371	4973	1845
21	Tobacco	17,432	74,557	233	—	—
22	Textile Mill Products	91,520	874,677	104	—	—
23	Apparel	34,365	1,252,443	27	1974	53
24	Lumber & Products (except furniture)	19,611	526,622	37	600	26
25	Furniture & Fixtures	89,341	364,166	245	616	151
26	Paper & Allied Products	211,363	587,882	359	190	63
27	Printing; Publishing, & Allied Industries	32,686	504,208	36	2876	104
28	Chemicals & Allied Products	123,564	772,169	100	400	81
29	Petroleum Refining & Related Industries	28,328	161,367	175	—	—
30	Rubber & Misc. Plastic Products	67,551	387,997	174	190	33
31	Leather & Leather Prod.	8,716	352,919	24	—	—
32	Stone, Clay & Glass Prod.	226,621	548,058	413	1612	666
33	Primary Metal Industries	19,611	1,168,110	16	2889	25
34	Fabricated Metal Products	130,743	1,062,096	123	2422	298
35	Machinery; except Electrical	58,834	1,445,558	40	5568	223
36	Electrical Machinery, Equipment & Supplies	119,848	1,405,382	301	6502	553
37	Transportation Equipment	82,804	1,541,618	53	5005	265
38	Professional, Scientific Instruments, etc.	13,074	341,796	38	—	—
39	Misc. Manufacturing Industries	200,473	369,071	543	376	204
90	Government	10,895	—	—	—	—
	Total	2,179,049[2]	—	—	—	4616

[1] Based on data reported in *Fibre Box Industry Statistics 1968*, Fibre Box Association.

[2] U.S. Bureau of the Census, *1962 Annual Survey of Manufacturers: General Statistics for Industry Groups and Industries* (M 62 (AS)-1 Revised) Table 1—General Statistics for Industry Groups and Industries: 1962, 1961, and 1958, p. 10.

[3] U.S. Bureau of the Census, *County Business Patterns, First Quarter 1962*, Parts 1 and 9.

Conclusion:

With a market potential for corrugated and solid fibre boxes totaling $4,616,000 in the Phoenix, Arizona area, the sales manager concluded that this company sales of $250,000 in Phoenix constituted 5.4 per cent of the Total market potential and was considerably less than he had originally imagined.

More importantly, he learned that the firm had no sales in a number of 2-digit industries which used a considerable quantity of corrugated and solid-fibre boxes. The furniture and fixtures industry (SIC 25), for example, was consuming approximately $151,000 of such boxes, yet the firm had no sales in this industry group. The stone, clay, and glass products in-

dustry (SIC 32) was even a larger untapped market with a corrugated shipping container consumption of $666,000.

In light of these and other findings, the sales manager decided that his sales potential for the Phoenix area should be based upon the company's sales accomplishment in the food and kindred products industry where its market share was 10.8 percent ($200,000 ÷ $1,845,000). Thus, the initial sales quota for the Phoenix area was set at $498,528 ($4,616,000 × 10.8 percent) or more than double the sales for the preceding year. Each industry group in turn was assigned a sales quory equal to 10.8 percent of its market potential, e.g. the apparel group (SIC 23) received a sales quota of $5724 ($53,000 × 10.8 percent).

SALES FORECASTING

A new product may either replace present products or it may perform a completely new function whose need may or may not have been recognized. If the new product is a substitute for a current one, it may only be sold for new facilities, it may fill a replacement market, or it may be so superior that the current products in use may be removed to make way for it. Different customers will perceive the product differently, depending on the company's marketing and product quality effort. Salesmen's estimates questionnaires sent to potential customers, and executive judgmental forecasts represent various approaches to forecasting. More expensive is the test marketing procedure of selecting a random sample of customers and exposing them to the product and selling effort. The percentage of the sample that purchases is an estimate of the percentage of all customers who will purchase.

Forecasting is complicated by a factor related or associated with advertising.[4] This factor is highlighted by the difference in views held by rapid consumarists, economists and those of industry. The consumerist believes that advertising is extremely persuasive and results in undesirable allocations of consumer expenditure. The economists generally hold that such expenditures are ineffectual and an economic waste. Industry obviously allocates funds to advertising and thereby must believe it is necessary—but how necessary and of exactly what value, is unknown. No one really knows exactly how advertising works.

This problem as it concerns forecasting is further complicated by the fact that most market research activity approaches its work with the hidden assumption that the marketing problem is to increase the company's share of a *static* market.

Sometimes the market researchers (upon whose results the sales forecast depends) do not deal properly with product differentiation, products often are *substantially* different (example: Tang vs. frozen or canned orange juice) whereas they act as if no real difference exists.

A more comprehensive approach to industry forecasting is outlined in Figure 9-7. This method involves statistical techniques, economic analyses, and mathematical models for projection.

Large companies are currently developing sophisticated computer-based Marketing Information and Decision Systems. These systems are total-business oriented procedures and methods for planned collection, storage and dissemination of information required for making marketing decisions. Built-in mathematical models often yield the results of integrated economic, marketing, production, and financial analyses to aid the decision maker. Figure 9-8 indicates the general nature of these systems with illustrative benefits. Figure 9-9 shows schematically the operative system at Mead Johnson.

Further, market researchers and marketers often are confused about the nature of competition. Consumerists and many government officials think only in terms of price competition. Yet, most (but not all) consumer goods marketers usually mean competition for differential advantage.

Finally, the factor involves another concept—that of "value added". Most people view this as an increase in value due to the investment or application of *factory* labor. Yet if one can sell a product for a higher price by advertising it strongly, hasn't value been added in the eyes of the buyer? Here is a big area for further study.

While no solutions are offered in the above discussion, it is hoped that it will provide the reader with a better insight to the problems of forecasting.

DEFENSE PRODUCTS MARKET RESEARCH

The small-business manager enters a high risk market if he directs his new products towards defense applications or many of the more complicated governmental markets such as NASA or AEC. Budgetary changes, competitive bidding, red tape,

Procedure for Forecasting Sales

Steps

Analysis

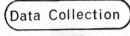

—historical price-volume movements
—trends in end-use applications, technology, substitute materials
—announced plant expansions, new suppliers, new processes, ore reserves
—competitors' long-range plans, marketing strategies, R & D
—trends in foreign trade, distribution facilities, freight rates
—projected movements in pertinent economic indicators

—major factors influenced demand, supply and price
—cause and effect relationships
—evaluation of industry problems, threats and opportunities for new business

—graphical projection of historical demand data
—correlation of historical demand with economic indicators, inventory and price changes
—interrelationships among substitute products, grades and geometrical demand
—selection of major variables, interaction terms, transformations
—assumptions stated and evaluated for realism

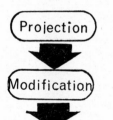

—statistical demand projection made for industry
—confidence limits established

—subjective modification of statistical projection for qualitative and irregular influences

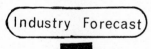

—total demand, by product grade, geographical market and end-use
—total supply, both domestic production and imports
—future demand-supply balance
—price outlock

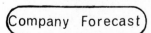

—projection of company's historical market share trend
—evaluation of competitors' long-range plans, product innovations, market strategy
—analysis of company's long-range plans, product quality and marketing strategy
—subjective modification and forecast of company's historical market share trend
sales and price forecast for company's participation

Figure 9-7 Industrial forecasting
Source: Donald J. Smalter, Director, Assistant to the President in Charge of Diversification and Planning,
Freeport Sulphur Company, N.Y.

BENEFITS POSSIBLE WITH A SOPHISTICATED MIS

	TYPICAL APPLICATIONS	BENEFITS	EXAMPLES
CONTROL SYSTEMS	1. Control of marketing costs.	1. More timely computerized reports.	1. Undesirable cost trends are spotted more quickly so that corrective action may be taken sooner.
	2. Diagnosis of poor sales performance.	2. Flexible on-line retrieval of data.	2. Executives can ask supplementary questions of the computer to help pinpoint reasons for a sales decline and reach an action decision more quickly.
	3. Management of fashion goods.	3. Automatic spotting of problems and opportunities.	3. Fast-moving fashion items are reported daily for quick reorder, and slow-moving items are also reported for fast price reductions.
	4. Flexible promotion strategy.	4. Cheaper, more detailed, and more frequent reports.	4. On-going evaluation of a promotional campaign permits reallocation of funds to areas behind target.
PLANNING SYSTEMS	1. Forecasting.	1. Automatic translation of terms and classifications between departments.	1. Survey-based forecasts of demand for complex industrial goods can be automatically translated into parts requirements and production schedules.
	2. Promotional planning and corporate long-range planning.	2. Systematic testing of alternative promotional plans and compatibility testing of various divisional plans.	2. Complex simulation models both developed and operated with the help of data bank information can be used for promotional planning by product managers and for strategic planning by top management.
	3. Credit management.	3. Programmed executive decision rules can operate on data bank information.	3. Credit decisions are automatically made as each order is processed.
	4. Purchasing.	4. Detailed sales reporting permits automation of management decisions.	4. Computer automatically repurchases standard items on the basis of correlation of sales data with programmed decision rules.
RESEARCH SYSTEMS	1. Advertising strategy.	1. Additional manipulation of data is possible when stored for computers in an unaggregated file.	1. Sales analysis is possible by new market segment breakdowns.
	2. Pricing strategy.	2. Improved storage and retrieval capability allows new types of data to be collected and used.	2. Systematic recording of information about past R & D contract bidding situations allows improved bidding strategies.
	3. Evaluation of advertising expenditures.	3. Well-designed data banks permit integration and comparison of different sets of data.	3. Advertising expenditures are compared to shipments by county to provide information about advertising effectiveness.
	4. Continuous experiments.	4. Comprehensive monitoring of input and performance variables yields information when changes are made.	4. Changes in promotional strategy by type of customer are matched against sales results on a continuous basis.

Figure 9-8   Marketing Information System
Source: Donald F. Cox and Robert E. Good, "How to Build a Marketing Information System",
Harvard Business Review, May–June 1967, p. 146

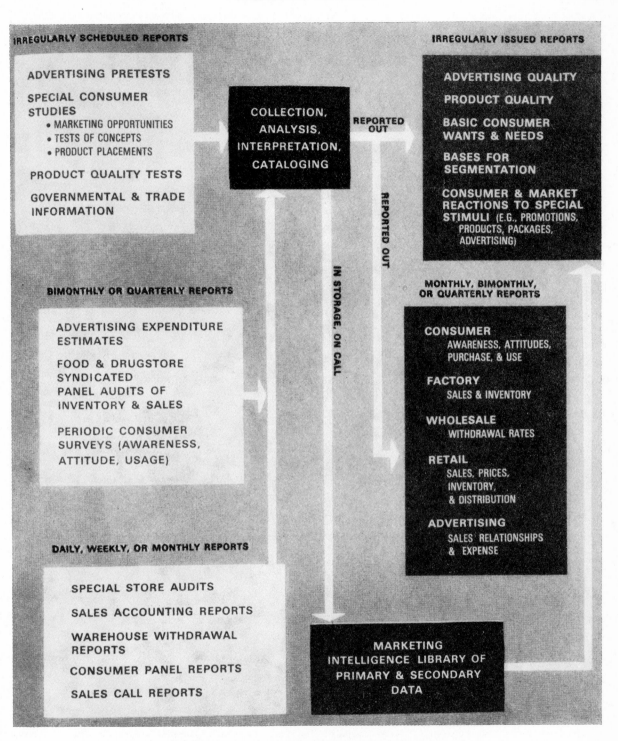

Figure 9-9   Mead Johnson's Marketing Intelligence System
Source: Lee Adier, "Systems Approach to Marketing", *Harvard Business Review*, May–June, 1967, p. 111

and rapid technological change make this a hazardous area. An approach may be to only offer to sell catalog items. Proposals for development and/or manufacturing of products is highly complicated in this market. If a company elects to enter this market, it is necessary to maintain good contacts among prime contractors as well as government officials. Further, the management of the company should obtain information on trends in defense and space procurement. It will probably pay the company to hire some people who have experience in selling, engineering and producing for this market. (See the reference list at the end of this chapter regarding market information sources).

A FINAL WARNING

The market researcher and top management should be guided by market research, but not "blinded" by it. Quantitative observation of these factors which may have considerable impact on the market are important. *Trends* should be sought, not just facts about the present situation. In complex situations, the small-business researcher may supply key bits of information which, when combined with the judgment of management, may at times surpass the most sophisticated models of the giant firms. This is evidenced by the small new companies which succeed in bucking entrenched products.

Finally, designers are often distrustful of consumer research since it is always unsettling to have one's good taste overruled by the average taste of the market—and it is an average sort of taste.

REFERENCES

1. For a list of such companies, write to the American Marketing Association, 230 North Michigan Avenue, Chicago, 60601. See also *Bradford's Directory of Marketing Research Agencies in the United States and in the World* obtained from 50 Argyle Ave., New Rochelle, N.Y., 10804.
2. For a discussion, with case examples, of sales forecasting of consumer durables and soft goods for small companies, see Robert G. Murdick and Arthur E. Schaefer, *Sales Forecasting for Lower Costs and Higher Profits* (Englewood Cliffs, N.J., Prentice-Hall, Inc., 1967).

3. U.S. Department of Commerce, *Measuring Markets*, (Washington, D.C., U.S. Government Printing Office, 1966, pp. 49–51).
4. This factor was clearly identified and views of others summarized by Kenneth A. Longman in *The Bulletin*, Institute of Management Sciences, Feb., 1971.

BIBLIOGRAPHY

Adler, L., "Systems Approach to Marketing", *Harvard Business Review*, May–June, 1967.

"Agricultural" Projections for 1975 and 1985", Organization for Economic Cooperation and Development, (OECD Publication Center), 1969.

Banks, S., *Experimentation in Marketing*, McGraw-Hill, New York, 1965.

Boyd, H.W., Jr. and Westfall, R., *Marketing Research: Text and Cases*, Homewood, IX; Richard D. Irwin, 1964.

Charnes, A., *et al.*, DEMON: "A Management Model for Marketing New Products", *California Management Review*, Fall 1968.

Cox, D.F. and Good, R.E., "How to Build a Marketing Information System", *Harvard Business Review*, May–June, 1967.

Crisp, R.D., *Marketing Research*, New York, McGraw-Hill, 1957.

Dichter, E., *Motivation Research Handbook of Consumer Motivations*, New York, McGraw-Hill, 1964.

Enrick, N., *Market and Sales Forecasting*, San Francisco, Chandler Publishers, 1969.

Frank, N.D., *Market Analysis: A Handbook of Current Data Sources*, Metuchen, New Jersey, Scarecrow Press.

Green, P.E. and Tull, D.S., *Research for Marketing Decisions*, Prentice-Hall, Englewood Cliffs, New Jersey, 1970.

Hainer, R., ed., *Uncertainty in Research, Management, and New Product Development*, New York, 1967, Reinhold Publishing Corp.

Hanan, M., *Market Segmentation*, AMA Management Bulletin, New York, American Management Association, Inc., 1968.

Journal of Marketing Research and *Journal of Marketing*, published by the American Marketing Association.

Kish, Leslie, *Survey Sampling*, New York, John Wiley & Sons, 1965.

Konopa, L., *New Product—Assessing Commercial Potential*, American Management Association, New York, 1966.

Lipsey, R.E. and Preston, D., *Source Book of Statistics Relating to Construction*, Columbia University Press, 1966.

Longman, K.A., "Marketing Science; Consumerists, Economists, and Marketers", *The Bulletin*, Institute of Management Sciences, Feb., 1971.

Lucas, D.B. and Britt, S.H., *Measuring Advertising Effectiveness*, New York, McGraw-Hill, 1963.

Luck, D.J., *et al.*, Marketing Research, Prentice-Hall, Inc., Englewood Cliffs, New Jersey 07636, 1970.

MacDonald, M., *Appraising the Market for New Industrial Products*, National Industrial Conference Board, Chicago, Illinois, 1967.

"Main Economic Indicators—Historical Statistics 1957–1966", OECD Publications Center, 1968.

"Market Testing Consumer Products", National Industrial Conference Board, Chicago, Illinois.

Marquis, D.G., "The Anatomy of Successful Innovations", *Innovation*, New York, 1969.

Murdick, R.G., *Business Research, Concept and Practice*, Scranton, Penn., International Text Book Co., 1969.

Murdick, R.G. and Schaefer, A.E., *Sales Forecasting for Lower Costs and Higher Profits*, Englewood Cliffs, New Jersey, Prentice-Hall, 1967.

New Products Marketing, editors of Printers' Ink, Duell, Sloan and Pearce, New York, 1964.

Pessemier, E., *New Product Decision: An Analytical Approach*, New York, McGraw-Hill, 1966.

"Proceedings of the National Inventions and New Products Exhibition and Conference", the Cleveland Engineering Society, 1960.

Reichard, R.S., *Practical Techniques of Sales Forecasting*, New York, Mc-Graw-Hill, 1966.

Reynolds, W., *Products and Markets*, Appleton-Century-Crofts, New York, 1969.

Roxburgh, D., ed., *New Product Development*, University of Strathclyde, Glasgow, Scotland, 1966.

Schoonmaker Associates, *A Market Research Handbook for the Electronics Industry*, P.O. Box 35, Larchmont, N.Y., 10538, 1970.

Smalter, D.J., Director, "Strategic Planning", International Minerals and Chemical Corp.

Smith, D., *How to Avoid Mistakes When Introducing New Products*, New York, Vantage Press, 1964.

Smith, W., "Product Differentiation and Market Segmentation as Alternative Marketing Strategies", *Journal of Marketing*, July 1956.

Sorenson, V.L., *Agricultural Market Analysis*, Michigan State Univ., 1964.

Talley, W., Jr., *The Profitable Product—Its Planning, Launching and Management*, Englewood Cliffs, New Jersey, Prentice Hall, 1965.

Tucker, W.T., *The Social Context of Economic Behavior*, New York, Holt, Rinehart and Winston, Inc., 1964.

Wasson, C., *The Strategy of Marketing Research*, Appleton-Century-Crofts, New York, 1964.

Wetson, J.P., ed., *Defense Space Market Research*, Cambridge, Mass., The MIT Press, 1964.

CHAPTER 10

EVALUATING NEW-PRODUCT PROJECTS

The most critical decision in business is the selection of products which the company will develop and (possibly) market. As we might suspect, the most critical decision is also the most difficult and complex decision to make. Firms have skyrocketed to great success or plunged into oblivion on results of new-product decisions.

It is believed by the authors and others that the most significant evaluation tool is the company's plan for the future. Any evaluation of profit or other benefits should be related to the company's desires as expressed in the plan for the future.

The authors recently queried major industrial firms believed to be aggressive and knowledgeable in their approach to new products—that is the successful identification, development, manufacture, and marketing of new products. Some declined to participate in the study simply because they did not want to disclose how they were handling this problem. However, their responses did indicate grave concern with the problem and the 37 participating firms provide an excellent insight into how today's successful corporations are attempting to cope with this most important problem. Figure 10-1 illustrates the first page of the questionnaire which posed three fundamental questions to these companies.

Almost 100% of the responding companies indicated that they used (1) technical evaluation, (2) market evaluation, and (3) economic evaluation, with economic evaluation being made upon completion of the preliminary design and upon completion of the prototype models. Most of them used all three at the concept state, but some eliminated the economic evaluation as being unrealistic at that point in time.

Generally speaking, their added comments, which usually came from an officer of the corporation and was often of surprising length, indicated that evaluation of projects was an on-going process. This is exactly as it should be since conditions do change, and it is necessary to have continuous evaluation.

Rather surprisingly, in one sense, was that no comparison of results to plans was mentioned. In another sense this was not peculiar because companies are just now beginning to see the benefits of long range planning.

It was stated in Chapter 1 that it was obvious that we should kill off the potentially unsuccessful product as early as possible. It was also stated that continued analysis was necessary. If we refer back to Figures 1-2 and 1-12, and apply a little common sense it is easy to see why the companies stated that evaluation was a continuous process.

Technical evaluations are briefly discussed in Chapter 6 on Research, Development and Engineering. Market evaluation was discussed in Chapter 9. The economic evaluations are partially covered in Chapter 12 (How to Price for Life-Cycle Profit). The total knowledge of all these chapters needs to be brought to bear on the problems of evaluation since all the factors mentioned are interrelated.

All but the very small companies try to routinize product evaluation—and the small ones should. Doing this assures consideration of the desired factors affecting the decision. Secondly, it permits evaluation and improvement of the techniques used; if one is not consistent such action is difficult to impossible. Finally, routinization permits delegation of data collection and even of certain evaluation procedures.

With respect to the selection of research projects in our survey almost all companies indicated the use of technological and economic forecasts. Most of the companies also indicated that judgment was involved, but some firms didn't indicate judgment to be a factor (we wonder if some of these did so because they did not want to appear unscientific). A minority of the firms took into account competitors' research and no one made use of operations research—this despite the fact sophisticated companies responded to the questionnaire.

It was indicated by a few of the firms that areas of corporate interest with respect to future growth were determinates in selecting research projects.

With respect to the methods of evaluation and selection identified as Question 3 of Figure 10-1, some firms indicated that judgement was involved, but that it was only used in conjunction with other factors. Virtually every one of the companies surveyed made use of market studies of customer needs and they made use of technical/marketing/ profit profile analyses. A majority, but by no means all of them, made use of return on investment ROI and other such methods. No one made use of

---

NEW PRODUCT EVALUATION

We make a:

Stage of product	Technical Evaluation	Market Evaluation	Economic Evaluation
1. a. Concept	☐	☐	☐
b. Completion of preliminary design	☐	☐	☐
c. Completion of prototype model	☐	☐	☐
d. Completion of pre-production run	☐	☐	☐
e. After a test market (if conducted)	☐	☐	☐

2. If you do research which is not related to specific products, indicate the bases used to select research projects.
a. Judgment .... ☐
b. Technological/economic forecasts .... ☐
c. Competitors' research .... ☐
d. Operations research .... ☐
e. Other _____

3. Which of the following methods of evaluation and selection of product projects do you employ:
a. Judgment only .... ☐
b. Market study of customer needs .... ☐
c. Technical/marketing/profit profile analyses .... ☐
d. Index methods (ROI, Sobelman, Mottley-Newton, Huetten-Sweany, Disman, etc.) .... ☐
e. Operations research approaches (Hess, Dean-Sengupta, Cetron, Belt, Krantz, etc.) .... ☐
f. Computer is used in the evaluation .... ☐
g. Other _____

Figure 10-1   Page one of survey research document to determine present company approaches to product evaluation

operations research, which is exactly in accord with what was found with respect to Question 2. A number of the firms did use point rating; the weighting of points by topic, group evaluations, etc. Only occasionally was a computer used and when it was used, the firms apparently were using it for such tasks as probability forecasting for ROI calculations.

Naturally the nature of the business had an effect upon the methods used. To some degree the sophistication of the firm and the kind of product lines involved had their effect. However, the above quite well states the issues with respect to the knowledgeable corporations who do have a record of success.

There are substantial lessons here to be learned for the smaller corporate executive who is attempting to make new product decisions on the basis of "seat of the pants" guesses. Also, a word of advice to all firms would be that if a firm is not consistent in its usage of techniques, that evaluation of the procedures used is difficult or impossible.

PERSONAL JUDGMENT AS A SELECTION TECHNIQUE

One possible approach to the use of personal judgment in the evaluation of new product projects is to first list all of the possible considerations that ought to be considered in the evaluations as well as all of the possible trade-offs. Going through the exercise of identifying the considerations and the trade-offs will force a somewhat systematic approach. If judgment is then made on a more-or-less intuitive basis, it is a far more systematic and likely successful procedure than doing so on the basis of a guess or arriving at a decision in some kind of an executive bull-session— without an organized approach to the factors involved.

If we go beyond the simple judgmental approach, we begin to apply more formal and quantitative procedures to assist with the decision making. These procedures may consist of simple evaluations by the assignment of numerical ratings at one end of this approach. At the other extreme, total corporate models and simulations could be employed. While such models have been devised, and apparently a number

are actually in use, our survey (1970) did not turn up any instances.

Since little can be done to assist in judgmental approaches other than to suggest that the executives taking this hazardous approach study the various forms accompanying this chapter and the others referenced in the various bibliographies to identify the questions that ought to be judged or evaluated.

With respect to the quantitative approach, space limitations force a consideration of only a limited number of the techniques and to some extent a somewhat limited consideration of these. However, the chapter bibliography refers to many other sources for the interested reader.

THE OVERRIDING CONSIDERATION

In all new product decisions, we must keep in mind the fact that there is one dominant criterion, long-run return on investment (ROI) of a desired amount. Short run objectives such as filling out the product line, customer service, social obligations such as pollution reduction, or growth and sales, may dominate the decision of a particular product. In the long run, however, these all add up to serving the needs of customers in a satisfactory manner at a profit within our legal-political-social-economic system. Therefore, every new product decision must be made with an eye to profitability to the company. We will therefore focus largely on ROI for most analysis. This is in accordance with what is actually being done by the more knowledgeable and successful firms in today's business environment.

PROJECT SELECTION
AT THE CONCEPT STATE

At the concept stage new product project selection in its most esoteric aspect is mainly concerned with the research end of the R & D spectrum. Unfortunately, there seems to be some confusion over the evaluation of technical research, because of the terms basic research, applied research and development as formulated by the National Science Foundation. No companies do research just for fun or because they think it is expected of them. All research is directed towards the fields of interest to the company, some more specifically than others. The smaller the firm, the more specific and more directed such research *needs* to be because the smaller firm cannot afford anything approaching the basic research end of the spectrum.

In order to assist in a discussion of this problem we will first define some of the terms to clarify the meaning of research and development as actually practiced in industry.

Proprietary Research

This is research on general problems in the fields of interest to the company. For example, early research on the electrical properties of crystals which might have applications in electrical circuits constituted proprietary research for companies such as AT & T, Raytheon, or General Electric. Research on construction of new synthetics is proprietary research for Du Pont. In each case, no specific product is pinpointed, but rather basic problems in the field of interest to the company are being worked on.

Applied Research

This is research directed toward a specific product. Much of the confusion arises because companies organize and manage this research in two different ways. In one case, applied research is first directed to advance the state of the art for specific attributes of a specific product. Then the engineering development of the product utilizes the results to design a new or improved product.

In the other approach, development engineering conceptualizes a new or advanced product and then calls upon applied research to solve specific problems beyond the state-of-the-art at present. In this case, instead of a serial approach, the development engineering group manages each project from concept to prototype.

Development

From what has been said above, it is apparent that development consists of applying current knowledge,

determining the need for research to fill gaps, conducting (or arranging for) research to fill the gaps in knowledge, designing and testing prototypes of devices, systems, or processes. Applied research and development, together, are directed at a product whose performance specifications have been established.

Product Design

Product design is the specification of the parts of a product and their interrelationship so that they become a unified whole and satisfy the requirements set for the product. A product design should be such that the product itself will perform its required functions effectively and reliably, that it can be economically manufactured and can be sold at a profit. It therefore must meet the purposes and the requirements of the consumer. Product design is the obvious next step to development where the development engineering merely conceptualizes a new or advanced product.

With respect to proprietary research, applied research, and development, the criteria for evaluation of each may of necessity be different. The closer we are to the research end of the spectrum, the more the unknowns. Hence, more subjective oriented evaluations are likely required.

In the case of proprietary research, we tend to ask "What problem shall we work on?" In applied research and development, the question likely asked is "What products or product shall we work on?"

The answer to both of these questions, to some degree depends on the nature of technology in the industry involved and to some degree on what the other companies are doing. This is why some of the companies in the referenced survey cited the fact that they did pay attention to competitor's research in selecting research projects.

What the technology will be can best be answered in many cases by looking to available technological forecasts and then perhaps sharpening these with respect to the company involved.

The choice of projects also depends on anticipating future customer needs, not just those which are required for today. Research projects do take time to complete, many times a time span of four to five years between the start of a research project and the time the product gets on the market is considered good progress.

At the research end of the spectrum different evaluation techniques tend to be required from those that can be used once the product begins to get into development engineering and especially into design engineering. At the research end of the spectrum more intuitive type judgments need to be involved because it often is impossible to predict with any degree of certainty the return on investment at the concept stage of a product. This does not mean that one ignores whether or not there is a market for the product. The use of this intuitive judgment should be aided by a list of questions or criteria, such as mentioned earlier, in order to direct it into its proper channels. The making of such a judgment should not be the sole responsibility of the research director involved in the decision making, it must include the marketing manager, the manufacturing manager and possibly others.

The track record of the decision makers need to be taken into account, especially when subjective evaluations are being made. If there has been considerable past success in selecting projects which not only work out well in the laboratory, but also lead to commercially profitable profits, then that man or team should be relied on more than an unknown man's judgment. Just because one makes good decisions in one company does not prove that he is going to make good decisions in another company which may have differing strengths from those of the firm that he left.

At the research end of the spectrum, it is very important to have a competent research director. There are many definitions for such a man, but one of the best criterion is the man's track record in selecting projects. In addition, a director's ability to attract outstanding research people is another important characteristic. Likewise is his ability to accept and work with less than the ultimate in equipment and budget and still complete projects at a reasonable rate. Finally and perhaps even more importantly, a good director of research has the courage to reverse himself and cut off projects when the apparent pay-off-to-input ratio for a project has become small, in his judgment.

AREAS OF EVALUATION

The well-established company which is properly managed will have on hand more ideas for new-product opportunities than it can afford to exploit. The problem is to select those which meet all minimum criteria established by the company and then, perhaps, select a smaller group which conforms best to the limited resources of the company. The four principal areas for evaluation of projects are:

1. Technological. Is the development feasible within the time limits established by company and market needs?
2. Marketing. Does the product fall within the field of interest of the company, its product lines, its distribution system?
3. Economic. Do the economics of the project indicate that costs, prices, and total investment justify the project?
4. Internal resources. Will development of the product conform to availability and limitations of company resources?

THE MULTI-PROJECT PROBLEM

One aspect of new product evaluation that is practically never considered is the fact that projects appear in a time stream. Companies usually consider only projects which are well defined at a particular point in time. They do not consider that selection of a certain group of projects may mean that they must forego possibly far better projects which may appear on the scene. The sketch below illustrates the situation.

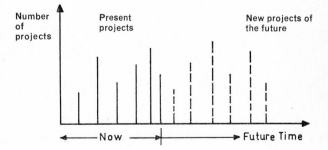

The analogy to the problem of the portfolio manager is very close. He must maintain different percentages of his assets in cash at different times so that he may be ready to purchase potential bargains. He must also maintain a balance of investments for income and growth. There are *always* opportunities in the future.

LIFE CYCLE OF THE PRODUCT

An analysis of a potential new product should take into account the life of the product and the "shape" of life cycle characteristics. Too often the economic analysis is based on assumptions of indefinite uniform expenses and income. Sometimes the artificial assumption of a three-year payback period is used as a sole criterion. The year-by-year cash flows in the face of economic, competitive, and technological changes must be estimated for purposes of project selection and long-range planning.

SEVERAL LEVELS AND TYPES OF EVALUATION NEEDED

The proper evaluation of R & D projects requires a different conceptual view than that generally being promoted in the literature.

Most of the academicians writing on this subject favor a "number" or quantitative system, preferably one expressed by mathematical relationships. By all means do use one if there is a calculated payout from the evaluation system. Such systems must take into account the cost of money—such systems *should* also recognize our creeping inflation, but few do. Speeded up inflation helped bring the giant Lockheed Corporation to its knees in 1970–71.

Industry writers tend to focus on some kind of rating system that considers a very wide variety of factors in almost every function of the business. Functions almost always included are Research, Engineering, Marketing, Manufacturing, and Finance.

Neither of the above groups seem to communicate very well with the other, or more importantly, seem to recognize some underlying fundamental facts.

The evaluation system that can be devised and actually used in the practical sense for a basic research project must of necessity be significantly different than the procedures used to evaluate a project when it is ready to move from engineering to manufacturing and marketing.

It is therefore recommended that the devisors *and* users of evaluation systems for *either* new product projects or Engineering and research projects recognize that different systems are needed at different stages of the project. This may have been stated before, but it is not well recognized or enunciated.

For example, it could very well be that the evaluation system used in Basic Research, Applied Research, and Engineering might each be different. This does not mean that they should not be related, in fact it is recommended that they be related and so devised that later evaluations flow from earlier evaluations in a somewhat natural and logical manner.

TIME-VALUE OF MONEY

Although many firms consider the time value of money in connection with specific investments in capital assets, there is little evidence that this concept is employed in new-product evaluation by the smaller firm. As we heard from our survey, it is almost universally used by the knowledgeable and sophisticated companies. Judging by the sample forms received, some were only beginning their use of this technique in new product evaluation.

In new-product evaluation, money which must be spent on research and development, advertising, marketing research, and distribution does not receive the same treatment as money to be spent on plant and equipment. Yet the timing of outflows and inflows of cash produced by a particular product is crucial. All cash flows should be reduced to a common point in time, usually the present.

The discount factor $1/(1 + i)^n$, where i is the cost of capital and n is the year from now in which the cash flows in or out, should be employed. The cost of capital is difficult to ascertain, but even if only a weighted average of the cost of equity, loans, and bonds is considered, it is better by far than neglecting the whole concept. The time-value of money is another reason why the analysis of the life cycle of the proposed product is so important.

A new element has entered into the calculation of the present value of a stream of future cash flows. This is the rapid inflation in our country which depreciates the real value of the dollars received in the future. This means that an additional (deflator) discount factor $1/(1 + d)^n$, d = inflation rate of the economy, should be used. An example is given below.

An alternative simpler approach with less theoretical basis is the use of a risk discount factor, $1/(1 + R)^n$, where R is increased by a desired amount each successive year in the future. It is apparent that combining the three discount factors of time, inflation, and risk makes projects with high payoffs in their initial years much more attractive, in general.

Risk analysis or other statistical decision methods must be used to obtain an evaluation of a project or product to take into account the uncertainties surrounding the inputs.

Almost every factor affecting a new product or even an ordinary capital investment involves un-

	Net Cash Flow ($)				Present Value	
End of Year	Project A	Project B	Cost of Capital Factor $i = 10\%$	Deflator Factor $d = 6\%$	Project A	Project B
1	−30,000	−50,000	0.909	0.943	−25,700	−42,800
2	10,000	0	0.826	0.890	7,360	0
3	20,000	10,000	0.751	0.840	12,600	6,300
4	15,000	40,000	0.683	0.792	8,090	21,600
5	5,000	30,000	0.621	0.847	2,300	13,910
					$ 4,650	−$ 990

Risk

Whenever we estimate future events, there is the risk of being wrong. We face two problems:

1. How wrong can we be?
2. What is the probability that we are wrong by a specified amount?

For example, suppose that we estimate the net cash flow as $ 20,000 in the third year for Project A. Actually we should have set up a table relating risk to possible return, as for example,

Cash Flow	Probability	Weighted Value
$ 15,000	0.3	$ 4,500
20,000	0.6	12,000
25,000	0.1	2,500
	1.0	$ 19,000

This suggests that if management judgments are extended to a set of possible returns in terms of risk, we should use the weighted estimate. Obviously finer intervals between amounts of cash flow could have been used, but the estimates of probability are quite crude so that little is gained.

certainties concerning the future. Better than merely hedging, application of risk analysis provides information which will lead to more profitable decisions. It still will not give perfect answers, but the answer is more realistic and the "hedge" is automatically a part of the answer.

David B. Hertz described a practical system or procedure generalized so that it could be applied to a variety of problems. Its essentials are summarized in Figure 10-2.

In applying the procedure, the first step is to identify the variables. Step 2 is to obtain an estimate of each variable that will occur or will be exceeded 90 percent of the time, the value that will occur or be exceeded 50 percent of the time and the one that represents the 10 percent point. These then permit generation of the probability distributions represented in the figure. A growth factor and/or an inflation

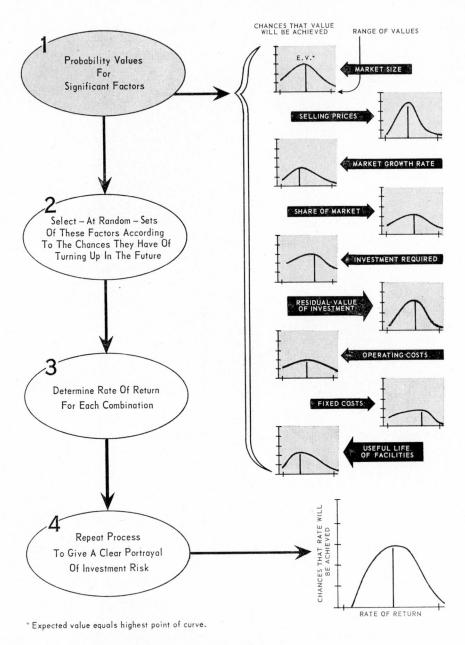

* Expected value equals highest point of curve.

Figure 10-2   Risk analysis for investment planning

Source: David B. Hertz, "Risk analysis in capital investment", *Harvard Business Review*, February, 1964

1. **Estimate most probable value**   : $4,500M.

2. **Estimate limits of practical (>.02 probability) range** : $4,000 – 5,500M.

3. **Divide range by five (i.e., $\frac{\$1,500\ M}{5}$ = $300 M).**

4. **Estimate probability of "best estimate"**   : 1 chance in 2 (or .5).

5. **Draw a smooth curve over range of values.**

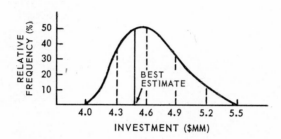

6. **Pick off relative frequencies for midpoints of each interval.**

7. **Calculate probabilities as shown below, left.**

Interval	Mid-point	Relative Frequency	Prob-ability
$5200-5499M	$5350M	.03	.02
4900-5199	5050	.20	.16
4600-4899	4750	.42	.35
4300-4599	4450	.49	.39
4000-4299	4150	.12	.08
		1.26	1.00

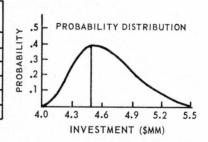

Figure 10-3 Steps in estimating the probability distribution of the required investment
Source: Robert F. Klausner, "The Evaluation of Risk in Marine Capital Investment", *The Engineering Economist*, Summer, 1969, p. 207

factor can be included. Step 3 would be to place the model details in a computer and, by means of random selections of each variable, simulate a single case. A large number of simulations are carried out until a final composite output curve is obtained.

A somewhat related procedure is outlined by Robert F. Klausner in Figure 10-3.[2]

While the applications here are in regard to capital investment, they apply equally, on a conceptual basis, to the evaluation of a new product.

Messrs Franz Edelman, Director of Operations Research for RCA, and Joel S. Greenberg, Vice-President of Venture Research and Development Group wrote on risk analysis and illustrated the general kinds of distributions they had encountered.[3] These distributions are shown in Figure 10-4.

Risk analysis is being used by more and more companies. Twenty-two of the 40 companies responding to a survey reported using this technique for operational and/or strategic planning.[4] (See Figures 2-3

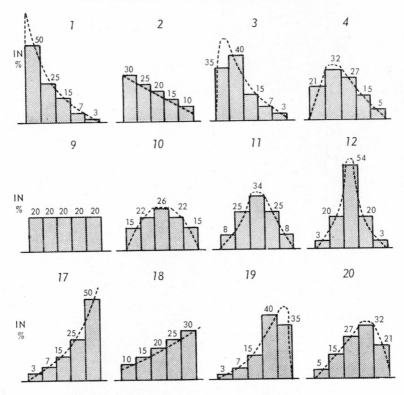

Figure 10-4 Uncertainty profiles encountered in risk analyses
Source: Franz Edelman and Joel S. Greenberg, "Venture Analysis: The Assessment of Uncertainty and Risk",
Financial Executive, August, 1969, p. 60

and 2-4.) New Product Venture Managers certainly should understand and use the proceedure and this does *not* require them to be an expert statistician or computer expert—such help is available from a large variety of sources internal and/or external to the company.

CONSUMER, INDUSTRIAL, OR DEFENSE PRODUCTS

In evaluating consumer and industrial product ventures, the ROI and the risk involved are related to the performance specifications of the product. Meeting the performance specifications or setting high performance standards are generally not critical for such products. Consider the success of the first crude ballpoint pen, the first moisture monitors for paper mills, or the early digital computers. Poor perform-

ance and occasional failures were tolerated. The products were measured by the manufacturer in terms of the amount of profits in the face of the risk involved.

Now let us consider defense products. Here risk is usually suppressed by various types of contracts which assure the company a modest return. Instead of profit as a measure of a potential product, cost-effectiveness is the measure. If a component or system going into a space ship or submarine does not fully meet performance specifications, it is not acceptable. There is no such thing as a profit based upon partial achievement of product objectives. There may, however, be penalties for excessive costs or time in reaching such objectives. This is where the risk lies, in technical performance and not in market potential.

We may summarize the areas of uncertainty at the start of development for consumer/industrial products and defense products as:

	Consumer/industrial	Defense
Engineering	Some to considerable	Considerable
Manufacturing	Some	Considerable
Marketing	Considerable	Little
Cost-Price-Volume	Considerable	Little
Cost-Effectiveness	Little to considerable	Considerable

COMMITMENT TIMING

Both technical development, manufacturing planning, and marketing planning must be carried along in parallel except at the research end of the spectrum of R & D activities. There are some expensive long lead-time commitments in manufacturing and marketing which must be made. Suppose that special machinery and tools are ordered and that commitments to advertising media are made at an early stage in product engineering. This would be done with the hope of getting the product on the market at the earliest possible date.

Now suppose a major revision in design or packaging is required which makes some of the tooling and some of the advertising artwork worthless. It is apparent that delaying major expenditures has some advantages despite possible lost sales. The problem is to balance these two considerations of early market entry and commitment of funds based on early designs.

INFORMATION

The key to making the correct new-product decision is *information*. Decisions at each stage of development are usually made with little information and lots of hunch. Information costs money and takes time to gather so that many managers are too impatient to involve themselves in the pains-taking search for information. It is only when the stakes become excessively high that they will, for example, conduct a test market study rather than risk a complete failure in the market.

New scientific methods for gathering information which is more reliable and for manipulating such information to provide useful indicators have been developed. Probability sample surveys, statistical design of experiments, unobtrusive methods of measurement, Bayesian analysis, modeling and simulation are examples of the techniques available.[5]

SUMMARY OF THE COMPONENTS OF THE EVALUATION PROBLEM

We have presented the components of the evaluation problem so that the business executive can explicitly state the trade-offs he makes when he examines a new-product proposal. It is likely that not all components have equal importance or significant importance in every case. At any rate, a study of each of these aspects of project evaluation may lead to a more rational and dependable evaluation of proposals, *in the long run*, than intuitive judgment of the proposal with no analysis.

NEW-PRODUCT ANALYSIS FORMS

In order to develop a systematic and consistent approach to gathering information, companies are developing forms and formal procedures. Although many such forms require such little information as to be almost worthless, some companies' forms cover every phase of new product development. A good example is the form used by Anchor Hocking Corp. which also provides for a post-audit of the project. See Figure 10-5.

PROJECT EVALUATION

New Product

Product Modification

New Market

Other (Define)

Project No.

Product

Start Date

Completion Date

Initiated By

PROPRIETARY: 'RESTRICTED FOR DISTRIBUTION TO

THIS DOCUMENT OR ANY PART THEREOF MAY NOT BE DUPLICATED NOR DISCLOSED
TO ANY PERSON NOT CONFIDENTIALLY BOUND TO ANCHOR HOCKING.

PROPOSED BY   DATE

General Description & End Use:

Market Considerations (Summarize Market/Sales Potential/Prices/Trends/Suppliers, Etc.)

GO

NO GO   DATE

Manufacturing Considerations (Summarize Facilities/Machinery/Lead Time, Etc.)

GO

NO GO   DATE

Page 1 of 2 Pages

RETURN TO MARKETING DEPARTMENT WITH ALL DETAIL AND SUPPORTING DOCUMENTS ATTACHED.

Figure 10-5

R & D Considerations (Summarize Development/Test/Results/Lead Time, Etc.)

GO

NO GO   DATE _____

Cost Considerations (Summarize Cost/Price, Etc.)

GO

NO GO   DATE _____

Page 2 of 3 Pages

EVALUATION HISTORY		
1st YEAR	2nd YEAR	3rd YEAR

TARGET VALUE
  PRETAX PROFIT (%)
  ANNUAL INCOME
  COMMERCIAL LIFE
  PROBABILITY OF SUCCESS (%)

TARGET EXPENSE (MFG)
  CAPITAL EQUIPMENT
  MOLDS
  PLANT FACILITIES
  INVENTORY
  START-UP COST

TARGET EXPENSE (R & D)
  EXPLORATORY RESEARCH
  PRODUCT DEVELOPMENT
  PROBABILITY OF SUCCESS (%)

RETURN ON INVESTMENT (%)

RECOMMENDATION

GO   ☐
NO GO ☐ _____   DATE: _____

PROJECT COORDINATOR _____

Page 2 of 2 Pages

Project evaluation

Source: Anchor Hocking Corp., Lancaster, Ohio 43130

	Very good	Good	Average	Poor	Very poor
I. MARKETABILITY					
A. Relation to present distribution channels	Can reach major markets by distributing through present channels.	Can reach major markets mostly by distributing through present channels, partly through new channels.	Will have to distribute equally between new and present channels, in order to reach major markets.	Will have to distribute mostly through new channels in order to reach major markets.	Will have to distribute entirely through new channels in order to reach major markets.
B. Relation to present product lines	Complements a present line which needs more products to fill it.	Complements a present line that does not need, but can handle, another product.	Can be fitted into a present line.	Can be fitted into a present line but does not fit entirely.	Does not fit in with any present product line.
C. Quality/price relationship	Priced below all competing products of similar quality.	Priced below most competing products of similar quality.	Approximately the same price as competing products of similar quality.	Priced above many competing products of similar quality.	Priced above all competing products of similar quality.
D. Number of sizes and grades	Few staple sizes and grades.	Several sizes and grades, but customers will be satisfied with few staples.	Several sizes and grades, but can satisfy customer wants with small inventory of nonstaples.	Several sizes and grades, each of which will have to be stocked in equal amounts.	Many sizes and grades which will necessitate heavy inventories.
E. Merchandisability	Has product characteristics at and above those of competing products that lend themselves to the kind of promotion, advertising, and display that the given company does best.	Has promotable characteristics that will compare favorably with the characteristics of competing products.	Has promotable characteristics that are equal to those of other products.	Has a few characteristics that are promotable, but generally does not measure up to characteristics of competing products.	Has no characteristics at all that are equal to competitors' or that lend themselves to imaginative promotion.
F. Effects on sales of present products	Should aid in sales of present products.	May help sales of present products; definitely will not be harmful to present sales.	Should have no effect on present sales.	May hinder present sales some; definitely will not aid present sales.	Will reduce sales of presently profitable products.
II. DURABILITY					
A. Stability	Basic product which can always expect to have uses.	Product which will have uses long enough to earn back initial investment, plus at least 10 years of additional profits.	Product which will have uses long enough to earn back initial investment, plus several (from 5 to 10) years of additional profits.	Product which will have uses long enough to earn back initial investment, plus 1 to 5 years of additional profits.	Product which will probably be obsolete in near future.
B. Breadth of market	A national market, a wide variety of consumers, and a potential foreign market.	A national market and a wide variety of consumers.	Either a national market or a wide variety of consumers.	A regional market and a restricted variety of consumers.	A specialized market in a small marketing area.
C. Resistance to cyclical fluctuations	Will sell readily in inflation or depression.	Effects of cyclical changes will be moderate, and will be felt after changes in economic outlook.	Sales will rise and fall with the economy.	Effects of cyclical changes will be heavy, and will be felt before changes in economic outlook.	Cyclical changes will cause extreme fluctuations in demand.

Factor					
D. *Resistance to seasonal fluctuations*	Steady sales throughout the year.	Steady sales—except under unusual circumstances.	Seasonal fluctuations, but inventory and personnel problems can be absorbed.	Heavy seasonal fluctuations that will cause considerable inventory and personnel problems.	Severe seasonal fluctuations that will necessitate layoffs and heavy inventories.
E. *Exclusiveness of design*	Can be protected by a patent with no loopholes.	Can be patented, but the patent might be circumvented.	Cannot be patented, but has certain salient characteristics that cannot be copied very well.	Cannot be patented, and can be copied by larger, more knowledgeable companies.	Cannot be patented, and can be copied by anyone.
III. PRODUCTIVE ABILITY					
A. *Equipment necessary*	Can be produced with equipment that is presently idle.	Can be produced with present equipment, but production will have to be scheduled with other products.	Can be produced largely with present equipment, but the company will have to purchase some additional equipment.	Company will have to buy a good deal of new equipment, but some present equipment can be used.	Company will have to buy all new equipment.
B. *Production knowledge and personnel necessary*	Present knowledge and personnel will be able to produce new product.	With very few minor exceptions, present knowledge and personnel will be able to produce new product.	With some exceptions, present knowledge and personnel will be able to produce new product.	A ratio of approximately 50-50 will prevail between the needs for new knowledge and personnel and for present knowledge and personnel.	Mostly new knowledge and personnel are needed to produce the new product.
C. *Raw materials' availability*	Company can purchase raw materials from its best supplier(s) exclusively.	Company can purchase major portion of raw materials from its best supplier(s), and remainder from any one of a number of companies.	Company can purchase approximately half of raw materials from its best supplier(s), and other half from any one of a number of companies.	Company must purchase most of raw materials from any one of a number of companies other than its best supplier(s).	Company must purchase most or all of raw materials from companies other than its best supplier(s).
IV. GROWTH POTENTIAL					
A. *Place in market*	New type of product that will fill a need presently not being filled.	Product that will substantially improve on products presently on the market.	Product that will have certain new characteristics that will appeal to a substantial segment of the market.	Product that will have minor improvements over products presently on the market.	Product similar to those presently on the market and which adds nothing new.
B. *Expected competitive situation—value added*	Very high value added so as to substantially restrict number of competitors.	High enough value added so that, unless product is extremely well suited to other firms, they will not want to invest in additional facilities.	High enough value added so that, unless other companies are as strong in market as this firm, it will not be profitable for them to compete.	Lower value added so as to allow large, medium, and some smaller companies to compete.	Very low value added so that all companies can profitably enter market.
C. *Expected availability of end users*	Number of end users will increase substantially.	Number of end users will increase moderately.	Number of end users will increase slightly, if at all.	Number of end users will decrease moderately.	Number of end users will decrease substantially.

Figure 10-6 Factor and subfactor ratings for a new product

Source: John T. O'Meara, "Selecting Profitable Products", *Harvard Business Review*, Jan.–Feb., 1961

SYSTEMATIC AND QUANTITATIVE EVALUATION

Systematic and quantitative methods extend from somewhat conventional evaluation forms to simple scaling of factors to sophisticated management science methods. We will give a capsule summary of a variety so that the reader may investigate fur-

ther those which appear appropriate for his company. Figure 10-5 is a good but somewhat conventional project evaluation form.

Factor Scaling or Weighting

An early listing of factors and a scale as developed by John T. O'Meara is shown in Figure 10-6.

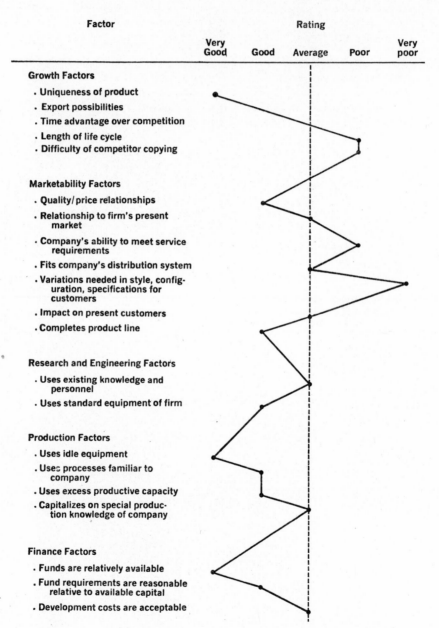

Figure 10-7   Illustrative preliminary screening profile for a new product year
Source: George A. Steiner, *Top Management Planning*, New York: The Macmillan Company, 1969

RATING SYSTEM

Criterion	Question	Range of answers	Numerical rating
Promise of success (P)	What is the best estimate of the promise of technical success consistent with known economies and the state of the art?	Unforeseeable Fair High	1 2 3
Time to completion (T)	How long will it take to complete the research effort from this time forward?	Greater than 3 years 1 to 3 years Less than 1 year	1 2 3
Cost of project (C)	How much will it cost to complete the research effort from this time forward?	Greater than $1 million $100,000 to $1 million Less than $100,000	1 2 3
Strategic need (N)	To what extent is successful research needed from a market standpoint?	No apparent market application; must be developed	1
		Desirable to maintain, reinforce, or expand position within market applications currently served	2
		Essential in relation to current or projected markets within market applications not currently served	3
Market gain (M)	What is the net market gain potential for the company after taking into account losses through product replacement?	Less that $1 million/yr $1 to $10 million/yr Greater than $10 million/yr	1 2 3

Figure 10-8a   Rating system for selection of industrial research projects (See next page for 10-8b)
Source: C. M. Mottley and R. D. Newton, "The Selection of Projects for Industrial Research", *Operations Research*, Nov.–Dec., 1959

A second example of developing a scale is the "profile chart" shown in Figure 10-7.

Mottley and Newton combine both project scores and available funds in numerical rating scale, Figure 10-8.

Perhaps the most comprehensive scaling system is that developed by John S. Harris shown in Figure 10-9a–10-9f.

Another concise scaling model with some points in its favor is shown in Figure 10-10a–10-10c where one or more concerned individuals rate the factors as to importance on a scale of 1 through 6 and the chance of success on a scale of 100%.

SIMPLE ECONOMIC ANALYSIS AND INDEXES

American Alcolac's Project Number[6,7]

This index of project worth depends upon management judgments on a scale from 0 to 1.00 for the success of technical development and commercialization.

$$\text{Index} = \left[\begin{array}{l} \text{Probability of} \\ \text{technical success} \end{array} \times \begin{array}{l} \text{Probability of} \\ \text{commercial success} \end{array} \times \right.$$

$$\times \begin{array}{l} \text{Annual} \\ \text{sales volume} \end{array} \times (\text{Price} - \text{cost}) \times$$

$$\left. \times \begin{array}{l} \text{Life expectancy} \\ \text{of the product} \end{array} \right] \div \text{Total cost}$$

EVALUATION OF PROJECTS IN RELATION TO PROPOSED BUDGET EXPENDITURES

Project no.	Rating of criteria					Project score	Budget request for next year	
							By project	Cumulative
	P	T	C	N	M	S	$ thousand	$ thousand
3	3	3	3	3	2	162	0	0
19	3	3	2	3	3	162	200	200
10	3	2	3	3	2	108	25	225
5	2	3	3	2	3	108	100	325
21	3	3	2	2	2	72	100	425
23	2	2	2	3	3	72	400	825
30	2	2	2	3	2	48	40	865
2	2	2	2	3	2	48	40	905
4	2	2	2	3	2	48	50	955
14	2	2	2	3	2	48	50	1005
1	3	2	2	2	2	48	130	1135
15	2	2	2	2	3	48	350	1485
25	1	2	3	3	2	36	40	1525
8	2	1	2	3	3	36	75	1600
29	2	1	2	3	3	36	75	1675
28	2	2	2	2	2	32	50	1725
12	2	2	2	2	2	32	100	1825
13	2	2	2	2	2	32	150	1975
6	2	2	2	2	2	32	175	2150
17	1	2	2	2	3	24	100	2250
22	3	1	2	2	2	24	125	2375
16	1	1	2	2	3	12	60	2435
27	1	1	2	3	2	12	60	2495
11	1	1	2	3	2	12	100	2595
26	1	1	2	3	2	12	100	2695
20	1	1	1	3	3	9	375	3070
18	1	1	2	2	2	8	60	3130
24	2	1	2	1	2	8	75	3205
7	1	2	2	2	1	8	100	3305
9	1	1	1	2	3	6	400	3705

Figure 10-8b   Examples of project evaluation in relation to proposed budget expenditures based on system shown in figure 10-4

Source: See Figure 10-4

MINUS

FINANCIAL ASPECTS | −2 | −1

−2 Less than 20%
−1 20% to 25%
+1 25% to 30%
+2 Greater than 30%
〉 Return on investment (before taxes)

Estimated annual sales

−2 Less than $100,000
−1 $100,000 to $1 million
+1 $1 to $5 million
+2 Greater than $5 million
〉 New fixed capital payout time

Time to reach est. sales vol.

−2 More than 5 years
−1 3 to 5 years
+1 2 to 3 years
+2 Less than 2 years
〉

−2 More than 5 years
−1 3 to 5 years
+1 1 to 3 years
+2 Less than 1 year
〉

RESEARCH & DEVELOPMENT ASPECTS

−2 More than 3 years
−1 2 to 3 years
+1 1 to 2 years
+2 Less than 1 year
〉 Res. investment payout time

Dev. investment payout time

−2 More than 3 years
−1 2 to 3 years
+1 1 to 2 years
+2 Less than 1 year
〉 Research know-how

Patent status

−2 No experience & no other applications
−1 Partly new with few other uses
+1 Some experience or new vistas
+2 Considerable experience or potential
〉

−2 Unsettled patent situation
−1 Open field or many licenses
+1 Restricted to few licenses
+2 Patent or exclusive license
〉

−2 Extensive educational program
−1 Appreciable customer education
+1 Moderate customer resistance
+2 Ready customer acceptance
〉

−2 Extensive advertising & promotion
−1 Appreciable requirements
+1 Moderate requirements
+2 Little promotion needed
〉

−2 Several directly competitive products
−1 Several competitive to some extent
+1 One or two somewhat competitive
+2 No competitive product
〉 Market development requirements

Promotional requirements

−2 Higher price, equivalent quality
−1 Competitive; or higher price and quality
+1 Competitive price but quality advantage
+2 Both price & quality advantage
〉 Product competition

Product advantage

−2 Probably 1 to 3 years
−1 Probably 3 to 5 years
+1 Probably 5 to 10 years
+2 Probably more than 10 years
〉 Length of product life

Cyclical & seasonal demand

−2 Seasonal and subj. to business cycle
−1 Seasonal
+1 Subject to business cycle
+2 High stability
〉

(•*The ratings for this aspect will depend on the individual company's type of business, accounting methods, and financial objectives. The values shown above are estimated on the basis of various published information to bracket the averages for large chemical companies.*)

Figure 10-9a to 10-9f   Profile chart used in overall evaluation of a new product. (Continued on next page).

PRODUCT:

Est. Annual Sales _____ lbs.

Price: $ _____

Annual Earnings: $ _____
  (before taxes)

Total Capital Investment: $ _____

PLUS

+1	+2

PRODUCTION & ENGINEERING ASPECTS

Required corporate size

−2 Can be made by any bucket operator
−1 Most companies could compete
+1 Average or larger sized companies
+2 Only a very large company

Raw materials

−2 Limited supply or suppliers
−1 Limited availability inside company
+1 Readily available from outside sources
+2 Readily available inside company

Equipment

−2 New plant needed
−1 Mostly new equipment
+1 Some new equipment
+2 Present idle plant useable

Process familiarity

−2 New process—no other application
−1 Partly new — few other uses
+1 Familiar process — some other uses
+2 Routine process or promising other use

MARKETING & PRODUCT ASPECTS

Similarity to present product lines

−2 Entirely new type
−1 Somewhat different
+1 Only slightly different
+2 Fits perfectly

Effect on present products

−2 Will replace directly
−1 Decrease other sales somewhat
+1 Slight effect
+2 Increase other product sales

Marketability to present customers

−2 Entirely different customers
−1 Some present customers
+1 Mostly present customers
+2 All present customers

Number of potential customers

−2 More than 500
−1 Less than 5; or 100 to 500
+1 5 to 10; or 50 to 100
+2 10 to 50

Suitability of present sales force

−2 Entire new group needed
−1 Some additions necessary
+1 Few additions necessary
+2 No changes necessary

Market stability

−2 Volatile market, frequent price cuts
−1 Unsteady market
+1 Fairly firm market
+2 Highly stable market

Market trend

−2 Decreasing market
−1 Static, mature market
+1 Growing market
+2 New potential market

Technical service

−2 Extensive service required
−1 Moderate service requirements
+1 Slight service requirements
+2 Negligible service required

Figure 10-9b   (Continued) Profile chart used in overall evaluation of a new product. (For examples of completed charts see Figs. 9c through 9f)

FINANCIAL ASPECTS
Return on investment (before taxes)
Estimated annual sales
New fixed capital payout time
Time to reach est. sales vol.

RESEARCH & DEVELOPMENT ASPECTS
Res. investment payout time
Dev. investment payout time
Research know-how
Patent status

PRODUCTION & ENGINEERING ASPECTS
Required corporate size
Raw materials
Equipment
Process familiarity

MARKETING & PRODUCT ASPECTS
Similarity to present product lines
Effect on present products
Marketability to present customers
Number of potential customers
Suitability of present sales force
Market stability
Market trend
Technical service
Market development requirements
Promotional requirements
Product competition
Product advantage
Length of product life
Cyclical & seasonal demand

Scale: MINUS / PLUS — −2 | −1 | +1 | +2

Figure 10-9c (*Left*) Before the chart shown in Fig. 10-9a and 10-9b was put into use, it was tried out on several products previously put on the market by Monsanto Chemical Company. One of these was Textile Preservative-B which had been a market failure due primarily to poor profitability and heavy technical service and marketing demands. As shown, this chart would have emphasized these points and could have saved much time and expense. (*Right*) Insecticide-N, unlike Textile Preservative-B, proved to be a market success. Based on developmental data, the chart missed what actually happened only on annual sales and lenght of product life.; both were underestimated. (These two charts reflect only the information available during development of the products.)

Source: See Fig. 10-9a and 10-9b

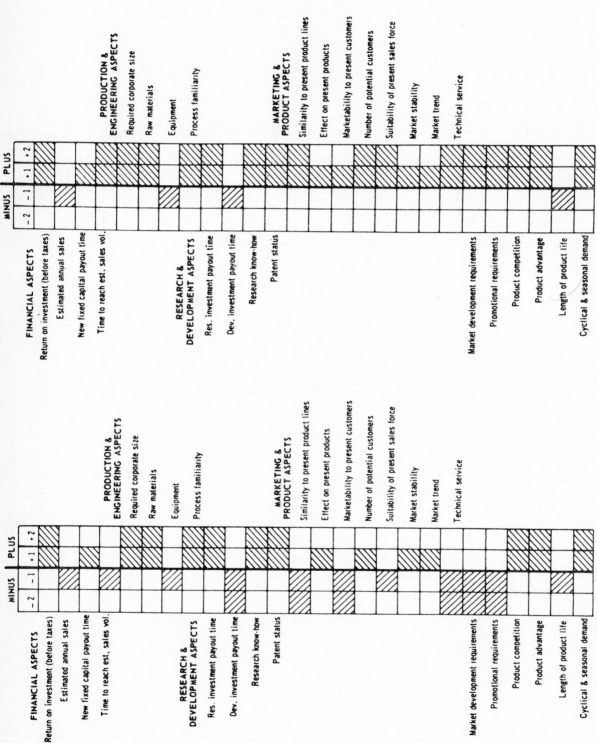

Figure 10-9d Where alternatives are available, such as in marketing methods, the profile chart provides a comparison of which is better. Drilling Additive-R could have been marketed in either of two ways. Case I (*left*) shows the effect of direct sales to the many drilling mud companies. Case II (*right*) shows what happens when the product is sold through a distributor spezializing in additives to drilling mud companies. Clearly, marketing is a controlling factor.

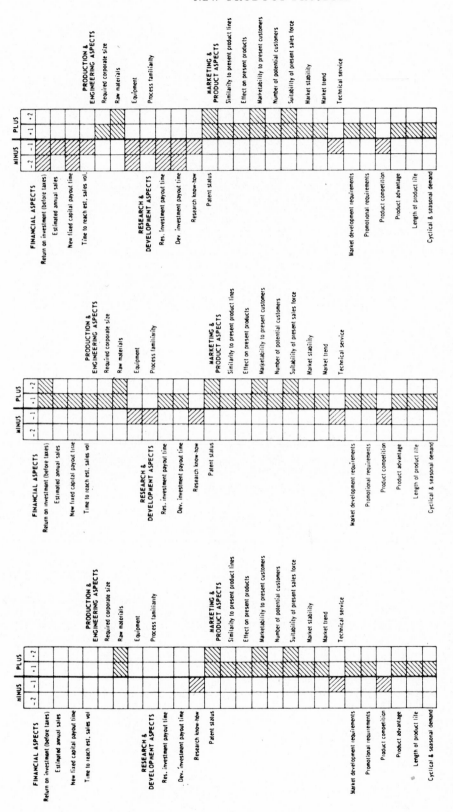

Figure 10-9e (*Continued*) Plasticizer-D provides an example of how a profile chart can change during the development of a product. At Stage I (*left*) it has shown promise in screening tests. Process work has not been started as yet—thus, neither the process nor economics is known. Several months later, during process research, the chart at Stage II (*center*) still rates the product high. Economics look good: An unavoidable by-product has been found, but it is expected to sell at a profit. Stage III (*right*) shows a much different picture. More work has shown that the by-product will not sell. This depresses financial aspects, and necessary pricing lenghtens the time to reach volume sales. Process research shows the need for a new plant. At this point, Plasticizer-D was dropped. **Source:** See Fig. 10-9a and 10-9b

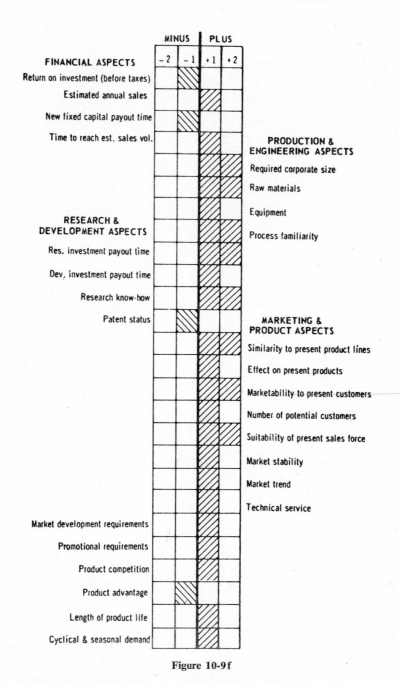

Figure 10-9 f

Figure 10-9: a–f Profile chart used in overall evaluation of a new product
This chart shows that Resin Intermediate-H, still in commercial development, has less than promising financial aspects. However, the production and marketing areas of the chart are favorable, providing reasons for trying to commercialize the product
Source: Fig. 10-9a and 10-9b
Source: 10-9: a–f were reprinted from *Chemical and Engineering News*; by their permission and that of author, John S. Harris, Vol. 39, No. 16 (April 17, 1961), 110. Copyright 1961 by the American Chemical Society and reprinted by permission of copyright owners

EXPLANATIONS OF FACTORS	Calcd. or Estimated % in Favor	Points	Rating	Special Comments
1. Chance of Technical Solution:	80	6	4.8	
The probability of success based on a particular company's technical capacity for solving a certain problem at a given time with the man-power that will be (or can be) allotted to the project. If technical people who have the responsibility for the project feel there is an 80% chance of solving the problem as defined, 80% will be used as the per cent perfection.				
2. Chance of Commercial Success:	99	6	5.9	
The chance of customer acceptance if all requirements of the project are fulfilled by the R & D effort. A high and well assured rating should appear here. If it is determined that solution of the problem as defined will yield a product that is assured of acceptance by the intended customers, the per cent perfection would be very high—90 to 100.				
3. Determination of Research Cost Relative to Market Potential:	90	6	5.4	
Whether research costs will be reasonable with respect to potential profits. Man-power, equipment, time requirements, etc., must be estimated. Additional products of similar type might be easier to create or develop from this point on. If research cost is estimated to be very .ow for the profits that can be expected in return, a high rating will be assigned.				
4. Estimated Size of the Market:	90	6	5.4	
This will influence the potential net profit that can be expected. If the market were not large enough to make a significant contribution to the company, a very low or zero rating would be assigned.				
5. The Product Cost in Relation to Its Selling Price:	75	6	4.5	
The essence of the profit picture. The actual manufacturing cost of producing the volume estimated should be calculated with respect to its over-all impact on costs and used to determine what profit margins can be anticipated.				
6. Research Cost Relative to the Company's Ability to Pay:	60	6	3.6	Danger-ously low
A practical measure of whether a project is of suitable size or too large to under-take even though it may look very attractive otherwise. If a company can easily afford the cost of the project, the rating will be high. As in the case of any critical area, the project should not be started unless there are other than normal reasons for continuing.				
7. Availability of Funds to Capitalize on R & D Investment:	90	6	5.4	
If funds are not available, large expenditures already made may be lost. If funds are available without qualification, give a high rating.				
8. Time to Be Ready to Market:	60	6	3.6	Danger-ously low
If the period is short between the time the project is started and the time the pro-duct is ready to sell, a high rating will be assigned.				
9. Life Expectancy of the Market Itself—Stability:	85	5	4.2	
The period which may be expected to elapse before change has eliminated or greatly reduced the demand for the type of product (project) under consideration. A market enduring into the foreseeable furure would give a high rating.				
10. Life of the Product before Requiring Additional Major R & D Effort:	70	5	3.5	
If no major modifications or obsolescence is anticipated in the foreseeable future, a high per cent perfection would be assigned.				
11. Intrinsic Value That Will Be Added to a Customer's Product:	85	5	4.3	
An upgrading of quality which will result from proper use of the new product. If the customer gains a distinct sales or price advantage, the rating will be high.				

Figure 10-10a A point rating system for new products (continued on next page)

Source: C.I.Sullivan, "Management Looks at R & D Project Evaluation", *Industrial & Engineering Chemistry*, Sept., 1961

EXPLANATIONS OF FACTORS	Calcd. or Estimated % in Favor	Points	Rating	Special Comments
12. Processing Advantages to the Customer: *May represent considerable saving and/or reduction of hazards. Any distinct improvement would help the rating. The degree of improvement determines value.*	95	5	4.7	
13. Competitive Situation (Strength and Potential): *Should be well understood because any new product is judged against competitive quality, price, and position in the market. If a normal sharing of the market is expected, a moderate rating will be assigned.*	50	5	2.5	Dangerously low
14. Availability of Raw Materials: *If the supply is unrestricted and will be so in the foreseeable future, a high per cent perfection should be assigned.*	90	5	4.5	
15. Availability of R & D Man Power: *If adequate man-power can be made available only by borrowing people and impairing other efforts, a relatively low rating would be assigned.*	60	4	2.4	Dangerously low
16. Patentability: *A product or process having sufficiently unique properties to provide patent protection would rate high.*	80	4	3.2	
17. Unique Properties: *May exist without the possibility of patent protection. If the properties can be used to improve the sales picture considerably, an appropriately high rating would result.*	90	4	3.6	
18. Controllability of Process: *If much trouble is anticipated, a near 0 rating would result and corrective measures are needed.*	80	4	3.2	
19. Effect on Customer's Selling Price: *An appreciable reduction in the cost deserves a high rating.*	80	4	3.2	
20. Company Goals (Diversifications, etc.): *If the project fits into over-all company aims (short and long range) it will have a high rating.*	100	4	4.0	
21. Waste or Fume Problems: *No problem means a high rating.*	80	4	3.2	
22. Operational Hazards: *If elaborate measures are required to provide adequate safety, there will be a low rating.*	80	4	3.2	
23. Use of Standard (Existing) Plant Equipment: *If standard equipment can be used, rating will be high. If changes or new equipment are required, rating will be adjusted according to the extent of the difficulty.*	90	4	3.6	
24. Stability in Economic Depression: *Ratings would be assigned according to the life expectancy in a depression.*	70	3	2.1	
25. Know-How (Familiarity With Field): *If no company background exists, a low rating would be assigned.*	60	3	1.8	
26. Relationship to Present Sales Organization: *If the finished product fits well into the existing sales organization and can be handled without additional man-power or special training, there will be high rating.*	70	2	1.4	
27. Breadth of Market: *If the product is to be used nationally by a large variety of customers, the rating will be high.*	90	2	1.8	
28. Difficulty of Being Copied: *A product which is hard to imitate, copy, or analyze would rate high.*	70	2	1.4	

Figure 10-10b   (continued on next page)

EXPLANATIONS OF FACTORS	Calcd. or Estimated % in Favor	Points	Rating	Special Comments
29. Anticipated Technical Service Requirements: *If a relatively small amount of servicing is required, the rating will be high.*	80	2	1.6	
30. Seasonal Market: *A product which can be sold at a steady rate all year will have a high rating.*	90	1	0.9	
31. Variations in Style, Type, Etc.: *Numerous styles or types would increase inventories and other expenses and be rated low.*	80	1	0.8	
32. Reputation in the Field or Related Fields: *If the field is the same or closely related, the rating is high.*	80	1	0.8	
33. Export Possibilities: *If there is an opportunity for a significant expansion into a foreign market, the rating is high.*	80	1	0.8	
34. Large Volume Individual Customers: *If there is one or perhaps two large volume individual customers and no small ones to offset having all the "eggs in one basket", the rating would be low.*	80	1	0.8	
35. Raw Materials to Improve the Company's Position in Other Raw Materials: *If the new product increases the purchase of certain raw materials and allows for better contracting, factor will be high.*	75	1	0.75	
36. Raw Materials Already in Use: *If the materials are already avaialble and require no additional facilities, the rating is high.*	70	1	0.7	
37. Maintenance Problems: *If reliable knowledge, preferably based on experience, indicates that equipment and process combined will result in a low maintenance cost, the rating is high.*	85	1	0.85	
38. Potential Use in Other Areas: *If there is a possibility that the product has potential value in areas other than those for which it was designed, assign a high value.*	80	1	0.8	
	2989	137	108.9	

Estimate average % of perfection: 2989/38 × 100 = 78.6%   *Over-all project rating 108.9/137 × 100 = 79.4%.*

Figure 10-10c

R. Manley Formula[7]

The maximum permissible research expenditures which will just give an acceptable profit is

$$N = 100 \times (P + W + R/2)/YS$$
or $$R = 2(YNS/100 - P - W)$$

where N = minimum acceptable net profit as a percentage of sales
P = investment in plant
W = investment in working capital
R = research costs, before tax

Y = number of years needed for total recapture of investment expenses
S = annual sales

Dean-Sangupta Index

This index has been formulated specifically by subsequent writers as:

$$\text{Index} = \frac{T \times C \times \sum_{t=1}^{N} R_t (1 + I)^{-t}}{\sum_{t=0}^{N} I_t (1 + i)^{-t}}$$

where i = cost of capital

T = probability of technical success

C = probability that the product will be marketed, if it is a technical success

R_t = return from the project in year t if it is both technically successful and marketed

N = number of years until the product is dropped

I_t = investment in year t

Present Worth and Rate-of-Return Techniques

The application of capital investment techniques in their barest form omits and obscures the greatest areas of uncertainty in new-product development. These are the marketing and commercialization problems. At the same time, such an analysis does focus on the equipment investment aspect and long range impact of new product decisions.

Let C = cost of new or additional equipment

E_j = net cash flow (may be positive or negative) in year j

i = cost of capital

r = rate of return

V = present value of the stream of cash flows

n = life of the equipment or the market life of the product, whichever is shorter, in years

The present worth method is the computation of the present value of the stream of cash flows. If this value V exceeds C, the indication is on the favorable side.

$$V = \sum_{j=1}^{n} E_j (1 + i)^{-j}$$

and $(V - C)/C$ = return on investment

In the so-called rate-of-return, discounted cash flow, or investor's method, the object is to find that rate of return r which will satisfy the equation

$$C = \sum_{j=1}^{n} E_j (1 + r)^{-j}$$

This is usually accomplished by trying different values of r until the right side of the equation is equal to the left side.

Sobelman Formula

The Sobelman Formula directs the present worth technique specifically to evaluation of new products.[8] The average annual profits and average annual development costs are discounted to the present. The difference of profit minus cost must be positive for the project to be considered.

$$z = \sum_{j=1}^{T^*} P (1 + i)^{-j} - \sum_{j=1}^{t^*} c (1 + i)^{-j}$$

where z = the value of the project

P = average net profit/year

c = average development cost/year

$T^* = T + \bar{T} (1 - t/\bar{t})$

$t^* = t + \bar{t} (1 - T/\bar{T})$

where T = market life or useful life, in years

t = number of years until the development is finished

$\bar{T}$ = average useful life for the class of products of which the project is a member

$\bar{t}$ = average time for development for the class of products of which the project is a member

MANAGEMENT SCIENCE APPROACHES

A number of aspects of project evaluation have been attacked by sophisticated quantitative techniques. The development of each of these methods is so lengthy that only a substance is given here. The reader is referred to the original publication for the complete development.[9]

Selection of Research Projects[10]

Atkinson and Bobis have developed a probabilistic model which has helped the management of American Cyanamid's Organic Chemicals Division to select projects and make budget allocations. Although a full explanation of the model cannot be given here, we will outline the key aspects.

First, the probability $P(C)$ that a project will be completed for an expenditure no greater than X dollars is developed as

$$P(C) = 1/[1 + \exp{(a - bX^a)}]$$

when a and b are constants used to fit this logistics curve to two data points.

The probability that the project will be completed in the i-th year, $P(C_i)$. is then computed. The overall probability of success, $P(S)$, multiplied by $P(C_i)$ gives the probability of success in the i-th year, p_i.

$$p_i = P(S) P(C_i)$$

The probability that the project does not fail or is not completed by the i-th year means that research expenditures will be required in succeeding years.

A life cycle curve for sales is then computed as

$$s_j = B/[1 + \exp{(g - jd)}]$$

where B is the asymptotic value for maximum sales and g and d are constants.

The delay between revenues from sales and completion of research is then estimated. From this, sales revenues in year j accruing from research in year i are calculated from another formula developed by the authors. All expenditures and revenues are then discounted to the present to yield the value of the project. By means of a computer simulation, a probability distribution for the gains from a project is developed.

Hazard Analysis[11]

A hazard state is a specific condition for which the magnitude of a loss exceeds a specific acceptable value. For example, suppose the criterion value is $100,000. Then a loss of $200,000 with a probability of 0.25 yields a product of $50,000. Since this doesn't exceed the criterion value, it is not a hazard state. If, however, a loss of $150,000 with a probability of 0.70 were associated with some stage of a project, the resulting product of $105,000 indicates that a hazard state exists.

There is almost a one-to-one relationship between new-product decisions and hazards. This relationship is shown by means of a *fault tree* as shown in Figure 10-11.

In some cases, it is possible to recover from hazards and in other cases, the hazard states are nonrecoverable states. The probability of proceeding to a successful end result may be calculated by first setting up a hazard system similar to that shown in Figure 10-12.

The DEMON Model[12,13]

Companies gather a large volume of data, much of which cannot be exploited. Reams of computer data output is not the answer to the new-product decision making. The DEMON Model (Decision Mapping via Optimum Networks) focuses on profit maximization, integration of financial, marketing, and production, and flexible planning for marketing. DEMON is a dynamic computerized model which provides for evaluations at key stages as shown in Figure 10-13 for a portion of the marketing network.

COMMITMENT TIMING FOR LAUNCHING A NEW PRODUCT

Preparation for manufacturing and for marketing before the product design is complete is required to shorten the time from product concept to market introduction. Such early preparation may make worthless a certain proportion of equipment, packaging, advertising layout, or dealer training. A model has been developed which establishes the date of commitment of funds in such fixed investments so that the "expected value" of the loss of investment due to a design or sales forecast change equals the expected value of a loss due to delay in getting our product on the market.

RUIN MODELS

Each time a company introduces a new product, it is making a bet. The payoff may be positive or negative. We can therefore visualize the company as a

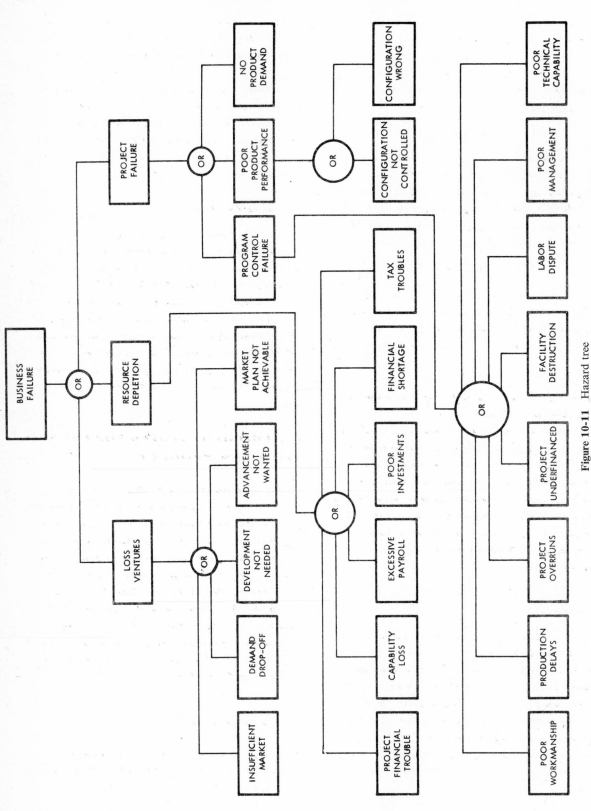

Figure 10-11 Hazard tree

Source: F. H. Krantz, *The Hazards of Project Decisions*, Space Division of North American Rockwell Corp., Report SD 69–26, March, 1969

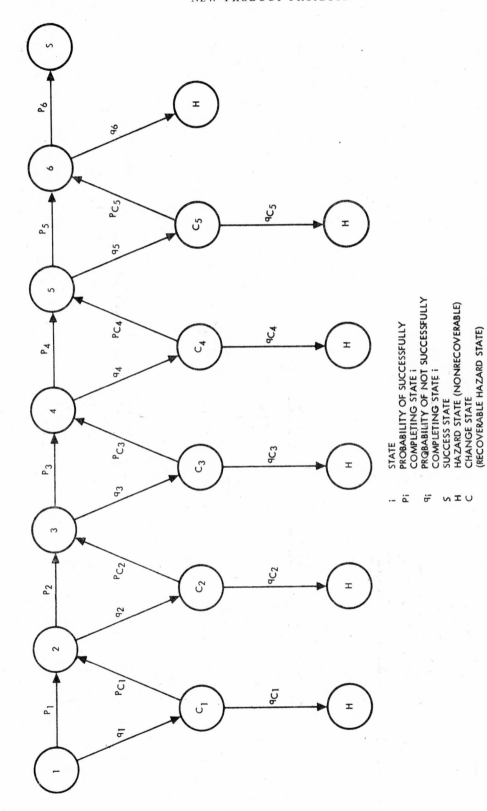

Figure 10-12 System development with changes

Source: F.H. Krantz, *The Hazards of Project Decisions*, Space Division of North American Rockwell Corp., Report SD 69-26, March, 1969

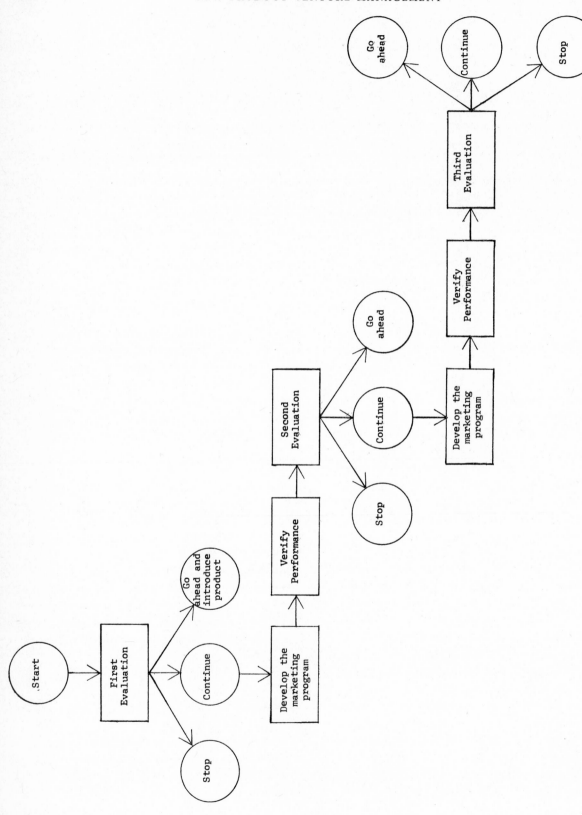

Figure 10-13 Portion of Marketing Decision Making

gambler betting over and over again. There is a certain probability of winning each time. The company may face ruin if the probability of winning is small each time, or the size of the loss is large relative to the capital of the company. The questions are: What estimated risk should the company take (to introduce a new product) in terms of its resources? What is the probability of ruin under this policy and is it acceptable?

If the company starts with C units of capital, invests one unit of capital on each new product, and the probability of winning one unit or losing it on each new product is p, then where q is $1 - p$,

Probability of escaping ruin $\cong 1 - (q/p)^C$

While this is a greatly simplified version of real life, it indicates the kind of approach used.[14]

PRAGMATIC METHODS

A company must contend with two very practical problems whose solutions appear at first glance to be in conflict. The first problem is to encourage the creative marketing and engineering people to produce a multitude of new product ideas. If rigid forms and detailed analyses must be prepared for each idea by these creative people, they tend to find other outlets for their creativity. Their regular jobs can absorb all the time that they can make available.

On the other hand, business evaluations of new-product ideas must be made. Firms cannot afford the luxury of pursuing many ideas to the point of commercial failure. Therefore, the most modern sophisticated techniques, within cost constraints, should be brought to bear upon the evaluations as the development of a new product progresses.

A simple solution to this dilemma may be possible. A relatively unstructured and brief form should be used to solicit new ideas. This form should ask only for a description of the product or the description of a market need and the author's reasons for believing this could be a profitable product. The short form should then be passed on to a business evaluation team. Such a team should be made up of a mix of individuals so that executive judgment,

functional competence, and management science skills are all present. At the initial screening, proposals would be classified on an A-B-C basis. A-rated proposals would be accepted for a significant expenditure of technical and marketing effort and money. Such proposals would be those with a high probability of success at this point in time. B-rated proposals would be those where there is a *possibility* of a good commercial success, say a 50–50 chance, but further investigation is required. A small step forward would be taken by a modest expenditure of funds for the purpose of gathering additional technical and marketing information. Final, C-rated proposals would be rejected on the basis of the first business analysis screening.

Flow Chart for New Product Evaluation

Mr. P. T. Ferrie, Manager of Business Development, Gulf Energy & Environmental Systems, Inc., presents a procedure for evaluating new product ideas which is in accord with the above recommendations. This procedure it described in the flow chart shown in Figure 10-14.

Evaluation Forms

A composite of the information required on the product evaluation forms of about 30 companies is provided by Figure 10-11. Individual companies show expanded versions of certain topics, particularly the technical evaluation. Relatively few indicated much detailed thought on the marketing aspects.

Figure 10-15 provides the basis for any company wishing to design or improve upon its evaluation form, expansion of some factors and omission of others are likely. Figure 2-7 through 2-7c illustrates still another approach.

SUMMARY

We have shown descriptive, quantitative, and pragmatic techniques for evaluating and selecting projects. Each firm must identify its key problem areas, its needs for information, and the appropriate

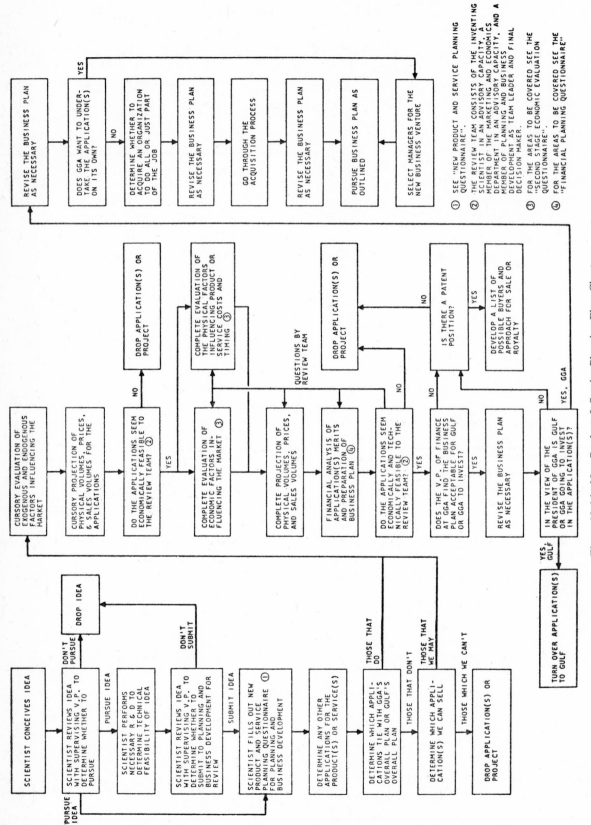

Figure 10-14   New Product & Service Planning Flow Chart

Source: P. T. Ferrie, Manager, Business Development, Gulf Energy & Environmental Systems, Inc., Feb., 1971

I Identification and Description

II Status Report
Brief summary of progress and expenditures to-date so that previously adopted projects may be reevaluated

III Evaluation of Technical Phases
A. Engineering analysis
B. Engineering exploration
C. Development model design
D. Development model construction
E. Development model test
F. Production model design
G. Pilot production test
H. Final engineering design and manufacturing drawings
I. Costs for each phase broken down by direct labor, direct materials, indirect expense, and general and administrative expense
J. Estimated start and completion times for each phase
K. Anticipated development problems
1. Unproved concept
2. Unsatisfactory concept of approach
3. Lack of personnel
4. Lack of facilities
5. Unsatisfactory definition of requirement

IV Evaluation of Marketing Characteristics
A. Types of customers that comprise the market, their needs, their buying practices
B. Size of market
C. Market trend and growth
D. Customer loyalty
E. Market share
F. Marketing practices: pricing, distribution, servicing, warranties
G. Competitors: strength and weaknesses
H. Anticipated marketing problems
1. Unsatisfactory sales forecast
2. Competitive situation

3. Customer make rather than buy
4. Indefinite requirements

V Operations Characteristics
Key skills, techniques, facilities; labor content; geographical considerations; proprietary and patent considerations; regulations

VI Manufacturing Evaluation
A. Available facilities
B. Capital equipment requirements
C. Manufacturing skills matched against requirements
D. Inventories required
E. Anticipated manufacturing problems
1. Undeveloped process
2. Lack of personnel
3. Tooling cost estimate too high
4. Lack of facilities: plant, equipment, tooling
5. High facility cost
6. High manufacturing cost
7. No cost estimate available

VII Financial Evaluation
A. Sales in dollars each year for three years
B. Cost of good sold: labor, materials, burden, each year for three years
C. G & A expenses
D. Marketing expenses
E. Target annual profit for each of first three years
F. Capital expenditures required
G. Working capital required
H. Inventories, in dollars
I. Return on investment

VIII Degree of Certainty at Each Stage
A. Certain and no anticipated problems
B. Certain, but anticipated problems
C. Probable (over 50% chance of success), but anticipated problems
D. Possible (under 50% chance of success), but anticipated problems.

Figure 10-15 Information requested on product evaluation forms

models to utilize such information. The key points to consider are:

1. What is the nature of the life cycle of the proposed product?
2. What are the most logical points in the product planning pre-launching phase to evaluate a particular product?
3. What combination of new product prospects may

be developed within the resource constraints which will yield the greatest present value of future cash flows (and intangible benefits)?

4. What information is needed to evaluate projects at each phase and what is the optimum amount in terms of cost and value? Value is, of course, a function of reliability and usefulness in decision making.

REFERENCES

1. Lt. John M. Byrne, Jr., presented this idea as a central theme in a paper at Rensselaer Polytechnic Institute on April 1970.

2. Robert F. Klausner, "The Evaluation of Risk in Marine Capital Investment", *The Engineering Economist*, Summer, 1969.

3. Franz Edelman and Joel S. Greenberg, "Venture Analysis: The Assessment of Uncertainty and Risk", *Financial Executive*, August, 1969.

4. Earnest C. Miller, *Advanced Techniques for Strategic Planning*, AMA Research Study 104, American Management Association, Inc., 1971.

5. See Z. C. Eulberg, "Soft Decision Engineering", *Optimum Systems Planning*, Proc. IFAC Symposium, Case Western Reserve U., Cleveland, Ohio 44106, June 20–22, 1968.

6. "Can You Rate Your Research", *Chemical Week*, May 30, 1959.

7. George Libik, Manley Formula—"The Economic Assessment of Research and Development", *Management Science*, Sept., 1969, pp. 49, 50.

8. Sidney A. Sobelman, *Modern Dynamic Approach to Product Development*, Picatinny Arsenal, Dover, N.J., Dec., 1958.

9. See Marvin J. Cetron, Joseph Martino, and Lewis Roepcke, "The Selection of R & D Program Content— Survey of Quantitative Methods", *IEEE Trans. on Engineering Management*, March, 1967, for a more complete listing of management science approaches to new product evaluation.

10. Anthony C. Atkinson and Arthur H. Bobis, "A Mathematical Basis for the selection of Research Projects", *IEEE Trans. on Engineering Management*, Feb., 1969.

11. See, in particular, F. H. Kranz, *The Hazards of Project Decisions*, Space Division of North American Rockwell Corp., Report SD 69–26, March, 1969.

12. See A. Charnes *et al.*, "DEMON: A Management Model for Marketing New Products", *California Management Review*, Fall, 1969.

13. A Charnes *et al.*, "DEMON: Decision Mapping Via Optimum Go-No Networks—a Model for Marketing New Products", *Management Science*, July, 1966.

14. See J. V. Uspensky, *Introduction of Mathematical Probability*, New York: McGraw-Hill Book Co., 1937 (chapter 8), and David W. Miller and Martin K. Starr, *Executive, Decisions and Operations Research* (2nd ed.), Englewood Cliffs, N.J.: Prentice-Hall, Inc., 1969 (pp. 511–517). See also Robert G. Murdick, *Mathematical Models in Marketing*, Scranton, Pa.: Intext Educational Publishers, 1971.

BIBLIOGRAPHY

Atkinson, Anthony C. and Arthur H. Bobis, "A Mathematical Basis for the Selection of Research Projects", *IEEE Trans. on Engineering Management*, Feb., 1969.

Byrne, Lt. John M., Jr., Paper presented at Rensselaer Polytechnic Institute, April, 1970.

"Can You Rate Your Research", *Chemical Week*, May 30, 1959.

Cetron, Marvin J., Joseph Martino, and Lewis Roepcke, "The Selection of R & D Program Content—Survey of Quantitative Methods", *IEEE Trans. on Engineering Management*, March, 1967.

Charnes, A., *et al.*, "DEMON: A Management Model for Marketing New Products", *California Management Review*, Fall, 1969.

Charnes, A., *et al.*, "DEMON: Decision Mapping Via Optimum Go-No Networks—a Model for Marketing New Products", *Management Science*, July, 1966.

Dimsdale, B. and H. P. Flatt, "Project Evaluation and Selection", *IBM Systems Journal*, Sept.–Dec., 1963.

Edelman, Franz and Joel S. Greenberg, "Venture Analysis: The Assessment of Uncertainty and Risk", *Financial Executive*, August, 1969.

Eulberg, A. C., "Soft Decision Engineering", *Optimum Systems Planning*, Proc. IFAC Symposium, Case Western Reserve U., Cleveland, Ohio 44106, June 20–22, 1968.

Fisk, George (ed.), *The Analysis of Business Systems*, Lund, Sweden: C. W. K. Gleerup, 1967.

Hertz, David B., "Risk Analysis in Capital Investment", *Harvard Business Review*, February, 1964.

Klausner, Robert F., "The Evaluation of Risk in Marine Capital Investment", *The Engineering Economist*, Summer, 1969.

Kranz, F. H., *The Hazards of Project Decisions*, Space Division of North American Rockwell Corp., Report SD 69–26, March, 1969.

Libik, George, "The Economic Assessment of Research and Development", *Management Science*, Sept., 1969, pp. 49, 50.

Miller, David W. and Martin K. Starr, *Executive Decisions and Operations Research* (2nd ed.). Englewood Cliffs, N.J.: Prentice-Hall, Inc., 1969.

Miller, Ernest C., *Advanced Techniques for Strategic Planning*, AMA Research Study 104. New York: American Management Association, 1971.

Murdick, Robert G., *Mathematical Models in Marketing*, Scranton, Pa.: Intext Educational Publishers, 1971.

Murdick, Robert G. and G. A. Steiner, "Hazard Analysis for New Product Development", Proc. American Institute for Decision Sciences, Blacksburg, Va., April 29–30, 1971.

Schrieber, Albert N. (ed.), *Corporate Simulation Models*. Seattle, Wash.: Graduate School of Business Administration, University of Washington, 1970.

Uspensky, J. V., *Introduction of Mathematical Probability*. New York: McGraw-Hill Book Co., 1937.

CHAPTER 11

HOW TO COST THE NEW PRODUCT

IMPORTANT BASIC COST CONCEPTS

From the managerial viewpoint, there are six cost concepts (not necessarily those an accountant would choose) which underlie all the detailed calculations, judgments, estimates, in the financial technician's ceremonies:

1. Planned costs vs. historical costs
2. Parametric costing—the allocation of costs among functions for maximum profits
3. Cost for goals and efficiency
4. Decline of unit costs according to an experience function
5. Breakeven concept and direct costing
6. Incremental cost concept

Costs must not be viewed in isolation. The decision to open a new product line should hinge upon its prospective contributions to the firm's long-run profit goals; not its short-term effect. A new product may at first provide the firm with real losses. Unfortunately, some never become a profit contributor in a direct sense. However, even in the latter case their may be other advantages such as a ready supply of an alternative to current suppliers of sub-assembly parts which may prove invaluable in instances of developing market shortages or monopolies (on suppliers, part, monopsony).

DANGERS FROM HISTORICAL COSTING

The big trap for the new product manager to beware of lies in the evaluation of alternatives through the use of the accountant's cost figures. Accountant figures used by the unskilled can lead to disaster, especially those which involve historical costs. These costs are past history. They were incurred at some past time and bear only accidental similarity to current values. Thus, when the new products manager foresees appropriation of equipment that is already in the firm's possession, the cost of this equipment should not be charged to him at a figure above its current cash value (current cash equivalent CCE), that is the price this equipment could command on the market, at that time. Yet, historical cost procedures will often charge the new product manager a much higher price.

If the equipment has alternative use in the firm, (it is not currently idle) then its cost should be the opportunity cost of using it, that is, the lost revenue from the alternative use.

Another danger lurking in the use of accountants' costs appears when overhead is allocated to new products on some predetermined basis. Again, the only relevant cost is the addition to cost precipitated by the production of new products—or incremental costs. Incremental costs, to repeat, are the addition to original total costs.

A third area for caution is encountered in dealing with sub-assemblies to be used in production of new products. These sub-assembled parts, also, are burdened with allocated overhead. This allocated overhead is composed of non-homogeneous costs, some current, some past, that may or may not be relevant in evaluating the total cost of the proposed new products and in coming to a decision concerning its future production. The allocation of costs to the new product directly should be carefully scrutinized. The use of some factor of allocation to apply overhead can be the cause of a "reject" decision. Overhead, regardless of the method of allocation, labor hours, labor cost, machine hours, etc., should only be composed of incremental cost. The addition of special machinery, or hiring of an addition foreman required by the addition of new products, are illustrations of such incremental costs.

Perhaps the most important thing to stress is that costs are assembled for different purposes. The accountants' historical costs apportioned and allocated in various (and sometimes questionable) ways should not be used without analysis and modification for making decisions on cost of new lines, and future profit contribution. Furthermore, in many instances, a product may be justified because of its values, such as providing ready supply of sub-assembled parts, preventing suppliers from dictating price, complementing an existing line, and so forth. In short, the new product manager must not limit himself to a simple dollar and cents analysis.

One final observation related to historical costing is that it is often coupled to (used with) the absorption cost approach. This procedure funnels fixed and sunk costs (costs which are viewed as sunk into or integral with the poduct) to products. The procedure can therefore mislead management in

(a) selecting between and/or adding new products
(b) pricing products
(c) computing costs by product line

Planned Costs vs. Historical Costs

For new product development, the fact that costs can be estimated in advance on the basis of various decisions is extremely important. When a new product concept first arises, management should not be gulled into believing that there is a single cost for developing the product and getting it on the market. In the first place, there are tradeoffs in time and risk. For example, management makes decisions concerning the manhours to be spent in each stage of development and analysis. There are usually higher risks attached to shorter time investments, but it is

management's responsibility to view the risk in terms of potentially greater payoffs.

Other planning which results in different cost patterns is based on the quality decision. For a new product, management should specify in advance the quality of the product in terms of the market and profit planning. Costs will also vary according to allocation of emphasis among engineering, manufacturing and marketing.

It must always be remembered that the costs developed in an estimate for a new product are *estimates*. Their accuracy varies with the information available, the skill of the estimators, the time to develop the estimate, and the attitudes of management. With regard to the latter item, too much pessimism will almost always cause the estimators to put in excess contingencies just as too much optimism and pressure for a low cost can have the opposite effect.

The point that is made here is that costs can be planned for over a wide range. Moreover, estimates of costs are not usually accurate except in the latter stages of the engineering effort—and then only when done by very skilled estimators working in the right environment and who enjoy a liberal portion of luck in forecasting the costs. Costs are not simply a package handed to management *after the fact* by estimators and accountants, but represent a key area of decision making for management.

Parametric Costing

The second basis concept deals with one of these important decisions which management must be aware of. The levels of expenditures for engineering, manufacturing, and marketing are parameters (optional values) which management may combine in various ways for any desired total budget level. For

($1000's)					
Step 1: Marketing effort	450	500	550	600	650
Step 2: Sales forecast	1000	1100	1320	1500	1580
Step 3: Other expenses	350	360	500	650	700
Step 4: Profit	200	240	270	250	230

Figure 11-1 Profit forecasting for different marketing levels

example, management could invest heavily in engineering, hence quality, at the expense of marketing effort. Or management could plan for a low allocation of effort to manufacturing, say, by elimination of quality control, in order to allocate more funds to marketing. Within the limitations of company policies and long-range objectives, management should examine a range of values of these "parameters" in order to find the best mix, i.e., greatest resulting profit.

Two figures will illustrate the point clearly. Figure 11-1 shows that there is no such thing as "*the sales forecast*", but rather the sales forecast depends upon funds expended, in this case, on marketing, assuming that other expenditures are held constant. It further shows that continually increasing expenditures *does not yield corresponding increasing profits*. There are diminishing returns.

Figure 11-2 shows how management may examine

Profit ($1000's)					
Marketing effort	450	500	550	600	650
Engineering development					
30	160	180	220	290	270
40	200	210	230	230	220
50	230	250	260	260	270

Figure 11-2 Profits for different mixes of marketing and engineering effort

variations in *two* parameters under its control, (1) engineering development and (2) marketing effort. We note that for the product under consideration a minimum of technical development with a fairly large marketing effort produces the maximum profit.

Often a pictorial version is helpful to the manager. Figure 11-3 shows how profits may be represented

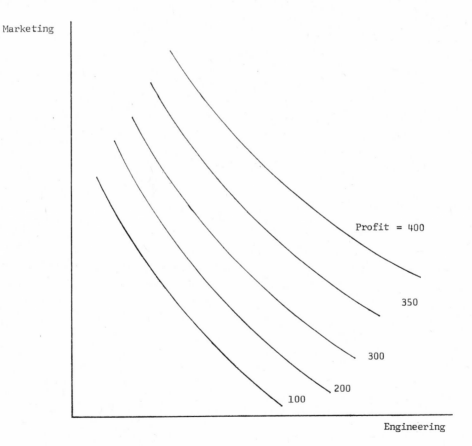

Figure 11-3 Profit contours

in terms of marketing and engineering effort in graphic form. Two things may be seen from Figure 11-3. If engineering effort is reduced to a very low point, proportionately greater marketing effort is required to maintain the same profit level. Also, to increase the profit level, considerably more of both resources must be devoted until finally the cost is so great that profits actually decrease with an increase in resources.

Cost for Goals and Efficiency

The typical unthinking company chant is "Reduce the costs! Reduce the costs!" Some aspects of cost reduction are commendable. However, one could, for example, lower costs by sacrificing quality, take increasing manufacturing risks, and decrease advertising and the sales force—all these actions would lower cost per unit. What is obvious but not frequently seen is that costs are based upon the goals set for the product and the efficiency with which these goals are achieved. The drive for reduction of costs should be based upon maintaining specified quality of product and support of operations.

Certain kinds of manufacturing, distribution, and office costs can be safely lowered through the techniques of industrial and value engineering, a fact reflected in the experience function. The experience function is discussed below.

Another factor that probably should be considered here is that of Organizational Slack. Many forms of slack exist—wages in excess of those to maintain the operation. This cushion which exists in almost any firm permits many of them to survive in the face of adversity. Under the pressure of potential failure—or the need to somehow mount an effort to introduce a new product—the organization discovers previously unrecognized opportunities for increasing the resources available.

Decline of Unit Costs—The Experience Function

According to research by The Boston Consulting Group, "Costs appear to go down on value added at about 20 to 30% every time total product experience doubles for the industry as a whole, as well as for individual producers".[1]

This means that if the business is run efficientl, and if the production cost of the 100th unit is $40, the cost of making the 200th unit is $32 if the 20% decline rate applies. Note that this reduction is assumed to be limited to value added by the company and hence does not include the cost of materials purchased. However, the actual experience of The Boston Consulting Group and the authors' is that purchased material has an experience curve of its own that causes decreases in price with quantity produced. A practical result of this is that initial quotes on "buy" parts for a new product will add up to one figure, the actual purchase prices will add to a lower figure if Purchasing is aggressive in trying to reduce costs. Moreover, the initial quotes on the second production run and the actual purchase prices will have a similar relationship—and both will be lower than the first two sets of price totals.

Breakeven Concept and Direct Costing

Direct costing is not essential to break-even analysis; however, it helps. Break-even points can be computed under absorption costing; all that is required is an adjustment for fixed costs elements involved in inventory charges. Furthermore, errors in interpretation may occur with direct costing for the assumption is made that variable costs are always the only relevant costs. This is not so. It is incremental costs, fixed as well as variable, that are relevant. The break-even concept is simply this. There is a gross margin or excess of revenue over variable cost per unit. This could be restated that gross margin is incremental revenue less variable cost. The cumulative gross margin increases as more units are sold. For a specified period such as a year or a product life cycle, there are certain fixed costs which exist whether or not any goods are produced and sold. The cumulative gross margin (excess of revenue over variable costs) must first pay off the period's fixed costs. After this break-even point, where total revenue equals total costs, the profit on all future units is the gross margin for the period involved.

The significance of this is that after the break-even point, fixed or overhead cost *should be forgotten and the objective should be to sell units for the best price possible as long as the gross margin is greater than zero*— admittably, this is an oversimplification of the strategy to follow. However, the approach given is opposed to the traditional accounting method which continues to charge a portion of fixed costs to all units, regardless of the quantity made and sold.

It perhaps should be added that "fixed or overhead" should not be combined synonymously, since overhead has a variable portion also. Furthermore, fixed costs that are not incremental may be ignored even before the break-even point. The point to stress is the margin over variable costs, the contribution margin. The contribution margin is available to cover fixed costs.

It should be understood that there can be (and usually is) a trade-off between large investment in equipment and investment in labor. A large equipment investment means a high break-even point and more risk. It also usually means small labor costs and therefore a greater contribution margin after the break-even point has been reached.

Another important value of break-even analysis for new products is that it provides an estimate of the number of units which must be sold to break

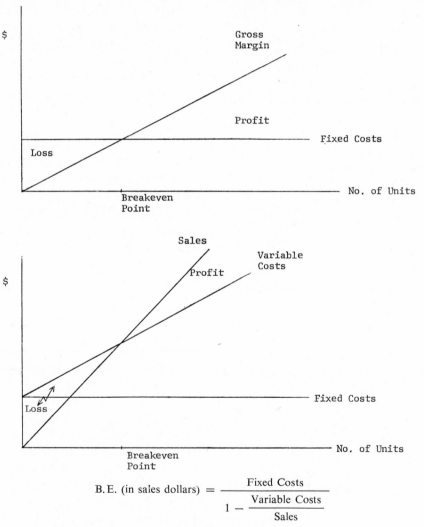

$$\text{B.E. (in sales dollars)} = \cfrac{\text{Fixed Costs}}{1 - \cfrac{\text{Variable Costs}}{\text{Sales}}}$$

Figure 11-4 Breakeven analysis

even. For example, if we estimate costs and prices such that 100,000 units must be sold to break even and the total market over the next five years is only 50,000 units, we must have some other very convincing arguments to bring out the new product.

Two sketches which clarify the idea of the break-even point are shown in Figure 11-4. The upper sketch shows the cumulative gross margin growing until it overcomes the fixed costs. The lower sketch shows the gross margin broken up into revenue (sales) and variable costs vs. number of units sold. As an example of the calculation of the break-even point, suppose

F.C. = $4000 for the period
V.C. as a percent of sales = 60%
Unit price = $5.00

$$\text{Break-even (\$)} \quad = \frac{\$4000}{1 - 0.60} = \$10,000 \text{ in sales}$$

Break-even (units) = ($10,000)/$5 = 2000 units

Incremental Cost Concept

Suppose a plant had idle plant and warehouse capacity and some "somewhat" idle permanent salaried employees. It is estimated that the cost of these is $30,000 per year. The company is debating whether to introduce a new product which it has developed. If it does so, the accountants plan to allocate $50,000 per year as the product's share of the total overhead. Additional data for the first year indicates the following:

Revenue	$100,000
Variable cost	60,000
Allocated overhead	50,000
Loss	$ 10,000

The company has no other promising products sufficiently developed so that the only alternative is not to produce the product. The empty space and idle machinery must still be paid for and the following table may be constructed:

Revenue	$	0
Variable cost		0
Overhead		30,000
Loss		$30,000

The incremental (additional) cost for producing this product for the year is $110,000 [variable costs plus *allocated* overhead (more than actual overhead)] − $30,000 (real or actual out-of-pocket overhead) = $80,000. Sales yield $100,000. Instead of a loss of $10,000 (the way the accountants normally figure), the incremental concept indicates that the company will bring in a profit of $100,000 − $80,000 (out-of-pocket variable and fixed costs) = $20,000.

The incremental cost concept says that when we consider introducing a new product, we should determine the *additional revenues* and the *additional costs* to find the *additional profits* (or losses).

COSTS IN RELATION TO RETURN ON INVESTMENT

Before detailing the costing procedures, we wish to show how costs are related to the construction of the Return on Investment. In this case, one chart is better than many words, so the reader is referred to Figure 11-5.

As we might suspect, accountants almost always have one or more ways of figuring a thing such as ROI. The chart in Figure 11-6 illustrates the five more important ways one can look at ROI. Also, the previous chapter contains additional material regarding ROI.

THE COSTING PROBLEM—THE COST ELEMENTS

Now that much of the overall approaches to establishing a cost have been covered, it is time to examine some of the specific cost elements that must be considered separately and in combination with each other. The following is a suggested check list of such items:

1. Pre-production engineering
2. Product support engineering
3. Facility cost
4. Equipment cost
5. Tool, jig, fixture, and miscellaneous materials handling equipment cost

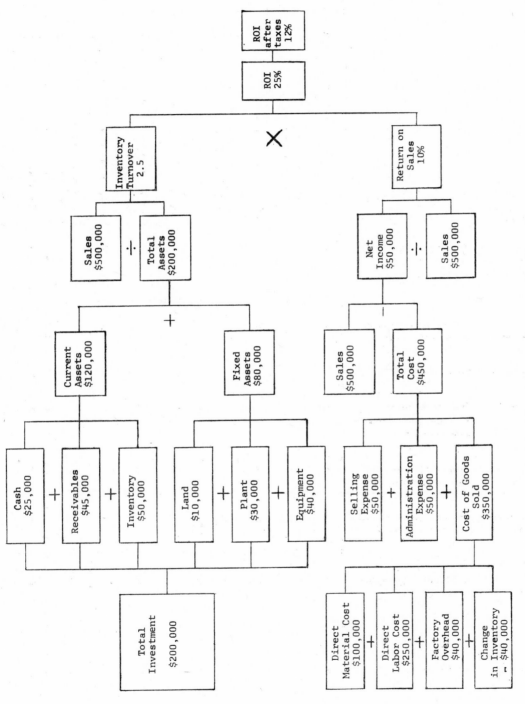

Figure 11-5   Costs and ROI, a simplified view

FACTORS INFLUENCING CALCULA-

Basic method	Other names or variations	Earnings or savings				Equipment or facility life				Investment cost	
		Operating expense		Operating receipts							
		Annual operating expense	Dollars adjusted for time distribution of expense	Annual operating receipts	Dollars adjusted for time distribution of receipts	Service life of proposed project	Salvage value of proposed project	Salvage value of old facility	Depreciations option may be selected	Installed cost	Capital additions adjusted for time value
1. Payback method	Payoff period, cash recovery method, payout period	X		X				X		X	
2. Return on investment	Accounting method, payback reciprocal	X		X		X		X		X	
3. First-year performance	First-year profits	X		X		X	X	X	X	X	
4. Total-life	Full-life performance, average, annual return, average cost	X				X	X	X		X	
5. Average rate of return	Profit return on average investment, average book method	X		X		X	X			X	
6. Present-worth method	Discounted cash flow, inventor's method	X	X	X	X	X	X	X	X	X	
7. Rate-of-return method	Discounted cash flow, investor's method	X	X	X	X	X	X	X	X	X	
8. Improved MAPI method	MAPI formula	X	X	X	X	X	X	X	X	X	

Figure 11-6

TIONS

Cost of money		Income tax	Investment credit against income tax	Inflationary or deflationary price changes		
Cost of capital or interest rate on borrowed money	Changes in time distribution of interest				Key advantages	Key disadvatages
		X	X		Quick and easy to compute. Drops out projects with very long lives. For high return projects with long lives, payback method gives a good approximation of complex methods.	Neglects time value of money and capital additions. Does not give a return on investment to compare with cost of capital. Fails to consider any revenue beyond the payback period.
		X	X		Gives a return on investment. Quick and easy to compute.	Neglects the time value of money. Generally assumes uniform annual receipts.
		X	X		Costs and receipts can be accurately forecast 1 year ahead.	Neglects cash flows beyond 1 year and neglects time value of such flows.
X					Rough and quick method of comparison of alternatives. Indicates cost per year. Permits comparison of projects with different service lives.	Neglects receipts or assumes they are the same for both alternatives. Neglects time value of money.
		X	X		Shows effect of decreasing value of investment over the life of the project. Easy to compute.	Gives a much higher rate of return value than other methods.
X		X	X		Flexible. Evaluates income and expenses as they occur. Good for ranking all sizes of projects.	Requires careful forecasting of expenses, revenues, and capital additions. Requires an estimate of cost of capital.
		X			Flexible. Evaluates income and expenses as they occur. Good for ranking all sizes of projects.	Requires careful forecasting of expenses, revenues, and capital additions. Awkward to solve the trial and error method. Assumes that cash is reinvested at rate of return of each project.
X Fixed		X			Standardized and simple. Sophisticated concepts underlie the method. Good for cost reduction, modernization and replacment projects.	For evaluating projects against existing project. Next-year comparison only.

Comparison of evaluation methods

Source: R. G. Murdick and D. D. Deming, *The Management of Capital Expenditures*, copyright used with permission of McGraw-Hill Book Company, 1968

6. Purchased material cost
7. Direct labor cost
8. Shrinkage
9. Scrap
10. Transportation
11. Overhead
12. Selling expense
13. General and administrative expense
14. Patent license costs
15. Special taxes

Each of the categories can easily be broken down into sub-categories and, in addition, new categories peculiar to a particular situation can also often be isolated and be considered separately. For example, if the product required the use of gem cutting techniques, it might be necessary to import one or more specialists from a foreign country. This could be extremely expensive and one could easily justify handling it as a separate major cost element.

While the development of the costs associated with many of the cost elements require use of separate cost analysis forms (An example is shown in Figure 11-8) it is also necessary to summarize total costs to determine if the desired has been reached. A typical form used for this purpose is shown in Figure 11-7 and is identified as a Cost Analysis. The order of usage on the form does not accord with the order of the cost element list since this is arranged solely for convenience of discussion. Bear in mind that the usage of this form as related to this discussion revolves around the pricing of new products. It can just as easily be used to price or analyze the cost of existing products. The example form illustrates how it could be used to cost a fictitious product. It is a conventional approach and implies that its usage will not take into account such things as fixed vs. variable expenses, etc. Actually, it is a form for accumulating costs, the details can be handled in any manner desired.

Pre-Production Engineering

Since this is primarily a dissertation on new product development, it would be wise to steer clear of any concepts that are unnecessarily difficult to define and for which there are conflicting definitions. For example, it is not necessary for the purpose of costing the prospective product to segregate "so-called" development engineering and product design engineering. If both are involved, they can be handled as a part of pre-production engineering. *Pre-production engineering cost can be defined as that engineering cost that will be necessary prior to the start of production.* A typical pre-production engineering estimate is shown in Figure 11-8 on a typical engineering cost estimating form.

Involved in pre-production engineering are such items as the following:

1. Engineering labor to investigate the problem generally
2. Junior engineer and/or technician labor to support the engineering investigation through lab work, library research, etc.
3. Drafting labor to make preliminary and final drawings
4. Packaging engineering costs to design the package and shipping carton
5. Specification engineering costs involved in integrating the special new product specifications into the established company standards
6. Model maker, assembly, or other similar labor costs to manufacture working models
7. Chemical engineering labor where this group provides consulting service (there may be other consulting groups within the particular company that need to be considered on a given product)
8. Technical publication costs, such as for writers, illustrators, etc., where one or more technical publications are needed in the marketing of the product
9. Engineering that may be contracted to another firm
10. Engineering material—raw, semi-finished—finished—which may be needed for any of the above labor classifications. Be sure to check each classification for related material costs
11. Engineering overhead on the labor
12. Procurement and transportation costs that may be chargeable against the material purchased
13. Travel of engineering personnel caused directly by the project

Cost Estimate		THE NEW PRODUCT COMPANY		BR. or Est. No. 2536

Cost Estimate
Bid Estimate
Engineering
C.P.F.F.
Fixed Price
Cost Indication
Make-Buy

THE NEW PRODUCT COMPANY
Plant - New York, New York

BR. or Est. No. 2536
Date January 5, 1960
Page 1 of 1

Distribution	Customer: Manufacturers of Military Electronic Equip. Customer No.:				
H. B. Allen	Article: Special high-temperature elec-trolytic capacitor having extremely low electrical leakage	Item #	Qty.	At (unit cost)	Amount
G. M. Clark					
J. E. West					
I. Newman					
	Representative unit	1	150M	$6.70	$405,000.00

		%	1						
1	Material		2.78						
2	Shrinkage	2	.06						
3	Procurement	5	.14						
4	Transportation	1	.03						
5	Total Material		3.01						
6									
7	Labor		.34						
8	Efficiency	90	.03						
9	Total Labor		.37						
10									
11	Overhead	181	.67						
12	Pre-Prod. Engr.		not charged						
13	Tools Etc.		.19						
14	Prod. Support Engr.		.13						
15	Engineering Labor		4.37						
16	Engineering O/H								
17	Total Mfg. Cost								
18	Interest								
19	Gen. & Admin.	5	.22						
20	Institutional Adv.	1	.04						
21	Royalties								
22									
23									
24	Total Cost		4.63						
25	Desired Profit		2.07						
26	Des. Selling Price		6.70						
27	Actual Profit		2.07						
28	Act. Selling Price		6.70						

Delivery and F.O.B. Point: New York, N. Y.

Comments: The above cost estimate is for a typical capacitor with a current selling price of $6.70 each.
Pre-Production engineering is considered as a legitimate charge against company R & D budget.
Pre-Production engineering is amortized over estimated first year's production for costing purposes.
Tool and Facilities are lumped into one charge and amortized over a three-year period for costing--
therefore one-third (1/3) of total charged to first year's production.

J. Blow	J. E. West	G. M. Clark	J. Adams
Product Manager	Engineer	Cost Estimating	Estimator

4G1319-2   M-1705-2

Figure 11-7 Cost analysis form for costing new products
Source: D.W. Karger, *The New Product*, New York: The Industrial Press, 1960. *Courtesy of the Magnavox Co*

PP. 756
REVISED
7.1.57

ESTIMATE OF ENGINEERING COST.
PRODUCT Special high-temperature
electrolytic capacitors
CUSTOMER Various

QUANTITY 150,000/year   PROPOSED SCHEDULE PERIOD 12 months

BID REQUEST NO. 2536   DATE _____

PREPARED BY I. Newman   DATE Jan. 5, 19 60
ENG. COST ANALYST I. Newman DATE Jan. 5, 19 60
PLANT New York, N.Y. SECTION Capacitor

CPFF ☐
FIXED ☐
OTHER ☐
R & D ☐
PRODUCTION ☒

ENGINEERING LABOR		MAN MONTHS	Pre-Prod. Engineering	MAN MONTHS	Support Engineering First Year					DESCRIPTION AND REMARKS
SENIOR ENG.	26									
ENGINEER "A" (Mechanical)	23	1.7	124,065							
ENGINEER "B"	21									
JUNIOR ENG.	19									
SR. LAB. TECH.	22									
LAB. TECHNICIAN "A"	20									
TECHNICIAN "B"	17									
ENG. AIDS (HOURLY)										
SR. DESIGN DRAFTSMAN	21									
CHECKER	21									
DESIGN DRAFTSMAN	19	.8	4,752.00							
JR. DESIGN DRAFTSMAN	18									
DETAIL DRAFTSMAN	15									
PACKAGING ENG. "B"	20									
SPECIFICATION ENG. "B"	18									
JR. SPECIFICATION ENG.	18									
MODEL MAKER "A"	19	4	22,000.00							
MODEL MAKER "B"	17									
MECHANICAL INSPECTOR	17									
MODEL MAKER APPREN.	15									
SR. CHEMICAL ENG.	26	11	95,810.00	12.	74,850.00					
CHEMICAL ENG. "A"	23									
CHEMICAL ENG. "B"	21									
JR. CHEMICAL ENG.	19									
CHEMICAL TECH. "B"	17	13	429,000	6	24,000.00					
EDITOR &/OR ARTIST	22									
SR. WRITER &/OR SR. TECH. ILLUST'R	20									
JR. WRITER &/OR JR. TECH. ILLUST'R	17									
ASSEMBLY SHOP (SALARIED)										
ASSEMBLY SHOP (HOURLY)										
FACTORY ASSISTANCE (HOURLY)										
TOTAL ENGINEERING LABOR			167,143.00		36,900.00					
ENGINEERING OVERHEAD @ 90 %			1,506,878.		882,000.					
ENGINEERING MATERIAL			5,546.00		8,000					
REPRODUCIBLE DW'GS			15,000							
TOTAL MATERIAL			55,100.00		5,000.00					
PROCUREMENT @10% R & D ONLY			551.00		500.00					
TRAVEL			1,000.00							
SUB-CONTRACT ENGINEERING										
PURCHASED TEST EQUIPMENT			5,575.00		155,250.00					
TOTALS			1,644,170.		1,092,550.					
UNIT COST			Not to be unitized		.13					

SECTION CHIEF _____ DATE 1/6/60
CHIEF ENGINEER _____ DATE 1-5-60
APPROVED
DIRECTOR OF ENGINEERING _____ DATE 1.5.60

Figure 11-8   Pre-production engineering estimate shown on a typical engineering estimating form
Source: *Ibid.*

14. Equipment costs associated with the pre-production engineering such as special machines, test equipment, etc.
15. Miscellaneous expenses. This category is provided to cover the more unusual costs, such as: outside laboratory service, consulting expense, patent license fees and associated legal expense.

The above check list covers the usual items of cost encountered in executing a pre-production engineering project. It would be virtually impossible to cover every category or kind of cost that might be encountered. For example, the check list in general would cover the situation where a proposed product might require the manufacture in the engineering department of a small number of test pieces that must be submitted to the government or to prospective customers for evaluation. On the other hand, this is the type of item that often is overlooked and only is noticed when the estimate is overrun. Multiple rechecks of any cost estimate are absolutely necessary if all of the costs are to be correctly delineated.

While pre-production engineering is a legitimate charge to a new product's over-all cost, it is rare that all of this cost can be recovered during the first year of production. One common way of costing the new product, so as to obtain recovery of the pre-production engineering cost and at the same time not make the burden so heavy as to force the selling price up to where the product cannot be sold, is to amortize the charge over a period of several years (usually 2 to 5 years).

It, of course, should not be overlooked, that the existing products of the company owe some of their revenue to the necessity of providing for the future of the company. If some of the new product pre-production engineering cost cannot be obtained from the profits of existing products—it will often spell the doom of the new product. A similar statement could be made regarding several of the other cost elements to be discussed.

Pre-production Engineering, in the example Cost Analysis shown in Figure 11-7, has not been amortized over any total expected output. In this case, the company felt this was a legitimate charge against existing products. The cost is shown for information purposes but not as a charge against the prospective new product.

Production-support Engineering

Production support engineering can be defined as those engineering costs that will be incurred during the production of the product on the factory floor. Even though the engineering department has engineered the product, produced drawings, tested working models, etc., their help and assistance will still be required after the product is put into production. The amount of engineering cost incurred during this phase of the product's history will be less than the pre-production engineering cost. It is, however, a tangible element of cost that cannot be overlooked an it will be larger during the first six months of production then after this period. The kind of items involved in the production support engineering are essentially the same as those listed under pre-production engineering and the same check list can and should be used.

Production support engineering is and was considered as a legitimate charge against the prospective new product in the Cost Analysis shown in Figure 11-7. It was amortized against the expected first year's production of 150,000 units.

Facility Cost

For ease in discussing this subject, it is well first to define what is meant by facility cost. It perhaps also would be wise to call the reader's attention to the fact that the definition of what is to be included in facilities will vary from company to company, to government agency, etc. The definition of the items to be included will generally be established by the Comptroller's department in industry and its counterpart in government. The guide or actual delineation ordinarily will be found in an accounting procedure or policy statement.

For the purpose of this discussion, facility costs will be defined as the cost associated with the establishment of any required new buildings, work benches, stock racks, pallets, and other general items that could have a future use on other products as opposed to special purpose items which can be utilized only on the product under consideration. This definition is believed to be of advantage to the estimator in collecting his data for the various cost elements. Normally most of these items are already available and he only has a small amount of miscellaneous costs—and as such the generalized definition given serves as a catch-all division. These could be sub-divided into so-called capital and expense items—a division that accounting will probably require. Accountants may use the term "revenue items" instead of expense items because they *normally* distinguish items charged to expense from items capitalized by the term "revenue items"—how to confuse the non-accountant!

The new product manager may also desire to make this latter sub-division if one or more members of management insist on charging part or all of the facility costs to the new product. Capital items are normally depreciated over a substantial period (10 to 30 years) and the depreciation is included in overhead which is charged to the product by an assessment to such factors as direct labor cost (the most common), direct labor hour, machine hours, etc. This procedure can be advantageous to product development by spreading the cost over time.

It is often possible to arrange with accounting and/or management, to amortize, for *product* costing purposes, the *expense* items over a time period, such as 2 to 3 years, instead of charging it off to the first year's revenues as would be done in a normal procedure. This aids the new product manager in justifying the product to management, since the charging against the product upon payment of the expense item invoice is an almost impossible situation. It inevitably seems to lead to a showing of a loss the first year which some managements cannot seem to accept. This latter procedure is the standard accounting department method for handling expense items. While the expense items may be charged off the company's books when the invoices are paid, the above procedure may be permitted in costing the new product. In effect, the product line is extended a no interest loan and allowed to repay it over an extended period. The effect is the same as that experienced with capital expenditures.

The facility costs will normally be provided by the industrial engineering and/or plant engineering functions. They can only do this after the product manager and the project engineer in the engineering department provide production design data, run rates, quantities to be produced the first year, future production forecasts, product drawings, specifications, etc.

In this initial effort to cost the new product it may be possible to merely "guesstimate" the probable facility cost, if any, rather than make a detailed estimate.

Few facilities, as defined in this section, will normally be required for the start of production of the ordinary new product—assuming that a well established company is introducing the new product. This is especially true if the same general type of product is being produced. It is primarily due to the fact that some surplus of the items defined usually exist. Such a surplus, coupled with the minimum requirements usually associated with initial production, can usually satisfy facility needs for start-up.

Often, when such needs are initially discussed it will be found that the estimating group, and their sources of information, will state that no surplus facilities exist. Only persistence and solid persuasive statements on the part of the new product manager or developer will force a solution to the problem that will not handicap the prospective new product with an unnecessary burden. No operating group wants to give up their safety margins on facilities, tools, equipment, etc. Ultimately, if the overall good of the company is sufficiently emphasized, such reluctance can be overcome.

While it may be necessary to purchase some few facilities, the problem can ordinarily be overcome as outlined above and by making some sacrifice of ideal layout and production process concepts. For example, it may be found necessary to plan for the work to be accomplished in several departments, rather than in one integrated production activity. A further compromise might involve spreading the work over several plant locations; however, this admittedly is often a dangerous and unwise solution because of the difficulty of adequate cost control and engineering assistance under this latter situation.

Another place to look for a solution to not only the facility problem, but also for the equipment, tools, etc., as later discussed, are the stocks of surplus items found in special storage areas around every plant. In one project, one of the authors required five different ovens (not actually a facility item). Four were located within the plant, but even after much "soul searching" by everyone the fifth could not be found. Everyone who should have known, said no more were available. However, a personal examination of a remote surplus equipment area in a rented building disclosed three practically new units. In fact, any one of these was ideal for the job requirement. The moral—don't ever give up!

Facility, equipment, and tooling costs for this project were all handled in a similar manner in the example Cost Analysis. They were amortized over the expected production for the first three years of the product's life.

Equipment Cost

The cost of manufacturing equipment generally is a variable function principally related to design parameters, the maximum anticipated run rate, and the minimum anticipated life span of the new product. Admittedly there are other factors affecting the cost of equipment, but these are the major ones. The same facts apply in a large degree to tool cost, and jig, fixture and miscellaneous material handling equipment cost.

The industrial engineering department utilizing the functions of automation engineering, tool engineering, process and methods engineering, and labor standards engineering plays a prime role with the product engineering group and the purchasing department.

Step 1 in industrial engineering's task is to tentatively decide which items to make and which to purchase, taking into account such factors as plant load, availability of facilities, tools, required personnel, and other pertinent cost elements.

Step 2, concurrent with Step 1, involves engineering an acceptable manufacturing process. This could involve automation to an ultimate degree, or it could be essentially an unmechanized process. The cost of equipment for each step in the process must be essentially balanced against estimated labor savings resulting from the use of equipment. It will also be found that mechanization and/or hand operations often affect the cost of purchased materials and/or parts (semi-finished and finished). One or the other approach often requires a slight material modification affecting purchase cost. Here is the point where product engineering must enter by performing one of the functions included in producibility engineering and aid in any required design revisions to keep cost to a minimum.

The purchasing department can also make a substantial contribution by directly suggesting changes that will lower the cost of purchased items. The vendors of such material also can often offer similar valuable suggestions—in fact, they generally appreciate being given such an opportunity. Engineering on the other hand is often reluctant to make the required concessions on tolerance, material, mechanical shapes, etc. This trial and error process can often extend over a lengthy period before the final version is reached. *It is a rare occasion where the indicated possible profit margin on a new product is adequate as predicted on the first, the second, or even the third cost estimate.*

Don't, if you're the new product manager, leave this work up to just the functional organizations doing the work. If you do, you will be in for a rude awakening. Work such as this is usually piled on top of an already loaded schedule and it normally is the last thing done, and then only given cursory attention. The new product manager must nurse it along—and he almost always must insist on trying different combinations. It is also of material help if he himself is able to contribute directly to the effort.

The new product manager must continually rescue the product from the scrap heap—not only in the estimating phase, but in the others involved in creating such a product. Estimating, however, will take up a major portion of his time.

Mechanization at times poses a difficult problem. Automation equipment is usually classified by the accountant as capital equipment (previously explained as involving "write-off" over a period of 10 or more years) but they seriously question the new product manager if he doesn't enter it into his pricing cost analysis as an accelerated "write-off" item (2 to 3 years maximum if it is specialized equipment not readily used on other products).

One "gimmick" that sometimes can be used by the new product manager is to convince management to use all or part of the first one or two years potential profits to pay for equipment, and tooling. The company thereby indicates willingness to support the effort to market a new product. Often it is necessary to resort to such a procedure in order to attain a required selling price or profit margin.

Tool, Jig, Fixture, and Miscellaneous Materials Handling Equipment Costs

This cost element, especially the first item, tool cost, can be subdivided into two categories: (1) vendor cost and (2) internal company cost.

As previously explained, the general parameters are similar to those of equipment cost. Also, the remarks concerning existing facilities apply to this item as well as to facility cost. The delineation of costs associated with this element will be concurrent with the work on facility, equipment, purchased material, and direct labor costs.

Purchased Material Cost

It is wise to have vendor quotations on parts to be segregated into: (1) special tool cost and (2) piece or material selling price. This has many advantages. It facilitates actions such as the following:
1. Analysis of the quotation
2. Usually yields the lowest quote on repeat orders
3. Obtains control of the tooling so as to: (a) prevent the vendor from using it to make parts for a competitor and (b) allow you to remove the tooling from the vendor in the event you want to use it to make the part or give it to another vendor to make the part
4. Permits the greatest degree of flexibility in handling the tool charges since it makes possible: (a) amortization over the first order (which the vendor would probably do if you didn't ask for the tool cost as a separate item), (b) amortiza-

tion over any arbitrary quantity for product costing, (c) to take it out of future profits (estimate or costing wise).

Another facet to consider in the analysis of material cost in an estimate is that actual purchases can often be made at 5 to 10 per cent under the original price quotations obtained for the estimate. Further, each subsequent order will almost always reflect a further incremental decrease in cost due to experience. Here much depends upon the types and kinds of materials involved, prior experience with the vendors, etc. The Purchasing Department Manager can be of great help at this point.

Direct Labor Cost

Establishing the direct labor expenditure required to manufacture a new product is an extremely difficult task—yet a matter of prime importance. It should occur concurrently with the effort to establish the equipment, facility, tool and material costs. Generally, one or more of these costs are at least partially dependent upon each other and almost always each of them directly affecting the amount of direct labor. If an advanced degree of mechanization is used, the labor will be minimum. How much we can afford to spend on equipment, tools, etc., is partially dependent upon anticipated production quantities.

Likewise, the presence or absence of competitive products has a great influence. If there is no competition, the selling price can often be established high enough to afford a high manufacturing cost. This, in turn, could make it possible to keep the capital investment low (few machines, etc.) and accept the usual high accompanying labor cost.

Design of the product affects each of the cost elements mentioned. Often, in fact it is usual where competition exists, that design must be modified so as to make possible a lowering of the manufacturing costs.

The more competition that exists, the more it is necessary to precisely determine each cost element; this is especially true of direct labor. The Industrial Engineering Department should make full use, not only of experience, but also of such techniques as pre-determined time systems (such as MTM), and standard data. Learning curves for similar products are also very useful.

Industrial engineering will usually break down the direct labor to a select time per operation (to the uninformed this is the time that it will take for a fully trained operator to perform the task when working with average skill and effort) to which is added a personal, fatigue and delay allowance. This yields an allowed time to which they add one or more of the following, either as a direct addition or as an allowance: rest period, material handling, instruction, group leaders, pilot run, initial training, rework, repair, and labor inefficiency, it is important to make them break down the direct labor on an important estimate and make them justify each item. The analysis of such data appears much more difficult than it really is—a little common sense goes a long way! Make them explain it in *your* language. Don't accept the results unless they appear to make sense.

Initial or start-up direct labor costs, mentioned earlier in this chapter, involve the higher labor costs experienced when a new product is put into production. Performance against an allowed time labor standard is poor in the beginning months of production due to pilot run cost (as much as 20 to 30 times standards allowed labor, training the operators, excessive rework and repair. These are the initial or start-up direct labor costs).

Shrinkage

Many problems can become buried under this term. It is intended here to cover the ordinary material losses, over-buys, and over shipments accepted. It is not intended that this item cover such cases where it can be expected that under ordinary conditions whole units or sections of a unit must be scrapped, such as occurs during certain destructive tests, or where the construction of the unit is such that it cannot be repaired if it happens to fail after assembly and adjustment. These latter instances should be covered under the cost element—scrap.

Material losses are bound to occur because of pilferage, carelessness in handling which causes

them to become lost or damaged, and unauthorized usage of parts by engineers and others for experimental purposes. Vendors, when shipping certain types of parts, are normally permitted to over or under ship by a small percentage of the total. Acceptable over-shipments (the usual case) causes unbalanced inventory and increases the cost of the product. Some parts are damaged in processing due to errors or accidents. All of these situations cause a shrinkage in inventory that must be compensated for in the cost structure.

Usually the cost estimating section of the Cost Department applies a percentage factor, based on guess and/or experience, against the unit material cost to increase this enough to compensate for shrinkage. In actual practice (not cost estimating) the Material Control Department arrives at percentage factors for shrinkage of the various classes of materials used based upon actual experience. These are used when applicable, by the cost estimating section. If, for example, a production release for 1000 units is issued and one part of a given class (one such part to be used in each unit) has an expected shrinkage of 5 per cent as defined above, they will actually order 1052 (1000/0.95 = 1052) parts.

Total shrinkage varies from a fraction of a per cent up to 5 to 10 per cent. The amount depends on the product, the classes of parts or materials involved, the complexity of the product, the degree to which engineering has completed its task, factory experience with similar products, the quantity to be produced, the controls to be in operation, the run rate, etc. On large quantity production of almost any kind of product it is well under 5 per cent. In material control—they pay most attention to controlling the more expensive parts and normally keep shrinkage on these items under 2 per cent, often down to $\frac{1}{10}$ of 1 per cent. Fewer controls are imposed on the low price parts and shrinkage is often allowed to go over 10 per cent. Handling shrinkage by part classification and/or cost is sometimes also followed in preparing the cost estimate.

It is well for the new product manager to remember that cost estimating and even material control will generally be doing some guessing on the amount of shrinkage to be encountered on even a known or normal product and are sure to be doing this on a new product significantly different from the regular line of products. Test the applied shrinkage factor with common sense reasoning. It could be much too low or much too high.

Scrap

Scrap, as used herein, was delineated as to the kind of costs involved under Shrinkage. It is usual to have no scrap in the sense that the word is being used. However, when such scrap does exist it affects both material and labor. It is usual to handle it as a percentage factor in the cost analysis, the same way as shrinkage.

In the case of material, it is usually applied before the application of shrinkage and the shrinkage is then applied to the sum of the base material plus the scrap. This is proper since shrinkage, as defined, would apply to both base material and the extra material ordered to cover scrap.

For labor, the labor involved in producing the scrapped parts is often accounted for by applying a percentage factor to the *total* expected direct labor (calculated as if no scrap was expected) required to produce the products (either per piece or for the total quantity)—not to base or allowed time labor.

It probably should be mentioned that the scrap labor cost and its associated overhead will be higher, the further along in the manufacturing process that the scrapping action takes place.

While this discussion of scrap and the previous one of shrinkage was aimed at the manufacturing activity, it also is applicable to a degree to the estimation of engineering material and labor, although it is not usual to attempt to define scrap or shrinkage for engineering. Occasionally, a situation arises where expensive components or equipment manufactured by a competitor are purchased with the intent to dismantle them for analysis. This could be an important cost element in such situations. It would need to be considered in the engineering estimate, just as shrinkage of engineering material must be considered, even though no attempt is normally made to define the amount.

Transportation

The expense of transporting required materials to the manufacturing plant are the charges to be discussed. Again, while the primary consideration is in regard to materials to be used in the manufacturing operation, it is also a factor in several of the other cost elements previously discussed, such as engineering, equipment, tools, etc.

A common way to handle this cost element in the cost analysis is to increase base material cost by a percentage, the amount generally being based on historical data. Usually, the percentage developed is for all products produced in a given plant. A more realistic way is to establish the percentage on a product basis. Accountants often shudder at this approach since their accounting systems are not ordinarily set up to segregate this cost element by product.

If the products manufactured in a given plant utilize many common purchased parts and/or material so that the transportation cost relative to material cost will be the same for each product, then covering the transportation cost by the application of a percentage against material cost for the entire range of products produced in this plant is fair and equitable. This would also be fair if the products used purchased items having in a like manner transportation costs in proportion to the value of the items purchased. The reverse situation could and often does exist.

When the new product requires the purchase of material having an associated transportation cost that is not similar to existing products, it can be a difficult cost estimating problem to solve. While the transportation cost of material and/or parts used in manufacturing a product normally range from 1 to 2 per cent, it can also be more or less and the end effect on price can be of important significance. This is so because cost elements often pyramid—for example, to the transportation cost must be added General and Administrative expenses, applicable taxes, interest charges, etc. in the example cost analysis.

The new product manager would do well to watch each and every cost element closely, even one which appears to have a small effect on cost. This is especially true where competitive products are involved.

The cost of transportation becomes even more involved when one or more plants of the producing company are shipping material to the plant scheduled to make the new product. Under such circumstances, company-owned trucks are often used or else the shipment is combined with other materials used on other products, so that the associated cost is significantly less than normal. Yet, the authors have found that, in this situation, the standard percentage cost is often applied to such shipments from subsidiary plants since all required material not actually made in the subject plant, is considered purchased material.

The transportation cost of heavy equipment purchased to manufacture the new product is normally included in the cost of the equipment. Here the traffic or shipping department can help in estimating the dollars involved.

Overhead

Overhead is almost universally handled as a percentage application against direct labor. It is to cover the *indirect manufacturing* costs—not such indirect expenses as advertising, general administrative, interest, selling, etc. Often overhead appears to the new product manager as his Nemesis.

Overhead can be divided into two fundamental divisions as discussed in the beginning of this chapter—and is often so segregated by accountants and managers. One of these divisions is defined as fixed overhead charges. While it's true that virtually nothing in industry is completely fixed, it is a fact that many indirect overhead charges are essentially constant as long as the plant or factory continues to operate. Examples of such charges are rent, building upkeep (landlord expense), certain salaries such as those of the factory manager and general foremen, heat, etc. The other fundamental division of overhead is the variable expense—these expense items depending most directly on the level of manufacturing activity. Examples are supervisors' salaries, cost accounting salaries, receiving and shipping department operating cost. The greater the level of manufacturing activity, the more personnel for these functions are required—hence the greater the expense. The variable overhead usually is less than 50 per cent of the total plant overhead.

Sometimes the new product manager can take some advantage of this situation. For example, if the prospective new product is a component used in the manufacture of an end product, such as a television receiver, management will sometimes agree to only charge the variable overhead against the direct labor during the initial production. In fact, this often is the basis for handling overhead when arriving at a "make-buy" decision. This procedure, when the product can be absorbed into the plant, will assure recovery of all extra real costs. Later, the new product's share of the fixed overhead can often be absorbed since the starting costs are then eliminated and a greater overhead can be accepted. This is a legitimate way to look at the introduction of new products into the line, but is not often used or allowed! It is a view similar to that expressed earlier in this chapter under the subtitle, Incremental Cost Concepts.

Another approach to the problem of handling overhead charges is to set up a special overhead account for the new product. For example, let us assume that the new product is being introduced into a company manufacturing an electro-chemical product requiring very large amounts of electrical power, extra expensive buildings, large amounts of process steam, significant amounts of expensive distilled water, extremely expensive process equipment, etc. Let us also assume that the new product essentially involves producing several small simple metal stampings and assembling them with tubular rivets (riveting machines are often rented). It would be unfair to saddle this product with the expensive fixed overhead charge enumerated. Under these circumstances a wise management will set up a special overhead account for the new product, only charging against it the actual costs associated with the product. Please bear in mind that the example given has been relatively uncomplicated and clearcut; it is not usually this simple in actual work situations.

A further improvement is to combine these two approaches, when appropriate and applicable, starting with only the variable overhead charge (this automatically eliminates the high fixed costs in the second example) and then, after production is rolling smoothly, set up and use the special overhead account.

The new product manager will do well to understand both general and cost accounting and use every means at his disposal to subdue this monster identified as *cost*!

There are other overhead accounts that have so far been ignored and unmentioned. For example—the question of engineering overhead—i.e. overhead within the engineering department on engineering direct labor. Engineering overhead costs are often a direct charge on engineering direct labor—especially in a plant accepting government or civilian contracts to perform specific engineering work. This is done to assure recovery of all costs, both direct and indirect, associated with such work. All remarks made concerning general overhead can be considered as generally applicable to engineering overhead.

In a similar manner, separate or special overhead accounts are often set up for maintenance departments, toolrooms, test equipment construction departments, and other similar departments. If the overhead charges in any of these activities are excessive, it may be advisable to contract for some of the work required from such departments from an outside company.

Selling Expense

Selling expense is often based on a percentage of manufacturing expense as a simple estimate. Today much effort goes into the determination of distribution costs, although it is a difficult task. If the new product fails within the product line it generally simplifies the problem, but it does not necessarily solve the problem. Let us consider an actual example. The company in question has sold its aluminum electrolytic capacitors to other home radio, television, hi-fi, and organ manufacturers through salaried company salesmen. They decided to increase their electrolytic capacitor line to include tantalum capacitors used primarily in the manufacture of military electronic equipment and hearing aids. Either more company salesmen or manufacturing representatives (Independent Sales Engineers) would be needed to supplement the existing sales force so that the additional plants involved would be contacted. Here, the expansion of the product line created an estimating problem—(1) Add more company salesmen? (2) Use manufacturing engineering sales representatives? (3) Compute the cost effect of one or both courses of action. The use of manufacturing representatives makes the problem of defining the associated selling expense relatively easy since they normally work on a commission basis to which must be added company administrative sales expense and advertising, if this latter item is to be included in selling expenses. Advertising is often handled as a separate cost element.

Often the company has several selling organizations and a choice exists as to which should sell the new product. Both the associated costs and the probability of successful marketing should be considered in deciding how to sell the product.

Advertising cannot be ignored since it is usually necessary to advertise the new product, if the sales department is to be properly supported. While some sales can be achieved without product advertising, its lack is a difficult handicap to overcome. However, some help can be expected from any existing institutional advertising and/or related product advertising programs. Such help should be taken into consideration when estimating the cost of advertising.

If the new product merely expands an existing product line, it is possible that no advertising cost, other than that normally associated with the product line need be considered. Yet, even in these cases, the expansion may necessitate extra advertising.

The chapter on promotion contains additional information on this subject. Exhibiting at engineering conferences and trade shows normally is considered to be a part of advertising and/or promotion.

If the new product is to be produced in a plant which bids on and accepts government contracts, the new product manager may encounter another problem—the distortion of civilian product selling cost because the government will not accept selling and promotion costs, yet the company must incur these if it is to continue handling such business. Here these costs are sometimes loaded on to the civilian products in the plant.

G & A, as the above is commonly referred to, like selling expense, virtually explains itself. It also is usually a percentage application against the manufacturing cost.

Little can be done about it and it normally is a standard charge for a given plant. If the new product can be shown to have little or no effect on the actual magnitude of this cost element, management might be persuaded to forego applying this charge during its introduction (initial production).

Patent License Cost

This sometimes is included under G & A. In any event, it usually is a percentage application against either Manufacturing Cost or Cost of Sales.

The new product may not involve any patent license cost, and if this is the case, it should not be charged some general percentage which is applied against all products involving such cost. In some cases, patents obtained as a result of new product development, may actually bring in income if other manufacturers are licensed under them.

Royalty payments are usually determined by applying the royalty percentage against the sales price obtained by the manufacturer. Sometimes the cost of packaging is excluded from the selling price for royalty computation. This slightly complicates the calculations involved in computing the correct percentage to use on the cost analysis form.

Special Taxes

This cost element usually appears where a state sales tax is involved. It is a tax levied on the selling price. It, therefore, like the patent license royalty rate, is somewhat difficult to handle. Once the selling price is established, the proper percentage is applied and the dollar amount determined. This amount is then applied against the Manufacturing Cost or the Cost of Sales to determine the percentage to show and use.

Summary Remarks on Costs

Costing is a most difficult, time consuming and tedious process. Do not slight this phase of new product development, or the chances that a new product will be introduced are indeed slim.

Licking the Cost Monster

It is not enough to know the cost elements and how each one contributes to the over-all cost. Neither is it enough to know ways to reduce some of the specific cost elements.

In order to really subdue the cost monster, every function mentioned must provide its maximum contribution. Unfortunately, the opposite is usually the case. Getting less than the maximum contribution is not due to incompetence or one of procedure—it is one of morale stemming from a lack of understanding of the problems involved.

Cost estimators and the men involved in the participating functions of purchasing, industrial engineering, and tool engineering are generally well organized individuals and like to have their work come to them in like manner. Unfortunately, when estimating and/or trying to "beat cost into line" on a development project, only partial information is available. The development engineer either assumes these functions can deduce the necessary information from the unorganized and incomplete data presented, or else believes it all an unnecessary chore. If this is coupled with the necessity of going through this messy procedure many times on the same product, the origin of an associated morale problem becomes apparent.

Knowing the problem and its origin, is half the battle in surmounting this obstacle. Literally, all elements of the organization concerned with subduing the cost monster must be brought into the act—not held off. If all the parties can be made to understand each other's problems and their collective relationship to the effort, then the problem is licked.

Just how these people are integrated into the program not only depends upon the organizational structure involved, but also upon the personalities and capabilities of the individuals concerned with the cost monster.

It is suggested that the personnel and/or training director be brought in to help bring about an understanding as to why and how these estimate requests originate and why they are so important to the company. This should help to substantially begin the defeat of the problem since it basically is one of misunderstanding. In spite of these helps, much "hand-holding" and explanation will be of vital necessity if these men are to work well together. The generation of real understanding is the only practical approach to really licking the cost monster.

In the preceding pages, it was mentioned that the product manager must analyze all costs charged to the new products to be sure that they are not burdened with costs for which they bear no responsibility. The concept of responsibility must constantly be kept in mind. In many instances, the new products manager is cajoled into accepting responsibility for cost because of some obscure or misunderstood accounting technique. *It must be kept in mind that accounting techniques attempt to allocate to all products not only costs that they initiate, but also costs that are distantly related and in many instances costs that have no relationship at all.* The accountant's task is to assign all costs to total output. In many instances however, the costs involved are cost of getting ready to produce and not direct cost of producing. Often the products manager believes he has compensated for this factor by only considering variable costs, however, as will be pointed out shortly, this approach can be potentially risky.

Naturally, *Capacity* costs and other costs of preparing for production must be covered in the long run if the business is to continue operations. But for short-run decisions, these costs are irrelevant. Because many of the costs of preparing for production are fixed in nature, accountants and management have tended to apply a variable or "direct cost" approach. This approach can also be subject to many hazards. Variable costs are relevant only to prospective production. For example, assume the opportu-

nity exists to produce 10,000 units on contract for $10.00 per unit. Cost analysis shows the following:

Cost of production	
	Per unit
Labor	$2
Material	4
Overhead—direct	2
Factory overhead	3
	$11

Omission of factory overhead will indicate a contribution margin of $2 per unit from production and sale ($10–$8). Naturally if the alternative to taking this contract is to do nothing, the firm should take the $10 offer. In this situation, only direct variable costs are relevant. Unforunately, this approach is also applied to situations involving past cost (incurred costs) resulting in incorrect decision. For example, using the same facts as above except that the contract price is $6.00 and the goods have already been produced, since as above the direct variable costs total $8.00 many managers would advise against taking the contract. The correct action is to view only present and future alternatives as being relevant and ignore incurred costs. Thus if the alternatives to the contract for $6.00 is to hold the goods in inventory, then the question to be answered is what will this action yield in economic benefit? The relevant data is the incremental cost of holding the inventory and the expected revenue at some future date. Included in the holding cost must be a provision for imputed cost of the investment. In short, the decision of whether or not to sell the inventory at $6 now must consider the "opportunity cost", or profits foregone from an available alternative course of action. Therefore, in our illustration the provision for the cost of capital invested in inventory is provided for by discounting the incremental cash inflows and outflows associated with "holding" back to the time of the decision. The discount rate which is used should be taken as equal to the cost of capital, that is, the rate which the firm must pay to obtain capital funds.

The Impact of Taxes on Cost

Many times the product manager will only be aware of the purchase price of special machinery needed in production of new products. Hidden from his view is the potential savings in cost from the tax reduction precipitated by the additional investment. Under the investment credit the firm is allowed to reduce taxes in an amount up to 7% of the cost of equipment. The credit is only available for qualified property. Qualified property is defined as depreciable tangible personal property, and depreciable real property with the exception of buildings and their structural components. The property must either be used in production or constitute a research facility. The credit cannot exceed 15,000 plus $\frac{1}{2}$ of the tax liability in excess of $25,000. Thus a firm with a tax liability of $85,000 is limited to a total investment credit for the year of $25,000 $+\frac{1}{2}$ (85,000 − 25,000) = 55,000. The purchaser is not entitled to the full 7% unless the property has an expected life of 8 or more years. If the estimate is less than 4 years, no credit is allowed.[2] The cost of special equipment subject to investment credit is therefore 93% of purchase price.

Depreciation

Not to be ignored from the standpoint of actual cost of special equipment is the tax advantage available from depreciation. However, to properly evaluate this factor the tax savings from depreciation should be discounted back to the date of purchase at the firm's cost of capital as illustrated in Figure 11-9. Instead of costing the firm $200,000 for special equipment, the actual economic cost is approximately $93,000.[3] That is, the firm can now borrow approximately $107,000 at 6% or less to buy the equipment, and be able to repay the loan over 5 years from the annual tax savings.

It should be observed that the method of depreciation can change the economic effect. In addition, if no previous equipment was acquired during the year, the first $10,000 of investment may be subject to an extra 20% first-year depreciation on top of the regular depreciation.[4] This 20% does reduce the remaining basis of the property subject to future de-

Data:

Asset cost	$200,000
Life	5 years
Tax rate	50%
Cost of capital	6%
Residual value	$40,000

Present value of tax saving using 5 year life and Double Declining Balance depreciation method:

Year	Depre-ciation	Tax benefit 50%	Present value 6%
1	$80,000	$40,000	$37,720
2	48,000	24,000	21,360
3	28,800	14,400	12,082
4	1,600	800	632
5	1,600	800	592
		$72,286	$72,286

Investment credit ($200,000 × 0.07 × 1/3) =	4,666
Residual value, year 5, $40,000, present value at 6% =	29,632
Total present value	106,684
Less cash outlay for equipment	200,000
Cost of machine adjusted for tax savings	$93,316

Figure 11-9 A concept regarding depreciation which is of value to the new product manager

preciation. However, the additional first-year deduction provides the firm with immediate funds from reduced taxes that may be needed during experimental periods.

The tax benefits from depreciation and investment credit are two strong points in the product manager's favor when fighting for funds. In addition, the special tax treatment of research and development expenditure should also be kept in mind.

Tax Treatment of Research and Development Expenditures

Certain research and development costs "... incident to the development of an experimental or pilot model, a plant process, a product, a formula, an invention or similar property, and the improvement of already existing property of the type mentioned,"[5] are afforded special tax treatment. Namely, the taxpayer may elect either to expense the item immediately or to treat it as a deferred item to be expensed over a period of at least 60 months.[6] If enough taxable income exists from other segments of the firm, immediate deduction for tax purposes will generate the greatest economic benefit, as well as immediate funds for further research.

This special treatment may apply to research or experimentation by a research institution, foundation, or outside contractor on the taxpayer's behalf. However, if another incurs expenditures for research and experimentation associated with the construction of depreciable property, he will be allowed special treatment only if the taxpayer ordered their construction and is to bear the risk. Therefore, the contract must not contain any guarantees of quality of production, yield, or performance.[5]

Excluded from special treatment

No special treatment will be granted to expenditures by others on the taxpayer's behalf for expenses other than research and experimental expenditures in connection with the acquisition or construction of depreciable property. Excluded, therefore, will be the cost of material, "... labor, or other elements involved in its construction and installation..."[6]

Also prohibited from special treatment are expenditures in the nature of ordinary quality control, "... efficiency surveys, management studies, consumer surveys, advertising or promotions".[7]

CONCLUSION

It should be obvious by now that the New Product Manager should have a firm grasp of accounting fundamentals and practices. The accountants can scuttle a project before it is even properly launched. It is not our intent by this statement to take away from the accountants the fact that theirs is a necessary and important function. However, it is emphasized that there are many approaches or options

open and without the understanding mentioned, the new product manager will not even know what they are or which one to exercise.

REFERENCES

1. *Perspectives on Experience* (Boston: The Boston Consulting Group, Inc., 1968), p. 12.
2. With a life of 4–5 years the credit is $\frac{1}{3}$ of 7%, with a life of 6–7 years, the credit is $\frac{2}{3}$ of 7%. Subsequent events may result in a life shorter than contemplated initially, in that situation, i.e., the actual life is 5 instead of the expected 7 years, the excess allowed credit must be refunded to the Gov. Unused credits may be carried forward or backward to obtain additional benefits.
3. An erroneous approach often used to arrive at the tax benefit is to take the total cost subject to depreciation and multiply by the tax rate then add salvage value, in this case, $180,000 \times 50\% - 90,000 + 40,000 = 130,000$ tax saving, and, therefore, an actual cost of $ 70,000, (200,000 - 130,000) an obvious overstatement of the tax benefit.
4. To qualify the property must have a life of at least 6 years.
5. Certain guarantees will not preclude special treatment such as, "... guarantee ... limited, to engineering specification..." Federal Reg. 1.174-2 (b) (3). Furthermore, the option to defer and write off over 60 months is not applicable to expenditures not chargeable to capital account or subject to depreciation or depletion. Federal Reg. 1.174 (a) (2).
6. Federal Regulation, Sec. 1.174-2 (b) (4). Note: Failure to specifically select either of these methods will probably result in a loss of tax benefit.
7. *Ibid.* Sec. 1.174-2 (a) (1).

BIBLIOGRAPHY

Bonchonsky, J.P., "Cost Control for Program Managers," *NAA Management Accounting*, May, 1967.

Cost Analysis for Product Line Decisions, New York: The American Institute of Certified Public Accountants, 1965.

Duro, R.A., "A System of Research and Development Cost Control", *NAA Management Accounting*, May, 1967.

Faulke, R.A., *Practical Financial Analysis*, New York: McGraw-Hill Book Company, 1968.

Gallantier, A.J., "Accounting Reports on Research and Development", *NAA Management Accounting*, November, 1967.

Haynes, W.W., *Managerial Economics: Analysis and Cases*, Homewood, Ill.: Irwin-Dorsey Press, 1963.

Holdham, J.H., "Learning Curves—Their Applications in Industry", *Production and Inventory Control Management*, Fourth Quarter, 1970.

Horngren, Charles T., *Cost Accounting: A Managerial Emphasis* (2nd ed.) Englewood Cliffs, N.J.: Prentice-Hall, Inc., 1967.

Huetten, C. and L. Sweany, "A New Product Philosophy", *Product Engineering*, May 9, 1960.

Jenkins, David O., "Cost-Volume-Profit Analysis", *Management Services*, March–April, 1970.

Murdick, R. G. and D. D. Deming, *The Management of Capital Expenditures*, New York: McGraw-Hill Book Company, 1968.

Nienow, Robert and Robert A. Coltman, "Putting R & D on a Profit-Making Basis", *Management Services*, May–June, 1969.

Niswonger, C. R. and P. E. Fess, *Accounting Principles*, Cincinnati, Ohio: South-Western Publishing Company, 1969.

Perspectives on Experience, Boston: The Boston Consulting Group, 1968.

Pessemier, Edgar A., *New Product Decisions*, New York: McGraw-Hill Book Company, 1966.

Shillinglaw, G., *Cost Accounting, Analysis and Control*, Homewood, Ill.: Richard D. Irwin, Inc., 1967.

Simons and Karrenbrock, *Intermediate Accounting*, Cincinnati, Ohio: South-Western Publishing Company, 1968.

Simons and Karrenbrock, *Advanced Accounting*, Cincinnati, Ohio: South-Western Publishing Company, 1968.

Summers, Edward L. and Glenn A. Welsch, "How Learning Curve Models Can Be Applied to Profit Planning" *Management Services*, March–April, 1970.

Tipper, H., Jr., *Controlling Overhead*, New York: American Management Association, 1966.

Vancil, R. F., *Financial Executives Handbook*, Homewood, Ill.: Dow Jones-Irwin, 1970.

Villers, R., *Research and Development: Planning and Control*, New York: Financial Executives Research Foundation, 1964.

CHAPTER 12

HOW TO PRICE FOR LIFE-CYCLE-PROFIT

FACTORS AFFECTING PRICING

The old guide for pricing of "Buy cheap and sell dear", if it ever had any useful value, would today be condemned to a deep burial. Pricing a new product is a highly complex affair which demands the greatest degree of both judgment and science. Let us list some of the major factors which must be considered in one way or another in price-setting:

1. Target return on investment
2. Type and mix of products
3. Competitors' strengths and responses
4. Development costs of the product
5. Cost of product to manufacture and sell
6. Position of the company in the industry
7. Type of market structure (monopolistic, competitive, highly product differentiated, few major companies)
8. Degree that the product differs from competitive products
9. Short and long term goals with respect to price and customer relations
10. Legal, government, and public influence
11. Stabilization of market price
12. Perishibility and cost of storage
13. Product life-cycle, with all its implications

In terms of these factors, the company must select a suitable and profitable price for its new product over the life of the product.

THE MARKETING CONCEPT AND PRICE-VOLUME PROFIT RELATIONSHIP

The marketing concept requires a "systems" approach to pricing. Within the limits of company policy (the long-range means for preserving the company image), the company should price to maximize profits over the life cycle of the product. The "systems approach" also requires that the company consider price as one part of the "marketing mix" of product (characteristics), place (distribution), promotion, price, and service.

A major weakness in pricing by small businessmen is their lack of understanding of the price-volume-profit relationship. There are two positions in time for which the pricing approaches are completely different.

1. Looking ahead from the beginning.

   The manager must plan to recoup all his investment in product development over the life-cycle of the product *and* make enough on the sale of each unit to cover variable costs, target profit, and contribution to overhead. He thus plans for prices which are both practical and profitable or he doesn't make the product.

2. Looking ahead after a large stock is on hand.

   Once the product has been manufactured, the producer has only two choices. He may hold the units in inventory, with all the attendant costs, until a more favorable time to sell may arise. The other alternative is to sell now at the market price without regard to cost. This latter alternative is

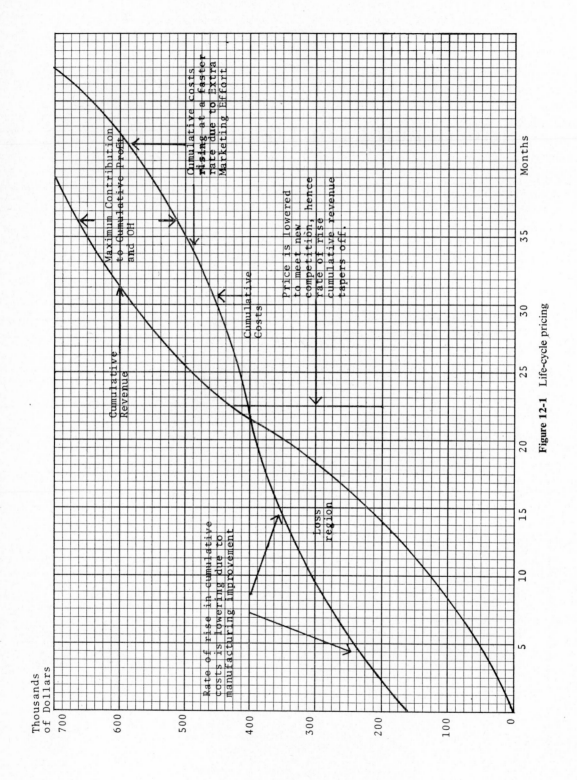

Figure 12-1   Life-cycle pricing

too often ignored by the small businessman so that he ends up with a warehouse full of obsolete deteriorating junk for which someone must pay to have it hauled away.

With regard to the first position in time, management must estimate the life-cycle to make sure that cumulative profits exceed cumulative variable costs *as well as product development costs*. The best project available is the one which makes the largest contribution to overhead costs and profits. Figure 12-1 shows a plan for pricing to meet competition in the maturity phase of the life cycle. The price-volume relationships should be forecasted along with costs to locate the time at which profit will have reached a maximum. Any sales after this point means that unit cost is exceeding unit selling price

with the result that cumulative profit (and overhead) contribution is decreasing. A form which is helpful in planning for pricing and later reviewing the achievement of plans is shown in Figure 12-2.

There are quite a few price-policy options available in planning for life-cycle pricing, and these will be discussed in detail further on.

The second situation where the company finds itself with a stock of goods on hand offers fewer options. The company may offer the goods at a price which will clear its inventory now. When inventory carrying costs are high, when the product is subject to rapid deterioration, or when a superior competitive product appears on the market, it is better to sell the goods for a fraction of their cost than hold the price high and sell nothing.

PRODUCT_____   PRODUCT MANAGER_____ DATE_____

RECOMMENDED MARKETING STRATEGY_____

TOTAL MARKET (UNITS)_____   MARKET PENETRATION GOAL_____%

PRINCIPAL   _____   EVALUATION _____

COMPETITORS   _____   _____

                 _____   _____

                 _____   _____

(1)	(2)	(3)	(4)	(5)	(6)	(7)	(8)	(9)	(10)
Year	Expected level of unit sales by the industry	Product's Unit Price			Product's Unit Sales				
		Expected price	Lowest likely price	Highest likely price	Expected annual level	Lowest likely annual level	Highest likely annual level	Expected cumulative	Actual cumulative
1									
2									
3									
4									

Figure 12-2 Price-volume planning form

Another option is available when the product will continue to attract customers. The company may then sell at a price which it feels will yield the maximum revenue. For example, it could set a high price expecting that only half its stock will be sold and the other half scrapped. Or it could set a lower price so that most of its stock is sold and cumulative revenue is maximized. There is no guarantee either situation will yield a profit, but maximizing revenue is the best the company can do. A policy of lowering price in steps as time goes by may be another option. One book publisher even *raised* the price of a certain book it had in stock in order to yield increased cumulative revenue. This indicates that the company belatedly recognized it had a monopolistic position in the face of a continuing strong demand for its product.

PRICE–QUALITY AND MARKET SEGMENTATION

The price-quality relationship is a very close one, and only for certain types of goods directed at certain market segments can advertising and promotion overcome the relationship. The very well-to-do person may pay a high price for a highly promoted prestige product and the poorly educated person may overpay for a highly advertised product out of ignorance. Research results have shown that in the absence of other clues, people judge the quality among products by their prices.

The new product price–quality relationship should be adjusted according to the market segment aimed at. Quality in the broad sense must also include utility to the customer as well as the inherent construction of the product. With this in mind, market segments which should be considered for the new product might be selected according to:
1. Socio-economic characteristics such as income, wealth, occupation, education, family size, age, sex, and recreations.
2. Geographic location such as urban, suburban, rural, region of the country, or climate.
3. Cultural characteristics such as ethnic group, language, heritage, race, and religion.

It is difficult to design a product which appeals to all segments of the market. An attempt to do so leaves the product vulnerable to the competitor who aims at a specific market segment. The price-quality relationship allows the manufacturer to make several models of different quality and price. For example, leading manufacturers of refrigerators, television sets, automobiles, tires, and watches produce a wide range of models. The low-price, low-quality models are directed at the lower income groups and other models are directed toward other segments of the market. In addition, manufacturers of items such as furniture, household furnishings, and clothing must produce variations in their products to reach different cultural or geographic market segments.

The lesson to be learned from the above discussion is: Identify carefully the market segment you intend to reach, and then adjust the quality and price to the market segment as your basic pricing policy.

LARGEST SHORT-RUN PROFIT

If the new product is a one-shot affair which is expected to face a strong demand, the price should be set relatively high to maximize the total profit. The introduction of the ball point pen is a good example of quick profit taking before the competitive price dropped to a fraction of the introductory price.

SKIMMING PRICING

Skimming pricing or "sliding down the demand curve" is a form of price discrimination over time. If the new product represents a significant and attractive innovation, the price may initially be set high. In Figure 12-3a, the high price P_1 will result in sales of quantity Q_1 to the higher income or more eager people in the market. After these people have obtained the product, the price is lowered to P_2 as shown in Figure 12-3b. If P_2 had been the initial price, Q_2 units would have been sold. However, Q_1 units at the higher price skimmed off the market. Thus $Q_2 - Q_1$ units are sold at the lower price. As the price is continually lowered in steps, as shown in

Figure 12-3c, the more eager buyers purchase units according to the price-quality demand curve.

The term "skimming" stems from the old practice of the farmer to skim the cream off the milk. There are four main reasons why a skimming price is advantageous for unusual new products.

First, it permits making maximum profit on the almost assured sales. This extra profit is often needed to help pay for the development of the product. Also, it helps cover the high costs associated with the initial stages of the manufacturing effort.

Second, the quantity of almost any novel new product that can be sold is less likely to be affected by price in the initial marketing effort. It is only after competitive products appear, that price becomes of prime importance. Also, it is often true that pure salesmanship, rather than price, is the initially determining factor regarding the amount sold.

Third, a high price will often produce the maximum dollar volume during the initial introduction of the product. Under these circumstances a skimming price will produce the maximum return and provide the funds often needed for expansion.

Fourth, the high price is often a good way to "feel out" the market. One can always reduce the price if it is necessary to achieve a desirable sales volume.

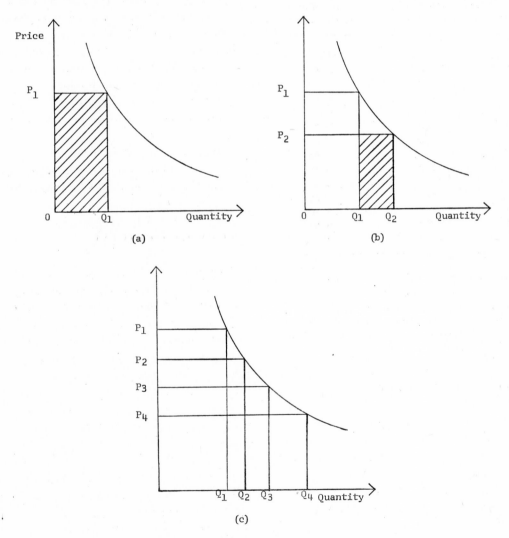

Figure 12-3 Sliding down the demand curve

On the other hand, however, it is difficult to successfully increase a low initial price because of unforeseen manufacturing or selling costs—to say nothing of the situation where the market would have obviously supported a higher price.

Fifth, if the price is continually being lowered, would-be competitors will hesitate to enter the market as they see declining prospects for profits.

Skimming pricing leads to lower and lower unit revenues and hence lower profits. This is strikingly shown for silicon transistors in Figure 12-4.

Year	Industry total accumulated volume (Million units)	Average revenue per unit ($ Constant)
1954	0.02	$23.95
1955	0.11	20.44
1956	0.53	19.94
1957	1.53	17.81
1958	3.6	15.57
1959	8.4	14.53
1960	17.2	11.27
1961	30.2	7.48
1962	56.8	4.39
1963	106.9	2.50
1964	224.0	1.35
1965	496.6	0.76
1966	977.8	0.58
1967	1456.9	0.52

Figure 12-4 Unit price decrease with volume for silicone transistors
Source: Derived from published data of Electronics Industry Association, *Perspectives on Experience* (Boston: The Boston Consulting Group, Inc., 1968) by permission

PENETRATION PRICING

A good basic objective in new product pricing is to build up a volume and cost advantage over competitors who wish to enter the market later. The price should be set so that competitors are prevented from gaining experience before the company introducing the product has gained experience and a large share of the market. Penetration pricing is the setting of a price so low, even below initial cost, in order to quickly reach high volume production. Costs will be reduced according to manufacturing progress improvements. Penetration pricing may be had

1. When the product does not command such an advantageous position as to permit a skimming price
2. When substantial economies can be effected in manufacturing and/or distribution through large volume production of the product.
3. If the new product is not strongly protected by patents, a major investment in specialized manufacturing facilities or some other similar element, penetration pricing tends to prevent the threat of strong competition soon after the introduction of the product. It discourages the competitor seeking to enter a lucrative market.
4. Where there is no elite market—that is, there are no reasonable number of buyers willing to pay a high price for the new product.
5. When the market is essentially non-existent at a price other than allowed by high volume production.
6. When a slightly lower price will result in a great increase in demand at some psychological level (such as the original $400 level for color TV sets).

STAY-OUT PRICING

"Stay-out" or preemptive pricing at first seems similar to penetration pricing. The initial price for the new product is set low, even below initial cost, until the company has established a very strong position in the market. Instead of maintaining constant price, or even decreasing the price with experience, however, the company gradually increases the price as its market position becomes assured. Although competitors eventually note the attractive profits, they are likely to regard the cost of bucking a well-established market as too high In addition, potential competitors realize that the innovating company has built up manufacturing and marketing experience which will permit it to drop its prices in the face of a threat of competition.

The real problem here is that raising the price for a product often is a near impossible procedure.

PUT-OUT PRICING

The policy of put-out pricing is the setting of the price of a new product so low such that the quality of the product combined with the low price will drive the older competing products out of the market. The legality of adopting such a policy should be carefully investigated in each situation before pursuing it.

The folklore of pricing practices is full of half-truths and/or attractive oversimplications.

Some of the theoretical or overviews of pricing so far have been given in a somewhat simplified manner. This in turn leads one to believe their application to be easy—in actual practice this is far from the truth. Pricing is often done by a mixture of hunch and accounting theology which has a distinctly medieval tone, even in firms which are strikingly well-managed—this statement by no less an authority on pricing than Joel Dean.

COST-PLUS-MARKUP PRICING

All that has been said before in this chapter must now be integrated with the comments in the previous chapter on costing and those which now follow on cost-plus-markup pricing.

This is a very popular pricing technique. The cost sheet in Figure 11-7 is essentially based on this concept and is absolutely typical *if* the "desired selling price" as shown on the sheet is actually the price charged the customer.

The method is simple, but it often leaves much to be desired. First, when rigidly applied it fails to take into account the buyer's needs and willingness to pay. In actual practice, the manufacturer must fix the price at a level acceptable to a substantial number of consumers, and not merely charge what the cost data indicate. Naturally, the new product manager will not be allowed to proceed unless price in the long run can be expected to cover costs and leave something for profit. However, in the short run, under certain circumstances, a price that does not cover all costs may be better than a higher price that fails to get business.

The concept of profit on an individual unit is somewhat illusional in view of the arbitrary and great variety of cost allocation in a multiproduct firm, as discussed in detail in the chapter on costing. For many pricing problems, the appropriate concept is not full costs, but direct or traceable costs. The marginal contribution to common overhead and profit by the product is what is strategic.

When a company has developed a unique product or unique manufacturing process for a product for which there is strong demand, it may resort to cost-plus-markup pricing. By charging off all development costs during the early stage of the life cycle, the maintenance of markup will lead to declining price after these costs are liquidated. At the same time, the company assures itself of a constant profit as a percent of sales.

If a constant price is maintained throughout the product life cycle, as costs decrease, the markup increases. Decreases in sales will eventually lead to reductions in volume with a corresponding reversal of the cost trend. In the case of low-volume, batch, or custom-made items, however, the cost-plus-markup pricing policy may be maintained as long as anyone places an order.

If a company has a highly efficient manufacturing operation, it may adopt cost-plus-markup pricing as a simple approach to pricing its new products. It must, however, *test the market for its products at about the introductory price.* For example, if the most efficient manufacturer in the world could produce color television sets only at a cost of $5000 per set, the fact that he was efficient would not likely yield high sales. On the other hand, a somewhat inefficient manufacturer may well be able to sell a color TV set for $400 in today's market because he is within the price range of the market. The difference in quality between complex products selling at the same price is not usually easy for the consumer to detect.

Generally, cost-plus-markup is a technological and non-marketing approach to setting prices. It fails to take into consideration the life-cycle of the new product, the market demand (price-volume relationship), the responses of competitors, and government and public sentiments and responses.

FULL-LINE PRICING

Related to the problems of full-line pricing is the uniform net profit concept. Also, it is an extension of the cost-plus markup formula to a multiproduct line. This approach or theory says that all the items should be so priced that "each one is able to pull its own weight". This means that each article is required to assume its full share of all fixed expenses, and the price is determined by adding a uniform net profit percentage to the total unit cost. Say the company has five items in the new product line and, after all the costs are allocated by one of the accounting procedures, the total unit costs at standard volume (say 85 per cent of capacity) amount to 40, 50, 90, 1.20 and 1.60. If the management decides to obtain 20 per cent profit on each item, the prices charged would be 48, 60, 1.08, 1.44 and 1.92.

The uniform net profit concept suffers from the same shortcomings as the cost-plus markup formula. Further, it does not take into account the fact that the various items in the product line may face different competitive conditions and have different elasticities of demand. When rigorously applied, the formula could prove to be a two-edged sword for restricting profits. It would tend to cut off profit at the top of the line by pricing the prestige article below what the consumers would probably be prepared to pay. Equally bad, it would reduce sales at the bottom of the line by overpricing items which usually are exposed to intense competition.

Let us examine the problems of full-line pricing a bit further. A well-established manufacturer may have a line of products such as a line of lathes and attachments. A new product which he develops cannot be priced without consideration of its impact on the whole line. For example, suppose he develops a chuck attachment because of a frequently stated need by his customers. To the manufacturer, this may appear to represent a marginal product unless sold at cost plus a target-return markup. His customers may resist the resulting high price and seek out other manufacturers for the device. This may lead to the transfer of all their business to such competitors. Therefore, our well-established manu-

facturer may do best by selling this chuck accessory at a very small profit, or even at no profit at all (by itself) in a package deal for lathes.

The opposite situation may exist when the demand for the basic product is very strong. For example, consider the case of the manufacturer of pleasure or recreation sailboats. He introduces deck paints which match the colors of his boats or their sails. He may very likely be able to charge a premium price for this product because of his line of boats and supplies.

The moral of full-line pricing is that customers like to purchase a *line* of products from *one* vendor, and they evaluate the line as a whole. If customers feel they can fulfill their needs for an entire line by going to another vendor at a lower cost, many will do so. Therefore, some items in a line may be so strong as to hold customers despite overpricing of accessories, while in other cases, overpricing of a single product in a line may lead to a mass transfer of business elsewhere.

Before examining some of the other more pragmatic and relative non-theoretical problems of pricing, the manager concerned with pricing should probably become acquainted with marginal theory as applied to pricing. It is the favorite of economists. Conceptually it states that, to maximize profits, price should settle at a level where marginal costs equal marginal revenue. Stated another way it postulates that the manufacturer should go on calculating the added cost for one more unit (or batch of units) of the product, and the price should be set where this additional cost equals the additional revenue generated from sales of the last unit.

Mathematically, the approach is sound. However, it breaks down badly when put to actual use, in large measure due to the following:

1. The traditional demand and supply curves of the economists almost never exist in real life.

2. Marginal costs are computed from average *unit* costs at different levels of output—but the unit costs in a multiproduct firm are based on assumptions that are far from perfect.

3. Even the largest business enterprise has very sketchy knowledge (if any) of what the sales of the new product would be at various prices. At

best, it may be able to approximate through experimentation the location of two or three points on the demand schedule.

With knowledge of only two or three points on the demand curve, it is difficult for a pricing executive to determine the shape of the curve between these points and beyond them. This plus the other factors causes the marginal theory to build theoretical models on figures that are either incomplete or subject to substantial errors of estimation.

"ETHICAL" PRICING

Occasionally a manufacturer will develop a new product which can be strongly protected against competition by patents and/or proprietary processes. The development of drugs offers a prime example. Because of the strong demand, the manufacturer may price his product to yield very high profits, as some evidence suggests for certain industries. On the other hand, despite the freedom from threat of competition, the manufacturer may set a "fair" return on his investment instead of gouging his customers. For a firm which is planning to be around for a long time, this policy would seem to have considerable merit.

DISCOUNTS IN PRICING

Discounts in pricing require that the manufacturer give close consideration to channels of distribution and legal restrictions or he may be quickly put out of business. It is a common practice for manufacturers to list a sale price with a discount rather than the actual transfer price. The following types of discounts are offered to purchasers:

1. Trade discount. This is the reduction in price given to members in the channels of distribution in anticipation of the job they are going to do. For example, a manufacturer may establish a trade discount structure of 40%–10%. If the selling price of the product to the consumer is $100, the retailer purchases it at a 40% discount or $60. The wholesaler's discount is 10% off what he sells to the retailer,

so that he purchases it for $60 less $6 or $54 from the manufacturer.

Where the small manufacturer and even large sophisticated manufacturers get into difficulties is when they sell through several channels, as for example, (a) wholesaler-retailer, (b) discount house-retailer, and (c) very large customers. If any channel thinks it is being shortcircuited and forced to compete directly with other people buying at a lower price and performing the same functions, members of the channel may drop the product or institute legal action (if a basis exists).

2. Cash discounts. A cash discount off the face of the invoice is offered to induce prompt payment of bills. For example, 2/10 net 30 requires that the entire bill be paid within 30 days but a 2% discount is allowed for payment in 10 days. With high interest rates in effect in the economy, the small cash discount offers little inducement.

3. Quantity discounts. Quantity discounts may be given for orders exceeding a specified dollar amount or number of units. *Cumulative* discounts apply to purchases over a given period such as a year, and in some cases may be discriminating and illegal. They are useful to the producer because they encourage large orders and reduce his inventory costs.

4. Seasonal discounts. If the new product is a highly seasonal item, peak production periods present a problem. By offering discounts for purchases made out-of-season, production and delivery schedules may be smoothed a little.

5. Special discriminating discounts. Discounts may be given to purchasers in certain geographical area in order to meet competition. Also, discounts may be given to certain types of customers in the channels of distribution or under certain reciprocal agreements. Again, the legality in each situation should be checked in advance.

LIFE CYCLE CONSIDERATIONS

Generally, the price of a product must be decreased over the life cycle of the product. While it is true that the cost of manufacturing may decrease with time, selling and promotional costs may reduce such possible benefits. Skillful pricing practices will help the entrepreneur obtain maximum cumulative profit over the product life cycle. We must also realize that all benefits should be converted to the same point in time (date) for comparison with alternatives. This may be done by finding the present value of each year's profit by standard discounting methods. Let us compare two pricing alternatives to see how we can evaluate the risk of selecting our policy over another.

Figure 12-5 shows a comparison of a high initial price policy vs. a low stay-out price policy. The high initial price reduces the life of the product for the company because competitors quickly jump in and drive the price down. Our company's share of the market rapidly decreases. In the case of Policy B,

---

Pricing Policy A

Assumptions:
1. A high initial price will shorten the life cycle of the product as far as our company is concerned
2. We will lower the price and conduct heavy advertising as competition builds up
3. Cost per unit declines only slightly and is assumed constant at 6%.

End of year	Price	Volume	Profit	Discount factor = 10%	Present value of profit
0 (now)	Initial investment −$150,000			1.00	−$150,000
1	$15	20,000	$180,000	0.909	164,000
2	12	40,000	240,000	0.826	198,000
3	10	25,000	100,000	0.751	75,000
4	7	15,000	15,000	0.683	10,000

Present value of life cycle profits = $297,000

Pricing Policy B

Assumptions
1. A low initial price will bring a larger volume
2. Maintaining a low price will keep advertising costs down and keep out the competition
3. Hence distribution costs and other costs are $5.50/unit

End of year	Price	Volume	Profit	Discount factor = 10%	Present value of profit
0	Initial investment −$150,000			1.00	−$150,000
1	$8	30,000	$105,000	0.909	95,000
2	8	50,000	175,000	0.826	144,000
3	8	50,000	175,000	0.751	132,000
4	8	50,000	175,000	0.683	120,000
5	7	50,000	125,000	0.621	78,000
6	7	30,000	75,000	0.564	41,000
7	7	10,000	25,000	0.513	13,000

Present value of life cycle profits = $473,000

Figure 12-5 Life cycle pricing

End of Year	Discount Rate for Risk	Risk Discount Factor
0	--	
1	--	
2	--	
3	5%	0.864
4	10%	0.683
5	10%	0.621
6	15%	0.432
7	20%	0.162

End of Year	Time-discounted Revenues from Policy A	Risk-discounted Revenues from Policy A	Time-discounted Revenues from Policy B	Risk-discounted Revenues from Policy B
0	-$150,000	-$150,000	-$150,000	-$150,000
1	164,000	164,000	95,000	95,000
2	198,000	198,000	144,000	144,000
3	75,000	65,000	132,000	114,000
4	10,000	7,000	120,000	82,000
5			78,000	48,000
6			41,000	18,000
7			13,000	2,000
		$284,000		$353,000

Figure 12-6   Discounting for risk

we keep out a large influx of competition and maintain a longer life cycle. We don't imply, of course, that Policy B is *always* the best.

Let us now introduce a simple risk concept. The further into the future we look, the greater the risk. New technology, new product substitutes, unexpected competition, or market changes present a hazard to our rosy predictions. One way of handling this is to discount the stream of profits further because of risk. The amount of discount must be based on executive judgment. Figure 12-6 shows a comparison of the two policies on such a risk basis.

A RISK ANALYSIS EMPLOYING EXECUTIVE JUDGMENT

It is a common and naive practice to simply set a price for a new product without regard to the resulting volume of sales which may result. Even when the yearly sales of units are predicted, no consideration is given to possible alternative outcomes. If we

use the concept of degree of belief as a "probability", we may gain more insight into the selection of a particular price.

To illustrate this point, suppose we wish to evaluate three possible prices for a new product which we will introduce. These prices are $3.95, $4.49, and $4.69. We wish to estimate the minimum sales volume at each price. To accomplish this, we try to establish a concensus among executives in answer to the question:

"At $3.95, what do you estimate the minimum sales volume will be—on the basis that there is only one chance in four that it will actually turn out to be lower?"

In other words, executives are asked for an estimate of the minimum sales such that they believe sales will be *at least* that amount 75% of the time they would make such a judgment in a similar situation and only 25% of the time would sales be less than the estimate. Figure 12-7 illustrates the presentation of these judgments at the 0.25, 0.50, and 0.75 level. The 0.75 case is where the executive sets a minim-mum sales volume which he believes has only a 25% chance of being exceeded when the product is on the market and 75% of the time sales are apt to be lower.

One large company uses 10%, 50%, and 90% indexes of belief (probability) for executive judgments. Many variations are possible, but quantifying judgments in any way helps executives think more precisely while at the same time allowing them to combine a number of possibilities regarding the future.

Price = $3.95

Probability	Estimated minimum volume (units)	Weighted volumes
0.25	12,000	3,000
0.50	20,000	10,000
0.24	24,000	6,000
Expected minimum volume =		19,000 units

Expected minimum sales volume = $3.95 (19,000)
= $75,050

Price = $4.49

Probability	Estimated minimum volume (units)	Weighted volumes
0.25	10,000	2,500
0.50	18,000	9,000
0.24	23,000	5,650
Expected minimum volume =		17,250 units

Expected minimum sales volume = $4.49 (17,250)
= $80,900

Price = $4.69

Probability	Estimated minimum volume (units)	Weighted volumes
0.25	8,800	2,200
0.50	12,000	6,000
0.25	16,000	4,000
Expected minimum volume =		12,200 units

Expected minimum sales volume = $469 (12,200)
= $57,220

Figure 12-7 Price and expected sales volume

CONCLUDING REMARKS

Pricing in many respects is more an art than a science. It involves an attempt to balance factors to which no precise weight can be attached. The estimation of the effects of various marketing policies (something backed up by experimentations in the field and sometimes on with experience as a guide) upon sales—both in the near and distant future—are involved. What is good policy for one company may be unworkable for another. Such decisions can only be sharpened by collecting all possible information. The less the information upon which to base the estimates, the more likely the decisions reached to be wrong.

The focal point should be profits, either short-term or long-term, and the best way to start is to study how the profit margins are generated in a multiproduct firm. This takes us back to the principles and practices of accounting. To this one must add the theories, lore, and philosophies associated with pricing. The third leg of the tripod upon which these decisions rest is that of information. Much of the information comes as a result of market studies involving the theory and practices of market research—a subject covered in another chapter of this book.

REFERENCES

1. For an excellent and analytically supported discussion of pricing and experience factors, see Perspectives on Experience, prepared by the staff of The Boston Consulting Group, Inc., One Boston Place, Boston, Mass. (1968).

BIBLIOGRAPHY

Cassady, Ralph, Jr., Competition and Price Making in Food Retailing: The Anatomy of Supermarket Operations. New York: Ronald Press, 1962.

Frey, Albert Wesley (ed.), Marketing Handbook. New York: Ronald Press, 1965.

Harper, Donald V., and William F. Massy. Price Policy and Procedure. New York: Harcourt, Brace & World.

Kallimanis, William S., "Product Contribution Analysis for

Multiproduct Pricing", *Management Accounting*, July 1968.

Lanzilotti, Robert F., "Pricing Objectives in Large Companies", *American Economic Review*, Dec., 1958.

Lynn, Robert A., *Price Policies and Marketing Management*, Richard D. Irwin, Inc., 1967.

Koller, Philip, *Marketing Management: Analysis, Planning, and Control*, Englewood Cliffs, N.J.: Prentice-Hall, 1967.

Marting, Elizabeth (ed.), *Creative Pricing*, American Management Association, 1968.

Montgomery, David B., and Glen L. Urban, *Management Science in Marketing*, Englewood Cliffs, New Jersey, Prentice-Hall, 1969.

Oxenfeldt, Alfred R., "Product Line Pricing", *Harvard Business Review*, July–August, 1966.

Phillips, Almarin, and Oliver E. Williamson (eds.), *Prices, Issues in Theory, Practice, and Public Policy*, U. of Penn. Press, 1967.

"Prices, Labor Costs and Profits", United Auto Workers, December 15, 1966.

"Robinson-Patman: Dodo or Golden Rule?", *Business Week*, Nov. 12, 1966.

Stigler, George J., *The Theory of Price*, New York: Macmillan 1966.

Stout, Roy G., "Developing Data to Estimate Price–Quantity Relationships", *Journal of Marketing*, April, 1969.

Walker, Arleigh W., "How to Price Industrial Products", *Harvard Business Review*, Sept.–Oct., 1967.

Watson, Donald S., *Price Theory and Its Uses*, Boston: Houghton Mifflin, 1968.

Dhalla, N.K., "The Art of Product Pricing", *Management Review*, June 1964.

Moulson, T.J., "How Much Profit Should a New Product Make", *Printers' Ink*, Duell, Sloan & Pearce, N.Y., July 23, 1965.

New Products Marketing, Editors of *Printers' Ink*, Duell, Sloan & Pearce, N.Y., 1964.

Perspectives on Experience, published data of Electronics Industrial Association, Boston: The Boston Consulting Group, Inc., 1966.

CHAPTER 13

PROMOTING THE NEW PRODUCT

by Dr. Richard E. Stanley, University of South Carolina

"Promotion is any communicative activity whose purpose is to move forward a product, service or idea in a channel of distribution."[1] By using various combinations of communications tools, promotions tell people of a firm's market offering and persuade them to buy it.

BACKGROUND FOR PROMOTION

Through the market communications, or promotional efforts of the seller, potential buyers are made aware of the availability and qualities of products and services, and attempts are made to persuade them to purchase the offering. Whether potential buyers are engineers, industrial purchasing agents, wholesalers, retailers or consumers, they can be reached and effectively sold if promotional tools are used with discretion.

The introduction of new products poses a special problem as their mortality rate is significant. This high risk coupled with the shortening of the new product life and profit cycle is forcing successful companies to use every available promotional means to get their new products distributed, known and bought quickly before profits start to decline. As a general rule, the profit margin starts to deteriorate before the sales curve of a new product has reached its peak because "sooner or later every product is pre-empted by another or else degenerates into profitless price competition".[2]

To get a new product launched successfully and quickly a firm must use every available means to reduce the risk.

Marketing research, which is conducted and interpreted properly, is the key to successful mew product introduction. The mass market is a myth because in reality, it is composed of many different submarkets. For example, the mass market for a new type of automobile tire might be divided into industrial buyers and consumers. Industrial buyers might further be subdivided into those who buy tires which become part of a finished product and those who buy for replacement to maintain their fleets. Consumer tire buyers can be classified as to income, safety-consciousness, etc. A new product should be promoted to these specific submarkets rather than the market as a whole in order to be of maximum appeal to potential prospects.

DETERMINING PROMOTION TARGETS

From the vast number of people in the nation, the introducer of a new product must determine those who are, or should be, the most logical prospects for his product. If his product is entirely new with nothing like it in the market, he may set up elaborate and time-consuming experiments to determine the most likely high-consumption groups. Or, he may proceed to define his prospect groups clearly on the basis of his judgments and the judgments of others. To the small businessman with a limited budget, the latter course may be the only one open.

What is needed are clear, exact specifications which clearly define the prospect groups to be reached. It is not enough to know that the best prospects are men—the promoter must know his promotion target by age, occupation, income, education, geographical location and perhaps religion, race and nationality in the consumer market. In the industrial market, he may need to know the size of company, type of manufacturing process, industry class, management structure; typical methods of purchasing, progressiveness, etc., about his promotion targets in order to reach them with maximum impact at minimum cost.

For example, the best industrial prospects for a new high-performance switch which has distinct advantages for the electric utility industry might be medium-sized, city-owned electric utility corporations with 10–15 million dollars in sales, with purchases of this nature being made by trained engineers and whose operations are confined to that section of the United States east of the Mississippi River. Likewise, key consumer prospects for a new type of food product might be housewives between the ages of 23–40 with two or more children at home, whose husband is a businessman or self-employed in one of the recognized professions, middle to lower-upper income group who live in the Northeastern section of the county. The secret to defining a promotion target is to do it in terms of prospect characteristics which will affect the sales of the product.

Until promotion targets are accurately defined, copy cannot be successfully written, media cannot be logically selected—in fact, nothing of a worthwhile nature can be done in regards to promoting the new product. Specifically defining promotion targets is an absolute must if a success is to be made of a new product introduction.

It should be noted that every new product depends initially upon cultivating target customers (who might logically use the product because of age, sex, income, geographical location, etc.), dissatisfied customers of other products, or "switchers". Product or brand loyalty cannot exist because the product is new.

"Switchers" are people who tend to try new products or brands just because they are new. The early users of a new product have been called the "high mobile" and tend to be people who wish to move up the status ladder.

Brand and/or product loyalty should be cultivated, but this is not applicable initially to a new product because primary demand, or demand for the class of product, must be developed first. Highly promoted brands within a product category seem to have exceptional brand loyalty.

PRODUCT MUST BE RIGHT

Each promotion tool makes its own peculiar, individualistic contribution to the introduction and sale of a new product. Even a maximum contribution by one or all promotion tools cannot overcome quality deficiencies, poor styling or design features, inadequate distribution and sales, or improper dealer service. Proper promotion works well when the product, sales and service package is right. It will not overcome deficiences in these areas.

THE PROMOTION MIX

To have purpose, promotion tools must be selected with a specific promotion target in mind. The particular combination of publicity, advertising, personal selling and sales promotion that a firm employs to launch its new product is its promotion mix *on that product*. All promotion tools are interchangeable and compatible. The final selection of a promotion mix for a new product depends upon the tasks assigned to promotion and the environment within which these tasks are to be performed. Decisions on the promotion mix should be made with the promotion targets' satisfaction as the key consideration.[3]

PROMOTION TOOLS

Each of the promotion tools has its own peculiar strengths and weaknesses. The trick in new product introduction is to take advantage of a promotion tool's strengths and offset its weaknesses with other promotion tools.

PUBLICITY

New product publicity consists of newsworthy information about the new offering which is placed in various media. Space or time charges of the media are free since the publicity release is treated as news by the editors. Although in some types of publicity the sponsoring firm is not identified, on new products, it is better for the firm's name to be included where possible.

Publicity is viewed as news by recipients and therefore possesses a high degree of believability—much more so than messages presented by means of other promotion tools. Since a new product has a reputation to earn unless it is released under the umbrella of a family brand, new product introductions should attempt to get as much publicity in media as possible[4].

For example, a company making packaging machinery might be trying to secure maximum publicity in trade publications for a new, sophisticated, packaging machine which offers buyers distinct advantages in speed, adaptability to different package forms and in reducing down time. First, the company might consider inviting the new products editors of the leading trade publications to the plant to witness a demonstration of the new machine. Related literature on the new machine could be distributed at this time. If the company considers this too expensive, perhaps a luncheon meeting might be arranged during which the new machine is unveiled and explained to the editorial group.

Publicity releases including photographs of the new machine and explanatory literature should be sent to editors attending the meeting and to trade publications not sending representatives. An attempt to place an article covering the development and applications of the new machine is also in order. Trade publications often use such articles, and they are among the best forms of publicity.

A publicity release is used at the discretion of the receiving editor, and it is up to him to decide whether or not to use all or any part of it, when and in what manner. The firm seeking publicity for its new product offering has no control over the publicity which is granted since it is not paying for time or space. Yet, to reach promotion targets it is often necessary to use a number of different media which would be prohibitively expensive except through publicity efforts.

ADVERTISING

Advertising is any paid form of non-personal presentation of goods, services or ideas by an identified sponsor. It is paid for in the sense that space or time charges are paid the media carrying the message. Because of this, the advertiser has a high degree of control over what goes into such space or time and is limited only by moral considerations, laws and at times certain restrictive practices of the media.

Advertising, in most forms, is employed to promote the new product to large audiences. It delivers a fixed message to a group, and this message cannot be changed to conform to the desires of each individual it reaches. Because of this and historical practices of some advertisers, advertising, in general, does not have a high degree of believability. Indeed, if just half of the recipients of an advertisement believe most of which is said or implied in the ad, that advertisement is doing quite well.

Highly complex products do not normally lend themselves well to effective promotion by advertising alone as it is difficult to get the complete story across. Likewise, extremely expensive products are difficult to sell entirely through advertising as severe price obejctions arise. In these latter two cases, it is best to couple advertising with personal selling or go with personal selling alone. In general, advertising is best used for low-priced, mass consumption items in the consumer market and to open doors for salesmen in the industrial market.

PERSONAL SELLING

Although personal selling is handled elsewhere in this book, a brief review of its characteristics as a promotion tool are in order here.

Personal selling is the most important type of promotion when viewed from the standpoint of our nation's annual business expenditures. It has the advantage of having a salesman in direct contract with a prospect with all the promotional flexibility such a situation allows. The salesman can adjust his sales talk to each individual prospect and thus can answer price objections on expensive products and go into as much detail as needed on complex propositions such as in selling industrial products where engineering features, performance factors, installation considerations, cost savings, etc., need to be carefully explained. Personal salesmen are especially adept at meeting objections and getting buying action from prospects—two areas in which advertising is notoriously weak.

The big disadvantage of personal selling is it is tremendously expensive when compared with other promotion methods. An advertising, publicity or sales promotion message can "call on" a prospect for a few cents while the per call cost of an aggressive salesman is hard to keep below five dollars and often is much higher. The hiring, training, compensating and maintaining costs of using a sales force as the sole promotion tool to contact prospects is usually prohibitive, so the other tools of promotion are used to do some of the work.

SALES PROMOTION

Sales promotion is any promotion other than publicity which supports and enhances advertising and personal selling activities. Sales promotion can be used to reach wholesalers, retailers, consumers or industrial buyers, help salesmen explain the new product to prospects and serve as a reference for customers.

A wide variety of sales promotion devices exist including sales literature, sampling, packaging, displays, premiums, banners, posters, signs, demonstrators, contests, trade shows, refund offers, sales meetings, product models, etc. Which devices to use depends largely upon present or impending competitive actions in the market.

Sales promotions are extremely active—they should not be fixed, rigid or bound by any pre-set formulas. They should be creative and possess the ability to change faster with conditions than other promotional methods.

The big strength of sales promotion is its extreme flexibility. It can be used at any stage of the new product introduction. It can hold customers who have been influenced by other promotional methods. It can enhance a selling delivered by advertising, publicity or personal selling. It can stiffen the backbones of wholesalers, retailers, manufacturers' agents, and company salesmen when the going gets rough. The form of a particular sales promotion is limited only by the ingenuity of its creator.

COOKING UP THE PROPER PROMOTION MIX

A company is perfectly free to determine its own promotion mix, or the promotion tools to be used and their budgets. There are no hard and fast rules

	Attention	Interest	Desire	Conviction	Action
Publicity	A	A	A	A	C
Advertising	A	A	A	D	D
Personal selling	E	E	E	A	A
Sales promotion	B	B	B	B	A

A—Very good for this purpose.
B—Tends to perform satisfactorily.
C—Average performance.
D—Does not perform well.
E—Usually too costly to use alone for this purpose.

Figure 13-1 Using promotion tools to complete a five-step sale

and few guidelines. It may be perfectly appropriate for a firm marketing a new product to a limited number of industrial buyers to use personal selling as its sole promotion tool. And, it may be appropriate for a cosmetics firm selling direct to consumers to depend mainly upon a sales force for its promotion efforts. What works for one company may not work for another. About all that can be done is to set down some general guidelines as shown in Figure 13-1.

In any sale, a prospect must go through the five mental stages of attention, interest, desire, conviction and action. The relative desirability of using each of the promotion tools to achieve each of the mental stages is shown in Figure 13-1.

To get maximum promotional effort at minimum cost, it is usually desirable to seek the right combination of promotion tools to meet specific promotion objectives. For example, on a new consumer product which requires a change in buying or living habits, an all-out promotion campaign may be needed. Publicity may be used to "kick-off" the promotion (get attention, interest, desire and conviction), be backed by advertising to present a controlled campaign message to prospects (reinforce attention, interest and desire), use salesmen to answer retailer and wholesaler objections and get them to stock the product (conviction and action) and depend upon the use of a sales promotion device known as sampling to get consumers to try the product and repeat purchase (conviction and action). Other new products, especially in the industrial market, may not require as extensive promotion efforts.

In determining the promotion mix for a particular new product, it is wise to consider some other factors which may affect the extent and intensity of promotion efforts. Some of these factors are the number of good prospects in the market, their degree of concentration geographically and otherwise, extent and nature of competition, degree to which prospects must be educated on the new product, price and profit margin available and the length of the distributive channel.

PLANNING THE PROMOTION CAMPAIGN

In order for promotion to achieve maximum effectiveness, it must be viewed as part of the total marketing program. Other parts of the program such as credit, transportation and storage can be used in the promotion effort just as promotion management can help these other marketing-related functions in the pursuit of their own area objectives.

The total marketing program should be in writing with overall marketing goals clearly established and tasks defined so that the various sub-areas, such as promotion, can develop its own objectives and ways of reaching them in order to accomplish what the total marketing program is after. The action of both the marketing plan and the promotion plan should be an integral part of any critical path delineation of the factors involved in the development and introduction of a new product. The marketing program is the key plan in the marketing area—the promotion program and all other sub-area programs are subordinate to it.

DETERMINING OBJECTIVES

The setting of overall promotion objectives is basic to the well-planned promotion program. These objectives can be drawn from a wide range of possibilities, and they should be set as specifically as possible. The general objective of "to increase sales" is of little value in guiding the promotion program. Is promotion to educate technical people on uses of the new product? Or, is it to create brand loyalty for a new product among a certain prospect group? Or, might it be to secure a certain number of retail outlets for the new product? The importance of setting specific promotion objectives is twofold: (1) It provides the promotion program with direction; and (2) It provides a basis on which evaluation of the program can be made.

Promotions can be designed to answer a number of questions which might be in the prospect's mind as indicated by a McGraw-Hill advertisement which makes the following statements from the viewpoint of the prosepct:

"I don't know who you are.

I don't know your company.

I don't know your company's product.

I don't know what your company stands for.

I don't know your company's customers.

I don't know your company's record.

I don't know your company's reputation.

Now— what was it you wanted to sell me?"

Once the basic promotion objectives have been set, specific tasks can be developed for each promotion tool. For example, publicity can be assigned the task of securing X number of lines of favorable publicity in consumer magazines; advertising might be charged with educating prospects to the uses of the new product; personal selling may have for its work the opening of a certain number of retail outlets; and sales promotion might be used to influence prospects to try the new product or to instruct, inform and elaborate on product benefits and applications.

DETERMINING THE PROMOTION BUDGET

If tasks are properly assigned to the promotion tools, an estimate can be made of the money required by each tool to perform its task. A skilled publicity man should know about how much money is required to secure the designated number of lines of publicity in a class of magazines; once the prospect group is defined, an advertising executive can determine the media to be used, size of space or time units, frequency and coverage of advertisements and with his knowledge of costs of preparing and placing advertisements can estimate the total advertising funds necessary to perform the tasks; with the knowledge of the cost of a salesman's call and the number of calls necessary to open up a new account, a sales manager can estimate the necessary personal selling budget; and once the types and magnitude of sales promotion methods to be used are decided upon, a cost estimate can be determined. Totaling these various estimates will produce an estimated promotion

budget based upon objectives and tasks to be performed.

Because of the skills necessary to make the above estimates, some companies use a percentage of anticipated future sales to set the budget for the promotion of a new product. This approach can lead to serious miscalculation of the promotion budget as the introduction of a new product usually requires a larger promotion budget than is necessary to maintain an established product. No guidelines or percentage figures exist on which to budget the promotion expense of introducing a new product. Some factors which influence the size of the promotion budget in an upward direction are: (1) Rapid turnover products which are purchased over and over again by customers; (2) A large prospect group to be reached; (3) A high number of competitors with intensive promotion efforts; (4) The lack of easily recognizable product differentiations; (5) The necessity of educating prospects to a new way of thinking or acting; and (6) Sufficient productive capacity to meet anticipated market demand.

COORDINATING THE PROMOTION EFFORT

An integrated promotion program will have one central selling theme which is used by salesmen, in advertising, on sales promotion pieces and where possible, in publicity releases. Salesman will use publicity clippings and advertisements to show distributors and dealers the support behind the new product. With each promotion tool supporting the other, a much greater impact can be made on a market than with different selling themes which water down the promotion effort. The "Pick a pair of six packs" selling theme used to promote Budweiser beer is an excellent example of reinforcing a sales theme by utilizing it in all promotional vehicles.

A recipe for marketing new products is aptly phrased by an executive vice-president of A. C. Nielson Company when he says:

"To a product with a good strong consumer plus add sufficient advertising over an 18-to-24 month period to produce a share of advertising about twice that of the share of sales you plan to attain. Season liberally with introductory offers to both trade and consumer and bring to a boil with a well-trained, hard-hitting sales force. Keep cooking in the front burner for the life of the brand, adding improvements from time-to-time along with enough advertising to maintain its share modestly ahead of its sales position."[5]

USING PUBLICITY TO PROMOTE NEW PRODUCTS

Publicity can prove the way for a new product's acceptance before advertising can have its sales-producing effects and salesmen can make their first calls upon prospects. Editors of magazines and business publications are always on the lookout for interesting news items and will seriously consider running informative new product stories. Even television stations use publicity releases which are properly designed for the media. Films, with a subdued sell, are supplied free to television stations. These films are usually long on product information of use to the audience and short on commercials.

A number of outlets for new product publicity are available as shown in Figure 13-2. When space or time are involved, the publicist receives this free of charge.

Business magazines and trade papers are always interested in information on new products. These media have a responsibility to keep readers informed on new products, new materials, new services, new processes and new techniques. Business papers are

---

Consumer magazines

Newspapers (especially women's sections and sections)

Business, trade and professional magazines business (especially new product sections)

Trade papers

Radio stations

Television stations

House organs

Figure 13-2 Some outlets for new product publicity

industry's clearing house for technical information and knowledge.

Yet, with all these outlets for new product publicity, amateurish efforts to secure publicity usually end up in an editor's wastebasket. So, unless trained personnel exist within the company, the services of an advertising agency or public relations firm should be retained. Many advertising agencies have hired publicity specialists to service their accounts, and there are many reputable public relations firms who can furnish a spot job or a long-range program on a fee basis.

New product publicity must be carefully planned. Publications must be studied for their editorial policies and viewpoints; television and radio stations have well-developed policies on publicity which must be understood; editors be contacted, releases written, filmed or recorded, and a plan for merchandising the publicity must be developed. These are not jobs for the novice.

WRITING PUBLICITY

Even though new product publicity is being placed by an advertising agency or public relations firm, the marketer should be able to recognize well-written publicity. Editors discard poorly-written publicity releases by the score.

Publicity releases have the best chance of being published when they contain information of interest to the publication's readers. They should be devoid of "puffery", be factual and excite the readers' interest. A publicity release to trade and business publications should contain such information on the new product as the engineering design, efficiency of operation, speed, price, sizes available and any specific new features that should be stressed. The publicity release will receive more editorial attention if it is not more than 300 words long and contains a $5'' \times 7''$ or larger photograph of the product in use. It is wise to tailor publicity release to fit each publication. General releases, written to blanket a number of markets, do not have the same chance of getting into print as specially-prepared releases.

A ten-point publicity program which includes some practical tips on securing new product publicity in publications follows:

1. Make sure that the product is really new or at least subsrtantially improved. Identify the release as a new product news release.

2. Date the release. If it is for future release, specify the future release date.

3. Put in a prominent place the name and address of the issuing firm and the name of the person to be contacted for additional information.

4. The publicity story should be factually and simply written on letter-sized (8½ by 11 inches) paper. Head the release with the basic name of the new product, not a coined company name.

5. List the features of the new product in descending order of importance in narrative form. Technical terms should be limited to trade or technical publications.

6. Condense the release until it is no more than 300 words. The most important information about the product should appear in the first paragraph.

JOHN P. CROWLEY LTD.
115 FERNWOOD PARK
ROCHESTER, N. Y. 14609
Telephone 716-654-8161

Advertising • Sales Promotion
Public Relations • Research

Delmar W. Karger
Dean, School of Management
Rensselaer Polytechnic Institute
Troy, New York 12181

May 7, 1970

Dear Sir:

I am extremely pleased at the prospect of having one of my releases considered for your book. The release which Mr. J. W. Moss referred to is enclosed as well as the product bulletin*and photograph which accompanied it. Of course the latter two items are a MUST when sending out a product release.

If I can be of any further help, please don't hesitate to contact me.

Sincerely,

John P. Crowley
President

JPC/nrc
Enc.

13-3a

JOHN P. CROWLEY LTD.
115 FERNWOOD PARK
ROCHESTER, N.Y. 14609
Telephone 716-654-8161

Advertising • Sales Promotion
Public Relations • Research

NEW PRODUCT RELEASE

THE SOLID STATE PT-100 FROM CHRONOLOGICS INC.

The PT-100 has adjustable timing ranges from
100 ms to 1600 seconds. The new solid state
design techniques incorporated in the PT-100
have created finer performance and greater
reliability than ever before possible. Accuracy
is $\pm$ 2% with repeatibility to $\pm$ 15% at constant
temperature. Maximum time for reset is 50 m sec.
Operating ranges are from 12 V to 110 V, AC or
DC, and four mounting options are available. The
timer is only 3x3x11/2 inches with Dial Accuracy
of 2% F.S. In small quantities the PT-100 sells
for less than $25.00 each. For further information
contact:

CHRONOLOGICS INC.
24 Martin Street
Webster, New York 14580

or call

716-872-1470

13-3b

13-3c

about **MAGNAFLUX CORPORATION**
7300 W. Lawrence Ave. • Chicago, Ill. 60656 • AC: 312 UN 7-8000

for release: IMMEDIATE RELEASE   *from:* Franklin S. Catlin

NEW PORTABLE MAGNETIC PARTICLE TESTING UNIT

SPEEDS INSPECTION OF WELDS AND STRESSED AREAS

A new compact portable magnetic particle testing unit, "P-100",
has been developed by Magnaflux Corporation, manufacturers of nondes-
tructive testing systems. P-100 is designed to provide an easy and
fast method of inspecting welds and a wide range of parts for surface
and subsurface defects. P-100 is also ideally suited for low volume
production testing applications and for sample inspection on volume
runs. The unit measures 9½"x9½"x18" and weighs 50 lbs. Its compact
size allows easy, one-man inspection in hard-to-reach areas.

P-100 can operate with either alternating current or half-wave
direct current. Varying part size and configuration are not
inspection problems due to a unique "Dial-Amp" current control, which
permits infinitely variable selection of magnetizing current levels
up to 750 amps.

Operation in the AC mode offers maximum sensitivity and speed
in locating surface defects. AC minimizes background interference,
permitting better signal interpretation and thereby increased defect
identification sensitivity.

13-3d

Page Two

Operation in the HW/DC mode allows detection of subsurface defects. The pulsating half-wave magnetizing current provides increased mobility of the magnetic particles during indication build-up and improved magnetic field penetration into the part for greater inspection sensitivity. False indications are minimized.

Little or no surface preparation is required on weldments or castings for either AC or HW/DC operation. P-100 is designed for one-man testing. Test set-ups are easy with three either/end connectors: an AC connector, an HW connector, and a common connector. Changeover from one mode to the other is accomplished by merely changing one cable connection.

Demagnetization after inspection is carried out by energizing the system with AC, and then slowly turning the current down.

For further information on this new portable magnetic particle testing unit, "P-100", write to: Magnaflux Corporation, 7300 West Lawrence Avenue, Chicago, Illinois 60656.

13-3e

About: Magnaflux Corporation
          7300 West Lawrence Avenue
          Chicago, Illinois 60656
          Phone - (312) UN-7-8000

From: Franklin S. Catlin

For: Immediate Release

A new compact portable magnetic particle testing unit, "P-100", has been developed by Magnaflux Corporation, manufacturers of non-destructive testing systems. P-100 is designed to provide an easy and fast method of inspecting welds and stress areas for surface and sub-surface defects. P-100 is also ideally suited for low volume production testing applications and for sample inspection on volume runs. The unit measures 9½"x9½"x18" and weighs 50 lbs. Its compact size allows easy, one-man inspection in hard-to-reach areas.

13-3f

13-3g

Figure 13-3a–g Two typical excellent new product news releases
Source: John P. Crowley, Ltd., Rochester, N.Y. and Magna Flux Corporation, Chicago, Ill.

7. Be sure the release includes such information as model, sizes, colors, costs, weight, how it operates, where it can be ordered, installation data and any unique manufacturing details.
8. Have a good quality, glossy photograph no smaller than 5 by 7 inches accompany the release.
9. Any technical literature on the product, case histories, etc., should be sent along with the release.
10. Be sure sales literature, specification sheets, etc., are ready for distribution as requests for these will be received.

To help guide the neophyte writer of new product news releases the editor of a major new products oriented magazine was contacted for samples of what he considered to be excellent releases. Two of these are shown in Figure 13-3a through 13-3g.

TIMING PUBLICITY

When promoting new products, don't let the advertising program begin until publicity has had an opportunity to "break" the story. Editors do not have much use for publicity releases after advertising has started on the new product because much of the news value is gone. Furthermore, publicity which precedes advertising has the effect of stretching promotional efforts over a longer period. Remember, publicity space and time are free while advertising dollars must be spent to secure equivalent space or time.

Business and trade publications often insist that new product announcements be released editorially before they appear in advertisements. Old news is no news to most business editors.

It helps to introduce a new product to buyers at a trade show. If possible, press conferences should be conducted early enough so that publicity breaks in publications just before, during or immediately after the trade show. There is little reason to conduct a press conference to talk about a new product which has been in use for months.

BREADTH OF PUBLICITY EFFORTS

There is much more to publicity than the writing of a new product story and sending it along with a good quality photograph to the editors of newspapers and magazines. A complete company publicity program should be planned to include all possible publicity areas such as product publicity, special or interesting product applications, new literature on products, news about the company and management activities, plant expansions, sales games, executive speeches on the industry, job appointments, industry awards, sales conventions, research reports, professional and charitable activities of employees, etc. A well-developed, consistent company publicity program will get the company known and make it much easier to introduce new products.

Publicity should be merchandised to get its full benefits. Any significant feature articles should be reprinted as sales promotion or direct mail pieces. Publicity clippings can be put into an attractive folder so that salesmen can show wholesalers and retailers that their market is being pre-sold by publicity as well as advertising efforts. When customers are shown such publicity they are more likely to promote and "push" the new product thereby making the salesman's job easier.

In order to measure the success of publicity efforts, one or two press clipping bureaus should be retained to locate publicity as it occurs. A count should be kept of new product stories, the space devoted to them and the number of inquiries which result from each. A simple cost of space or time check can then reveal the value of space and time received in dollars and cents. In addition, the media which return the greatest number of inquiries should be noted for future reference. The quality of such inquiries should be noted by determining which ones ultimately led to sales. Of course, inquiries must be turned over to the sales force for proper action, for without such action, they are virtually worthless.

After the initial publicity campaign, advertising can further impress the publicity-conditioned market for a new product by reinforcing the basic product story.

USING ADVERTISING TO PROMOTE NEW PRODUCTS

The average person is daily bombarded with about 1500 advertising messages. However, only a few of these advertisements register any telling effect upon an individual as he has, for survival's sake, developed an armor of apathy. To penetrate this armor, a new product advertising campaign must be properly conceived and ingeniously executed.

Some products are more advertisable than others. It will help a new product advertiser to determine how well his product will respond to advertising. This can be done by evaluating the product according to five conditions which influence the opportunity for effe ctiveadvertising. These are: (1) A favorable primary demand trend for the product; (2) A chance for significant product differentiation; (3) Importance to the prospect of hidden product qualities; (4) Opportunity to use strong emotional appeals; and (5) Circumstances which favor the accumulation of sufficient funds with which to advertise.[6]

If the demand for the class of product is growing, such as in the case of sugar substitutes, the product is more advertisable than if demand for the product class is shrinking, such as has been true for snuff. This does not mean that a product in a shrinking demand category cannot be advertised, as the advertiser may attempt to capture a large portion of a dwindling market. It simply means his advertising will be less effective than if the demand for the class of product is expanding.

If the product can be significantly differentiated from other products in its class, advertising will be more effective. Examples of significant product differentiations are the free pouring feature of a brand of salt and the stannous fluoride ingredient of a leading brand of toothpaste. The advertisers of gasoline, sugar, and coal have had great difficulties in developing significant product differentiations. If a new product has no significant differentiation, it is questionable whether it should be introduced into the market at all.

Hidden product qualities help an advertiser develop preference for his product based upon product features which cannot be objectively recognized by the buyer. The "sanforized" label in clothing which means the garment will not noticeably shrink, the vitamin "C" in orange juice and the mildew resistant feature of some house paints are examples.

Some products can make strong emotional appeals to buyers such as the "love of family" appeal made by some insurance companies, the appeal to mastery and advancement made by home study schools and the appeal to health used by many proprietary medicines. People, especially consumers are much more likely to buy on an emotional basis than a rational basis, and this can be used to advantage in launching a new product.

Sufficient funds to advertise a new product are a practical necessity. A high profit margin per unit, potentially large sales volume, or fast repeat purchasing of the product may furnish sufficient advertising funds. If sufficient funds are not available, the advertiser will have to reduce the market area he is trying to influence or perhaps even forego the use of advertising at all.

A careful analysis of the new product in accordance with these five factors of advertisability will give the advertiser some knowledge of how successfully he can employ advertising as a promotional tool. Once the basic decision to advertise has been made, the selection of an advertising agency for the new product is the next task.

SELECTING THE ADVERTISING AGENCY

Most advertisers, who are trying to influence a geographical market broader than one locality, will benefit from the services of an advertising agency. Advertising agency personnel are specialists in writing copy, doing layouts and selecting media—jobs which few advertisers are equipped to do for themselves. In addition, most advertising agencies receive the majority of their compensation in the form of a 15 percent discount from the media which is supposed to take care of any planning, copy, layout and media selection services performed for the client. Of course, any extras beyond these basic services are changed directly to advertisers.

An important decision which faces a new product advertiser is the selection of an advertising agency. Advertising agencies differ in their skill, degree of familiarity with a class of products and in other ways. A good advertising agency is one which is familiar with the strengths and weaknesses of the various media that should be used for the products involved, has excellent creative ability and has had experience with advertising programs similar to the one the new product advertiser is contemplating. It is best for an advertiser to choose an agency which has had experience in the advertiser's type of merchandisr, trade channel and with advertising budgets of similar size. Two excellent sources for locating advertising agencies are *Standard Advertising Register* and *McKittrick Directory of Advertisers*.

WORKING WITH THE ADVERTISING AGENCY

New product introductions are the acid test of the worth of an advertising agency. The results of an agency's creative efforts are much more readily observable on a new product's sales than on the sales of an established product.

In order to get maximum new product sales results from an advertising agency, it is necessary to estab-

Basic Services
Planning
Copywriting
Layout
Media selection

Research Services
Market research
Copy research
Media research
Consumer research

Trade Promotion Services
Wholesaler promotions
Dealer promotions
Booklets, pamphlets, broadsides
Catalogs, catalog sheets, specification sheets
Exhibits

Sales Training Services
Planning sales meetings
Salesman's manuals and portfolios
Visual aids

Product Services
New product development
Product design
Creation of brand names
Creation of trademarks
Complete packaging design

Merchandising Services
Displays
Package inserts
Banners, streamers
Price cards, counter cards

Direct Mail Services
Letters, folders, booklets
Brochures
Sampling
Couponing

Other Services
House organs
Premiums
Contests
Instruction booklets
Calendars
Annual Reports
Pricing

Publicity and Public Relations Services
New product publicity
News stories
Company image building
Consumer relations
Employer—employee relations

Figure 13-4 Complete advertising agency services

lish a good relationship with the agency. This requires five things on the part of the advertiser.

1. The agency must be brought in at the beginning of the new product introduction. Mutual confidence, respect and "no secrets" communications must exist between advertiser and agency.
2. The advertiser must know the range of marketing talent available in the agency. A good agency is a pool of the finest marketing talent available, not just an "ad-maker". All the agency's talent is at the disposal of the advertiser. Figure 13-4 gives an idea of the range of agency services.
3. There should be a written marketing plan with specific objectives to be reached on the new pro-

duct. This plan should contain all the facts about the product and its market.
4. Be prepared to pay an agency for value received. It is necessary to compensate the agency for a full new product effort. An agency cannot be expected to use its best talent on a new product introduction unless it is paid accordingly.
5. Delays in clearing agency work should be kept to a minimum. Congenital indecision on the part of the advertiser leads to flagging interest in the new product on the part of the agency.[7]

If the advertiser will abide by these five "directives" he can expect maximum help from his advertising agency. An agency which has only second class citizenship is unlikely to turn out first class work.

CREATIVE ADVERTISING STRATEGY

An advertising agency's very existence depends upon its creative ability—its ability to come up with the big selling idea and communicate it to the right prospects. All other agency functions are secondary.

The "big idea", or what is often called the unique sales proposition, is the central theme of the advertising campaign, and it can be conveyed copywise, artwise or otherwise. A unique sales proposition (USP) is necessary in advertising, especially consumer advertising where the armor of the consumer's indifference must be penetrated. A good advertising agency should be able to create a central selling theme which will attract the right prospects. Examples of such themes (big ideas, USP's) are the tatooed Marlboro cigarette man, the "Think Small" Volkswagon theme and the "You wonder where the yellow went" jingle—type theme used by Pepsodent some years ago. A good campaign theme will be attractive to the right group of prospects, tie in logically with the new product and its qualities and be capable of being used in multiple media.

Most campaign themes are expressed in the written or spoken words of the advertisements and are part of the copy. Advertisers should not attempt to write their now copy or depend upon amateurs to do it for them. Professional advertising agency copywriters should be used for this purpose. However, the advertiser should be able to recognize a competent piece of copy when he sees one. Therefore, the following rules for evaluating advertising copy are presented.

1. Copy should be written to the "average person" in the prospect group the advertiser is trying to reach. Good copy sounds like a personal letter written to each member of the prospect group.
2. The most important idea should come first in the copy. Product qualities should then be presented in terms of benefits from the most important to the least important.
3. "You" and "yours" should be used in the copy in the place of "we", "our" and similar terms.
4. Copy should be written in language that the prospect group uses and understands.
5. Specific and full information should be provided within space or time limitations.
6. Key copy ideas should be repeated in various guises.
7. Copy should not exaggerate, misrepresent or be untruthful. It needs to be sincere in order to get prospects to believe in the product.
8. Some sort of buying action should be called for on the part of the prospect.

Advertisement illustrations help to convey the central campaign theme and should be selected with care. Although the advertising agency should be allowed to do the selecting, the advertiser should evaluate their choice with the following criteria of good illustrations.

1. Illustrations should be keyed to the self-interest and understanding of the prospect.
2. Illustrations should include all or some detail of the product. A photograph of the product in use is usually best.
3. Illustrations should be technically accurate and believable to the prospect group.
4. Illustrations should support and reinforce the copy theme.

MEDIA SELECTION

Media selection is part of the creative strategy of an advertising campaign and as such, will be determined by the advertising agency. Media decisions involve which general class or classes of media to use newspapers, magazines, direct mail, television, radio, outdoor, transit or business papers. In addition, specific mediums must be chosen within each media class, the advertising frequency, dates, sizes, time periods, colors, costs, etc., must be chosen, and all of this incorporated into a media schedule. The key idea in media selection is to get the advertiser's message to the right group of prospects at a time when they will be reading, listening, or watching the media vehicle. Each media class must be chosen in terms of what it can do for the advertiser. A short discussion of each media class and its strengths for new product introductions follow:

Newspapers

News is the very essence of newspapers. Newspapers mean new things to the consumer, and millions of newspapers are bought daily to satisfy the request for "what's new?" Every year, automobile manufacturers make heavy use of newspapers advertising in introducing their new models. Basically, there are five specific reasons for the use of newspapers in new product introductions.

1. Newspapers can be used in a market-by-market introduction of the new product. Many advertisers do not have the funds for simultaneous, nation-wide distribution. Newspapers put the advertising in the specific markets where it is needed.
2. Newspapers are very flexible in introducing new products. Short closing dates for ads allow changes to be readily made in the size, color, illustration and copy of newspaper ads.
3. Local wholesalers and retailers can easily tie-in their advertising with newspaper ads run by the manufacturer.
4. Many newspapers give the advertiser valuable merchandising assistance. Dealers are given the dates when the manufacturer's advertising is to run, are urged to stock up on the product and may even be given point-of-purchase help.
5. Advertising testing can be done very economically in newspapers. Campaign themes, copy appeals, layouts, colors and sizes can be checked before the total advertising budget is committed. Changes can be made in the campaign if necessary before large expenditures have taken place.

Magazines

People who read magazines usually have better incomes, are better educated and are more receptive to new ideas than nonmagazine readers. Many magazines are slanted toward specific interest groups such as *Good Housekeeping, Field and Stream* and *Popular Mechanics*. Beyond this outstanding ability to reach well-defined markets, magazines have other advantages of interest to the new product advertiser.

1. Many consumer magazines such as *Life, Reader's Digest* and *Better Homes and Gardens* sell advertising space in regional editions. The advertiser whose product distribution is limited need no longer buy unwanted circulation. He can put the prestige of a major national magazine behind his new product from the first, and his advertising can "break" on a region-by-region basis if such is the basic marketing strategy.
2. Magazines offer fine reproduction of art and color. The product can be shown in exact and specific detail.
3. Magazine advertising has a long life and gets multiple readership. Unlike newspapers, magazines are often kept for weeks and months and pick up additional readers beyond the original subscriber. Magazine ads often keep pulling inquiries for months after the advertisement has been run.
4. Magazines are often read slowly and at leisure. Therefore, they are a logical choice for new products and services which require an educational campaign.
5. Many national magazines are authorities in their fields, and some of this prestige rubs off on products advertised in them.
6. Tie-in sales promotion material is provided by many magazines and is very helpful when introducing a new product.

Direct Mail

Direct Mail is known as the "rifle" of advertising. It can reach prospects in a certain block of a city or restrict its readers to company presidents, farmers or Chamber of Commerce members. It is the most flexible of all the media. The effectiveness of direct mail advertising depends to a considerable extent on the mailing list used. Names and addresses of potential customers can be gathered by the advertiser himself or bought from a list broker. If the list is a current list of the right prospects, direct mail offers the advertiser some unique advantages.

1. It is very personal when addressed to a specific person. Direct mail pieces addressed to the "occupant" lose this peronalized quality and are often discarded without opening.
2. It has none of the space or time limitations of other media. The advertiser decides (within post office regulations) the type of direct mail piece to be sent and by the mailing date, determines approximately when it will be received.
3. It adapts itself to large or small advertising budgets. Mailings can be elaborate and extensive or simple and restrictive.
4. Direct mail is not in competition with other advertising as only the advertiser's message is delivered.
5. Copy themes, appeals and ideas can be tested at small cost.

Television

For new product introductions to consumers, television has an impact which is hard to match with any other media. The combination of sight, sound and motion in television comes closest to matching personal selling. However, its use in reaching industrial buyers is limited because of its mass appeal. Television has some other outstanding advantages which should be considered by the new product marketer.

1. Television has a high degree of territorial flexibility which can be adapted to the new product's distribution pattern. Spot TV is often used in major markets when a new product launching takes place. Combined market coverage on a simultaneous basis is possible with network TV.
2. New products, which need to be demonstrated to prospects, are logically introduced on television.
3. Selected audiences can be reached by TV through careful choice of the type of program and time of broadcast.
4. Television has a reputation for news. The "timeliness" characteristic of TV makes it possible to tie new products in with local events.
5. The increasing use of color in programming and the growing number of color TV sets makes it possible to reach large audiences with faithful reproductions of the product and its package.

Radio

This media provides the warmth of the human voice. When time costs are a consideration, radio should be carefully studied. Some of the plus factors offered new product advertisers by radio are:

1. It is geographically flexible media. Time can be bought on individual stations in particular markets or network arrangements can be made.
2. Compared to television, radio advertising requires much lower out-of-pocket expenditures. Because of this, it is especially useful where the repetition of a copy theme or brand name is essential to the new product campaign.
3. Different groups in the population such as housewives, children, etc., can be reached by careful selection of stations and times. Large segments of automobile drivers listen to their car radios during peak traffic hours.
4. Copy testing of new product campaigns is inexpensive and quick.

Outdoor

Outdoor advertising, such as billboards, is not very effective for introducing new products unless it is used in conjunction with indoor media. Outdoor and radio—gives size and color plus the chance to tell an involved story; outdoor and newspapers—outdoor advertising can catch them on their way to retail outlets while newspapers furnish more detailed information; and outdoor and magazines—magazines give broad coverage while outdoor advertising puts emphasis on local markets. Large size, rapid penetration, color reproduction, fast package identification and low cost are the chief attributes outdoor advertising can bring to a new product introduction. In addition, outdoor advertising is easy to merchandise to retailers is they notice it on their way to work.

Transit Advertising

Transit advertising campaigns are especially useful to keep pressure on the market after a new product has been introduced. Car-cards on the inside of buses and the outside posters on the sides and rears of vehicles are suited mainly to reminder—type advertising. Where public transportation is utilized frequently by the advertiser's prospect group, car-cards are often the last contact between the advertiser and prospect before she enetrs the retail store.

Business Papers

The over 3000 business publications are the most widely used media in contacting business and industrial buyers. They are a virtual "must" in marketing a new industrial product. Business papers are industry's clearing house for new products, ideas and technical information. A prime responsibility of a busines publication is to keep readers informed on new products, new materials, new services and new techniques. Practically every large segment of American industry has its own business publication—*Iron Age* and *Steel* for the steel industry, *Oil and Gas Journal* for the petroleum industry and *Women's Wear Daily* for retail store buyers are examples. Each issue of a business publication must have new, interesting material. In a number of studies, business papers have been identified as the number one method for keeping up-to-date on new developments.[8] They provide the advertiser with the opportunity to expose his new product to the buyers in the industry he wishes to reach with little waste circulation. They form the backbone of most new product campaigns aimed at business and industrial buyers.

USING SALES PROMOTION TO PROMOTE NEW PRODUCTS

In new product introductions, sales promotion is used to supplement advertising and personal selling efforts. It helps to produce sales volume called for by the marketing plan and is designed for immediate action.

Sales promotion on a new product involves three main tasks: (1) Promotion to the company's own salesmen; (2) Promoting to the trade—wholesalers and retailers; and (3) Promoting to the ultimate consumer. Let us examine each of these jobs in turn.

Sales promotion to the company's own salesmen involves sales meetings, contests, premiums, sales portfolios, visual aids and anything else that can inspire the salesmen, motivate them to push the new product and make their selling job more effective. The company sales-force is usually the key to getting necessary new product distribution among wholesalers and retailers.

Distributors and dealers must be willing to stock and promote the new product on their own. To make them more effective such sales promotion devices as showing the product at trade shows, contests, premiums, brochures, "special deal" allowances, "free" display cases and signs are used. Middlemen must be kept excited about the new product and cannot be allowed to adopt a "ho-hum" attitude.

Consumers are also vulnerable to properly used sales promotion devices. Such things as trading stamps, sampling, contests, in-store demonstrators and point-of-purchase material can help to make that all important initial sale. Then, the new product must fulfill its promises if repeat purchases are to be expected. Sales promotion should be brought in at the start of a new product campaign—not tacked on as an afterthought.

TYPES OF SALES PROMOTION DEVICES

A wide variety of sales promotion devices are available for new product introductions. The following examples are representative of the more commonly used devices but are by no means a complete listing.

Literature

Brochures, booklets, pamphlets, etc., are useful new product promotion devices and can be used to inform company salesmen, wholesalers, retailers or consumers. They can be used to promote industrial or consumer products. Usually, they provide complete information on the new product—much more extensive than is normally given in publicity releases or advertisements.

Sampling

This is the acknowledged top technique for introducing new products, but it is also the most expensive. Obviously, it is usually limited to low cost products and would find only limited use in the industrial market. Sampling puts the new product into the hands of people in their homes or businesses free of charge. It is the best way to make certain a new product will be tried. However, repeat purchasing of the product must be frequent enough to make sampling pay off.

Couponing

This is the second best device for introducing new products. Whether they're mailed, on the product package or included in a newspaper or magazine ad, coupons have been proven new product sales builders in the consumer market. If the manufacturer wants to keep control of the operation and be sure the product is being tried, the mail-in, refund coupon is the answer.

Packaging

This is the silent salesman for the new product. Besides protecting and containing the product, promotional messages can be given to lookers or buyers through illustrations, colors, offers, etc., on the package itself. A well-designed package is especially important when selling to ultimate consumers.

Point-of-Sale

A unique display at the point-of-sale can help a new consumer product get off to a flying start. Bakery goods, canned goods, cereals and dairy products are tremendously responsive to point-of-sale display. On the other hand, coffee, tea, cocoa, soaps, frozen foods and meat respond best to price cuts and other

devices. In the grocery field, unplanned purchases average about 34 percent of purchases made, and this figure is even higher when the product is promoted at the point-of-sale.[9]

Premiums

Premiums are not usually used in new product promotions directed at consumers. They tend to confuse the consumer and draw attention away from the qualities of the new product.

Price-off Offers

These are seldom used in promoting a new product to consumers because the price of the new product is not clearly-enough established in the consumer's mind to know whether it is a bargain or not. The question, "Off of what?" often arises. However, these offers are often made to wholesalers and retailers.

Banners, Posters and Signs

All have "stopping value" and are standard in many stores. These are especially valuable when they are in the near vicinity of the new product display.

Demonstrators

In-store demonstrators tend to be an expensive way to reach consumers. However, their use is sometimes justified for high traffic stores when the product has a rapid turnover rate.

Contests

These are not generally used in new product introductions to the consumer. However, various types of contests have their place in promoting the new product to the company's salesmen or to its dealers and distributors.

Trade Shows

When introducing an industrial product, it is often wise to take exhibit space in the main trade shows of industries which might be logical customers. Good salesmen, manning exhibits in such shows, can generate considerable interest, excitement and orders for the new product.

Sales Meetings

These are restricted to company salesmen, and/or dealers and distributors. Information on the new product and promotion plans can be passed along. Enthusiasm may also be generated at such meetings.

EVALUATING THE SALES PROMOTION PROGRAM

Before the sales promotion program is turned loose, the program planner can get a good idea of its probable success by asking six pertinent questions:

1. Is it useful to the salesman? The program should help make the salesman's job easier by creating interest and lowering sales resistance.
2. Is it trade oriented? The program should be designed to meet the capabilities and needs of the middlemen who are to take action.
3. Is it workable? The program should be tried out on salesmen, distributors and retailers. This will reveal how good a promotion program it really is, or what adjustments are necessary.
4. Is the language correct for each level? Salesmen, distributors, dealers and consumers all have their own selfish interests and peculiarities of language. Speak to each group in language it can respond to and act on.
5. Will the program get needed participation? The program should get as many people as possible involved. Salesmen, distributors and dealers need to carry it out. Can they do it? Will they do it?
6. Will the program move the new product? Unless it will help in selling the new product, it is quite useless.[10]

PROMOTING NEW INDUSTRIAL PRODUCTS

In promoting new industrial products, promotion agencies may be somewhat familiar with the market but seldom do they know as much about the particular group the company is trying to reach as the company. The company has much more knowledge of distribution channels and the market. Outside agencies must look to the company for this information before they can do a proper creative job.[11]

As previously mentioned, business or trade publications are normally the backbone of the new industrial product promotion effort, and it usually helps to give trade press editors a look at the product and supply them with information just prior to its introduction. The product should be exhibited in the proper trade shows and be listed and described in trade catalogs. Samples of the new product are necessary for the proper training of salesmen and distributors. Clippings of publicity and preprints of advertisements should be furnished to salesmen.

PROMOTING A NEW PRODUCT ON A LOW BUDGET

In the industrial market, a small promotion budget, even one as low as $25,000, can be stretched. Experience has shown that a well-organized trade publication advertising and publicity campaign can be designed to fit almost any reasonable budget.

In the consumer market, a new product may have to be introduced on a market-by-market creep-out rather than a national rollout if the promotion budget is slim. This approach means the company picks a small geographical market and concentrates its promotion efforts on it until it is captured—then, the profits from the first market are used to develop the second market, etc. Anheuser-Busch used this approach in promoting its Busch-Bavarian beer when the product was in its infancy.

The seller with limited new product promotion funds can also concentrate on mail order selling. Advertisements for the new product are placed in the classified sections of newspapers and magazines and orders are solicited. Direct mail advertising is often employed to secure initial orders on new products.

Whatever the method used, the seller should be careful not to bite off a bigger piece of the market than he can digest. If necessary, it is better to start small and develop a healthy appetite and the promotional strength to satisfy it.

REFERENCES

1. James U. McNeal, *Readings in Promotion Management*, New York: Appleton-Century-Crofts, 1966, p. 1.
2. "Why Are New Products So costly?" *Printers' Ink*, Vol. 273, No. 10 (December 9, 1960), p. 48.
3. James U. McNeal, *op. cit.*, p. 4.
4. A family brand is a brand name which applies to all of the individual products in a product family. For example, Kellogg's is a family brand for products which include Kellogg's Corn Flakes, Kellogg's Rice Krispies, etc.
5. James O. Peckham, "Ad Spending for New Brands Must Be High for First Two Years", *Advertising Age*, Vol. 34, No. 47. Reprinted with permission from the November 18, 1963 issue of *Advertising Age*, copyright 1963 by Advertising Publications Inc.
6. Neil H. Borden, *Economic Effects of Advertising* (Homewood, Ill.: Richard D. Irwin, Inc., 1942), pp. 424–428.
7. John R. Rockwell, "A New Kind of Relation Emerges", *Printers' Ink*, Vol. 287, No. 9 (May 29, 1964), pp. 142 – 143.
8. Angelo R. Venezian, "New Products' Strongest Ally", *Printers' Ink*, Vol. 287, No. 9 (May 29, 1964), pp. 216 – 222.
9. Samuel Bader, "The Sign: Its Power Ever Rises", *Printers' Ink*, Vol. 287, No. 9 (May 29, 1964), p. 35.
10. Joel Harnett, "The Means are Many, the Goal But One", *Printers' Ink*, Vol. 283, No. 11 (June 14, 1963), pp. 363 – 364.
11. "Industrial Marketing Outlet", *Printers' Ink*, Vol. 290, No. 8 (April 9, 1965), p. 49.

BIBLIOGRAPHY

Bader, Samuel, "The Sign: Its Power Ever Rises", *Printers' Ink*, Vol. 287, No. 9 (May 29, 1964), pp. 134–135.

Banning, Douglas, *Techniques for Marketing New Products*. New York: McGraw-Hill Book Company, Inc., 1957.

"Budget Guidelines Wanted for Introduction of New Product", *Industrial Marketing*, Vol. 52, No. 2 (February, 1967) pp. 25.

Donovan, Joseph T., "Outdoor: Strong, Simple, Fast", *Printers' Ink*, Vol. 287, No. 9, (May 29, 1964), pp. 223–226.

Golden, Hal, "President's Guide to Product Publicity", *Business Management*, Vol. 21, No. 4 (January, 1962), pp. 12*.

Gumbinner, Paul G., "In Defense of A Slighted Medium", *Printers' Ink*, Vol. 287, No. 9 (May 29, 1964), pp. 213–216.

Harnett, Joel, "Sales Promotion: Marketing's Tiger by the Tail", *Printers' Ink*, Vol. 290, No. 5 (February 26, 1965), pp. 47–59.

Harnett, Joel, "The Means are Many, the Goal but One", *Printers' Ink*, Vol. 283, No. 11 (June 14, 1963), pp. 358 – 360*.

Harnett, Joel, "When Magazines Should Come First", *Printers' Ink*, Vol. 287, No. 9 (May 29, 1964), pp. 209–213.

"Industrial Marketing Outlet", *Printers' Ink*, Vol. 290, No. 8 (April 9, 1965), p. 49.

Jones, Ernest A., "What Advertising Can Do—and How!" *Printers' Ink*, Vol. 287, No. 9 (May 29, 1964), pp. 139–141.

Lesly, Philip, "No More Elephants in the Elevator", *Printers' Ink*, Vol. 283, No. 11 (June 14, 1963), pp. 392–396.

Lynch, Virgil A., "Blueprint Your New Product Publicity", *Industrial Marketing*, Vol. 43, No. 11 (November, 1958), pp. 156*.

McClure, J. Warren, "Where News is Always Present", *Printers' Ink*, Vol. 287, No. 9 (May 29, 1964), pp. 192–194.

McGannon, Donald H., "TV: You Can't Succeed without It", *Printers' Ink*, Vol. 287, No. 9 (May 29, 1964), pp. 201 – 204.

McNeal, James U., *Readings in Promotion Management*. New York: Appleton-Century-Crofts, 1966.

Peckham, James O., "Ad Spending for New Brands Must be High for First Two Years", *Advertising Age*, Vol. 34, No. 47 (November 18, 1963), pp. 1.

Rockwell, John R., "A New Kind of Relation Emerges", *Printers' Ink*, Vol. 287, No. 9 (May 29, 1964), pp. 142–146.

"Speed: GE's Formula for a Four-Week Product Debut", *Industrial Marketing*, Vol. 51, No. 12 (December, 1966), pp. 71–72.

Venezian, Angelo R., "New Products' Strongest Ally", *Printers' Ink*, Vol. 287, No. 9 (May 29, 1964), pp. 216–222.

Whelan, Susan M., "Where the First Sale is Made", *Printers' Ink*, Vol. 287, No. 9 (May 29, 1964), pp. 132–133.

CHAPTER 14

SECURING CAPITAL AND GOING PUBLIC

VENTURE CAPITAL

According to Stanley M. Rubel venture capital is what is used to finance relatively small-sized companies before they can qualify for public underwriting.[1] This kind of financing would include start-up situations and any intermediate financing required up to the time of a public offering.

Venture capital sources sometimes insist on temporary stock control, especially when such a financing group assumes most or all of the capital risk. At other times they will take minority equity positions.

Venture capital sources are not usually interested in securing operating control of a business. They are, however, interested in securing a more than average return for their investment and are therefore interested in equity positions as well as the mere lending of money for convential interest.

Mr. Rubel in the referenced text lists over 450 companies that control an estimated 1.5 billion dollars in capital devoted exclusively to venture capital investments.

The sources indicated range from individuals who operate independently to major firms. Included in this group are small business investment companies (SBIC's) and men who operate in the corporate finance departments of investment banking firms.

The companies each have their preferences as to the kind of business in which they are interested. However, they almost always are seeking new projects for companies having exciting growth potential.

Some of the firms can provide a wide range of financial and managerial services while others tend to be passive investors and generally keep themselves from being involved in the daily affairs of the companies in which they invest. However, the most successful venturers appear to be those, according to Rubel, who are actively involved in the companies they finance.

While some of the venture capital sources like to keep their commitment to a given firm below $100,000, there are many who will commit up to a half million and some are willing to go for one million dollars or more.

Selecting or finding a venture capital firm suitable to a given company's purpose is somewhat similar to finding an underwriter for a public offering. In both cases it is important not to create the impression that one is shopping. If a firm receives the idea that a company's proposal has been turned down by one or more other firms, they are most likely to also turn down the proposition-feeling that others have evaluated the situation and found it unattractive.

In trying to select a venture capital firm to approach one ought to try to do a little sleuthing to find out what their current capital situation is with respect to new investments, the kind of companies in which they are primarily interested, the kind of "positions" they have taken in the past, so that you can compare their past and probable future actions with what you would like to have happen to you.

Do not approach a venture capital firm by sending in a request through the mail. You would *not* do this when trying to find an underwriter for your public offering and you certainly should not do it in seeking a venture capital firm. It is best to secure an introduction, if possible. Introductions can also be accomplished by the firm's bankers, accountant, lawyer, or a business friend or a specialized consultant. However, keep in mind that if you use professional services to secure the introduction, that you usually are committed to providing a finders fee.

A great deal hinges on the initial impression made on the venture capital firm. The presentation of the company, its opportunities and its needs ought to be professional in every respect. The venture capitalists obviously will be looking for signs of ambition, business knowledge, integrity, growth possibilities, and the successful application of management skills and abilities. Obviously they will want complete detail background on the principals in the firm, background information of the industry, the firm's principal competitors, financial statements, projections, cash flow forecasts, descriptions of marketing programs, development programs, etc. Do not underestimate the need to make a most knowledgeable and professional presentation.

Rather obviously the venture capitalists will be looking for quality management. Beyond that they will be looking critically at the company, its products, the industry in which it is operating, the financial situation, etc. The venture capitalist obviously will not put his money in a firm he does not believe has an excellent chance of succeeding and in which the rewards are not likely to be substantial.

With respect to the information needed before a deal is concluded, the venture capitalist will want everything mentioned to date and essentially everything that is later mentioned in this chapter with respect to underwriters and/or the Securities Exchange Commission (S.E.C.) with respect to a public stock offering.

The actual deal will need to be negotiated between the President of the company and the venture capital firm. This negotiation cannot be delegated. As to the exact terms, they will vary from situation to situation. In some cases a simple common stock investment might be made. However, in most cases there is some kind of debt paper as well as an equity position involved. Further, the debt paper often contains a variety of restrictive provisions designed to protect the venture capitalist. However, keep in mind that these restrictions are not aimed at crippling the prospective firm because the venture capitalist cannot win *unless the firm succeeds*.

After the business grows and matures, it is to the advantage of both the company and the venture capitalist to have the company secure funds through a public stock offering. If there is no public market for the stock, the venture capitalist will not be able to obtain the benefits of his equity psoition.

Going public means the open sale of stock to the public. This can take place if the corporation sells stock, if existing stockholders sell stock, or if both the corporation and the stockholders sell stock.

The public offering of securities is governed by the Securities Act of 1933, as amended. It is administered by the Securities & Exchange Commission (S.E.C.), and the securities laws of the various states (commonly called "Blue Sky" laws). The latter laws are administered by the Securities Commission or other designated officials in each state.

WHY FIRMS GO PUBLIC

Traditionally, the public sale of stock serves to provide for the expansion of resources and production capacity where risk is involved. The desire to undertake a major new product venture and all kinds of things may well provide the motivation. If a company has a major new product which they wish to place on the market and which will take a significant amount of capital or if the company wants to provide for the systematic product diversification (which also requires significant capital) they may decide to obtain this capital via a public offering. Another reason is where a new product venture has modestly succeeded, and the people involved want to at least partially take out some of their "locked-in" gains—a public stock offering does this.

There are a number of advantages to going public. For example, the credit rating of a publicly-owned company is enhanced. The fact that shares are publicly held and that the market holds them in reasonably high esteem is evidence, in combination with a good balance sheet, of financial soundness and responsibility. It naturally commands more respect from suppliers, customers and suppliers of credit than a non-publicly held company.

The acquisition and retention of company personnel can well be an important factor. A public company has the advantage of providing financial benefits, such as significant stock option to its employees. A non-public company can make available stock, but it is generally meaningless because there is no market for such stock. Professional and management talent tends to be more readily attracted to a public company simply because of its greater visibility and the longevity and continuity of operations appear to be more certain.

A rather generalized but very important reason often is the fact that the market value of a private or closely held company is almost always *no more* than its book value. Further there is no market value to the stock except what might be generated through a liquidation or selling of the company. In contrast, a company's stock often exceeds its book value by a significant multiple! Going public, therefore, not only enhances the personal net worth of the original owners, but more importantly for the "long-run" it provides more liquidity for diversification. In closed or privately-held corporations, stock normally has no greater value than actual book value.

If a company has large outstanding debt, the fixed interest charges may be quite a burden. By going public, the company may be able to retire this debt, eliminate the interest payments, and put its resources to work more profitably.

The estate tax advantages sometimes provide part of the motivation for going public. The market value of public stock easily determines the value of the deceased stockholder's estate. Liquidity is provided in meeting the state tax charges—this could be a problem if the owner of a privately-held company did not have significant liquid assets to pay taxes. It is often true that differences in opinion occur between the Internal Revenue Service and the executors of an estate where a company is privately held—the differences are over the value of the private company. The public value of a share of stock in a publicly held company is never disputed.

A public offering enables private owners to convert part or all of their accumulated earnings into cash at the lower capital gains rate.

Perhaps one final reason for going public would be the prestige associated with a publicly-owned company. In some cases this is a strong motivating factor.

THE CONSIDERATIONS INVOLVED IN GOING PUBLIC

Most small company owners, or even owners of relatively large privately-owned companies, are concerned about losing control when they go public. Public financing does not have to divest the original owners of their majority or controlling interest.

The matter of losing control in the thoughts of owners ranges from losing the power to generally direct the corporate effort to interference in determining compensation, dealing with employees, setting prices, etc.

There is little to fear if only 30–35% of the company's voting stock is offered, as is commonly the case, even selling off 60% usually causes no problems. This stock is usually dispersed among a large number of stockholders. Only if a private placement is made to one or a few institutions is there the hazard of outside pressure on management.

The time of the offering is *an important* consideration since the popularity of the industry group into which the company falls has some influence on the price at which the stock can be marketed relative to earnings per share. Industry analyses are available from several public sources, such as Standard & Poor's.

In order to go public, one must "shed the light of day" on expenses and profits. This sometimes poses problems to management in a non-publicly held company.

SOME FACTS CONCERNING GOVERNING STATUTES

The Securities Act of 1933 is primarily a disclosure statute in that it seeks to protect the purchasers of securities by requiring adequate disclosure by the source of the security.

The state "Blue Sky" laws range from those permitting public offering without any filing or on mere notice of filing to those fixing minimum standards which a public offering must meet. Some of these latter vest in the securities commissioner authority to approve or disapprove of an offering.

A practical rule of thumb indicates that an offering is public and subject to the various securities acts if it is made to more than twenty-five offerees, or if any of the individuals receiving the offer are not in a financial position to risk the investment or if they lack the sophistication to understand the nature of the risk involved.

One way of trying to avoid coming under the act is through a public offering made only to residents of the state in which it is incorporated and doing a substantial portion of its business. Even though such an offering may be exempt from the registration provisions of the securities act, the anti-fraud provisions of the act are still applicable. Companies considering an intra-state offering must understand that it is difficult to comply with this exception from registration and the SEC will take cognizance of the action.

Another consideration with respect to the time of a public offering concerns the fact whether or not sales and profits for the recent accounting period have been adversely affected by a strike or other unusual and non-recurring problem. If so, it may be wise to wait until a proper growth pattern can be re-established so as to present a more attractive picture to underwriters and the buying public.

Another consideration could be that a key labor contract is due to expire within the time involved and, if so, "is a strike a possibility"? Again, under such circumstances, it may be advisable to postpone a public financing until the terms of the new contract are known.

Since some dilution of ownership on the part of present shareholders will likely be experienced, they may want to wait in case it is a rapidly growing business and defer public financing if financing for the immediate future though debt issue is available — such action might make possible delaying the public

offering for a year or two so that the same number of dollars could be raised by selling a smaller proportionate equity interest to the public.

A PUBLIC OFFERING UNDER THE ACT

The sale of securities may be exempt from SEC registration if it does not constitute a "public offering", if it is not greater than $300,000, or if it is an intra-state sale only.

The registration statement (usually Form S-1) requires that a Prospectus be filed which contains certain required basic information.

The Securities Act of 1933 requires a waiting period of twenty days between the filing data and the solicitation of offers to buy. Therefore a preliminary Prospectus is usually circulated in order to give the public and prospective buyers time to consider the offering. On the cover page of each preliminary Prospectus, there must be printed in red ink the fact that the stock is not being offered for sale. Part of this legend may say for instance;

This Prospectus shall not constitute an offer to sell or the solicitation of an offer to buy, nor shall there be any sale of these securities in any state in which such offer, solicitation or sale would be unlawful prior to registration or qualification under the Securities Laws of such State.

Because of the red legend, the preliminary Prospectus is often called the "Red Herring" Prospectus.

It is common that after the SEC has reviewed the registration statement and the Prospectus it sends a "deficiency letter" to the company noting what they consider necessary changes.

The filing of the statement is no guarantee of its accuracy nor does it constitute approval by the SEC. Once the company files a correcting amendment in accordance with the "deficiency letter" it starts a new twenty-day waiting period.

When the SEC declares the Registration Statement effective, offers for the purchase of this security may be accepted providing a final Prospectus, this time without the red herring legend, is delivered to the purchaser prior to or upon the confirmation of the sale of the security. The entire process from the date of filing to effectiveness usually requires from four to eight weeks, although on occasion it can be much longer.

Because of the usually required changes and variable time factors involved, it has now become common for the original registration statement to have on its front cover the following statement:

"The Registrant hereby amends this Registration Statement on such date or dates as may be necessary to delay its effective date until the Registrant shall file a further amendment which specifically states that this Registration Statement shall thereafter become effective in accordance with Section 8 (a) of the Securities Act of 1933 or until the Registration Statement shall become effective on such date as the Commission, acting pursuant to said Section 8 (a), may determine."

The effect of this is to do away with the old procedure of filing delaying amendments, and it also means that the filing of an amendment does not start a new twenty-day waiting period. The advantage is that a delaying period cannot be started until the registrant files a socalled acceleration request after which the registration will normally become effective in one or two days.

Should the offering be for $300,000 or less, an alternative procedure known as Regulation A can be used. Under this procedure, a filing is made in the SEC Regional Office in the region where the principal place of business of the company is located. Filing papers on Form 1-A contain, for circulation among potential subscribers, a document called Offering Circular rather than a Prospectus. No Red Herring offering circular is permitted, which means that the offering circular cannot be circulated in the investment community prior to the date upon which the commission permits the offering to be made. The time to clear a Regulation A offering varies from two weeks to three or more months.

Generally the Prospectus and the offering circular require the disclosure of similar information which includes history of the company, the precise nature of its business, information concerning its products, properties, personnel, sales, patents, competition, the company's financial condition, its principal

shareholders, the names and backgrounds of directors and officers, any important contracts with suppliers and/or customers and all other information which would be of significant interest to a potential investor.

Some of the common deficiencies noted in Prospectuses or offering circulars are:
1. Failure to state the speculative aspects and/or the harzards of the business.
2. Failure to set forth completely the full extent, nature and effect of transactions with insiders.
3. Failure to indicate complete earnings and normal growth-profit relationships.
4. Failure to set forth and discuss adverse developments that may occur after the balance sheet date.

FINANCIAL STATEMENTS NEEDED

In order to make an offering for over $300,000, a company must make available an *unqualified* certificate from an independent certified public accountant with respect to a balance sheet of a date no earlier than the end of the last fiscal year, except in the special circumstance when a registration statement is filed immediately after the end of the fiscal year and before the audit report is available. In this case one may temporarily use the audit from the prior year. The audited income statement must be for at least three years ended on the date of the audited balance sheet. There must also be a summary of earnings covering a five year period, the first two years of which may be unaudited. The rules as to consolidation are more complex than the last sentence suggests.

In addition, if such audited financial information is of a date more than ninety days prior to the date of filing with the SEC, an unaudited income statement from the date of the audited balance sheet to a more recent date and for the comparable period during the prior fiscal year is required as well as an unaudited balance sheet of a more recent date. Rather obviously, if the company has been in business less than three years, it only must go back as far as does its history. If subsidiary companies are involved, their financial statements must be consolidated with those of the main firm.

If an offering is made under regulation A, the financial statement requirements are then changed. An unaudited balance sheet dated within ninety days of the date of filing, together with unaudited income statements for the two fiscal years prior thereto and for any interim period between the close of the last fiscal year and the balance sheet date, is needed. However, one can be sure that audited statements carry far more weight with the SEC and providing unaudited statements is not good practice. In fact, the underwriter may absolutely require audited statements.

If the company is in its early stages of development and without a substantial operating history, it then may file a form which requires the furnishing of an audited statement of assets and liabilities and audited statements of cash receipts and disbursements.

A barrier to proceeding with a public offering sometimes occurs when a company has accomplished prior sale of stock or other securities. Such financings, taken singly or as a whole, could constitute a prior illegal public offering in violation of the registration, anti-fraud, or both provisions of the Act. In such case, the company may be required to make a registered recision offer to prior stockholders and/or bondholders, offering to refund their money. Otherwise the company may be required to establish on its books a "contingent liability" to such stockholders and/or bondholders for having made an illegal offering. As a practical matter, such a problem might preclude making a public offering for a number of years.

UNDERWRITERS

Why Utilize Underwriters?

The officers of the company may want to consider "going it alone", based upon their having been approached by friends and business acquaintances saying, "I would be interested in buying some of your stock". The experience of many companies who have tried the do-it-yourself route has usually been disappointing. The friend who was thought to have ten thousand dollars ready to invest will usually end up wanting only five hundred dollars worth of stock when confronted with the request for cold cash. The underwriter, in addition to purchasing the company's securities or providing a market for them, performs many other functions for the company engaged in its first public financing. Such services or advice include:

Expert advice as to the type of securities which would most likely assure the success of the effort.

Distribution of securities to a large number of investors in relatively small individual quantities, thereby avoiding large blocks of stock in the hands of non-management investors who could seriously depress the market if they should decide to sell.

Financial counsel of a general nature. Frequently this includes the recommending and/or furnishing of experienced men for the company's board of directors.

Sponsorship of the company's stock in the aftermarket.

The prestige arising from the company's connection with a respected investment banking house.

Choosing the Underwriter

Here the problem is to first find out what investment banking firms in the company's geographical area specialize in "originating" or acting as managers of syndicates for the marketing of new offerings or securities. Many large brokerage firms do little or no "originating", but will take part in syndicates managed by others or in the group of dealers who assist in marketing some securities offered in an underwriting. The firms specializing in "originating" have developed staffs of experts who work with the managements of companies in planning securities offerings and who are capable of taking charge of setting up underwriting syndicates and dealer groups.

Large commercial banks, lawyers who specialize in securities work, and national accounting firms all are in a position to supply helpful information on underwriting firms.

The smaller underwriting firms with local networks of offices will be the most likely prospects for a company whose business activities are largely local in nature. Larger underwriting firms are generally more interested in managing securities of larger companies or those likely to grow to national proportions in a relatively short period of time.

The ability of the underwriting firm to maintain a strong aftermarket following the offering will be of importance to the company in making its selection.

While competition between investment bankers is keen, it is difficult to do much shopping around. If such shopping is not done very carefully, the company will find itself unable to secure a good underwriter. It generally is advisable to consult with one firm at a time. If discussions with a particular firm are promising, take enough time to develop these somewhat before prejudicing the new-born relationship by promptly seeking better terms elsewhere. If the conversation does not appear to be promising, they can be terminated and another firm tried.

Types of Underwriting

There are three basic forms of underwritings by broker-dealers. These are (1) a firm underwriting or firm commitment, (2) a best efforts all-or-none offering and (3) a straight best-efforts offering.

A firm offering is one in which the underwriter agrees to purchase all the securities to be offered (at a discount called the "commission" or "spread") from the public offering price. The purchases made by the principal underwriter, called the managing underwriter, and by any other underwriters whom the managing underwriter brings into the offering— these latter are called co-underwriters. All of this group offer to sell their securities to the public as principals. They do so either directly or through other brokers who are called "selling group" members. They do not act as agents for the company.

In this form of underwriting, the underwriters do not sign the purchase agreement until the day of, or the day before, the effective date of the registration statement. However, if a registration if filed by a company with a reputable underwriter, it is most unusual that the underwriter will not proceed with the offer unless there occurs an adverse change in the circumstances of the company or a serious dislocation of the market.

In a best efforts all-or-none offering the underwriter usually signs an agreement well before the effective date stating that he will act as agent for the company to offer securities to the public and will use its best efforts to sell them on an all-or-none basis. This means that unless all of the securities are sold within a designated period, usually thirty or sixty days, the offering is terminated and all monys received to that date are returned in full to the subscribers. In a few cases, a variation of this form of underwriting, the offering is effected (the money not returned) if a specified portion of the securities are sold.

If a pure best-efforts offering agreement is consummated, the underwriter agrees to use its best efforts, as agent for the company, to sell securities during the designated period of time and all sales are final regardless of how many securities are sold. Obviously, this latter form is the least desirable way to proceed, particularly for the company and for the securities purchaser. It is not commonly used except for the smallest and most speculative of issues.

On occasion a person acts as a "go between" to effect the introduction of a company to an underwriter. In this case it is not uncommon to provide for the payment of a Finder's Fee, either in cash, in stock and/or in stock options. In such cases, it is important that any agreement with respect to compensation be reduced to writing as quickly as possible and to provide in the agreement that no compensation will be due and payable if for any reason the offering is not successfully consumated. It might be added that "finders" are not required since underwriters will gladly talk to responsible officers of the company.

Underwriting firms sometimes are willing to enter into non-binding agreements, commonly known as "letters of intent". These set forth the important points of the agreement between the company and the underwriter. They are only an expression of good faith or intention and are not legally binding. The binding agreement only comes at the last minute.

The Concerns of the Underwriter

This subject is introduced because if one wants or needs to get public capital, then the firm needs an underwriter. Unless he is satisfied with regard to the identified issues he may not want to proceed. Knowing these concerns in advance enables the firm to get ready for the questions, often internal corrective action is required *before* the company can go public.

Some of the concerns of the underwriter with respect to a prospective client includes concerns responses or statements relative to the following items:

The financial position of the company, especially its working capital position.

Growth in sales and/or earnings during the past several years.

How do sales and earnings growth compare with those of the industry in which the company falls.

The company's reputation—in general, the quality of its products, its reputation in the financial community, among the people who sell to it, etc.

Present and expected competition.

Quality and experience of top management.

Depth of management.

Will top management accept the burden of responsibility to a public stockholder group?

Compensation of officers and how it compares to the general industry pattern.

Are existing employment contracts (if any) of such a nature that they might prove burdensome to the company?

The efforts of the company, past and future, for research and development.

The uses to which the company proposes to put the funds received from the prospective offering and whether the proposed use of the funds will likely contribute to future profits.

If the investment banking firm and the company have just formed a new relationship (have not carried on discussions with each other over a period of a year or more) the investment banker or underwriter may request a general management survey of the company (usually at the company's expense) before the underwriter makes its decision whether to accept the business. Such a survey would include a consideration of its products, its markets and marketing organization, its present and future prospects, etc. If the prospective company is engaged in the exploitation of natural resources, an independent engineering report on reserves will usually be required. The underwriter is required to investigate.

The underwriter's own staff will usually prepare a detailed memorandum on the company being considered as an underwriting client for circulation among the partners of the firm. This inter-firm memorandum with any other available data will be considered at one or more meetings of the partners at which such matters as size of offering, types of securities to be offered, possible price range and general make-up of the potential underwriting syndicate (if any) and dealer group (if any) will be discussed.

Issues to be Negotiated between the Underwriter and the Company

The basic issues involve the size of the offering, the price-earnings ratio of the security, the type of securities, etc. If the Certificate of Incorporation does not provide for an adequate number of authorized but unissued shares, action by shareholders as well as directors is required. With respect to type of security, most companies today think primarily in terms of common stock. Under certain conditions the company and the underwriter might want to consider preferred stock, convertible debentures, warrants, or any other combination of the foregoing. Further, one might elect to offer a non-convertible note together with warrants.

The public offering price for shares of common stock will usually be based upon analysis of the per share price-earnings ratio of comparable companies whose securities have been seasoned in the public market. Typically, the originating underwriter will prepare a chart comparing the company with a number of other companies engaged in the same general business; if this is not possible, in comparison with similar businesses. Some of the items on the comparison sheets usually include total shares outstanding, net after tax profits, ratio of current earnings per share to current market price, ratio of book value per share to current market price, per share dividend yield, comparable earnings growth, etc.

It is not always in the best interests of the company to make its initial public offering for the highest possible price per share. If the price is too high, the market for the shares will sag, brokerage firms will lose interest, demand for the stock will wither and the price may remain depressed for some time. On the other hand, if the offering price is conservative, the stage could be set for an upward trend which will get the company far more attention in the financial community and thereby ultimately enhance the value of the stock.

The underwriter's discount (commonly called "spread") is related to the risk the underwriter takes. Common stock calls for a greater percentage spread than preferred stock, debentures or bonds. A well established highly reputable corporation will face a smaller spread than will a new company whose shares have never been marketed.

Sometimes the originating underwriter may only be induced to accept and manage a first public offering by a relatively new and speculative company if it is granted warrants to purchase a block of the company's shares for a period of years at a price related to the public offering price. Another device occasionally used in such a situation is so-called "bargain" stock. Here the originating underwriter will obtain part of its compensation through "letter stock" purchased from the company (or from principal stockholders) as a block of the old outstanding before any recapitalization at a price substantially below value of the new shares to be offered to the public. Such stock is, of course, unregistered and commonly known as "letter stock".

Agreement as to price-earnings ratio and the size of the offering generally determines the structure of the immediate future capitalization of the company. Usually in order to get the price per share within a price range that the underwriter thinks is suitable for a first offering, the outstanding shares usually need to be split in some fashion in order to generate more shares of stock. Also, if cash needs to be raised for the company, and more will be said about this later, additional shares need to be authorized by the board of directors.

In a first offering a full "bail-out" (a term used where the offering is made on behalf of shareholders as contrasted with one made on behalf of the company selling treasury unissued shares) normally will not be acceptable to the underwriter. In a first offering at least some new shares, as well as old shares usually are necessary.

An offering involving the sale of stock owned by selling shareholders is known as a "secondary offering". Principal shareholders often like to include several of their own shares in the offering, either to diversify their investment, because they wish to create a market for the stock or in some cases because they wish to make additional shares available for trading to satisfy listing requirements on one of the stock exchanges. Listing requirements on a stock exchange require a specified minimum public distribution of stock and further the distribution must be among specified numbers of stockholders holding various lots of shares. These listings requirements change from time to time and are different for the American Exchange as opposed to the New York Stock Exchange. A company making a first offering obviously does not at the same time apply for listing on the exchange. However, they should keep in mind some of the requirements for listing.

The percentage discount or spread can range from six to twelve or more per cent.

EXPENSES

While there is no fixed rule, it is common to anticipate costs for an issue of one million dollars to total between twenty-five to fifty thousand dollars for legal, accounting, printing and other such costs. Typically these costs would include the following categories of expenses, and the amounts indicated are estimates and/or educated guesses by knowledgeable people:

SEC Registration Fee

This usually the smallest item, being one-fiftieth of one per cent of the maximum aggregate public offering price of the security with a minimum fee of $100.00.

Accounting Fees

These vary in size and most companies already utilize a CPA firm. However, in order to go public it is wise to use a nationally recognized public accounting firm. These fees can easily range from $7500 to $20,000 for a first registration of a company with a single set of financial statements.

Federal Issue and Transfer Taxes

The federal original issue and transfer taxes are applicable. However, the state situations vary. In New York, a transfer tax is levied which applies to a sale by selling stockholders to underwriters if the sale or transfer occurs in New York.

Printing Costs

The materials filed with the SEC as well as the Prospectus is usually printed, however lithographed, multilithed, mimeographed or even typewritten material can be used. Other exhibits to the registration statement can be reproduced in the small quantity needed by less expensive means than printing. However, specialized printers are usually used and, in part due to timing requirements, the minimum will be about $15–16,000.

Printing and Engraving Costs of Stock Certificates

The managing underwriter would usually be satisfied with a simple lithographed certificate. However, the company often insists on hand-engraved certificates. In a case of a simple certificate these costs are quite low.

Legal Fees

Total legal fees can easily range between twenty to forty thousand dollars, the bulk of the fees of course going to the counsel doing most of the work. If the corporate legal counsel is experienced in securities work, the underwriter's counsel will usually confine his task to reviewing the registration statement, preparing the underwriting documents and examining the matters necessary to the rendering of his closing opinion to the underwriters. However, it is quite common for the underwriter's counsel to bear the prime responsibility. Typically, the underwriter's counsel will do the "Blue Skying" of the issue (remember the Blue Sky laws of the various states?). It is not unusual to have the maximum amount of the fee of the underwriter's counsel to be borne by the company to be specified in the underwriting agreement. If the underwriter covers his counsel's fees, the discount will be deeper in order to cover the costs.

Blue Sky Filing Fees and Expenses

These costs (exclusive of legal fees) will actually depend upon the number of states in which the underwriter (and his group if he has one) desires to market the issue. A typical range of costs would be fifteen hundred to thirty-five hundred dollars.

Registrar and Transfer Agent's Fees

Appointment of an independent transfer agent and registrar for the stock will almost always be required before a public offering is made. Charges are based upon a fixed fee for each certificate issued and registered and each certificate transferred. Charges incurred in connection with an initial public offering usually range upward from a minimum of two to four thausand dollars.

Insurance Policies

An offering by selling stockholders is sometimes accompanied by the procurement of insurance to protect both the underwriters and the selling stockholders against possible risk or loss from liabilities under the Federal Securities Act. Such liabilities might arise out of the erroneous statements or omissions in a registration statement. Typically one million dollars or protection costs somewhere in the order of ten thousand dollars.

It perhaps should be noted that such coverage is not easy to obtain. A limited number of American insurance companies write it only for issuers whose net worth exceeds $50 million, and the London market, where most of such insurance is written, is at the time of this writing revising the form of their policies.

Where some of the principal stockholders are selling shares as well as the company selling additional stock, the selling shareholders normally will bear their proportionate share of the underwriting expense. This is not always the case and in some cases some of the larger stockholders might well have purchased stock with the understanding that they could at a later date be enabled to sell some of their letter stock shares (unregistered shares) when the company made its next public offering without incurring any additional expense.

The underwriter's agreement which is executed just before the registration statement becomes effective is a document containing much "boiler plate" and is usually ten to twelve printed pages in length. Typically such agreements cover:

Warranties of the company relating to completeness and accuracy of the registration statement.

Warranties on the part of any selling stockholder as to title, validity and transfer ability of their shares.

Agreement by the company and by any selling stockholders to sell and by the underwriters to purchase the stock at a designated price and to make a public offering at the initial public offering price stated in the Prospectus. This of course is slightly modified depending upon the type of agreement reached with the underwriters as previously outlined.

Designation of the time and place of closing. Closing usually occurs at the transfer agent's office

seven to ten days after signing of the underwriting agreement if it is a firm underwriting.

Agreements by the company relating to qualification of the offering under the blue sky laws of the various states designated by the underwriters, delivery to the underwriters of sufficient quantities of the Prospectus, development and filing of the necessary amendments to the registration statement where necessary during the offering period, and the furnishing of subsequent financial reports to the underwriters and the security holders that will be acquired through the offering.

Agreement regarding the expenses of the registration, including in some instances certain expenses of the underwriters.

Agreement by the company and in most cases by selling stockholders if any to indemnify the underwriters against liabilities arising under the Federal Securities Act or otherwise on account of false statements or omission in the registration and Prospectus together with a cross-indemnification by the underwriters as to statements made in the registration statement on the basis of written data furnished by them unless there is insurance provided to cover such liabilities.

The agreement will contain provisions concerning default by any member of the underwriting group. Finally there will be a series of conditions specified concerning the effectiveness of the registration statement, opinions of counsel, certificates of company officers and selling stockholders as to accuracy of their warranties, letters of assurance and other such matters.

TIME REQUIRED AND THE STEPS INVOLVED

The heart of the matter, to some degree, is the date at which the required financial statements will be certified. They are the heart of the registration statement and the accounting firm must therefore be very closely involved.

A typical timetable could be as shown in Figure 14-1.

The tentative timetable is extremely "tight" and

Date	Matter	Responsibility
Feb. 10	Tentative agreement with underwriters	
Feb. 15	Questionnaires to be sent to officers, directors and 10% stockholders as to stockholdings, remuneration for services and interest in material transactions	Company Secretary and Counsel
Feb. 15 March 1	Company documents to be gathered for review and reproduced as exhibits, where required	Company Secretary and Counsel
Feb. 15 March 1	Interviews with Company officers, preparation of memoranda regarding history of business and its operations	Company Counsel, officers and employees
March 1–10	Preparation of prospectus (exclusive of financial statements) and of other portions of registration statement	Company Counsel and Underwriter's Counsel
March 10	Audit as of December 31, 1959, to be completed and financial statements to be furnished to printer	CPA firm
March 10	Registration Statement to be sent to printer for proof pages	Company Counsel
March 10– March 15	Registration statement proof pages revised and new proof pages obtained	Company Counsel and Underwriter's Counsel
March 18	Registration statement in final form to be printed and signature pages to be signed	Company Counsel, officers, directors and CPA firm
March 21	Registration statement filed with SEC in Washington, D.C.	Printer and Company Counsel
March 21	Preliminary blue sky survey to be distributed	Underwriter's Counsel
April 8	Telegraphic delaying amendment to be filed with SEC pursuant to Rule 473, with confirmation mailed to SEC	Company Counsel
April 15	SEC letter of comments ready for delivery (arrangements should be made to have an agent pick up letter in Washington, D.C. and read it over the telephone to a stenographer, to avoid delay in mailing)	Company Counsel
April 15– April 20	Preparation of first amendment to registration statement	Company Counsel and Underwriter's Counsel
April 18	Due Diligence meeting (to acquaint underwriters and dealers with the Company and the offering)	Company officers and Underwriters
April 21	First amendment to registration statement filed with SEC with letter requesting acceleration of effective date to April 25	Company Counsel
April 2	Sign Agreement Among Underwriters	Underwriters
	Sign Underwriting Agreement fixing price	Company and Underwriters
April 25	Price amendment filed	Printer and Company Counsel
April 25	Registration statement declared effective by SEC	
April 25	Final blue sky survey distributed	Underwriter's Counsel
May 2	Closing	All hands

Figure 14-1   Timetable for going public

Source: Reprinted from the April 1960 *Business Lawyer* with the permission of the American Bar Association and its Section of Corporation, Banking and Business Law

generally more time should be budgeted totally, and especially for the waiting period between the filing date and the proposed effective date. The actual time required could be significantly greater.

Night and week-end sessions of work are commonplace in a situation such as that scheduled in Figure 1. However, it is unwise to "cut corners" in order to meet deadlines since the quality of the registration statement will suffer with the almost inevitable result that there will be even greater delays in its processing by SEC.

Post-Offering Obligations

Companies which register their securities must file regular periodic reports with the SEC. Such reports include an annual report on Form 10-K, monthly reports on Form 8-K in any month in which a reportable event occurs such as a charter amendment, an acquisition, the commencement of significant litigation, or any other important corporate event. A semi-annual sales report on Form 9-K is also required which include, of course, pre-tax earnings, tax provisions and net earnings as well as sales. Further, in connection with the references to Form 8K, 9K and 10K, the SEC is currently considering the so-called "Wheat proposals" and the whole reporting system may be substantially revised.

At the end of the first fiscal year following the public offering in which the company has five hundred or more shareholders of record and gross assets of at least a million dollars, it must register under another statute with the SEC as a so-called twelve (G) company. The result of this latter requirement is that all subsequent proxy statements must be processed by the SEC and appropriate reports on Forms 3 and 4 must be filed by officers, directors and ten per cent stockholders with respect to any changes in their holdings. Also, public companies must hold annual meetings with their shareholders and they must generally supply quarterly as well as annual reports to shareholders. The quarterly reports are not necessarily an absolute requirement of the SEC, but they are desirable nonetheless in order to keep their shareholders informed.

Principal shareholders and officers of the corporation as well as members of their immediate family are now not free to sell their shares on the public market without filing a registration statement—there are only very limited exceptions to this requirement.

CONCLUSION

It was deemed important to go into considerable detail with respect to this subject in a book on New Product Venture Management since many of the smaller companies need to go public *in order to exploit new developments*. Also, one way of diversifying a company's activity and in many cases to acquire certain kinds of talent is to acquire another firm. This can best be done if the company's shares are public. Finally, availability of the kind of information contained in this chapter is not readily accessible to the ordinary company officer. These are the primary motivations behind the inclusion of this material.

REFERENCES

1. Rubel, S. M., *Guide to Venture Capital Sources*, Capital Publishing Corp., Chicago, Illinois, 1970.

BIBLIOGRAPHY

Blackstone, George A., Post-Effective Amendment to "Guideposts For A First Public Offering", American Bar Association, Section of Corporation, *Banking and Business Law*, May, 1968.

Borden, Arthur M. and Bull, John H., "Introduction to Going Public", *Datamation*, August, 1968.

"Going Public—Fashion, Fad or Frenzy?", *Credit and Financial Management*, January 1962, National Association of Credit Management, 1962.

Robinson, Gerald J., *Going Public*, New York: Clark Boardman Co., 1961.

Rubel, S. M., *Guide to Venture Capital Sources: 1970–71*, Chicago: Capital Publishing Corp., 1970.

Wheat, Francis M. and Blackstone, George A., "Guideposts for a *First* Public Offering", *The Business Lawyer*, Section of Corporation, Banking and Business Law of the American Bar Association, April 1960.

Winter, E. L., *A Complete Guide to Making a Public Stock Offering*, Englewood Cliffs, New Jersey: Prentice-Hall, 1962.

INDEX

Advertising 243, 253
  agency 254
  agency services 255
  copy 256
  creative strategy 256
Agency law 123
American Alcola 181
American Cyanamid 192
Atkinson, A.C. and A.H. Bobis 192
Attribute listing 63

"Bail-out" 271
"Bargain" stock 271
Belief, degree of 3
"Blue sky: laws 264, 266, 273
Board of Directors 21, 22
Booz, Allen & Hamilton, Inc. 14, 42,
    47, 48, 49
Boston Consulting Group 7, 204
Brainstorming 62
  reverse 63
Brand 242
Breakeven 204
Breakeven analysis 205, 206
Business, parameters 138

Capital, sources 263
  venture 263
Carborundum Company 137
Catalog techniques 63
Check list technique 63
Commercial success, rate of 89, 91
Commitment timing 175, 193
Committee fundamentals 52
Company, defining the business 137
Consumer 1
  characteristics 148
  goods 1
  market 144
  market research 144
Contract law 123
Contracts 123

Coordinator 55
  corporate 55
Copyrights 122
Corporate Board 21
Corporate strength 39
Cost, basic concepts 201
  direct labor 216
  elements 205
  equipment 215
  historical 202
  incremental 202, 206
  material 216
  overhead 219
  patent license 221
  planned 202
  ROI 207
  scrap 218
  shrinkage 217
  tool, jig, fixture 216
  transportation 218
Cost analysis form 211
Costing, historical 201
  parametric 202
  product 132
CPM (see Critical Path method)
Criteria, new product 34
Creative climates 68, 69
Creative individual 69
Creative melee 65, 66
Creative performance, prediction 61
Creative person 61, 62
Creative thinking 60
Creativity 61, 69
Critical Path method 29, 42, 44
Customer, characteristics 145

Dean-Sangupta index 191
Debt/equity 7
Decision making, marketing research
    141
Decisions, project 5
  resource 5
  venture 5

Defense products, market research 162
"Deficiency letter" 266
Deflator 171
DELPHI technique 65, 98
DEMON model 193
Depreciation 223
Design, Negligence 124
Development 168
Direct costing 204
Disclaimer 126
Disparate thinking technique 63

Edelman, Franz 173
Engineering, pre-production 210, 212
  prime responsibilities 96
  production support 213
Engineering & research 89
  criteria for expenditures 89
  evaluation 103
  expenditures 89, 91
  growth of expenditures 90
  1953-1971 90
Entrepreneur 1, 3, 19
  key formulas 76
  profile of 55
Entrepreneurship 1
Equipment cost 215
Evaluation, engineering 104
  individual 104
  quantitative 180
  research 104
Evaluation methods, comparison 209
Experience function 204

Facilities, evaluation 22
Facility cost 213, 214
Factor scaling 180
Fads 76
Failure, business 6
Ferrie, P.T. 197
File-wrapper estoppel 115
Forecasting, sales 149
Frame distortion 93

Free association   63
Freeport Sulphur Company   159
Full-line pricing   234

General Electric   31, 93, 98, 100, 101,
      107
   key result areas   23
General Dynamics Corp.   2
Goals, company   103, 104, 105
   engineering   104
   individual   103, 105
   long-range   22
   marketing   137
   new product venture   22
   output vs. method   106
   research   104, 105
   research, development and engineering
      103
Going public   263, 265
   considerations   265
   financial statements needed   267
   statutes   265
   timetable for   274
Greenberg, Joel S.   173
Growth   7
Gulf Energy & Environmental Systems,
      Inc.   197

Harris, John S.   181
Hazard Analysis   193, 195
Hazards, decisions   6
Hazard tree   194
Hertz   138
Hertz, David B.   172

IBM   31
Ideas, external sources   81
   from abroad   84
   printed and published sources   86
   solicited   81
   unsolicited   81
Idea stimulators   78
Induced disassociation   63
Industrial product, market analysis   155
   research   153
Industrial research laboratories   82
Information   93, 175
Innovation   69, 70
   and social values   70
   government impact on   70, 71
   management of   70
   opportunities   71
   sources   60
   technological   59
Integrated program plan   100, 101

Invention, outlets for   84
   outside offers   116
   patentable   113
   records   79
Investment planning   172

Kepner-Tregoe   67
Keuffel and Esser   137
Klausner, Robert F.   173
Know-how   119

Laboratory, college or university   83
Liability, product reliability   127
Licensing, benefits   121
   costs   121
   foreign   119
   risk   121
Life cycle   13, 14
   price   235
   pricing   236
   profit   227
   product   12, 170
   renewed   14
Linear chart   97
Linear responsibility charting   56
Lockheed Aircraft   2
Loyalty   242

Make-buy   80
Management committee   51
Manager, professional   1
Manpower, evaluation   22
Market, potential   144, 149
   research   153
   segment   230
   segmentation   145
Marketing, balanced action   135
   decision making   196
   evaluation   22
   functions   130
   no-no's   136
   organizing for   134
   processes   134
   role of   129
   versus R & D   136
Marketing concept   129, 227
Marketing research   153
   decision making   141
   defense products   162
   library   142
Market potential   153
Material losses   217
Measurement criteria   23
Media, selection   256
Morphological analysis   65

Mottley and Newton   181
Multi-project problem   169

NASA   92
Network   29
New ideas   75, 76
   company's acquisition   81
   direct creation   76
   in-company sources   76, 77
   purchasing   81
   reports   80
   sales department   81
   searches   79
   service department   80
   sources of   76
New product   1, 130
   analysis forms   175
   attrition   15
   basics   12
   CPM   44
   criteria for   34
   definition   8, 12
   department   54, 130
   development   12
   diagrams   31
   early entry into the market   7
   economic analysis   181
   effectiveness of expenditures   15
   evaluating projects   165
   evaluation   166, 169, 182, 183, 192
      management science approaches
         192
   evaluation forms   197, 199
   factor ratings   179
   failure   130
   flow chart   198
   functional responsibilities   131
   how to cost   201
   ideas   41
   industrial goods   2
   launching   133
   launching network   133
   manager   55
   manufacturers dependence on   1, 2
   market conditions for   139
   mortality   3
   network   43
   organizing for development of   50 51
   organization for   48
   personal judgment   167
   projects   177
   publicity   247
   publicity program   248
   rating system   181
   sales, 1972   2

New product *cont.*
  sales promotion 259
  screening process 26
  suggestion system 79
  standards and measurements 41
  timing 131
  venture management 180
  winners 139
New product development, organizing
  for 49
New product evaluation, flow chart
  197
New product ideas 75
New York Stock Exchange, listings
  requirements 271
NMT 42
Non-patent protection 119

Objectives, long-range 40
  strategic 21
Offering circular 267
O'Meara, John T. 179
Organization, informal 56
  problems with upper level manage-
    ment 56
  symptoms of problems 48
Osborn, Alex 67

Patentability, requirements for 114
Patent committee 116
Patent program 115
Patents 82
  and Government contracts 118
  anti-trust actions 122
  claims 113
  design patents 117
  foreign 119, 120
  infringement 113
  policies 117
  types available 85
Personal selling 243
PERT 29, 42, 43
  procedure 42, 45
Planning, exploration 29, 31, 32, 33
  long-range 21
  methodology for 32, 33
  nature of 19
  operation, advanced techniques 27
  objections to 19
  price-volume form 229
  reasons for 20
  strategic advanced techniques 28
Planning project 30
Present worth 192

Price-quality 230
Price-volume-profit 227
Pricing 131
  cost-plus-markup 233
  discounts 235
  ethical 235
  factors 227
  full-line 234
  life-cycle 228, 229, 236
  new product 132
  penetration 232
  put-out 233
  skimming 230, 232
  "Sliding down the demand curve"
    230, 231
  "Stay-out" 232
PROBE 98
Problem definition 64
Process newness 11
Proctor and Gamble 137
Producibility 103
Product, choosing a name 133
  components of value 108
  costing 132
  differentiation 254
  evaluation amd screening 131
  industrial 148, 149
  liability and reliability 124, 126, 127
  life cycle 12, 170
  opportunities 23
  planning 19
  pricing 132
  screening check list 132
Product development 94
Product newness 7, 9, 10, 11
Product manager 53
  roles of 53
Product planning 23
  basic concepts 24
  basic program for 39
  diagram 29
  network 29
  opportunities for improvement 47,
    48, 49
  organizing for 23, 24, 25, 47
  policies for 40
  procedure 28
  systematic approach 24, 25
Profile of company 21
Profit, short-run 230
Profit, contours 203
Project, comparison 99
  decisions 5
Project evaluation 182, 183, 191
  hazard analysis 193

Project manager, organization 53
  matrix organization 54
Project planning 30
Project rating 35, 36, 37, 38
Promotion 241
  budget 246
  coordinating 246
  magazines 257
  mix 242, 244, 245
  newspapers 257
  objectives 245
  planning campaign 245
  targets 241
  tools 242, 244
Prospectus 266, 267
  "Red herring" 266
Publicity 243, 247
  breadth 253
  new products 247
  program 248
  releases 243
  timing 252
Publicity releases 247
Public offering 266
Purchasers, three major classes of 12
R & D (see Engineering and research)
Put-out pricing 233

Rand Corporation 98
Rate-of-return 192
"Red herring" prospectus 266
Registration statement 267
Replacement market 149
Research 94
  applied 168
  management of 95
  planning and control of 102
  priority 168
  strategic concept 93
Research and development expenditures,
  tax treatment 223
Research and engineering (see Engineering and research)
Research, development and engineering
  95
Research institutes 83
Research laboratories 83
Resource, decisions 5
Risk 1, 4, 126
  analysis 171, 172
  and time 7
  discount factor 171
  executive judgment 237
  expenditures 4
  growth 7

Risk *cont.*
  nature of 2
  new product 241
  reducing 141
ROI 34
  costs 207
Rubel, Stanley M. 263
Ruin, probability of 197
Ruin model 193

Safety 2
Sales, executive group judgment 152
  one-man judgment 152
  sales force composite 152
Sales forecasting 149, 150, 151, 158
  procedure for 159
Salesmen 136
Sales promotion 244, 259
  banners, posters, signs 260
  contests 260
  couponing 260
  demonstrators 260
  devices 259
  packaging 260
  point-of-sale 260
  premiums 260
  price-off offers 260
  sales meetings 261
  sampling 260
  trade shows 260
Sample survey 148
Sampling, techniques 151
Scientific method 67
Screening, profile 180
SEC (see Securities Exchange Commis-
      sion)
Secondary offering 271

Securing capital 263
Securities Act of 1933 264, 266, 267
Securities Exchange Commission 264,
      266
  registration for 272
Selling, personal 243
Service marks 122
Segmentation 145, 146
  market 147
Selling expense 220
SIC 154
Skimming 230, 231
  pricing 232
Small company, strategy of 107
Smalter, Donald J. 159
Sobelman formula 192
"Spread" 271
Standard Industrial Classification (see
      SIC)
Stayout pricing 232
Stock issue, accounting fees 272
  blue sky filing fees and expenses 272
  federal issue and transfer taxes 272
  insurance policies 272
  legal fees 272
  printing and engraving costs of stock
      certificates 272
  printing costs 272
Strategy, marketing 138
  small company 107
Suits, Dr. Guy 93
Sullivan, C.I. 191
Synectics 63
  flow chart 64

Task force 51
Taxes 221

Technological forecasting 98
  department of defense 98
  sources 99
Technological innovation 59, 60
TEMPO 98
Test marketing 153
Time-cost delay 93
Time-value of money 170
Timing 93
Trade-marks 122
Trade secrets 119
TRW, Inc. 98

Underwriters 268
  agreement 273
  concerns of 270
  discount 271
  issues to be negotiated 270
Underwriting, types of 269
Uniform net profit 234

Value, product 108
Value analysis 107
Value engineering 65, 107
Venture 1, 4
  decisions 5
Venture analysis 174
Venture capital, sources 263
Venture capitalists 264
Venture manager 75
Venture team 51

Warranties, reserves 125
  risk 124
Weighting 180
Westinghouse 98
Work sampling 105

Xerox 1

DATE			
MAR 0 6 '87			